THE RESTLESS WIND AND SHIFTING SANDS

To: My handsome grandson Justin.
with love.
Grandpop

THE RESTLESS WIND AND SHIFTING SANDS

Harry J. Sweeney

iUniverse, Inc.
New York   Bloomington

The Restless Wind and Shifting Sands

Copyright © 2009 by Harry J. Sweeney

All rights reserved. No part of this book may be used or reproduced by any means, graphic, electronic, or mechanical, including photocopying, recording, taping or by any information storage retrieval system without the written permission of the publisher except in the case of brief quotations embodied in critical articles and reviews.

iUniverse books may be ordered through booksellers or by contacting:

iUniverse
1663 Liberty Drive
Bloomington, IN 47403
www.iuniverse.com
1-800-Authors (1-800-288-4677)

Because of the dynamic nature of the Internet, any Web addresses or links contained in this book may have changed since publication and may no longer be valid. The views expressed in this work are solely those of the author and do not necessarily reflect the views of the publisher, and the publisher hereby disclaims any responsibility for them.

ISBN: 978-1-4401-5931-2 (pbk)
ISBN: 978-1-4401-5929-9 (hc)
ISBN: 978-1-4401-5930-5 (ebk)

Printed in the United States of America

iUniverse rev. date: 12/21/2009

To Joan

The Prophet said, religion is very easy, and whoever overburdens himself in his religion will not be able to continue in that way. So you should not be extremists, but try to be near to perfection and receive the good tidings that you will be rewarded; and gain strength by worshipping in the mornings, nights.

(Hadith: Bukhari 1:38)

CONTENTS

Chapter 1 . . . . **1**
Palestine – apostasy – predestination and martyrdom – life in general – the West does not understand us – Londonistan and Ameristan – the Sunni Shiite schism – Americans are not the Meccans of centuries ago – war is deceit – the Banu Quraiza (800 beheaded).

Chapter 2 . . . . **39**
Who cares about Abu Ghraib? – multiculturalism, political correctness, and apostasy – Nasser – Banu Quraiza and American militia – jihad, women, and head scarves – arranged marriages and honor killings – hanging the innocent – reform – American troops and child martyrs.

Chapter 3 . . . . **87**
American troops, Holy Trinity – Allah, predestination, martyrdom – gun control madness – the mother-in-law – al-Qaida and the Taliban – a highjacked religion? – the coalition versus al- Qaida – killing insurgents in Iraq and killing babies in America – we are not threatened by unbelievers – apostasy and martyrdom.

Chapter 4 . . . .
What happened to 72 Virgins? - fighting in Anbar; obligation only to tribe and family – Iran and Iraq – Wahhabis - President Ahmadinejad, Iran, and Europe - Ahmadinejad, Oriana Fallaci, End of Days - Afghanistan – that Old Time Religion - what could be better than killing people for offenses against Allah? - Hamas-Iraqi versus al-Qaida.

Chapter 5 . . . .**184**
The women's viewpoint - ancient Chinese strategies in Iraq - Iraqis

fight al-Qaida, laugh at Abu Ghraib – the wives discuss their husbands - the scandal: Muhammad and Zainab - on reading the Qur'an - The United States and the first Barbary pirates - people of Anbar versus al-Qaida - Muhammad at Yathrib; on robbing caravans – on Palestine.

Chapter 6 . . . .**233**
Reform: a capital offense - on Aisha - Qur'an sura 33; the Islam ideology - waterboarding -unemployment and marriage - the Qur'an and women's fashions - "is not your wife your tilth (tilled land)?" - young Muhammad - Ahmadiyya movement - prayer times.

Chapter 7 . . . .**282**
Turkey and American Democrats - female genital mutilation - honor killing - sharia funding and zakat - HIV - "Kill them wherever you find them!" - Muhammad's early life - on reading Qur'an Sura 2.

Chapter 8 . . . .**329**
On reading Sura 4 - on reading Sura 5 - killing apostates - on reading Sura 6 - on understanding Sura 6 - "Strike from them every fingertip!" - discussing Sura 8 - discussing the sharia in London - discussion of Sura 9 - predestination, martyrdom and white grapes - "They have little fighting credibility."

Chapter 9 . . . .**385**
"It is an ideology and a bunch of outdated traditions." - The Winchester and the Kalashnikov - "If the Americans leave, most of us probably will die." - the hijab - "It is every Muslim's duty to root out sinners and punish them." - discussing Sura 10 - some thoughts on Sura 11 - violent verses - Arab dialogues - violent verses in Suras 4 and 5.

Chapter 10 . . . .**439**
The Truce of Hudaibiyya - Sadr City - "Would you kill him if you knew he would kill children at play?" - Muqtada Al Sadr - the Hijira - divine mystery, Sunni Shiite schism, Battle of New Orleans - the sharia - the crusades - female circumcision is mutilation - The Ottoman Empire - where do we go from here?

x

FOREWORD

Harry J. Sweeney has produced a clever means of explaining the intricacies of Islam that puzzle much of the Western world today. In his book, The Restless Wind and Shifting Sands, Sweeney uses a fictional dialogue, satire, and three fictional Iraqi Arab characters, Modi, Mani, and Radi, to explain the facts about Islam.

The three characters, of course, represent moderate, mainstream, and radical Arab Muslims. Through their daily conversations, the three give their different opinions of Islam as they go about their daily lives. They are the best of friends, as are their wives, and the discussions cover almost all phases of Muslim life– including, but not limited to, talking about sharia–Islamic law, predestination, honor killing, female genital mutilation, and the hanging of a teenage girl because of her own family's abuse. They even discuss "Palestine."

The three Arab characters and their wives, just as easily could be Muslim residents of Turkey, the Comoro Islands, the Western Sahara, Egypt, Saudi Arabia, Yemen, Bangladesh, Indonesia, or any of the inhabitants of the other 57 nations that make up the Organization of the Islamic Conference.

These vignettes reveal the basic tenets of Islam as practiced by the world's 1.4 billion Muslims.

The book is clear and easy to follow. I recommend it to anyone who seeks a better understanding of Islam and the challenges it poses for Western civilization.

Dr. Steven Carol
Prof. of History (retired)
Official Historian
Middle East Radio Forum
Author of *Middle East Rules of Thumb: Understanding the Complexities of the Middle East*

PREFACE

This book is unusual. Unlike other books that describe each scene and each character, this book does so only when it is absolutely essential to provide information that does not appear in the dialogues. The book leaves something for the imagination, but not too much. From the very first word, the book started out that way. The conversation between three Iraqi friends about Palestine provided a much better analysis of the situation than sound bites from the Middle East or reports from others who have only learned part of the problem.

The tragedy of 9/11 touched me deeply, as it did so many other people who love the United States. Like so many others, I had to know who was responsible and why they felt they could justify murdering so many innocent people. Forty years of intelligence work and investigations prepared me for the research and investigation that were required to ferret out the information that I needed. The books I considered critical to begin the task came from India, Afghanistan, and Pakistan as well as from Europe and the United States. They included not only different translations of the Qur'an and the hadiths, but also the writings of Maududi and Qutb, two very influential Muslim writers. Through e-mail and personal contacts, I had joined with other scholars, renowned specialists in the field, to advance the work of Islamic research.

As an advanced Middle East scholar, I continued writing essays and articles, and I provided analyses of current Islamic events on radio. At the invitation of Politico Mafioso, I began writing a series of articles which became the conversations of Modi, Mani, and Radi. I knew that with this series of conversations, I could tell the story I wanted to tell and give everyone a glimpse of the mysterious Middle East and the people who live there, work there, and practice their religion and culture of Islam.

Harry J. Sweeney
September 2009

I wish to thank my colleagues, Dr. Steven Carol and Carl Masthay for their help and encouragement on this book. My son, Kurt deserves special thanks for his assistance in many ways.

CHAPTER 1

Conversation 1: Palestine

Three Arab friends in Baghdad, Iraq: Modi, Mani, and Radi are discussing politics, as usual. Modi is the quieter, pensive man wearing the typical city cap, called the *takiyah*. He is sometimes considered a moderate because of his non-belligerent attitude toward the West. Mani, like Modi, also wears the white *takiyah*, but is not as quiet as Modi and has no antipathy toward the West, but at the same time, he is not impressed with western countries. Mani is considered by his friends as mainstream, preferring that the Arabs be left alone. Radi, unlike his two friends is not at all quiet. He is very excitable and nervous, afraid to be seen as soft on anything. He wears the traditional kafiyah of the desert, along with traditional desert attire. He is known to be radical because of his extremist views on Arab culture and Islam. Despite their differing views, all three men are fast friends and enjoy dining and praying together.

Modi: I did some research on our Palestine and discovered that the entire area was set aside for the Jewish homeland with the proviso that land also be set aside for a Palestinian state. I don't know why everyone is fighting about it. Why don't we all just return to the original set of specifications, put everyone where they are supposed to be, and let it go at that? There is plenty of land.

Mani: Who told you that lie? No one has the right to do that. It is our land and nobody invited the Jews! Whoever thinks that way does not live here.

Radi: Yeah. He should have his head cut off. Palestine for the Palestinians! Who was it who gave it away?

Harry J. Sweeney

Modi: It was first the League of Nations, and then the United Nations followed suit and decided on the Balfour Declaration. It was a huge chunk of territory. It was not as large as the Jews' original homeland here, but enough for them and the Palestinian state.

Mani: It doesn't look that large to me. Where do you get the "large chunk" business? Now, Modi, you know, the Jews never had a homeland here! They are newcomers to the area, interfering with our own homeland.

Radi: Yeah. You should have your head cut off.

Modi: Well, it *was* a large chunk, but King Hussein's father, King Abdullah, bluffed the Brits, and he tore off about 75 percent of the territory. It has been said that the new Jordan became the "Palestinian State" that they talked about. Mani, almost everyone knows the Jews were here before some other folks we know. The Roman Empire forced them to leave that homeland. You remember that one imam that visited last year mentioned the suicide of the Jews at Masala to avoid surrendering to the Romans?

Radi: Oh yes. He enjoyed telling that story

Modi: That tragedy happened in Palestine in the year 73 CE, before the area was renamed Palestina by the Romans.

Radi: I don't believe that. The Jews were never here; they are newcomers.

Mani: You will not convince him, Modi. Now, you were saying Jordan took three fourths of that territory away from us—without a vote or anything? Didn't the Palestinians have anything to say about it?

Radi: Vote? What is that? Modi, can I cut off his head?

Modi: No, Radi. Settle down. Look, there were no "Palestinians" to ask, remember? There were only Arabs. When the Ottoman Empire fell apart, the territory was vacant; at least as far as legitimate owners were concerned, except for those acres that were ceded to certain Arab chiefs. The Jewish settlers bought much of that land themselves.

Mani: The Jews bought our land?

Radi: Aha! I'll cut off *their* heads.

Modi: No, Mani. The Jews bought land from Arabs so that they could settle there and farm the land. It did not matter if there were Arabs here and there; they were not displaced unless they caused trouble. Some caused trouble, but others continued to live there in peace.

Mani: So, how did all the trouble start?

Radi: Trouble? Who is making trouble? My sword will drink his blood.

Modi: There was a great deal of trouble between the Jews and the Brits because they did not want the Jews moving here in such numbers, even though it was supposed to be their new homeland. Nevertheless, they had nowhere else to go, especially after the Holocaust, so they fought the British and some of the Arab tribes. They also had problems with some Arab nations that did not want a Jewish state in the Middle East. However, the UN would not accept the reason that Allah owned the so-called "Ottoman lands," and that the land could not be negotiated. The Arabs believed the land should not have been for sale or parceled out to any state that was not an Arab state. They still believe that even the tiny enclave that is now the State of Israel is occupying too much Arab territory and should be removed forever.

Mani: That sounds right to me. The entire world belongs to Allah, and we are responsible for returning it to Him.

Radi: Now you're talking. Let's go cut off some heads.

Modi: It is not a good idea to rid the world of other people. We have

Harry J. Sweeney

learned centuries ago that it is not a good idea to depend on our own leadership—if they won the world—to be completely faithful to Allah and fair to all of the population. You must always remember that power not only corrupts, but the corruption most often includes arrogance and injustice. Just look at the history of the first few leaders, the Caliphs. Some of them actually knew the Prophet personally. One was his best friend and his father-in-law. Yet the period was so bloody with the assassination of leaders that it finally led to a split between Sunnis and the Shiites. Even now, the Sunnis and Shiites are bent on killing each other. Our own Salafists are not too friendly with us if we are not absolute puritans! I sometimes wish there were a greater religious authority looking out for us. We really do need an international organization to interrupt us on occasion and keep things on the right track.

Mani: You mean the United Nations? I like them. They give us everything we want; pardon my snickering. Those Europeans are eating out of our hands. Allah wanted us to rule the world; that's why he invented political correctness. You say the Salafists think we're infidels?

Radi: Infidels? Is that true? Hey, come to think of it, father told me we are Salafists! Are you two really infidels? I can have fun with infidels!

Modi: Radi, you never told us your family was Salafist. You must believe that only the laws from the time of our beloved Prophet (peace be upon him) and his companions are valid. That creates a terrible situation for other believers who are more modern in their outlook and want to move on. We have a better handle on psychology, sociology, and other people sciences and can avoid much of the present bloodshed.

Mani: One of these days I might find out what that all means, Modi. I am not so sure the imams would agree.

Radi: I haven't cut off a head all day; I need some exercise. Are there any Europeans around?

The Restless Wind and Shifting Sands

Modi: Radi, why don't you settle down, get married, and raise a family? We know about your girlfriend. She is more than you deserve.

Mani: Yeah. Your mind seems to work on only one track? Why don't you go make some babies and do something important?

Radi: I would like to do that but don't have enough money to get married. So I get frustrated. Since I cannot even talk to a female unless I am married to her, the only fun I get is cutting off heads. Are you guys going to be busy the next few minutes?

Modi: You bet. But I think I can help you out of your dilemma about girls. I know a place where you can have as many as 72 girlfriends and it is no sin to hug them, kiss them, dance with them, or anything you want.

Radi: Really? Oh, my. That sounds great. Where do I sign up?

Mani: I just happened to know a chap in a popular brigade in town; Modi, let's walk him over there. I know they're hiring.

Harry J. Sweeney

Conversation 2: Apostasy

Modi, Mani, and Radi discuss the news of the day.

Modi: I saw in the newspaper this morning that London is establishing a secret organization for apostates.

Mani: Well, I can understand any apostates' wanting to keep their whereabouts secret.

Radi: Yeah! If I knew about him—zap—off with his head.

Modi: You don't understand, Mani. The Brits want to hide them from us. It is especially from you, Radi; they think you are too violent!

Radi: Oh yeah? They have not seen Mani in action yet. He does the same things I do; I just enjoy it more.

Mani: Yeah! To me it is just a duty to kill an apostate. That's what is written for us. You know that yourself. I remember the hadith: Bukhari 4:52:260.

Modi: I know what is written, but I cannot reconcile it with other documents that say that there is no compulsion in religion, Dawud: 14:2676.

Mani: That only means that we cannot force someone to convert if he doesn't want to convert. It does not mean that once you have converted you can do what you want or even leave the religion.

Radi: Yeah. I agree with that. They should have their heads cut off.

Modi: Radi, death is not the answer to everything. I for one am not really sure that apostasy is that big a deal, at least not big enough to bring about the death penalty—especially not from any person on the street. If he wants to serve Allah some other way, why bother as long as he is serving Allah.

Mani: It is not a question of our opinion in the matter. It is written that he should be killed, so that's it.

Radi: Yeah. What's so hard to understand about that? It is written.

Modi: Suppose that your cousin decided to be a Christian, converted to Christianity secretly, and then a year later decided Christianity was not for him and rejoined his old faith, this time a more ardent believer? What would you do if you discovered what he did?

Mani: I have to think about that. I suppose I would do nothing. If he is a good believer, that is all that matters.

Modi: Well, what is wrong with letting each person alone to find the error of his ways and return to us?

Mani: If we let him alone, he might not return.

Modi: What harm would he cause if he does not return?

Radi: He cheats us out of the zakat (poor tax) and he can't join jihad with us.

Mani: Those reasons are rather petty, Radi.

Radi: Abu Bakr did not think so.

Mani: That was about 1400 years ago. Modi, I suppose it would be a matter for the authorities; I just am not equipped to answer such an important question.

Modi: That is my true point, Mani. How can we let just anyone on the street kill whomever he thinks is an apostate?

Mani: You are giving me chills. Can we change the subject? What about those believers in America who are demanding foot baths in school and at work?

Harry J. Sweeney

Radi: What about them. They must use the basin to wash their feet each time before prayer. Don't they?

Modi: No—I knew we could catch you on that one, Radi. It is written that you only really need to wash the feet with water every 1½ days—if you wear shoes and socks after you wash the feet for the first prayers. The other four times that day you can go through the motions by passing your wet hands over your shoes. Of course, most people do that for only one day at a time, unless they are traveling. If it was good enough for our most beloved, it should be good enough for the other guys.

Radi: Hey! Are you sure about that? That would save me some time; I wouldn't have to take my shoes and socks off five times per day.

Mani: I heard something about that. Are you sure it is lawful?

Modi: Look, the law has fifty-one pages covering ablutions, and it describes everything.

Mani: You know what? The law has all the answers. Why don't we just stick to the law for everything?

Modi: Do you think the law always makes sense?

Mani: I would not keep saying that so loudly. For one thing, you got Radi sharpening his knife again. And look, if he wanted to remove your head from saying that, I couldn't stop him. He is right.

Radi: Did someone call me?

Modi: Yeah, Radi. Would you two really kill an apostate? Why? What about his relatives and friends? Wouldn't they claim revenge?

Mani: Now we have you on that one. Everyone has the right and the duty to kill an apostate if one has access to his person. Also, the law says that anyone, even the worst of people, can kill an apostate with

The Restless Wind and Shifting Sands

no retribution allowed. So, if you decided to become a Christian, for example, even your parents and siblings would be required to take the action if they could get to you. I remember hearing about an Egyptian professor who was chased down the street by his father. The old man emptied his revolver at him. And they are not allowed to take any action against someone who beat them to it.

Radi: Yeah. It's not as if we were getting away with anything. It is actually a violation if we don't (chuckles). I could do it in a second with no consequences.

Modi: Except I would haunt the hell out of both of you.

Mani and Radi: How would you do that? The book says no consequences.

Modi: But I'd be a Christian then—and I'd be allowed to do it. Ha! Especially you, Radi. Every time you put your knife down, I'd hit it on the sharp edge with a rock! And every time you fell asleep at night I would fill your head with dancing girls—you'd never get to paradise!

Mani: But there is nothing preventing me from killing you now; you are not a Christian!

Modi: Afraid so! It is written that thou shalt not harm another believer except for cause—and you guys don't have cause. Well, my watch tells me it is time for the noon prayer. Let's go wash. And Radi, this time, leave your socks on, dummy!

(Radi chases in mock anger)

Harry J. Sweeney

Conversation 3: Predestination and Martyrdom

Modi: I see the American newspapers are writing about us moderates again. They wonder why we can't do something about Radi.

Mani: I noticed that. But they talk only about you and Radi; they seem to ignore me. I guess they don't know I exist.

Radi: Yeah, can you believe it? They can't tell the difference between you two guys anyway; they just know *they don't like me*. And those Americans think you can do something about me. *I dare you to try.*

Modi: Radi, they don't like the way *you interpret* our Sacred Book and the law. They think it's the *interpretation* that causes the fighting between us and them. Why do they always get things backwards?

Mani: I agree with that. If Allah says kill the infidels wherever you find them, doesn't that mean the same thing to the three of us?

Radi: You bet! I keep my blade sharp for those infidels, whoever they are. But Modi, you even have some Christian friends! That is against our laws! *Do not take Christians and Jews for friends.*[1]

Modi: Well, Radi, a Jew is an infidel, I know. Have you ever met one or even seen one?

Mani: What does that have to do with anything? Allah did not like them, He said so; so neither do we.

Radi: Yeah. That goes for me too. I would kill them all. Bring 'em on.

Modi: Does that go for Christians, too? More people you have never met—oh, wait! Didn't some Christian soldiers find your grandmother in that house that was blown up by a martyr and then rush her to the hospital to save her life?

---

1   Qur'an 5:51.

The Restless Wind and Shifting Sands

Mani: Yeah. I am still angry about that. If they had let her alone, she would have died a martyr and gone directly to paradise. Now she is worried sick because she does not know if she is one of the ones Allah has chosen.

Radi: Yeah, Modi. You know that everything is preordained. Everything is already mapped out, and you don't know which way you are going when you die. No matter how good you have been or what good works you have done, your path is already chosen. The only way you can change it is by martyrdom. If you are not chosen for the path to the fire, you may do something sometime, even at the last minute and burn in hell forever. It is not up to you.

Modi: So you are telling me that, to you, just staying alive is taking a terrible chance with fate.

Mani: Yes indeed! That other grandmother in the news had the right idea; she lived a full life and then became a martyr—just in case.

Radi: But we can't always be that lucky. We might get really angry about something and do something wrong, and then be hit by a truck and burn in hell forever because someone made us angry.

Modi: Oh, my! So the only guarantee you have is martyrdom. But have you really looked at the Sacred Law about that? Martyrdom is not a guarantee by any means. People have been doing it because they want to get that guarantee to paradise, others because they want those virgins, still others—the young people—because they see no decent future for themselves and martyrdom celebrates them as heroes while they are still alive and provides a great reward to their families.

Mani: So, what's wrong with that?

Modi: True martyrdom requires that you do it *only for the love of Allah*

Harry J. Sweeney

and for no other reason. It is a matter of intent[2]. I for one am not going to bet all eternity on what my true intentions are at any time.

Radi: But if you have no intention of being a martyr and an American bomb falls on you, it is said you are a martyr even if you did not know you were in a target area. What about that?

Modi: I will let the imams fight about that one. I'd just as soon be out of town.

Mani: Well, Radi, I guess that leaves martyrdom up to us.

Radi: What do you mean *us*?

---

2   *Reliance of the Traveller*, Nuh Ha Min Keller translator, Amana Publications, Beltsville, MD, 1994.

The Restless Wind and Shifting Sands

Conversation 4: Life in General

Modi: Well, guys, we are getting up in the world. Did you know that nearly one in every five people in the world professes our faith?

Mani: That's a lot of people. And if they all pay their tax, that would be billions of dollars available worldwide every year.

Radi: You got that right! That is 2.5 percent of the value of everything you own every year. Americans complain about income tax, Ha! And complicated? My cousin in Chicago has to subscribe to audit software to keep track. And by the way, the dollar is losing traction all over to the euro. Lots of countries are switching.

Modi: I know. I have already switched to euros. Radi, your cousin is among almost 6 million others in North America. Would you believe there are more than 32 million of us in Europe?

Mani: Well, that is not even one tenth of what's in Africa.

Radi: I'd like to get a share of what is coming out of Europe and America. I bet it's more than enough to wage jihad forever.

Modi: But why wage jihad when you could use the money for other purposes.

Mani: But we are commanded by the Qur'an to wage jihad until the entire world believes as we do. And besides, what would most people do with more money? You know that this life is only temporary; you are not supposed to settle down in it and enjoy yourself; you must work hard for the next life. The next life is the important one.

Radi: Mani is right. The sooner we get out of this life on earth, the better. The longer we stay here, the more tiresome it becomes. Why do we have to live so long? I am anxious to get to paradise. My Phoenix cousin keeps telling me how good he has it, and I keep telling him that

Harry J. Sweeney

if he is enjoying life now, he will be in the fire forever. But he laughs and tells me it's only a dry heat. I don't know what he means by that.

Modi: But Radi, you must get some fun out of life. You can't just run around with your friends at night looking for people to hack up. Don't you ever get the idea that good legal philosophies have no time for vigilantism? I have no problems with someone tipping off the authorities about crimes and criminals; however, when people take on the task of judge, jury, and executioner, you can let me off. I will not buy a ticket on that train.

Mani: Leave him alone. As long as he is not bothering us, who cares? Let him lop off as many heads as he wants.

Radi: Yeah, you mainstreamers got it together. You know we are right in what we do, and we can count on you to keep the money coming and the press quiet. That "hi-jacked religion" theme was a good one, almost as good as the one about the "religion of peace." We just could not do what we do without you.

Modi: I know you are both right according to our laws, but I just cannot help thinking that I was not made to enjoy constant strife. It seems too unnecessary and destructive. It doesn't matter to me that Christians and Jews do not think as we do. I think we should just live and let live.

Mani: You can think that way for a while, but eventually you have to join the jihad. Allah will ask you on the Day of Judgment if you joined the jihad—you already know that. It will not be enough to say you did nothing against us! He will say that unless you joined the jihad with us you were actually against us and against Him! He will have you thrown into the fire.

Radi: Maybe He'll let me cut off your head first. Listen to Mani. You moderates are doomed on the last day. Don't you believe that?

Modi: I look at that elephant every day of my life. I know what is

The Restless Wind and Shifting Sands

written, but it does not feel right. I don't want to hurt anyone. I hate the noise of the explosions and the gunfire and the people—kids even—bloody and blown apart. I hate seeing the kids die.

Mani: But that's the beauty of it. Those of us caught in the explosions and the crossfire will automatically zoom to paradise because we are martyrs even if we didn't know it. But the unbelievers, pardon my snicker, will all go to hell and burn forever. We can watch them writhe and cry out in anguish as we enjoy our sumptuous meals in paradise.

Radi: Even you, Modi, with your messed-up thinking. You too could be a martyr—in fact, that would be best for you. It would save you from the fire because you won't join the jihad. That is a violation! Martyrdom is your only escape.

Modi: Radi, you keep saying life is too long. I think it is too short. I would like to go to school or something, achieve something good for myself and my family. Maybe I could write a book.

Mani: If it agrees with our scriptures, I have already read it. If it doesn't agree, I won't read it. It's as simple as that. Nothing personal.

Modi: But life is personal, Mani. It's a people-to-people affair with people getting along with each other, trading, entertaining others, and being entertained. Life can be great! And we have a world big enough for everyone.

Radi: That talk is trash. I am not listening to you anymore. Modi, don't say things like that to anyone else. You are a goner if you do.

Mani: Radi's right. Next time I do my ablutions, I will do my ears especially well to get all that nonsense out. I have heard too much. Allah may be wondering why we don't report you.

Radi: We don't have to report him. I can lop off his head and then let everyone know why. No big deal. But…perhaps he will learn to be a better person, like us.

Harry J. Sweeney

Modi: Yeah, right. Perhaps someday I can find the answer to the question: why do so many of our actions that seem so terrible, actually turn out to be correct and lawful here?

Mani: See…now just go with the flow.

The Restless Wind and Shifting Sands

<u>Conversation 5: The West does not understand us!</u>

Modi: I guess you guys heard that the new sheikh in town, Gordon Brown, thinks we are not an army, just criminals. He is going to send in his peelers to arrest us.

Mani: Yeah, that's funny. I thought Tony Blair did not quite understand us, but this guy…

Radi: What's a peeler?

Modi: Well, you know that some American senators had the same idea. Can you imagine serving warrants for Usama bin Laden in Pakistan?

Mani: I would like to see that news video if it happens.

Radi: C'mon, guys; what's a peeler?

Modi: I thought that "religion of peace" applied to Radi and friends was fairly humorous, but now I hear that we all hate America because we were deprived of a good education and social programs…and that is the reason why our guys are attacking them all over the world.

Mani: I heard about that too, ha! Ah, those British and American politicians. I get my kicks watching Dr. Zawahiri making fools out of them. The good doctor tells them things, but they don't know what he means. It seems as if whatever they do not understand they just ignore.

Radi: Now look, I want to know what a peeler is, and I want to know now.

Modi: Radi, it is British slang for policeman, like bobby or cop. Mani, all these politicians have to do is look at the three basic masterpieces of Islam to discover the answers to all their questions. But they are either too busy playing house or too complacent to look.

Mani: I never really thought of them together, but you are right. The Qur'an, the sira, and the hadiths. But I would bet, if we were allowed to bet, that they would spend more time with the Qur'an than the other two documents. Even Radi knows better than that.

Radi: I know better than what?

Modi: What we were discussing is that the Americans and Europeans seem to think that the Qur'an is the totality of our religion and our culture. They do not realize that all through the Qur'an we are commanded to obey Allah *and His messenger.* It is written that we must all emulate the Prophet of Allah in all things, for he led the perfect life.[3] That is why we had been called *Muhammedans* for so long.

Mani: Righto! Everyone thought we worshipped Muhammad. I can understand how they got that impression—we really dote on his life, for good reason. One would think that the West would have caught on to that by now. It's not the Qur'an they should be researching—if they are researching anything, which I doubt—but the *sira*, the biography of our most beloved and the Ahadith, what Muhammad has said about everything. And how he lived.

Radi: I have been trying to collect the hadith sayings, but I don't know how many there are.

Modi: Just with the four most popular hadith writers: Sahih Bukhari, Sahih Muslim, Sahih Malik, and a partial collection of Sahih Dawud, there about 18,000. Of course, many of them are repeated and told in a different way by different witnesses.

Mani: My father was a good businessman, and he used to read me one hadith from Dawud many times. I think it was Number 170. It described how the spoils of the raid on Khaybar were divided afterwards. First they were divided in half, and one half went to the people with the Prophet, including the Prophet himself. The rest went to Allah and His

---

3   Qur'an 33:21.

The Restless Wind and Shifting Sands

Messenger for future needs. If we are still doing this, I am missing out on something. Radi, what do you know about this?

Radi: There is always profit in war. In some places, we can walk away with lots of cash for what we do. Sure, there are many austere ones who are hot-to-trot to get themselves killed, but once they get over the nonsense and realize the more hell they raise, the more money they can make, then they go ape for a few raids, go home with their pockets filled, and let some of the others take their turns. A really good horror story brings lots of cash from Europe and America.

Modi: I suspect one chap was worth millions before the Americans caught up to him.

Mani: But he is OK now. He is in martyr's paradise.

Radi: After what Modi said a couple of weeks ago, I am not too sure about that. Modi said it is in the law that you must be totally committed to the love of Allah and have no other reason to don the martyr's belt; otherwise, your sacrifice is for naught.

Mani: I remember that. He poked his finger in the air and said, "Fighting for territory, politics, spoils, honor, money, or even just for comradeship is not jihad. And purposely sacrificing one's life for any or all of these petty reasons and not simply for love of Allah will get us an early hell." I checked, Radi, it is in the law (takes a piece of paper from his pocket). Here it is, section a3.3 (1). I would have bet that it wasn't. Maybe that's why I am not a betting man.

Modi: Told ya!

Harry J. Sweeney

Conversation 6: Londonistan and Ameristan

Modi: Look at this newspaper! The UK believers have claimed sovereignty over both the United States and Great Britain!

Mani: What does that really mean? Has the sharia been accepted there?

Radi: Only in a few places. But the British appear not to be doing a thing about our guys there raising all that fuss. They are shouting, threatening death, scaring the hell out of people with taunts of beheadings and unleashed jihad. Even the moderates like Modi here are just standing around not saying anything.

Modi: But that's just in London! Much of the British leadership seem to be so politically correct, I do not believe they can bring themselves to say or do anything that would be offensive to anyone, even you guys.

Mani: I have heard that, "Do not offend the people who came to kill you!" But isn't that the way it is in the U.S.?

Radi: I certainly hope so. Aren't the leaders the same in America as they are in Europe? Aren't they the same people?

Modi: No, many Americans are different. I know, I know, you have watched some senators and representatives clown around on CNN and C-Span, and they give you fits of laughter. Believe me, these are only the politicians! The American people are a lot different from that.

Mani: I don't understand. Aren't the leaders from among the people?

Modi: They can't possibly be from the same tribes. The people for some reason seem to give their allegiances to politicians who don't even like them. Look at what's happening here. On one hand, the American people want to win their war against Radi's buddies in Iraq as quickly as they can, yet half the leadership appears to treat that as unimportant.

The Restless Wind and Shifting Sands

A group of politicians claim the armed forces aren't getting anywhere, but they are the ones holding the troops back.

Radi: You are right, Modi! My friends are getting killed like crazy, and we are trying as best we can to hang on. Thank Allah that the American politicians keep telling us to hang on a little longer and eventually they will pull the troops out. If they ever stop doing that, we will have to pack up and leave. Those troops are too much for us when they act independently. But to know that we have only to wait a little longer, whew! Allah is really helping us there.

Mani: We are helping you there also, Radi. Without us mainstream believers, you guys would have no source of recruitment. We are the backbone of the radical movement and you know it!

Modi: I can see that. Yes, the radicals recruit from the mainstream, and the mainstream recruits from newbies. But do not discount the help we moderates bring to the cause. Those of us in America could be writing letters, marching, advising the administration to get rid of its radical advisors, but few of us do. My guess is that they want to keep a low profile because of what happened to the Japanese-Americans in World War II.

Mani: Yeah, you could be right! I am surprised that you are a moderate because we all know that moderates are as much a target as unbelievers. When we take over all these countries—or whenever the countries are just handed to us—you people will be the first to lose your heads, after the Leftists, of course.

Radi: Yeah! I am really eager to get my hands on some girly boys, whatever they are!

Mani: Radi, can't you talk about anything else?

Radi: Darn! That's no fun.

Harry J. Sweeney

Modi: Radi, killing people is not supposed to be fun! That is why I remain a moderate,

Mani. I just do not hold with indiscriminate killing and general mayhem.

Radi: I do.

Mani: You, Modi, do not seem to care about establishing an international caliphate and having everyone respond to the call "*Allahu Akbar*" five times or more each day.

Modi: I would not go that far. I just do not believe in slight breaches in culture or tradition as an excuse for killing. Too many people are different, and they should not be killed along with their families because they are different.

Radi: Nah! That is the main reason they should all be killed. By being different they are a threat to believers. We should obey the book: "Kill them wherever you find them!"

Modi: Radi, you know that had to do only with the Meccans during the Hijira many centuries ago! That verse has nothing to do with today! Perhaps a caliphate would be a great idea for the Muslim world—if it would cut down on the indiscriminate violence and establish order in our world.

Mani: You are changing the subject now that Radi has challenged you. You keep saying that about some of the verses, and it is not true! Allah never sent another prophet to us to say that all of those ayats about violence were changed and that we should not hate and kill Jews and Christians any more.

Radi: Yep, he is right. Besides, Allah said He was not going to send any more prophets. So whatever has been said way back then is still in effect today. And believe it; I am going to kill them wherever I find them.

The Restless Wind and Shifting Sands

Modi: We don't know any of this for certain, you guys. Sure it was written, and we know that Allah revealed it to our Most Beloved verse by verse. I understand all of that; however, whatever happened between the revelation and the collection of the verses is not known. Could some human have made a mistake in the process?

Mani: That is the difference between you moderates and us. You know you believe it, but you do not want to because it does not fit your modern view of "live and let live." You are spoiled rotten because you have thrived without jihad and want this good life to continue.

Modi: There's nothing wrong with the life I live. It is a good way, and I am still a believer and do the things believers do. I enjoy my wife and children. I want to see them grow up in peace and safety. I am a good believer!

Mani: Except that you take Christians and Jews for your friends, you allow your neighbors to eat pork and drink alcohol without confronting them, and you do not support jihad! Allah will spit you out!

 Modi: I pay my *zakat*, and much of that goes toward supporting jihad.

Radi: Modi, you know in your heart it is not enough! You must wage war!

Modi: On my own neighbors?

Mani: On your own family if necessary! Half a believer is not a believer. You are either with us 100 percent or against us! There is no other way.

Modi: You are forcing me to make a choice between what I know is right and what you think is right! Isn't the world big enough for all of us? Can't we all just get along?

Mani: Nope! This is our way! This is the way it has always been. This

Harry J. Sweeney

is the way it will always be as long as Radi and I are alive to see it stays that way.

Modi: I see you are not giving the world much choice in the matter.

Mani: No! It is either us or them! No negotiation, no treaties, no surrender! We cannot live with the world the way it is—with all those other people in it!

Radi: We were ordered to kill them all, and that is exactly what we will do, no matter what! Oh, we had better hurry; it is almost time for prayers. I do not want to be late. Do we need ablutions?

Modi: Only if you did not remain pure between prayers.

Radi: Arrgh! See you at mosque.

The Restless Wind and Shifting Sands

<u>Conversation 7: The Shiite-Sunni Schism</u>

Modi: Did you guys see the news about al-Qaida threatening Iran?

Mani: Yes, I did. I thought the Iranians were hand and glove with Shiites and Sunnis here.

Radi: I never trusted the Shiites. They are not true believers!

Modi: How can you say that? They *are* true believers. Their history goes back as far as us Sunnis. The only difference is the right of succession. We are all children of Allah anyway. There is no good reason why we should not worship together. We should be one people.

Mani: No, *our* history is longer. They were captured by our victorious armies much later.

Modi: Oh, you mean the country of Iran. Yes, that's true. The people of Iran, Persia then, were mainly Zoroastrians before converting. I was talking about the Shia. Remember, the Shia were "The Party of Ali." Ali was the first man who converted to Islam and also our Most Beloved's nephew and son-in-law.

Radi: They were the ones who started all of the trouble after our beloved prophet died. They should lose their heads.

Modi: Radi, our Most Beloved was so many things to his community, from simple imam to virtual king,[4] that it was almost impossible to step into his shoes. We were fortunate in having Abu Bakr, the prophet's best friend, and others—and of course Ali, holy men all.

Mani: I remember there was a problem caused by the Shiites and now they flog themselves every year with those chains, celebrating the Feast of Ashura.

---

4   Muhammad and the Unbelievers, Center for the Study of Political Islam, page 1.

Harry J. Sweeney

Radi: Yeah; I remember hearing about that, and I saw it on TV once. Bloody.

Modi: Well, you cannot say that the Shiites started the trouble. There was a very simple difference of opinion between two groups that were trying to do what they thought was right. They formed two parties. The party of Ali thought that succession should be kept in the family of our Most Beloved, and so the husband of Fatima, the daughter of our Most Beloved, was Ali. Also, he was a close relative as well as a holy man intimately connected to our Holy Documents. To the Shia he was the most logical to succeed and to first wear the mantle of caliph or successor.

Mani: I thought the first caliph was Abu Bakr.

Modi: You are right. The party of the Sunnah, the Sunnis, did not like the idea of a dynasty, so they decided that the caliph had to be the best person, relative or not. Since Abu Bakr was our Most Beloved's best friend and he relied on him extensively, the Sunnis felt that he would be the best person to succeed and be the first caliph.

Radi: Ha! Did he kill Ali?

Modi: No, Radi. Ali and Abu Bakr were two holy people and would not do things like that. Ali just stepped back and let Abu Bakr assume the mantle.

Mani: How did the trouble start if Ali just stepped back? We know there was a lot of trouble back then, and neither side forgets!

Modi: Abu Bakr ruled well, but upon his natural death, he named Umar as his successor—which is allowed.

Radi: I am still waiting to see how the trouble started.

Modi: Since Abu Bakr named Umar, Ali again stepped away. But Umar was assassinated, and Uthman was selected according to a new process.

The Restless Wind and Shifting Sands

Uthman was assassinated in turn, and finally Ali was asked to assume the mantle. He refused at first but finally agreed. Unfortunately, Ali was assassinated by members of what became the Umayyad dynasty.

Mani: I remembered that the Umayyads strayed from the straight path, and it came to Hussein, Ali's son, to try to overturn things.

Modi: Not quite, Mani. But there was grave concern that the religion was being dishonest and not rightly guided. With 72 people, including women and children, Hussein was not attacking but leading a procession of the prophet's family to reason with the believers to return to the true religion of his grandfather. But he was attacked by an army of the caliph, and all the men murdered.

Radi: Were they beheaded?

Modi: Yes, Radi, they were. And the Shiites were so shocked they withdrew, mostly to Iran. But they never forgot the massacre, and every year they continue Hussein's procession, flagellating themselves with whips in commemoration of the terrible event. And even today they reject the first three caliphs and insist Ali should have assumed the mantle first.

Mani: But that was hundreds of years ago.

Modi: Not to your friends and the Shia; it could have been last week or last month. Time does not dampen things here in the Middle East. You know as well as I that some families will wait several generations for an opportunity to take revenge on someone. Some poor great-great grandson will be attacked and killed by a neighboring family and never know why until his last breath.

Radi: How well I know, pardon my snickering. He never saw me coming.

Modi: I don't know about your friend here, Mani.

Mani: I thought he was yours. Anyway, I guess I had missed some of that history.

Modi: Many have. There is a lot more to it. Today the Sunnis are vexed because Iran wants to be the big power in the Middle East, and the Sunnis do not want that. Now that some American officials are becoming very cool about our war here, Iran is making its move in Lebanon and Syria. Al-Qaida is the only force in the Middle East, outside of Egypt, that thinks it can hold them back.

Radi: So we may be looking at another big war. Oh, goody! Heads will roll!

Mani: Shut up, Radi. Anyway, the shadows are lengthening. We need a little peace and solace. Let's go wash up. Modi, I need to be a better friend to you; I know I am very hard on you. I am just afraid you are not on the right path.

Modi: Perhaps Allah will help. He knows what's in our hearts. I hear Balil. Let's go, Radi!

The Restless Wind and Shifting Sands

<u>Conversation 8: Americans are not the Meccans of centuries ago!</u>

Mani: I saw on CNN that some American politicians and pundits want to abandon the fight. Allah has shown them the way.

Modi: Yes, I saw that. Unbelievable. And they don't see the problem here.

Radi: After they surrender and leave, how soon can we attack them? My blade will get rusty if it doesn't get some action soon.

Modi: Our friend Radi is still fighting at Badr. Just listen to him.

Mani: Yes, he is getting fiercer now that he knows there might be an end here. He is like a shark that smells blood in the water.

Radi: By my brandishing this knife, I serve notice that I will make our Most Beloved laugh by launching this body into their midst without a flak vest and driving my knife hither and yon, to send those heathens to hell.

Modi: You have been reading Ishaq's sira again. Ha! I never heard it like that.

Mani: When I hear him go off like that, I feel some stirring inside.

Radi: You should; we will do what we were born to do—kill the unbelievers until the entire planet is ours. We will be like Sa'd, from Ishaq 446, and leave none of them alive.

Modi: You are this way because the American leaders are talking about surrender?

Mani: I told you, he is now like a shark, Modi; he smells blood in the water.

Radi: I will cut the head off each enemy I subdue only after I let him watch as I take all of his possessions. I will give up one fifth to our leader, but I will keep the photos of the families and look up each in turn. There is no sin in tilling those fields. There will be slaves. Ha!

Modi: Radi, you are giving me chills.

Radi: Modi, you too may taste my blade if you run with the dogs. Allah has promised that He will be with us, giving us strength and endurance, and He will strike terror into the hearts of the unbelievers. We will cut off heads and fingertips, Modi. And it will be just the beginning for you. The torment of the fire of hell will be yours forever.[5] I will hate to see you writhe and scream in pain, but I will watch.

Mani: (Walks around and looks at Radi's back) Nope, don't see any wind-up key.

Modi: How do we turn him off?

Radi: Modi, there is no turning me off. I will not turn my back to the unbelievers or you. I will not retreat. Our Lord has commanded that anyone to do so will earn Allah's wrath and his new home will be in hell. He will meet a torturous end. I will be fierce and strong! I will take the heads of the men and confiscate their women and children. I will be God's terror in the land of America.

Mani: Radi, when the soldiers leave and we follow, Modi will be with us, with the faithful who are called by Allah to fight. Allah will breathe on him and fill his heart with the blue fire, and he will taste the blood lust of the victors of Badr. It will be he who introduces steel into the neck of Abu Jahl and enriches himself with the fortunes and the wives of the slain.

Modi: I hope you are wrong, Mani. It is not right. The Americans are not the Meccans, and this is not year 624. Some American politicians might be confused, but not the soldiers. The Americans came here to remove Saddam and help us rebuild; they have been attacked by

---

5   A reference to Sura 8:12.

The Restless Wind and Shifting Sands

insurgents, some of whom are now sorry they did so, even the ones still alive. The Americans will kill you on their own soil and not just the army. You think our insurgents and foreign fighters are tough. You had better think more than twice.

Radi: Allah will blind them, and they will not see us. Believers from everywhere will join this jihad. We will overwhelm the Americans.

Modi: You are reading material that will shorten your life, Radi. Be reasonable. Think about what you are saying.

Mani: You can't change him, Modi. I told you, he smells the blood of surrender and retreat and that brings out the Great White in him. He will not be satisfied now until he follows the troops to America and attacks them there. I see many of his friends are also ready to go.

Radi: I want to go to the big city of Washington. We will round up all the leaders and their families, and they will build a big ditch.

Modi: I don't want to hear any more of this. Besides he would not be a Great White; he is more like a hammer-head. How many times do we have to murder the Banu Quraiza?

Mani: It is Friday, and we have a good speaker today. He will calm Radi down.

Mani: Perhaps the ablution water will cool his passions.

Radi: My passions are too hot for ablutions to cool me down.

Modi: Oh yeah? I am going to throw you in!

Mani: Me too, Radi. I'm going to help Modi. (They all laugh)

Modi: (To Mani) I hope the American congress doesn't do this thing. I am afraid of the results. You know how many people there are like

Harry J. Sweeney

our Radi? Too many. But then, there are many more that are not bloodthirsty as he is.

Radi: Allah knows about them too. As Mani said about you, Allah will breathe upon them and bring them to jihad.

Mani: Modi, he is right! We all will have to join in; all of us. Radi was not kidding. It's the way things are. *Insha'llah* (if God wills it).

Modi: Now I hope I myself can calm down. Something is running up and down inside me. Now I am also running a sweat…

Mani: That is Allah calling you to jihad. You are hot to fight the infidels!

Modi: No, I would bet on those two cups of coffee I had at Radi's.

The Restless Wind and Shifting Sands

<u>Conversation 9: War is deceit!</u>

Modi: Mani, has Radi wound down yet? He was pretty tight last week.

Mani: Not really. He believes the American power majority is still attaching the white flag to the rope. I think Radi is wrong about that. Americans are much smarter than that. Our Most Beloved has said, "War is Deceit." Surely we have deceived some American politicians into believing that they are losing. Hah! I can hardly stand it. How dumb! How damned dumb!

Modi: We? You are aligning with the radicals?

Mani: Well, Modi, we were never very far away. We always wanted to see which way the wind was blowing. Now it seems it is blowing our way. There are American reporters who do not seem to get the idea that when they tell us how many troops they are sending and what they are obliged to do and what they are restricted from doing, they play right into our hands. We have their playbook.

Radi: Hi, guys. Yep, you are right, Mani. The American news programs give us the numbers, the itinerary, and the objectives so that we can get there first. It is almost like having a spy in their meetings.

Modi: Mani tells me you guys listen and read everything that goes on.

Radi: Of course. We have physicians, psychologists, analysts, and all kinds of experts digesting and analyzing all of those interviews on CNN, Fox, Headline News, and a few others.

Modi: There are quite a few other TV stations. Do they all broadcast that type of information?

Radi: Are you kidding? I don't even think they know anything about us. If they do, they certainly are not telling anyone.

Harry J. Sweeney

Mani: What do the experts do after they listen to the CNN and Fox interviews?

Radi: They analyze the data to see if the source is OK and knowledgeable, then determine the information's value and priority, and then send the analyses and recommendations to our own headquarters people.

Modi: It must be interesting work.

Radi: Most of the time it is, but sometimes when a couple of politicians argue, some of us go into fits of laughter, and we have to watch again to see if we missed anything someone else might have said.

Mani: What about that one former big shot, the old guy? Isn't he a friend of ours?

Radi: I have never been sure he knows what he is saying. It always seems to sound good as far as we are concerned, but such a big shot saying things against his country gives me the willies! I am surprised the Americans haven't put him away somewhere.

Modi: Mani reminded us that it has been written that "War is deceit." Perhaps the Americans are deceiving you guys with that older guy.

Mani: Nobody is that good a deceiver. Perhaps I should take that back; too many politicians, including ours are getting good at it.

Radi: Yes, Modi, war is deceit. Never give up or give in, simply appear to do so, gain strength while the enemy stands down, and remembering the Treaty of Hudaibiyya,[6] strike again with more force before he is ready. When we fight against Israel, if they want a cease-fire, we keep on fighting and redouble our efforts. If they don't want a cease-fire, we get our guys in the United Nations to give it to us. They are always very obliging.

---

6   *Mohammed and the Unbelievers*, Center for the Study of Political Islam, CSPI Publishing, 2006, pp 123-125.

The Restless Wind and Shifting Sands

Mani: Yes, Modi, it is like a big football game with all of the referees on our side.

Modi: And all the fans too, I see. And most of the announcers are as well.

Radi: Now you get it. Allah and the United Nations have an understanding; whatever it is, America is always wrong, and we can never lose!

Modi: When will they ever learn?

Harry J. Sweeney

Conversation 10: The Banu Quraiza[7] (800 beheaded)

Modi: Radi, why are you laughing so hard?

Radi: (Laughing so hard, tears run down his cheeks) I just heard that woman politician's speech about us and Guantánamo.

Mani: What was so funny?

Radi: (Still laughing) We are very busy all over the world, deceiving and killing Americans, not giving much of a damn about their rights or rules of engagement or anything like that. Now the stupid Americans want to give us all lawyers—thousands of lawyers (another fit of laughter) to see that we get our rights! And (laughs more) they are going to allow us discovery! (All three laugh) Yes, they may have to give us classified information that may be relevant—stuff that we can immediately pass on to all of our guys everywhere.

Modi: I have no idea what is going on in the minds of some Americans. They don't seem to know they are in a war to the death with no quarter at all given by Radi and his friends, and it almost seems as if the Americans are putting out a welcome mat.

Mani: Yes, it is just as the Book says: Here I am come kill me! Or, from a tree: "Hey, you warriors, there is an American hiding behind me. Come kill him." Allah is truly clouding the eyes and brains of some Americans so that it will be so much easier to kill them.

Radi: The Americans are now the Bin Quraiza. Their politicians will not let them fight us when we are at their very gates; perhaps their leaders will look for the best deal no matter how bad each deal is. But the best deal for them will still be hell-fire.

Mani: Bin Quraiza? You mean Banu Quraiza?

Modi: Same thing. While the Battle of the Trench was still not complete,

---

7   Ibid, pp 101-103.

our Most Beloved was advised by the Angel Gabriel to attack a nearby Jewish tribe, the Bin Quraiza. If given the opportunity, the Jews would ride against the believers and attack them, but on their own soil they would be too righteous. The warriors among them would silence their women and children, but for the others there was too much sentiment. They could break out of their village and die like men, but they did not want to break the Sabbath. Instead of fighting at all, they asked for a mediator. The mediator, Sa'd, told them they should simply surrender and let themselves be killed. They agreed to do so because it was the only option given and they wanted to be politically correct. And so they were taken to Medina where all the men were beheaded—including the male children; more than eight hundred people in a single day.

Mani: I remember that Aisha watched the executions that day.

Radi: The wives, children, and property were all divided up. Riches! And remember, *we must always emulate our Most Beloved; he lived the perfect life.*

Mani: Nobody can disagree with that! Everyone is commanded to emulate him.

Modi: And the Americans are supposed to be worried about the world condemning them about Guantánamo.

Mani: What world? The Europeans? What have they ever done that they can condemn the Americans? Hah! We are the world!

Modi: Yes, I heard the words: "The Americans have shocked the conscience of the world." They have forgotten about 9/11!

Mani: They have forgotten a lot of things. Embassy bombings, Blackhawk Down, the first World Trade Center attempt! They forgot Beirut and the Towers in Saudi Arabia. How can the Americans ever shock the conscience of the world if *we* can't even do it?

Radi: What world can they be thinking of? There is only one world,

Harry J. Sweeney

and we are masters of that one. At least we will be as soon as we defeat the Americans. Oh that's right, we did. One senator has already pronounced, "The War is lost."

Modi: I surely thought the Americans would do much better than that. Their congress seems to be tripping all over itself to let us win.

Radi: Modi, I told you what it was. Allah has said in previous troubles that he would say the word and the enemies would destroy themselves.

Mani: It certainly seems to be happening.

Radi: I see I am going to be very busy. Perhaps I should go sharpen my blade.

Mani: Why bother. Let the American congress do it for you.

Modi: You guys are kidding yourselves. The American Congress will eventually get it straight. They wake up and look around once in a while.

Radi: Yeah? My blade will sever many heads; many will my victims be. Uh, oh!

Mani: What's the matter?

Radi: We had better hurry or we will be late for the noon prayer! We must hasten there to purify ourselves first.

Modi: Yes, Radi, be sure to work on that tongue of yours.

CHAPTER 2

<u>Conversation 11: Who cares about Abu Ghraib?</u>

Modi: I have been looking over our loving scriptures again and I continually come across the admonishment that there should be no compulsion in religion.[8]

Mani: I remember telling you that the saying applies only to forcing defeated enemies to convert. Of course, it is necessary to have some dhimmis; the entire Muslim world runs on dhimmi money. Our religion, as you should know, is based upon absolute belief and obedience of the people. Actions that are not harmful in themselves but demonstrate disobedience to Allah are considered *kufr;* that disbelief must be punished.

Radi: Mani is right, Modi. When the imams say "arise," all followers all over the world must immediately stand and await the next command. The imams must not be questioned.

Modi: That does not make sense. The imams don't know everything. Many imams want this terrorism to be called a "holy war," but it is not a holy war; it is simply a disagreement among believers. Some want the Americans to stay and help rebuild the country, and others want them out. There is nothing holy about this war.

Mani: I have to tell you, what you are saying is *kufr!* You could be cut down just for saying it. The Americans declared war on Islam!

Modi: See, that's where you are wrong, Mani. They declared war against the government of Saddam Hussein. The American army ran in and defeated Saddam's armies in no time at all, but some inept American

---

8   Qur'an 2:256.

Harry J. Sweeney

civilians screwed it all up. And, of course, Radi and his friends did not help. But the Americans helped us get rid of our tyrant!

Radi: I will never help the Americans. Why should I? They kill our people.

Modi: The Americans kill anyone who is shooting at them and killing them with roadside bombs—which incidentally kill our people as well.

Mani: They are also occupiers who came for our oil! They are here illegally, not sanctioned by the United Nations.

Modi: The Americans want nothing more than to help us get started, and then they want to leave. And quite frankly, Mani, tell me how much oil they have taken. And you mentioned the United Nations. Many of those UN members are still upset because the U.S. shut down their businesses netting millions in bribe money in the oil-for-food program. Saddam sold our oil under the table supposedly for food and medicine. How much food did you see, Mani? How much medicine has reached our people?

Radi: Oh yeah! What about Abu Ghraib? What about that?

Modi: Ha! You nitwit! Who cares about that? A couple of low-level soldiers made some of our guys look silly! How many mass graves were needed afterwards? None, right? Not a single person was hurt. If Saddam's mass graves and murders were not outrageous, what is the big deal about a few Arab fighters wearing dunce caps? Look at what Radi's friends do with American prisoners? Hah! No answer! They chop them up into little pieces and hang them from a bridge.

Radi: They deserved it!

Modi: Who the hell are you to say they deserved it? They were not soldiers, Radi; they were contractors, plain old everyday workers like you and me. And they were here to make a decent wage while helping

The Restless Wind and Shifting Sands

us to rebuild. I would bet not one of them ever fired a single round at an Arab. You know something, Radi, you like the French so much because of Monsieur Chirac, but if you pull that stuff on French forces in Lebanon and they send in the Foreign Legion, there won't be any of you left to complain about atrocities. The Legion did not much care about political correctness. I'll tell you something else; you let the US Marines in to do whatever they have to do without absurd micromanagement, and you will have to wait for a new army to grow up—the U. S. Marines don't care for political correctness either. And the British troops, if let go to do the job their way—you will be grass and they are the lawn-mowers.

Mani: Why are you so anti-Islam today? You don't know what you're saying!

Modi: How dare you say anti-Islam! I have just grown a little tired of listening to raving and maniacal garbage from you and others about what is going on here and who is going to do what. You don't see what is going on and don't want to know the truth. None of you people want to help; you only want to criticize the Americans. You and the Arabs in Palestine just do not know who your best friends are!

Radi: It is written we must kill the infidel wherever we find them.[9] We find many here, and we will find more in America! We will kill them all. Their women and children will be our spoils of war. We will own their fancy cars and their nice homes. It is already written.[10]

Modi: There is more written, Radi, than you know about. There is a Golden Rule that says "Do unto others as you would have them do unto you." Don't you believe that? Oh, I forget myself. We do not have that rule in the Middle East.

Radi: Let me give this to you straight: if our Most Beloved did not say it, it is not worth listening to or considering. It is trash!

---

9   Qur'an 2:191, 2:256, 9:5.
10   Qur'an 8:41 8:69, 33:26.

Harry J. Sweeney

Modi: What about: "Live and let live"?

Mani: It is not at all Islamic. Social awareness, kindness, and compassion apply only to our relationships with other followers. Everyone else is destined for the fires of hell, and anyone so destined can be ignored, banned, taxed, tortured, raped, or killed without sanctions because they are hated by Allah.[11]

Modi: You two are actually condemning all people that do not happen to be believers.

Mani: No, Modi, they have all condemned themselves. How many times do I have to tell you: Bismillah,[12] our Most Beloved delivered to all of mankind the Qur'an, whose originator was Allah? The Qur'an cannot be changed or interpreted—or corrupted like other scriptures given to the Jews, so it will be eternal, and everyone will know the same ideas and commands from The Most Merciful. It is so easy.

Radi: That is so, Modi. Those people who reject the commands of the Qur'an of Allah and the emulation of the perfect life of our Most Beloved are *kafirs*, ungrateful to God, and must be eliminated until all the towns all over the world ring with the glories of only Allah.[13]

Modi: Have you ever considered thinking your own thoughts and not looking at the world according to what was written more than a thousand years ago?

Radi: What? How dare you? That is blasphemy! That could make you an apostate!

Mani: Yes, Modi. If you say things like that and Radi just hauls off and separates your head from your body, I can only watch. He is right.

Modi: Great friends you are. All I want you to do is think for yourself and make decisions based on what YOU think is right.

---

11   Qur'an 2:6, 3:151, 5:76, 48:13.
12   In the name of Allah.
13   Qur'an 2:216, 5:33-34, 22:19-22, 76:4.

The Restless Wind and Shifting Sands

Radi: Why should we. Allah has already made those decisions for us centuries ago. We are His followers; we obey Allah.

Modi: What if something happened and a believer erred in reading some written word in the middle of a verse a thousand years ago? People have misunderstood meanings before. Some of those ayats, those verses, were written on banana leaves, and the language was not advanced enough to guarantee a word would mean one thing and not another; they used no diacritical marks. Memory was actually much more reliable, even though the diligent believers tasked with memorizing verses had been through several battles. Mani, I couldn't guarantee I could remember anything, especially verses, had I experienced the raids and the battles during that time. You don't think some meanings could be lost and others mixed up—lots of people were killed with verses still embedded in their memories? Were the verses lost?

Mani: That could not happen.

Modi: Why not?

Mani: Allah would not let it.

Modi: Aaaargh! I quit. Let's go eat or something. How about a pork sandwich?

Mani: Dammit, Radi, kill him. (They give chase, laughing.)

Harry J. Sweeney

Conversation 12: Multiculturalism, Political Correctness, and Apostasy

Modi: Good morning. Radi, you were not at morning prayers, outside with our neighbors. We even saved you a spot stone free. Someone's father asked about you. Maybe he has a daughter that needs a husband.

Radi: I was out all night with friends; we were looking for an apostate we heard about. We didn't find him. I just rolled out, did a quick ablution, offered my life again to Allah for all his benefices, and then rolled back in. What? Someone's father looked for me? Oh, I know. I have been too busy to visit.

Mani: If you would get married, Radi, you could be home snuggled up with a loving wife instead of dealing with things that are none of your business. Didn't the cold water wake you up this morning, you look terrible?

Modi: No, he wore a mask all day, so he only had to pass his hands over the mask.[14]

Mani: (Laughing) You are sick, Modi. Did you see the news item that reported the British school board announcing the death of Western Civilization?

Modi: Yes, I did. Talk about sick! This monster has been dogging their tracks since the end of the big war. The British leadership, as usual, got things wrong again. Remember that British imam who gave that big talk about a year ago, Radi?

Radi: Oh yes. That imam was fire and brimstone all right. He had the British pegged: not worth fighting. He said they will implode.

Mani: I recall that the imam told us the British leadership blamed

---

14   A reference to the ablutions rule that if one wears socks right after one ablution, one need only rub hands over the socks instead of removing them and washing with water. The limitation on this is 1½ days; then wash the feet again.

The Restless Wind and Shifting Sands

British, as he described it, "questionable culture" for causing all of those wars, so I suppose that is why they won't teach their historic culture any more.

Modi: Right. And since Christianity and Judaism were part of that culture, they blamed them both for the rottenness in their history. What a piece of work! I have no idea what they think the Jews did. It must have been a whopper.

Radi: But what does all of that mean to us?

Mani: If it is really true, it would mean the British now would be empty; they would have no culture to fall back on. Without culture, there are no traditions or clues on how to react to life and emergencies. The military and police have their own traditions, but they are now limited by political correctness and multiculturalism. For doing what they can't get arrested for there.

Modi: Mani is right. Political correctness means that they cannot tell the population that radical Islamists are responsible for the bombings, even if they have direct proof. And multiculturalism means that the British and Muslims must live side by side with two different systems of government at a certain level. If we want more than one wife, the government just looks the other way. But the British citizens can't even think about it.

Mani: Yes. And if we kill our daughters for wanting to have a British boyfriend, that is OK too. Or if someone like Radi wants to kill an apostate, he is not charged.

Modi: Not all the time, Mani. Sometimes they arrest the parents and bring them to trial. If they can find them. Although they'd rather not pursue anything that "is a matter of religion." They cannot differentiate between religious demands and traditions. It is the same with killing an apostate; the British bring the person to trial sometimes and his lawyer argues it is his religion. One of these days, some law firm is

Harry J. Sweeney

going to actually study the Qur'an and sharia and discover they have been hoodwinked.

Radi: Is France that way also?

Modi: Almost, They do not seem to charge groups with political crimes or conspiracies, or to show group responsibility for crimes; they must show that each of the individuals committed a crime, even though the crimes were committed by a hate group.

Radi: You are saying that if *Islamiya,* for example, blew up a couple of buildings and a railway station, they can't blame *Islamiya* and round up the members?

Mani: Not publicly, no. They must put the blame on the actual individuals who did the deed. I would guess if someone squealed and an investigation showed that the organization was indeed responsible, the French would go after each of the individual members of the organization who gave the order.

Radi: Sounds like my kind of place.

Modi: I did not say that the French *keufs*[15] would not beat the hell out of you if they caught you with explosives or running from a burning building.

Radi: You already know what we would do. We would gather a few of our people from the neighborhoods and go looking for them with Kalashnikovs and knives ready. They would not live for a trial. It's cost effective.

Modi: Like any apostates you might find?

Radi: Yeah, yeah. Too bad he got away.

Mani: Tell Modi who gave you authorization to kill an apostate.

---

15   French verlan (inversion of syllables: à l'envers) slang for policeman (*flic*).

The Restless Wind and Shifting Sands

Radi: He really doesn't know? Modi, we are mandated to kill apostates—even the sharia acknowledges there are no sanctions or any consequences at all for killing one.

Modi: But why must an apostate be killed?

Mani: Because it is so written.[16]

Modi: But *when* it was written, apostates were those who were considered traitors and could have caused harm by telling the Meccans or the Jewish tribes about plans or weaknesses of the believers in Medina. It could affect the outcome of a battle. Today, if a woman wants to marry a Christian or a Jew, who cares? Why should she be killed? It makes no sense.

Radi: It is written. It is not required to make sense.

Modi: I will ask you what I had asked Mani. If your brother decided he was simply tired of religion and just left home, not to join another religion but to live freely without any religion for a while, would you kill him?

Mani: Yes, before you could say Abu Musaad al Zarqawi.

Modi: *Et tu, Brute?*

Radi: What?

Modi: Nothing. I am disappointed. I thought you guys loved your family more than that.

Radi: More than what? There are 101 important priorities in life; religion represents 100 of them and family 1. We love our families—

---

16   Qur'an Verse 3:90 "Those who disbelieve after they have believed, or whose unbelief has increased, their repentance will not be accepted." Hadith Bukhari 9:84:57 Statement of Allah's Apostle: "Whoever changed his Islamic religion, then kill him."

Harry J. Sweeney

our children. Even if we have to kill any of them for violating our scriptures. Allah always comes first.

Mani: Actually, first, last, and always.

Modi: But you see your children every day, you love them, and they love you. They would do anything for you.

Radi: I hope they would never let me get so mad, drunk, or so sick that I would renounce my religion.

Modi: But when you sobered up, you would be a fine believer again. Your lapse would be only temporary. If your family killed you, you would be a dead apostate. Dying in that state would put you in hell forever, according to what you told me earlier.

Radi: Yes, that is the way things are.

Modi: Then wouldn't it be better if your family let you alone for a while, perhaps to come to your senses?

Radi: You are messing with my mind. That's a waste of time.

Modi: Yes, a mind is a terrible thing to . . . never mind.

Mani: I hear Balil. Radi, go first. You make Modi nervous.

Radi: Ha! I'm gonna lop off his head if I ever find out what he means. I know he is insulting me; I just don't know how.

The Restless Wind and Shifting Sands

Conversation 13: Multiculturalism, Political Correctness, and Nasser

Mani: Modi, the other day you were telling us about European culture dying or being killed off by their educators.

Modi: Yep. It is not just the people who teach; there are some people in authority with strange notions about education.

Radi: Well, what about religion in general?

Modi: The religions that they consider part of their historical culture are Judaism and Christianity. To their way of thinking, a little skewed, somehow the two religions were responsible for all the wars that have devastated both the British Isles and the Continent.

Mani: You already said that. Does it include the crusades?

Modi: The crusades are part of it. But just like here, if you talk to anyone who has been educated in universities you hear just about the same theme: any political system other than socialism is bad. Socialism will save the world from itself.

Radi: But we are not socialists. Nasser appeared to be, but he was not accepted in much of the Arab world. He pushed a pan-Arab agenda. But he relied too much on the Soviets.

Mani: Nasser was OK but militant only in nationalism, not in his religion. He suppressed the Brotherhood and had Qutb executed. We can't forgive him for that. But if the Europeans are down on religion, why are so many of us emigrating there?

Modi: Radi, you are right: we are not socialists, but we are pretty close. But about our migration to Europe, there are more than a few reasons for that. One reason is that the Europeans were very confused by their politicians who are not keen on their past histories. They are just not having children. They love their social programs, but soon they could

Harry J. Sweeney

lose them because there would be no one to pay for them. When you kill your babies, who is there to look after you in your old age?

Radi: Oh! So they bring our guys in to work and help pay for those programs.

Modi: Exactly. So some of us go there to work and live and grow old in Europe. But others have been thrown out of all the Middle Eastern countries and can go only to Europe—Europe can't throw them out if they can't return to their own countries. It's their stupid law! I can never figure out why the West tries to commit suicide.

Mani: They can't throw out even the terrorists who are plotting and scheming and raising havoc?

Radi: Yeah. I heard that from some folks I know in London. You won't believe what they can get away with there. They would be killed here for doing what they can't get arrested for there.

Mani: Like what?

Radi: Demonstrating against the government and screaming defiance at the top of their lungs in the town squares; they threaten everyone with death.

Mani: If Europe is down on religion, why is our religion tolerated when our guys flout it?

Modi: We were not part of their historic culture. We are part of the "suppressed minorities" so loved by the politicians; and the European leadership considers us something like a back-to-nature religion, the pure and honest peons who only want to work, pray, and serve Allah.

Mani: But that's who we are!

Modi: But in serving Allah, we also serve ourselves. I know that in the past, by absorbing the riches of the lands we conquered, we sometimes

The Restless Wind and Shifting Sands

enriched ourselves, adding their inventions to our inventory, adding their achievements to our own, and encroaching farther and farther into their world to take it from them and to absorb the people as well or just enslave them like we did to so many over time. But there were times when we simply destroyed everything.

Radi: Mani, Is he insulting us? What is he talking about?

Mani: Now wait a second! Just what would you have us do?

Modi: What is wrong with not fighting with them and not scheming to take their lands? They invited us to come into their countries and be like them—oops, no. I got that wrong. They were supposed to invite us into their countries to live and work right alongside them, and become integrated and merged into their culture, and they into ours. We were all to become one people together. But as usual, the politicians got it wrong again.

Mani: How's that?

Modi: They have this insane idea that we must come into their country and set up our own cultural communities separate from theirs, parallel communities that do not even have to speak each other's languages. It's called multiculturalism. It is a product of their unworkable notion of equality.

Mani: Equality?

Modi: Yes. To them, individual freedom and privacy is not as important as being equal to everyone else—even if you are not. They actually think the culture of some Borneo headhunters is equal to Western culture.

Radi: By Allah, that indeed is insane.

Mani: It has already led to lots of trouble in France and England, Holland and Denmark also. The politicians seem to say, "Let the poor, underprivileged people from the Middle East live in their culture and

Harry J. Sweeney

practice their religion in peace, no matter how it shocks the knickers off of us!" However, some of that "culture" is against European laws.

Modi: Yes. Many of our people who go there expect a different life—to remain true to their religion but live like Europeans, and the leadership just will not allow it—they think they are favoring us by doing this and now our kids—even those born there—are killing them because they have an identity crisis caused by this awkward and discredited idea of multiculturalism. They don't know who or what they are, European or Arab. The teachings of one doesn't match the democracy of the other. When they begin to adjust to the Western culture, even some very progressive professors tell them no, don't adopt our culture; it is corrupt. The authorities appear not to see the problem, so it continues.

Mani: And I can see Radi's friends eating that chaos all up and taking advantage of it.

Radi: Pardon me if I snicker. The name of the game is recruiting. Five minutes with one of those kids and he's ours. Even the kids who are not of our religion want to convert and be part of something, anything.

Modi: Yes, your radical friends are taking advantage of British and European soft-headedness. Instead of being part of something, they are tearing it apart.

Radi: It is their fault! You said it yourself: the immigrants are not allowed to merge with the populations. Don't we have groups there that try to explain these things to their hosts?

Mani: From what I've seen, once those silly politicians get an idea in their heads, trying to talk them out of it is like talking to cement.

Radi: Aha! I've got it. I know what is happening. Just like other battles, Allah is blinding our enemies to what the truth is, making them do things even against their own nature. And He does this because he has chosen us as his special people to take his planet back.

The Restless Wind and Shifting Sands

Mani: Yes, Modi. Radi is right. Allah is the owner of our universe and the CEO of every nation and every business. All we do is for Him. We owe everything to Him and will gladly give it all up for Him.

Modi: Everything is for Him? What about your families? Your wives?

Radi: It is written, our wives and slaves are our gardens to till as we please. When I am married, I intend to till and till and till.

Mani: Better use a lot of fertilizer, tiller!

Modi: Ha! He's nothing but fertilizer!

Radi: I'm going to kill you both. (gives chase, laughing).

Harry J. Sweeney

Conversation 14: Banu Quraiza and American Militia.

Mani: Radi, it looks as if most of the Americans now favor ending the Iraq war and will be putting the other party back in power. I just saw it on CNN.

Radi: I hope Modi doesn't know yet; I want to tell him. Hah!

Modi: I heard all of that. Radi, you are a real buddy.

Radi: Modi, We talked a few days ago about the Banu Quraiza, a Jewish tribe in Medina. Well, it seems America is the new Banu Quraiza.

Mani: Yes. The "old" president and some generals have told everyone time after time that if they surrender in Iraq, we will most assuredly follow them home. He seems to understand that we will definitely attack them in their own country. Why don't the rest get it?

Radi: I don't understand the ignorance that bounces around the American congress. You know, our Most Beloved, the man who led the perfect life, back in the seventh century had many spies in Mecca, always letting him know what was going on there, and had spies among the Jewish tribes for the same purpose.

Mani: Yep. And he also knew over a thousand years ago that war is deceit, he said so. He would never continually tell the Meccans what was on his mind. He always made plans to surprise them somehow.

Modi: That is ancient news. He did not care how outnumbered he was, he was confident of his leadership because he knew what he was doing. He did know warfare and rewrote all the rules. Our Most Beloved was a great general, no doubt about that.

Radi: You watch, Modi. The Americans will leave Iraq as if they had lost great battles because the leaders think they know it all—and they do not. And then the American leadership will become the chieftains of the Banu Quraiza.

Mani: I agree. They will ask about treaties to protect themselves from us, and our friends in congress, just like our Most Beloved's spies, will let us know how badly they want those treaties. That makes me think I smell something like Hudaibiyya.

Modi: You think the American leadership will want protection from us so bad they will sign anything to get it?

Radi: Yes. And more than that. We will require the American leadership to push through many rules that will be of great benefit to us and very humiliating to the American people. They must provide us with lots of money and provide the transportation for our people to immigrate there.

Mani: We will demand the sharia for all believers in America, but first we will start pushing our own people into their congress and senate—then we will ultimately have full sharia. And the laws against the American people will be tightened.

Radi: With the full sharia, their loving Constitution will be gone.

Modi: I do not think the Americans will take to being dhimmis. I doubt very seriously you can pull this off. The American people are great fighters.

Mani: They, like the Banu Quraiza, will have no choice. They wanted to fight too, but their weaklings among them talked their elders into surrendering to us. It reminds me of all those politicians that wring their hands, sweat like crazy, and hide from the people.

Modi: One of the biggest problems for the American leadership or educators is that they do not know our history or our culture. They do not really know who we are. Some of us old moderates keep trying to tell them, but they won't listen.

Harry J. Sweeney

Radi: You may be right. What if the American people knew about what happened to turn a handful of people into the masters of all Arabia in just a few years?

Mani: Yeah, and then turned that into ownership of half the world, almost winning the rest of the world. If Charles Martel had practiced political correctness, the entire world would have been speaking Arabic today.

Modi: If they knew about those things, they would probably march on Washington and throw a lot of inept people out of office. It would be fun to watch, almost as much fun as watching Radi running for his life.

Radi: But I would miss watching the faces of the American men when we tell them, as we did the Quraiza, that they will walk into a long ditch to make it easier for our boys and men to lop off their heads. We may have hundreds of those ditches.

Mani: I know Modi will want to believe that the Americans will fight and never walk into the ditch.

Modi: You guys have not seen the American militia.

Radi: We have seen their great American Army, their Air Force, and their Marines. We are not afraid of them.

Modi: But they are not the militia.

Mani: (Looks at Radi and back to Modi) I don't get it. Are you talking about their National Guard? The leadership would have surrendered them all. We will kill all the warriors first, as we did before.

Modi: Their leadership cannot surrender the militia. See, there are still things you guys with all of your intelligence do not know about.

Radi: I don't understand. If the militia cannot be surrendered by the American leadership, what is it? With all our forces of believers from around the world, why should we be concerned about the militia? Just what is it?

Modi: It is the entire population of the United States, that's what.

Mani: Right! We should be afraid of them?

Modi: You know what the leadership is like. Well, these people are just the opposite. They are also well armed with their own private weapons of choice, and they know how to use them effectively. They know their countryside, and lots of them even make their own ammunition.

Radi: What?

Modi: You remember how you used to complain about the American snipers in Iraq and Afghanistan. One shot—one kill! How do you feel about coming up against a few million of people who do not waste ammunition and never miss?

Mani: Ha! Before that happens, we will make the American leadership take their guns away from them.

Modi: That has been tried before many times. In fact, every year some of their leaders try to push for laws to do just that. The Americans always fight back.

Radi: What? The American leadership is trying to disarm its own people? What kind of craziness is that? You must be kidding, Modi.

Mani: Yes, Modi. No leader in his right mind would even think of doing something that stupid. What is wrong with them?

Modi: Many politicians do not believe in the individual, only the mass

Harry J. Sweeney

of people in general. But the American people have been nice enough to let them know the only way they can take their weapons from them.

Radi: Oh? How's that.

Modi: They can pry them from their cold, dead hands.

The Restless Wind and Shifting Sands

Conversation 15: Jihad, women, and head scarves.

Mani: Modi, I hope you have all that anti-believer stuff out of your system.

Radi: Yeah! Another outburst like that and I will be your Khalid.[17]

Modi: OK, guys, look: I am not anti-believer. I am a very ardent believer. I love my religion as much as you two.

Radi: You don't act like it.

Modi: An ardent believer does not have to run up and down the streets waving a sword or firing a Kalashnikov, cursing people he does not even know. An ardent believer can be tolerant with nonbelievers.[18]

Mani: Only if the unbelievers are dhimmis. But an ardent believer joins the jihad!

Modi: He does so when there is a good reason for jihad. The war against the Americans in Iraq is not a jihad! I keep telling you, not one drop of oil have they taken from us. In addition, everything they do points to their trying to help, not overcome.

Radi: They are just like the Europeans, occupying our lands in order to suppress us and our religion. It is a war against our beliefs.

Modi: Now wait a minute. If you are bringing into the mix the judgment of history about the West and us, I can trump that noise. If you recall, the Europeans occupied believers' land for only 50 years, and during that time our religion and culture suffered no damage from European administration. On the other hand, we occupied some European lands for 1300 years. During that time, there was nothing but suppression

---

17   Ishaq, *The Life of Muhammad*, margin notes 834, 835. Khalid was so violent the Prophet announced to Allah three times that he was innocent of what Khalid had done.

18   Qur'an Sura 109:1-6.

of everything European. The Europeans that chose to live with us were humiliated and treated with utter disgust and atrocities.[19]

Mani: We treated everyone with the respect or disrespect they deserved.[20] But the Americans have not been much help here.

Modi: They made mistakes because the Americans do not know or understand us. Look at the French; they know us and understand us. Are they helping us? No! They just want our money and our oil. Are they helping the Americans to understand? No! They want the Americans to fail. They would rather see us in turmoil so that they can come in when the Americans leave and take what they can get. Of course, with Chirac gone, perhaps they may surprise us.

Mani: The French have been our friends for decades.

Modi: Yes, as long as they could make money from us.

Mani: But you, Modi, must become stronger in your faith!

Modi: I do everything our faith demands. But I don't require my wonderful wife to wear a *burqa*, and she can leave the house anytime she wants. I take enough static from my neighbors about that. They'd be happier if I beat her every day with a stick. We have been so happy with each other; I had forgotten things I was taught years ago.

Mani: Well, I can understand about the *burqa* and leaving the house. But you do have to beat wives off and on. And no one is allowed to ask you why you did it!

Radi: I know about not asking why, but I can't agree with how Modi

---

19   *Cancer in America*, John U. Hanna, pages 4, 5.

20   Qur'an Sura 9:029, SHAKIR: Fight those who do not believe in Allah, nor in the latter day, nor do they prohibit what Allah and His Messenger have prohibited, nor follow the religion of truth, out of those who have been given the Book, until they pay the tax in acknowledgment of superiority and they are in a state of subjection.

treats his wife. Women should be invisible! They should be dressed in formless *chador*s or *abaya*s with hood and veil. They should be no more than shadows! And they should never, ever leave the house without permission from their husbands. I would not let mine leave at all, not even to go to mosque. And all women should be chaperoned whenever they are outside the house. Wives can never be trusted. And a husband should control his wife totally. She is his from the top of her head to the bottoms of her feet.

Modi: Gee, Radi, are you ever going to get married?

Mani: The imam keeps bringing him nice, believing women, but he keeps turning them down. They are all covered up so thoroughly he can't see what he is getting. But he still claims that one woman will be his someday. I am beginning to doubt it.

Radi: (Modi and Mani chuckle) That's not right and you know it.

Modi: From what I understand, Mani's only slightly exaggerating.

Radi: You may laugh, but Allah will punish you for not being stronger!

Modi: Well, am I supposed to be like the believers who let the fourteen little daughters burn to death in a fiery schoolhouse because they didn't have their head scarves on?

Mani: I would have let them out, I think! I believe so. Maybe not. I don't know.

Radi: They were martyrs to their faith; the men did right! They were strong in their religion. God will reward them.

Modi: What about humanity? Doesn't that count for something? Allah is merciful, remember?

Harry J. Sweeney

Radi: Our Most Beloved was strong in his religion, and he did not shrink from his duty even when hundreds of Jews had to be killed.[21] Allah can be merciful; we cannot. Your marriage contract requires you to pay a dowry and provide lodging, food, and clothing; the wife commits herself to be there for you, whenever you want her.

Modi: We don't have free will?

Radi: Only within the limitations of what Allah has planned for you. You cannot defy destiny, except through martyrdom.

Mani: Modi, why can't you just tell Radi you will try to be stronger in your religion. You can see bickering is not getting us anywhere.

Modi: Mani, I am striving—my own jihad—to be stronger and better, more knowledgeable in my religion. In doing so I found that it does not require me to be meaner, more violent, or more intolerant of others.

Radi: See! He is insulting us again. I should lop off his head.

Modi: That's what I mean, Mani, no tolerance at all. Each little thing off base and he wants heads to roll in the street. Look at whom we execute: the poor guy who accidentally swept some dust on the wall of a mosque, girls who don't want to marry some old geezer their fathers picked out, someone who just wants to leave the religion and do something else to worship his Creator. We need to rethink some of these rules.

Radi: See! He is condemning us again! Modi, how many times must I tell you all of these rules are eternal! They can never be changed, ever! And anyone who even brings up such heresy needs to die!

Modi: See, Mani; he has his religion and I have mine. He doesn't believe what I believe, and I cannot believe what he believes. It is unfortunate that it's the same religion.

---

21   A reference again to the Banu Quraiza.

The Restless Wind and Shifting Sands

Mani: You two are incorrigible.

Radi: So are you—whatever that means!

Harry J. Sweeney

Conversation 16: Arranged Marriages, Honor Killings.

Mani: Modi, what on earth is wrong with you? You look like you just found out your family was Jewish.

Modi: Worse than that! I have a terrible family problem.

Mani: Whew! If it's worse than that, maybe I shouldn't hear it.

Modi: It's about my little sister.

Mani: I thought she went to Denmark with your parents on holiday.

Modi: I thought so too, but it turns out they were going to marry her off to an old friend of my father's.

Mani: That's nice! An arranged marriage.

Modi: Nice?! She's twelve for crying out loud! Twelve! Just a baby! A forced marriage!

Mani: Nothing wrong with that. Keeps her out of trouble.

Modi: She thought they were going to look at some schools there. She really wants to get an education and do something important.

Radi: There is nothing more important for a woman than to obey, honor, and support her husband.

Modi: I am tired of hearing that, Radi. We are talking about my little sister.

Radi: Oh! I remember her. She must be ready for marriage by now.

Mani: Don't say that, Radi. Modi thinks she is a baby. Be civil!

The Restless Wind and Shifting Sands

Radi: I don't know what we're going to do with you, Modi. Our women have been doing that for centuries. That is the way they are brought up—absolute obedience!

Modi: Centuries of mistakes do not make anything right. The marriage is not the worst part. When she found out what was going on, she ran away.

Mani: Oh no! Have they found her yet?

Modi: They know where she is; a group of people there took her in, and they are protecting her. They won't give her up. My parents want me to go there and get her; they think she will listen to me.

Radi: They want you to talk some sense into her?

Mani: Radi, you know what happens when daughters do that.

Radi: They want Modi to kill his little sister?

Mani: That is why he is so down. You already know how it works. I bet they told him he either must do it himself or else bring her back so that they can do it. It's the knife or the stone—or consent to be married. It may be too late for that; the family is dishonored already. It is an honor killing! A blessed event!

Radi: And Modi does not want to do it because it's his little sister? Now that's where the rubber hits the road; he is either a believer or not. He has to save his family's honor. If he doesn't, there will be dreadful consequences.

Mani: Yes. The family will be dishonored twice. Modi and his sister both will bite the blade. Modi, you have to go and do it.

Modi: No! If I go, I will help her. She deserves to have a life, and she deserves to be educated. She does not need to suffer the life of a shadow of a person depending on the attitude of a husband for either

Harry J. Sweeney

a mediocre life at best or a terrible and painful one—and a very short one.

Radi: You make it sound worse than it really is.

Modi: Remember that imam that they killed because they claimed he was a sorcerer? I did some favors for him once, and he told me he would give me a special power: I can point my finger and change anything I want, but just one time! So, I am pointing at you and will change you into a woman!

Radi: What? (Covers his face) You better not! I will kill you for that!

Mani: Radi, Modi is only kidding you. He does not have that kind of power; he was just making a point.

Radi: (Holds his heaving chest) That joke is not funny. I could never be a woman.

Mani: Modi, what are you going to do? You cannot dishonor your parents.

Modi: I am not going to see my sister married, hurt, or killed. I will let my parents know that no one except me knows what really happened. If I visit my sister, we might both run away somewhere, perhaps to America. Whatever I do, it will be to avoid harm to my sister.

Mani: What good will that do?

Modi: I am not finished yet. I will tell them to let my sister go and make up a story that will save their honor. If I hear that they continue in their efforts to find her, I will go there and interfere. Then they will have to find someone to kill me. That will not be easy.

Radi: Ha! They could hire me.

The Restless Wind and Shifting Sands

Modi: If that is the kind of friend you are, Radi, how can we continue to pray together to the same God?

Mani: Modi, it would not be personal with Radi. He just follows his religion, as we all must do.

Modi: I told you guys before—that is not following religion; it is giving in to your basic instincts because your traditions allow it. Many, many believers know what the religion says, but they do not kill people who are in no way harming them. When it comes down to killing someone, it is more important than what you read; you must wait until you have a clear and unambiguous sign from Allah before you can act. And even then, you must think about it.

Radi: I just received a clear and unambiguous sign.

Mani: Uh, oh! I did not like the sound of that.

Modi: (Looks seriously at Radi) What kind of sign, Radi?

Radi: My stomach is making unambiguous noises and I did not have breakfast. Is that clear enough?

Modi: One of these days Radi. One of these days.

Mani: Both of you guys are nuts!

Harry J. Sweeney

Conversation 17:

The conversation between a judge and a girl while he actually placed the noose around her neck was not recorded. Perhaps it was more interesting than fiction could imagine. The girl was 16 and the charges for which she was convicted stemmed from abuse of her by family members during a protracted period. She was an orphan, living and working in their home.

Girl: Judge, how nice to see you. I did not expect you to come see me off. I thought you despised me.

Judge: I see you still have a mouth.

Girl: It is my only defense in this male-dominated world.

Judge: It was not much of a defense and definitely a hindrance. You do not show proper respect for your elders.

Girl: Oh, heavens! You would not allow me to have a defense counsel and would not allow me to say anything in my defense. What was I supposed to do, let you bad-mouth me like my male relatives were doing?

Judge: I was not obligated to listen to a defense lawyer, and you did not have four female witnesses or two male witnesses who saw each act.

Girl: Right. Now don't you think that rule is just a little silly? Actually, I did have four male witnesses, but they were the culprits. You did not question them at my trial. That would have turned things around if you made them tell the truth.

Judge: All of those male "witnesses" were whipped.

Girl: Yep; their trial followed mine so you could convict me first without their guilt on record. So, today, I am waiting for the noose

The Restless Wind and Shifting Sands

and the crane to lift me high above the city to slowly strangle to death. Where are the males? Are they watching?

Judge: They were judged fairly according to our laws.

Girl: You will pardon me if I don't kiss your feet for that. *Our* laws, indeed.

Judge: You are still mouthy and disrespectful!

Girl: Tell me, learned one, just whom should I respect?

Judge: (Picks up the noose and adjusts it) You did not have your female witnesses in court to defend you.

Girl: Of course not, you old fool! Their husbands would not allow them to go. Did you expect anything different? If they went, and they were allowed to tell the truth, I would be innocent of these false charges—charges you know are false.

Judge: (Places the noose around her neck and adjusts it again) But that's the law!

Girl: It is only a law, and a bad law at that, because you morons and people like you want it that way in order to escape any responsibility for your cruelty to women and children. How old is your wife, Judge?

Judge: (Pulls the noose tight and causes pain) That is none of your business.

Girl: Ha! Struck a nerve, did I? What will you do when you tire of her, accuse her of being unfaithful and then forbid her to testify? I really feel sorry for her. And sorry for the system that takes people like you seriously. You are a disgrace! I could forgive you if you asked, but it is not just me. I guess thousands of innocent women have preceded me, and for them and those to come after me, I cannot forgive you.

Harry J. Sweeney

Judge: (Signals the crane operator to drop the hook slowly) You are just about to meet your judgment, and you are still disrespectful to the officials appointed over you.

Girl: You know something, you old fool: the people in the heavens beyond this earth are not who you think they are. I have had time to think and dream, and they came to me in a dream and said that I was not to be afraid. They sat with me in my dream and told me they know I am innocent and that they do have a special place in the fire for people like you.

Judge: (Lifts the metal ring at the tail of the noose and places it on the steel hook) No one beyond the heavens would ever come to visit a piece of trash like you in a dream.

Girl: Look skyward with me, Judge. Please look up there! The little breeze feels nice on my face. There are many things in this world and the next you do not know. Well, if you look up there, you can just about see them—yes, they are there all right. And I am going to tell them all about you. You use religion to satisfy your own needs and your blood lust. The males that raped me were all taught that women are nothing but trash and for their use to do with as they will. The law defends their animal instincts, but you are worse. You are educated and should know better, but you don't. You and people like you are monsters of the earth. I am well rid of you.

Judge: (Signals the operator to begin lifting the hook) You are on your way to the flames.

Girl: (Speaks with difficulty) I go to God. He . . . waits. Lord, I'm coming. . . com. . . .

Judge: What is the matter with her? Nobody visited her in a dream. I am looking, but cannot see the heavens; the sun is altering my vision. Who would ever visit her? I need to go rest; that crazy girl has upset me. A visit in a dream! I still do not see anything in this glare.

The Restless Wind and Shifting Sands

The crane operator stopped the ascent of the girl's body, leaving her twisting slowly in the mild breeze. The operator noted the judge still looking upward toward the body. He shook his head then and wondered what was in that judge's mind.

Harry J. Sweeney

<u>Conversation 18: This dialogue is a continuation of number 17.</u>

The girl appears to the judge in a dream.

Judge: Why are you waking me? It is still night.

Girl: I am not waking you. You were already waking. You did not say your night prayers. You must pray five times each day. Naughty boy!

Judge: You upset me so badly this morning; I fell asleep with a headache.

Girl: I see. Well, sleeping through means you can make it up. If *you* were upset by hanging me this morning, how do you think I felt?

Judge: It was nothing personal.

Girl: Oh, but it was personal. You took my life. That is personal! It was all I had.

Judge: I had to do that; you broke the law.

Girl: That is why I am here to speak to you about that. I met several people since I have been gone from the earth—and by the way, I am not going to the flames, as you can see.

Judge: You are upsetting me again. You are not going to the flames?

Girl: Do you remember the phrase, "Allah knows what is in your heart"? That is why I am not going to the flames, and that is why I am allowed to visit you. Allah knows what is in my heart—and also what is in yours!

Judge: I do not understand.

Girl: I can say that Allah knows of my innocence—that should mean something important to you! You must think about it. I can say no more about that. Think, Judge, think! Please, think about what I say to you!

Judge: If you are innocent, what about the law?

Girl: Forget the law for a moment! My new friends here said that I may say only so much. You must use your mind to use the information I give you to figure out the rest. I cannot run your life.

Judge: What sort of information?

Girl: Now listen to me! You may take it from my friends here; I am innocent of the charges for which I was hanged. I am happy, content, and am not destined for any fire or any other punishment. I am in paradise! Does that help? You must listen and understand!

Judge: What am I to understand from what you say?

Girl: You make me want to weep for you. Think! Please think! You are not talking to a lawyer, judge. Think only about what I said. I just said something important!

Judge: Are you saying the law is wrong?

Girl: Aha! I am sorry; I cannot break the rule by being direct. You must do the thinking and the deciding, not me. Please dwell on what I can tell you.

Judge: Have you seen the Prophet there?

Girl: I have not been here that long. You hanged me only this morning. Now you are going off on a tangent. Please stay focused.

Judge: I need to know so many things.

Girl: I am glad you said that. I already know the answers to so many things. You want to know the true source of the Qur'an because you

Harry J. Sweeney

have always had a modicum of doubt. You want to know if our Most Beloved actually did lead a perfect life, and thus he should be emulated by all men. All of those answers I now have.

Judge: Will you tell me?

Girl: I so much wish I could. I can tell you that all the answers will be the same. It is for the living to discover the truth and the way, but not from the dead. Allah has given the living the ability to ferret the truth out for themselves. Many people will see the fires because they have discovered only *their* truth—the truth they wanted. It is not Allah's truth.

Judge: What is Allah's truth?

Girl: I cannot tell you; however, it is all around you.

Judge: How do I recognize it?

Girl: It is beautiful. It is a summer afternoon by a quiet lake or a visit from an old friend, long forgotten. Allah's truth is a gift that suddenly appears in your heart and your mind, making you feel happy to be alive and at peace with your neighbors. It is the look in an elderly wife's eyes, when finally you think enough of her to take the heavy pail from her and carry it home.

Judge: That does not make sense to me. You must always be wary of your neighbors. If you do not stop them from sinning, they will affect others as well. If you do not punish all the transgressors, everyone will transgress. And your wife requires special alertness; if you do not keep her busy all the time she will stray or plot against you. She will find your stores and steal your money.

Girl: Judge, I asked you if you remembered the phrase, "Allah knows what's in your heart." You indicate that you did. Did you see anything wrong with that phrase?

The Restless Wind and Shifting Sands

Judge: Of course not. Allah truly knows these things.

Girl: Judge, a young girl is brought before you and accused of having an elicit encounter with a man twice her age. You look at her, and she is small, dainty, humble, and devastated. You look at the man accusing her and see a strong, rough beast of a man that is a known bully and has been in similar situations before. He is loud and continually demands hell-fire for her. What is your first thought concerning the case?

Judge: I must follow the law and seek witnesses.

Girl: I expected that answer, but hoped against it. You do not see any incongruity between the man's charges and the girl? Suppose the man's wife points to the man, her husband, and says he raped the victim and the victim tried to stop him. What would you make of that?

Judge: Nothing. The girl needs four female witnesses. You know all of this.

Girl: Yes, I should. But what does your mind tell you about the case?

Judge: To follow the law. Why are you asking me these questions?

Girl: You need to know the right answers. I am pleading with you to open your eyes and go beyond what you have been told. I cannot tell you more. I want to more than you could know, but I can't; you have to figure it out. But it is important that you look at your answers again and see what is in your heart to make that reply. Please. So far, you cannot seem to grasp the point.

Judge: But I have only been given the law.

Girl: You have also been given a mind and heart. You must seek Allah's truth in all things. You must seek Allah's truth, not yours. The law does not command that you be stupid. When the facts have been told, and not held back, regardless of a lack of witnesses, Allah's truth is often clear. Once the truth is before you, your duty is clear.

Harry J. Sweeney

Judge: You will not tell me what Allah's truth is.

Girl: I came as close as I could, and my time here is finished. I must return.

Judge: Will you visit me again?

Girl: Only if you wish me to.

Judge: I must learn more about Allah's truth.

Girl: I told you, judge, it is all around you—the beautiful things around you. It is light and color and nice sounding, like the whisper of wind in the trees. It is your granddaughter laughing in her crib. Allah's truth is everywhere, except perhaps in the darker corners of some minds who prefer scurrying around in the darkness, looking . . . oops! I am saying too much. If I say too much, I cannot come back. Pray to Allah, Judge, to open your eyes, and pray until you cry real tears. If Allah smiles upon you, His truth will appear clearly, and you will wonder why you never saw it before. I must go now. Good-bye.

Judge: Wait. Just another minute, please. (The girl is gone)

In a few minutes, the judge awakens and remembers the conversation. He looks at his clock and sees it is again time to pray. He can also make up for his missing prayers. He tries to push aside the conversation, but he cannot. He elects to do the prayers in his room. He wants to avoid questions if he spends longer than usual at prayer. He also knows that his eyes are already welling up with tears that no amount of face rinsing will dissipate.

The Restless Wind and Shifting Sands

Conversation 19: Reform

Mani: Good morning, Radi. Where is Modi?

Radi: (Bears large knife) I made a good moderate of him.

Mani: What? You are kidding me. There's Modi now. Hello, Modi.

Modi: What is all the fuss? Radi is playing with his pet knife.

Mani: He is in good humor this morning.

Modi: Oh? You found someone to decapitate, eh? Who was it? Did someone turn Christian or Jew? Did you catch a heretic?

Radi: You don't appreciate our nocturnal patrols to keep Islam free, do you?

Mani: Keep Islam free of what? Heretics? Apostates?

Radi: Last night we discovered a whole nest of people who were talking about reform.

Mani: Reform? Whoa! I bet that went over well with your gang.

Radi: Yeah, we wiped them out—everyone.

Modi: Wait a minute here! You took it among yourself to kill people without taking them to court or anything? That is not justice!

Radi: When will you learn, Modi? All of us must stop people who would hurt Islam.

Modi: How would reformers hurt Islam? Aren't they trying to make it better, easier? If someone discovers something wrong, doesn't he have an obligation to change it?

Harry J. Sweeney

Radi: See! You do not understand at all! How can you reform something that is perfect? Islam is perfect! It was given to us by Allah! It is perfect and so cannot be changed. That includes the Qur'an and the hadiths. They must endure unchanged forever!

Modi: Radi, nothing in this life is perfect. Everything that is touched by humans has a fault somewhere. None of us is perfect.

Radi: Tell him, Mani, our Most Beloved was perfect and led a perfect life. We must emulate his every step.

Mani: I have to agree with Radi. The Messenger indeed was a perfect man, and he led a perfect life. It is so written.

Modi: He never made a mistake?

Radi: No, never.

Modi: His *Satanic Verses* was not a mistake?

Radi: (Brandishes his knife) Mani, I'm going to kill him.

Modi: Typical Salafist response, Mani. Kill everyone who does not agree entirely! What a world that would be.

Mani: You should not have brought up those verses. Many people are still very upset about that.

Modi: So he made a mistake, so what. (Looks directly at Radi) He admitted that mistake, Radi. He tried to end the persecution of his people and bring them back from exile, and so he agreed to accept two Meccan gods. It did not take him very long to realize it was a mistake, and he did correct it. So what? It was nothing; he was human. He tried to accommodate the Meccans to save his people; when he realized it was an error, he fixed it. If anything, it showed his concern for his people. Remember, Allah forgave him for that. Allah knew what was in his heart.

The Restless Wind and Shifting Sands

Mani: Radi is never going to accept that, Modi. I am not certain that I can accept it.

Modi: If it were proved to be true, Mani, would the Prophet be any the less in your eyes?

Mani: Of course not.

Modi: Radi's either, I know. Therefore, we won't pursue it because it does not really matter. It is the refusal of some believers to accept it that is the problem.

Mani: Why is that a problem?

Modi: Because no one is perfect, and how can anything written as rules for all humanity to follow be perfect for all ages?

Radi: What about the American Constitution that you admire so much?

Modi: Nobody ever said it was perfect, but it is better than anything anywhere else. No honest-to-goodness American would ever change its basic philosophy and its reason for being.

Mani: Then why are so many people in America, even Supreme Court judges, demanding to change some of it!

Modi: Because they're not committed to the form of government the Constitution represents—a republic, Mani. They would prefer a one-world government of political correctness and multiculturalism, more like that of Europe.

Radi: So it is not right to reform the American Constitution but it is right to reform Islam? Sounds like bigotry to me.

Modi: I do not suggest reform for our religion. We could use some fresh air in our political ideology, though. You can look at it any way

Harry J. Sweeney

you like, but the American Constitution is much different than our scriptures. It is not based on warfare. It does not tell them to kill the British or the Tories wherever they find them.

Mani: I think he has you there, Radi. I think we should drop the idea of comparing Islam to the Constitution.

Modi: How could there ever be a comparison? The Constitution mainly spells out the rights of the people. The scriptures we are discussing spell out the responsibilities of the people toward Allah. I would hope that a political reform movement would give some attention to the rights of the people.

Radi: I don't believe anything you say. I cannot.

Modi: I know that, Radi. Mani has a tough time with it also.

Radi: Even your words are foreign to me. I can never ever listen to or allow any suggestion of reform. Reform is completely out of the question now and forever. I look at the word reform as the head of a snake. As soon as it raises its ugly head, it must be killed quickly.

Modi: Radi, I have often thought that you live in a black-and-white world. Colors must really confuse you sometimes. The Ottomans found that you cannot rule half the world from their headquarters unless you allowed regional changes. Only the Salafists have not learned that lesson.

Radi: We will still defeat the West, and the new caliphate will rule the entire world.

Modi: If the religion allows itself to be changed, it can take its place as a major religion in this world of ours. If it doesn't change, non-believers see it as becoming a danger to the rest of the world because of what it teaches. You just cannot go around preaching "Kill everyone but us."

Radi: Why not?

The Restless Wind and Shifting Sands

Modi: See, Mani. He doesn't know why not.

Mani: I don't really see it either, Modi. I guess I am against reform also.

Modi: Sometimes I have the impression we are not all in the same religion.

Harry J. Sweeney

Conversation 20: American troops and child martyrs.

Mani: (Walking away from mosque) Well, Modi, what did you think of the speaker today? Very powerful, eh?

Radi: Yeah! He really crushed the idea of the American troop surge in Iraq doing any good. He absolutely stomped on the surge! I bet he even convinced Modi. That reminds me: Modi is springing for lunch today.

Modi: I agree that he was a very powerful speaker. His images and his rhetoric stunned the crowd and brought them to their feet many times shouting God is Great! However, forceful speech and colorful images do not equal the truth. There should have been some truth somewhere in what he was talking about, but there wasn't.

Mani: How can you say that? He is the best speaker we have seen here in a long time.

Modi: Now listen closely. I did not say he was not a good speaker. I said there was no truth in anything he talked about. He made no reference to anything tangible. For example, he said, "Our fighters have been able to withstand every new weapon and technique the enemies have thrown at them and still came back for more." What new weapons have come into Iraq? I have seen some new weapons coming in for us from Iran, and the Americans had to strengthen their vehicles to compensate. We also received some new automatic weapons from Iran, which they probably received from China.

Radi: Are you trying to say the speaker was a liar?

Modi: In a word, yes. If anybody has been using new stuff, we are the ones. You might say that the Americans are the ones able to withstand every new weapon and technique we have thrown at them.

Mani: I do not know about you. You have just spoiled the man's entire speech for me. You should be ashamed of yourself.

The Restless Wind and Shifting Sands

Modi: Why do you guys always fall for the same propaganda? You know that some of these Friday afternoons are a giant pep rally to tell you how good we are and how evil America is. I have noted these speakers spice things up a little with recycled tales of how the Prophet fooled the Meccans, only this time about how our sneaky little people spent the entire night rigging a road bomb to go off by way of a cell phone once an unwary coalition vehicle passed nearby. To makes things worse, they do not seem to care how many of our people are also nearby.

Radi: Our people are heroes for taking American lives. They gladly give their own.

Modi: Heroes do not go around at night setting explosive devices to kill people who came to help you get rid of a tyrant and set up your own government. Heroes do not murder ten of their own people to get to one coalition soldier.

Mani: The American troops are better equipped than we are. We have to use alternative methods to kill them.

Modi: Look, Mani. The Americans have no intention of killing us. Why can't you understand that? Look! If no one fires a shot at them or blows up a truck, their patrols are as peaceful as a religious procession—probably quieter too.

Radi: He is insulting us again. I have had enough. He will bite my blade.

Modi: I do not want to belabor the point, but last week, Mani, when your old car broke down in the middle of the road, an American patrol had just turned the corner.

Mani: Yes, I know. I was in fear for my life.

Radi: If I were with you, we could have martyred ourselves together, Mani, and killed many.

Harry J. Sweeney

Modi: (Shakes his head in disgust) Those American soldiers never looked at you as an enemy, Mani. Moreover, that young freckled kid who walked over and watched what you were doing was really interested in helping you. He showed you the distributor wire had popped out. He also waited until you restarted the car before he was satisfied and rejoined his waiting buddies.

Mani: He just wanted to show me up to make me look foolish.

Modi: You did not need his help to look foolish. And if he did not come along, your car would still be there and you would really look foolish. Mani, I saw you nod a "*shukran*" to the young fellow, and I saw him smile before he moved on as if he knew the word "thanks" in our language. You are not fooling me. If it were not for all these stupid people filling your head with nonsense, you would like the Americans.

Mani: Don't you dare say that. (Looks around) Are you trying to get me killed?

Radi: I do not see a particularly good point in all of this talk.

Modi: Try this on for size. Look at the people on any given day as the American patrols saunter down our streets. Do all the men run and hide? Do the women all run out and gather up their children from play and hide them? Do the children run away from the Americans or do they run to them to say hello and perhaps wrangle some chewing gum or a candy bar or something? Perhaps one might say everything goes on as usual? And seeing Americans does not strike fear in our hearts?

Mani and Radi say nothing.

Modi: Let me ask you this: if our real brave fighters wanted to throw in some RPGs, or mortars, or machinegun fire to kill the Americans, who aren't really bothering anyone, would the fact that our children are milling around the Americans make any difference to the fighters? I take it from your silence you know I am right. Let me ask another

The Restless Wind and Shifting Sands

question. If our brave fighters could slip homicide vests on some of our kids and then detonate those vests as soon as the Americans were near, do you suppose that they would think twice about doing it?

Radi: Of course not. The children then become martyrs of Islam.

Modi: They have no right to make martyrs of children. They have no right to put women, children, and old folks at risk because of their notion about how the world should be. Just who do they think they are?

Radi: We are the rightful rulers of this planet!

Modi: Oh yeah? Did Allah anoint you boss?

Radi: You know it is in our scriptures. Everything belongs to Allah and we are his chosen people. We are to fight and kill everyone who stands in our way.

Mani: Radi is right, Modi. You can't get out of that one.

Modi: If Radi were right, Allah would not have allowed America to become the greatest country in the world. Saudi Arabia and others have great oil fields and lots of money, but where are they? They are still fighting among themselves. Where would the Saudis be today without America's protection? We had one of the greatest of empires once—half the world—and venality, along with incompetence, made it a laughing stock until it finally crumbled.

Mani: Are you trying to say we must quit the jihad?

Modi: Jihad, my foot! We are not engaged in jihad; these are stupid little games of defiance and denial. Look, our children are our future, and you are killing them—you are killing our future! What is left when the children are gone?

Harry J. Sweeney

Mani: I think Modi might have something there about the children, Radi. What do you think?

Radi: I know I am going to kill him but not until after lunch. He's buying.

Mani: Radi, you are impossible—and a cheapskate.

CHAPTER 3

Conversation 21: American troops, Holy Trinity.

Mani: Modi, you don't look very well this morning.

Radi: Yeah, you look like death warmed over.

Modi: The coalition searched my house last night. I was up for almost an hour.

Radi: Aha! Now you know what being a moderate gets you. Mani, we may have a new recruit here.

Modi: Don't get your hopes up. The soldiers did not hurt anyone, and when they learned I spoke English, it was more conversation than anything else. They wanted to know if anyone was making roadside bombs in the compound. I told them if my neighbors and I knew someone was here doing that, we would kill him! People like that put us all in danger.

Mani: That is not showing loyalty to Iraq!

Modi: That is crap, and you know it. We do not have an army and a police force we can trust yet. Why? Because bastards you call friends attack and kill them as soon as they graduate. The Americans are the only force keeping us safe.

Radi: Al-Qaida will soon defeat the Americans and establish our own Islamic country.

Modi: Oh, yeah? Based on what? Do you honestly believe that after Saddam Hussein you would welcome the Taliban? No reasonably

Harry J. Sweeney

intelligent person in this world could even wish Taliban rule on his worst enemy.

Mani: It would be much better than this police state!

Modi: What police state? I just said we do not have a police force. You two just do not know how good you have it. The Taliban had a beard police that measured everyone's beards. If it did not measure up, you were beaten every day that you were on the street.

Radi: What is wrong with that? We are supposed to have full beards.

Modi: Well, it so happens that sometimes I like to shave and go without a beard for a while. It is nobody's damned business whether I have a beard or not! But that is not the worst.

Mani: They had other police?

Modi: Yep. They had the ethical police. If you attended a soccer match and called out anything but "God is Great" when someone scored, you were beaten severely for that. All those lunkheads had to do was find one or two females on the street without a male escort, and they had a grand time beating them, *burqa* or not.

Mani: That doesn't sound right.

Modi: Well, what on earth do you think Extremist Islam is? If you keep listening to Radi and those other people, you will find yourself back in the Dark Ages without music, dancing, or worthy books, and if you had TV, it would be filled with Zawahiri's tirades. Interesting, huh? Look, I can understand the people's admiration for some of the things bin Laden has done; however, the man himself is a bore. And Zawahiri—I would rather listen to my mother-in-law.

Radi: I knew you were becoming a traitor.

The Restless Wind and Shifting Sands

Modi: My moderate friends and I are not the ones killing other Iraqis, Radi. You guys cause us more hardship and deaths than the coalition. When was the last time coalition troops set up a car bomb outside a mosque? When did they ever send homicide-bombers into a wedding feast? When did they ever put a suicide vest on a 6-year-old girl or a 70-year-old grandmother? When did they ever declare total war on all civilians?

Mani: He has you there, Radi. Modi is making sense. The coalition forces do not really make war on anyone. I find myself hoping they will stay until we have a real government and a real police force.

Radi: I am going to kill him...unless he is protected by his American friends.

Modi: I wish I had American friends. It would be nice to send my family there while we were dodging bullets and bombs from your friends, Radi. If people in my family are killed because of some stupid things you guys are doing, I am coming after you.

Mani: That does not sound like a moderate.

Modi: Make no mistake, you two. Being a moderate does not mean I will not fight; it means only that I know who my real enemies are, and I don't listen to some uneducated, stupid knucklehead tell me we are still fighting against the polytheists from the seventh century.

Radi: But that is exactly what we are doing. And you must kill them wherever you find them.

Modi: When is the last time you were face to face with a polytheist?

Radi: The Americans are polytheists.

Mani: What? How do you figure that?

Harry J. Sweeney

Radi: They believe that God had a son and in all there were three gods. They also prayed to the Mother of Jesus and all of the saints.

Modi: Real people have not believed that since the seventh century, Radi. Back then, people did not know all that much about Christians. Most of their information came from Nestorians or others who had broken from mainstream Christianity and believed whatever they wanted. People who are still screaming about that today are in a time-warp mentally. When are you ever going to learn? Anyway, what the hell difference does it make what anyone else believes? If you hate Americans for what they believe but they don't hate us for what we believe, it makes them right and you wrong!

Radi: When we rid ourselves of the Americans, we will take care of moderates like you who have abandoned their religion.

Modi: I am truly a better believer than you, Radi. I have never killed another believer. You have.

Radi: Only those who deserved it.

Modi: You are neither judge nor jury and have no right to call what you do lawful. On judgment day Allah is going to require an accounting for all those needless, mindless deaths.

Mani: I need to change the subject before we have another fight. Modi, how long were the soldiers in your house?

Modi: Less than an hour. The only thing broken was my door lock. I told them not to bother repairing it; I would do it.

Mani: Did they find any explosives in your compound?

Modi: No, but I did get a good laugh out of them while they were looking.

The Restless Wind and Shifting Sands

Mani: What did you say?

Modi: I said, if they were looking for more of those Iranian toys, I would not worry about them being any good for anything—most of the toys are now made in China, so they will probably be recalled.

Harry J. Sweeney

Conversation 22: Allah, Predestination, Martyrdom

Mani: Hi, Modi, Radi. Good news today.

Modi: I can hardly wait. Al-Qaida surrendered?

Mani: Be serious and be cheerful. Believer recruiting is up in Europe. Many Europeans have become believers.

Radi: That is good news. We will be the majority before long. Then we will have a whole new continent of our own.

Modi: I would not celebrate just yet. People are leaving the religion also.

Radi: How can that be? They know the penalty for that is death.

Modi: Some courts do not see it that way. Of course, too many still do, to their shame. I bet recruitment would not be up very much if the recruiting clerics "came clean" about what happens if they changed their minds later on.

Radi: By then they will know how beautiful the religion is.

Modi: You will never learn, Radi. It is the people who make a religion wholesome and beautiful. It can also happen that rotten people can take an otherwise decent religion and make it rotten and stagnant.

Mani: Yes, that is what is written about Judaism and Christianity.

Modi: Judaism and Christianity never really matched the evil things that were written about them in our scriptures; however, aside from that, both have evolved over the centuries and have become quite humanitarian. This religion of ours could use some fresh air and a new perspective—and perhaps some social programs.

The Restless Wind and Shifting Sands

Radi: Modi, you say one more thing about reform, and you and I will fight.

Mani: I am sure that Modi didn't mean it. Tell him, Modi.

Modi: Radi, you and Mani and I are good friends. We are believers, but we still see things differently. We do many things together, including praying to Allah. We all love Allah, but I do not fear Him. I expect to be punished for a few minor lapses, but I do not foresee burning in hell or anything like that. Allah knows what is in my heart. I see Allah as a kindly forgiving God; others see Him as a warlike, vindictive God that gives no slack to anyone and willfully creates life so He can eventually destroy it by inflicting eternal punishment, deserved or not. I just cannot believe that.

Mani: Modi, you must fear Allah. He will exact revenge if you do not!

Radi: You will burn in the fires forever.

Modi: See what I mean? Look, the common belief is that whenever a human being is created that person's life is completely planned out, including when he will die and how he will spend eternity. Allah, it is said, knows all and causes all things to happen.

Mani: I understand that.

Modi: In the course of the fighting between the believers and the Meccans, the believers were exhorted to do their best because they would die at the scheduled time no matter what they were doing; so it would be much better for them if they were killed in battle. Besides, they were told, dying in the way of Allah created an escape from the preordained schedule. Remember, believers had no way of knowing if they were destined for the fires or not, regardless of the lives they led.

Mani: I never quite understood that part of it.

Harry J. Sweeney

Modi: Everything was preordained, including going to the fires or to paradise. Things people did were also planned in advance, including poverty, success, failure, and so on. People just had no way of knowing where they would end up, and they had no control over the outcome.

Mani: So, to break out of that cycle, martyrdom became a guarantee of paradise. It was the only guarantee of paradise.

Modi: Exactly. The radical leadership is still exhorting us in the same way, except that many of us do not believe that anymore. They are now forced to use kids—our future—as martyrs to achieve a tactical or public relations advantage. Shameful!

Radi: I do not know why you make sense; however, there is no way I can believe you.

Modi: I understand that, Radi. Much of your "known" world would crumble into dust if suddenly you felt you agreed with me.

Mani: I understand what you are saying, Modi, but I too am distanced by your logic. Why do our scriptures disagree with you? I simply must rely on the scriptures.

Modi: Perfectly understandable. However, if you look at the history of our scriptures, it would be logical for you to question some of the meanings, especially in light of the different world we live in.

Radi: No! The Qur'an was created by Allah Himself and not one word can be changed forever! Anyone even thinking about what you said should be killed outright!

Modi: You said, "Anyone even thinking about it should be killed outright."

Radi: Yes. I stand by that statement and am willing to back it up. To even so much as touch that document in your home, you must do your ablutions and ensure that you are clean in mind and body.

The Restless Wind and Shifting Sands

Mani: I agree with Radi about touching and opening the Qur'an. I am just not sure about anything else. I can tell you that I am not going to do or say anything that will bring the wrath of the radicals down upon my family or me.

Modi: That is part of the problem, Mani. The Moderates and the Mainstreams would at least look at the problem and debate it if the Radicals allowed it!

Mani: Too many people have been killed swimming upstream against that tide.

Modi: So you would rather live under strict guidance of the Radicals than break out and think for yourselves. You do not want to be the good people who make this a beautiful religion. You do not want to play a great supporting role in the course of human events; you would be satisfied to be in line with Satan.

Mani: Satan! Don't pull that on me, Modi. We Mainstreams are not evil. We love our religion, and we believe our scriptures.

Modi: But you will not even give any consideration to the idea that anything could have happened somewhere along the line to require a new analysis of their meanings. You know what is written, and it is bloody. Because of it, our entire history is bloody. It has to be time to stop and take another look at everything. Allah could not possibly mean that the believers must kill everyone else.

Radi: Yes, He can and does. He owns the entire planet; everything is His.

Modi: I got the idea, Radi. If Allah already owns everything and has seen fit to populate each country the way He has, what makes you think he wants you to kill everyone, undo everything that He has done, and follow the dictates of the imams? Are you trying to undo a mistake that Allah made? Do you think He might have screwed up somehow?

95

Harry J. Sweeney

Mani and Radi look toward the sky for expected thunderbolts.

Mani: This conversation is ended, Modi. It is time for coffee anyway. Coming, Radi?

Radi: Is it my turn to pay?

Mani: No.

Radi: Then count me in.

The Restless Wind and Shifting Sands

Conversation 23: Gun Control Madness

Mani and Radi are laughing loudly as Modi approaches.

Modi: What is so funny?

Mani: (Tries to control his laughter) We watched Fox News this morning (laughs), and they had a story about a 13-year-old boy suspended from school (laughter) for drawing *what they thought might be a gun!* (He and Radi laugh more.) In addition, get this, (more laughter) the school officials "considered it an absolute threat!" (All three laugh.)

Radi: I can't stand it; a kid's drawing is an absolute threat! (All three laugh all over again, tears streaming down their faces.)

Mani: These are our mortal enemies? Grown-up school officials terrified of a vague outline of a gun, doodled by a kid?

Radi: (Still laughing) It seems to me we can just walk right in and take over the country. We wouldn't have to be armed, just leave the arms home and bring pictures of them.

Mani: (Laughing) Yeah. Terrorists now do not have to sneak in actual dirty bombs, just send photos or a diagram. (All three laugh.)

Modi: (Tries to stop laughing) I have to say it is not only funny, but also tragic. Can you imagine such crass, stupid crybabies as adults, let alone education authorities?

Radi: Tell me again about your great American militia, the people who make their own ammunition and are fiercer and braver than any of our armies. (He and Mani laugh.)

Modi: (Still smiling) It is a good thing that this type of person is not typical of the American. These people have to be the sissies of the world. They want everything just so: pajamas must be fireproof, kids aren't allowed to fight, all games must not have winners or losers, and

Harry J. Sweeney

test scores must not be posted—no child must have to acknowledge that other kids can be smarter, faster, tougher, or just all around better than they. It is too much pressure.

Radi: If I had not seen the news item, I would not have believed you.

Mani: Yes, Modi. What is the matter with people like that? America is facing multiple enemies from all over the world. The government cannot secure its own borders, people are pouring in to do harm to the American people, and some people want the people to give up their guns.

Radi: Maybe the people should mail in photos of their guns. (Laughter)

Modi: Yes, I told you about this once or twice before. There are those who do not believe in the individual; hence, there can be no individual right to defend oneself. To engage in self-defense requires an individual decision and not the deliberations of a committee. I am tired of saying it. They would rather that people, when accosted by predators, should simply die quietly and promptly without wasting anyone's time.

Mani: That is sick!

Radi: Maybe, but it is good for us. It will be much easier to kill them all. Just dig a ditch shoulder high, invite all the men to walk into it, and then have teams of believers with swords behead them as they walk along the ditch.

Modi: Americans won't do that.

Radi: But some would, remember Jonestown?

Modi: But the rest of the country would fight like lions, even harder than lions.

Mani: Why would the rest fight harder?

The Restless Wind and Shifting Sands

Modi: They wouldn't have all those sissies holding them back and trying to get them to stop defending themselves.

Radi: Ha, Modi, I think you have something there. Therefore we must make a note. When we attack America, don't touch the sissies until the others are dead or captured. Afterwards we can take our time removing their heads.

Mani: Radi, I swear you have a one-track mind.

Radi: About the drawing again, Mani. I assume the teacher saw the drawing on the kid's desk. He would be in real trouble if he just stuffed it in his pocket.

Modi: Why do you say that?

Radi: (Laughs) Because then he would have a concealed deadly weapon. (They laugh.)

Mani: Radi, you do have a sense of humor after all.

Modi: Of course he has; you should see him at an ambush.

Radi: You never saw me at an ambush.

Modi: I could just imagine it. You must really drool until it is time to squeeze the trigger.

Mani: Enough of that. We still have lots of time till noon prayers. How about a late breakfast?

Radi: Modi's buying this time.

Modi: Oops. I don't think I brought enough money with me this time. Let's swing by my house first.

Radi: No need. Here is some paper and a pencil.

Harry J. Sweeney

Modi: (Looks puzzled) What are these for?

Radi: (Starts running, calls over his shoulder) Just draw a few thousand dinars.

Modi: (Laughs and runs after Radi) You SOB!

Mani: Here we go again.

The Restless Wind and Shifting Sands

Conversation 24: The Mother-in-law

Again departing from Modi, Mani, and Radi, we look into another situation of interest to some of us in the Western World.

Mother-in-law: My son did not like his dinner.

Basma: From what I saw, he did. You are the only one complaining. My husband, did you enjoy the dinner? (Her husband looked at both women and left the room without saying anything.)

Mother-in-law: See! He is not satisfied. He will divorce you one of these days.

Basma: How can you say that? I always buy only those things he likes, and you know that. You accompany me to the shops only to goad me into buying what you want. My husband gives me enough to buy what we need. If I buy something for you, that means I can't buy something for him.

Mother-in-law: Aha! You are saying my son is not generous; he is stingy! I will tell him that.

Basma: You will tell him what you like, true or not true. For the past 2 weeks you have filled his ears with your little fiction stories. Since his father died, we both have made you more than welcome; however, you say things and do things that make both of us unhappy.

Mother-in-law: Are you saying I am no longer welcome in my son's home?

Basma: I would never say that. I am simply pointing out, my husband's mother, that you and I should strive together to make your son very happy.

Mother-in-law: We will see about that. (She leaves the room without offering to help.)

Harry J. Sweeney

Later that evening. . . .

Amal (Basma's husband): My wife, I have ordered you not to argue with my mother. She is very upset with you.

Basma: If I do not argue, I would be accepting her criticism as if it were true. She will get worse. I love her as you love her, but I do not know what to do to please her, other than admit to lies.

Amal: I am ordering you again not to argue with my mother.

Next day. . . .

Mother-in-law: My son asked that you go to the home of his first cousin and retrieve money that is due today.

Later Basma returns empty handed.

Basma: (Knocks at the door) Mother-in-law, please open the door. My husband's first cousin knew nothing about money due.

Mother-in-law: Go away! You do not live here and are not wanted here. Go away or I will summon authorities.

Basma: (Knocks louder) Open up or I will tell my husband you locked me out.

Mother-in-law: Ha! What husband? (Laughs loudly) Did you not see the message taped to the door?

Basma sees the paper taped to the door and opens it up. It is a message from her husband; it simply states, "You are divorced."

The document is valid, and the divorce is final as of her next period if she is not pregnant. Even if the husband decided to take her back, he could not do so until after she has first been with another man—which

The Restless Wind and Shifting Sands

would mean another marriage and another divorce. Basma, of course, is devastated and can do nothing about it.

A few months go by, a friend visits her. . . .

Friend: I cannot imagine how you felt when you read that little message.

Basma: My world ended. I had no alternative but to go to my father's house. I could not go anywhere else. My mother was sympathetic, but not father. He wanted me gone; married off to anyone who would take me. He was embarrassed that my husband divorced me. If he did not take me in for a while, I would have nowhere to go. It is good my former husband never accused me of anything; my father would have to kill me. He was angry enough as it was.

Friend: You must have had suitors. You are a nice person, and people know it.

Basma: I had some suitors, but a quirk of some kind always stood out and disqualified them to me. I just could not take a chance on another bad marriage. Father was always livid when I turned someone down. He thought I should be happy to marry anyone who asked. Another friend told me about a gentleman in the Shiite area. The man offered a temporary marriage, a *mut'a*, to find a wife. As Sunnis, we could not do that, but the Shiites could. I sent a message to their local imam that I would appreciate such an opportunity. The imam interviewed me first. The man's first wife died, and he wanted a companion as well as a wife. Can you imagine that? He wanted a wife to be his companion!

Friend: You entered a temporary marriage?

Basma: Yes. Every detail was discussed and agreed upon for a week's trial, including compensation after the week was up. Nothing was left untouched.

Friend: Well? What happened?

Harry J. Sweeney

Basma: He was a very nice man, older than my first husband, but nicer and gentler. He was very considerate of me and was very proper concerning prayer times and Friday Mosque. He allowed me to attend mosque. By the third day I had no intention of leaving this man.

Friend: What did you do to convert the temporary marriage into a permanent one?

Basma: Nothing. When he awakened on the last morning, I was busy doing my chores, working on his breakfast, and making myself as cheerful as I could for him. I knew breakfast is his favorite meal and made sure he would enjoy it.

Friend: So, what else happened?

Basma: We went about our daily routines until dusk. He looked up from his reading and looked at me. I had started to mend an old shirt he liked to wear in the garden. I looked at him just for a second and went back to my mending. I thought I saw a smile start, but with the evening shadows, I was not sure. My mind told me that I needed him and he needed me. In a little while, he took my hand and we retired for the evening. When our hands touched, he knew I was his and so did I.

Friend: You did not have to go through another marriage rite?

Basma: No. It just took mutual understanding and acceptance. If I did not walk away, the marriage solidified.

Friend: Did you ever look up or ask about your first husband?

Basma: No. I never thought of it. I guess I am just too busy being the best wife I can be to this wonderful man. When I see a lovely, robust rose, I enjoy the rose and for some reason do not think about thorns or insects. I know they are around, but they just don't seem important.

The Restless Wind and Shifting Sands

<u>Conversation 25: Al-Qaida and the Taliban</u>

Modi: Good morning, old pals of mine. Nice day.

Mani: Uh-oh! Radi, something is up with Modi. He is almost too eager to share it with us.

Radi: I noticed. Shall we just ignore him?

Modi: Another al-Qaida chief is now in American custody.

Mani: I saw that. He was betrayed by local citizens.

Modi: Mani, you are wrong. Al-Qaida is the betrayer, not the local people. The local people know who the bad guys are.

Radi: Al-Qaida is not the betrayer; they are the heroes who are fighting for our freedom and for Islam! Everyone who disputes this fact should be killed!

Modi: Get real, Radi. Al-Qaida is just another extension of the Taliban. If anything, they want to destroy the idea of freedom—freedom comes with democracy. Democracy terrifies them. They want to see everyone, man, woman, and child, in chains.

Mani: Now just how do you figure they could do that? There aren't enough chains.

Modi: Mental chains, the chains with which the logic-blind, hairy-faced, mean-spirited imams from the seventh-century time-warp keep wrapping up the unwary worshipper in those Saudi-financed mosques. They have been trying to turn out mealy-mouthed zombies for years if they cannot successfully turn out trained killers. They have been successful in the killer category, recruiting people who will kill at the drop of a hat—and they will drop the hat. In addition, the only reward they ask is a quick death. The best armies in the world could not recruit people like that.

Radi: None of that is true. We have very kind, very learned imams who remind people what their responsibilities are according to our scriptures.

Mani: That is right, Modi. The Saudi imams are only bringing us back to the true religion.

Modi: Get real! That is so much crap I am amazed that you don't see through it, Mani. Radi I understand. He has his own agenda. He likes to hurt, maim, or kill people who make mistakes. He will fight to the death to keep such a regime in power and so many victims in his grasp. He enjoys meting out punishment to the "sinners."

Radi: You have me all wrong, Modi. I love my religion and I hate sinners. Sinners need to be punished to keep everyone in line.

Modi: Do you understand what Radi is saying, Mani? It is about what I told you. He will kill to keep everyone in line. Is that not suppressing freedom? Is that not suppressing democracy? Why must everyone be in line?

Mani: He is just practicing his religion.

Modi: NO! That is not religion! That is totalitarian, and it is murder! Religion is love and tolerance, not hate and murder! We have no right to point at this person and call him a sinner. That is only between Allah and him! Everyone else should butt out! Religion is kindness, gentleness, love, and patience. We believers must ourselves believe that love of Allah is an individual thing, not a communal or universal ritual. We are all human, and sometimes we make mistakes or need a change in schedule from doing the same things over and over. We must not look askance at those who want to do things differently.

Radi: Our scriptures have laid out for us what we are to do.

Modi: Our scriptures have only given us a start. They have shown us what we had to do in the seventh century to build this religion. Later

The Restless Wind and Shifting Sands

on, as the rest of the world grew physically and changed psychologically and socially, some of our best imams began to grow also, and we learned new rules and could entertain new tolerance. We began to climb out of the Dark Ages. At that time another plague road out of the Najd, like the al-Saud before him, but this time killing with his words as well as his sword. We were told there would never be reform and we are to eliminate from our consciousness any hope of modernizing beyond the death of our beloved prophet.

Mani: You must admit he had many followers.

Modi: I disagree! However, that is a story for another day. The problem with some of our worshippers is they are never satisfied that they worshipped long enough or ardent enough, so they always fall for the people who encourage the thought. Who really cares whether a person prays five times per day or just one? Do you think Allah in all his wisdom and kindness cares how many times per day each of us prays?

Mani: But that is one of the Pillars. We must pray five times per day.

Modi: It is one of the Pillars, yes; however, the idea did not originate with the Qur'an. Truth be told, it was most probably a Persian idea. In fact, each of the Pillars, except perhaps the profession of faith, predated Islam. That is not important. I would not be surprised if other religions did not have similar professions of faith before the coming of Islam.

Radi: But Islam is the completion of all the other religions.

Modi: That is what I hear all the time. We never hear anything else. And what does it matter which came first or which came last? That trivia is unimportant. Radi, we are getting away from the main point. Al-Qaida is not fighting for our freedoms. It is true to some extent that the coalition is fighting for our hearts and minds. What that means is, they want us to believe in them. They want us to understand that we are not their enemy and so we have nothing to fear from them. They do not interfere with our government—I for one wish they would build a fire under it. On the other hand, al-Qaida is fighting for our souls.

Harry J. Sweeney

That means they want us to believe the strict dogma of the Salafists and Wahhabis—the people we used to laugh and jeer at before they got the oil money. It is payback time, and they want to control all of Islam. What that means is, that they want to control every action and every thought of every believer. If you even appear to be less than ardent in your prayer or even more than ardent, you may suffer for it.

Mani: You must be exaggerating. Nobody wants that much power; nobody would dare give anyone that much power.

Modi: Ask the people who lived in the recently cleared al-Qaida run area. Research the history of the Taliban in Afghanistan. Read up on Wahhabism. Look, we all want to worship Allah; however, we do not want the ethics police coming into every home before dawn and marching everyone to the prayer ground—and beating you if you dare to yawn. You have daughters, Mani. You could not educate them under the Salafists or let them play beyond a certain age. You may be told at any age you must turn them over to the Taliban who have already selected husbands for them. Would you defend this country against such a Taliban, Mani?

Mani: I think so, but how could I if they are simply stricter in their religion than I? Perhaps it is what I need—to practice being a better believer. I want to be the best and strictest believer I can be.

Modi: Why? Allah knows you and loves you as you are! We are not competing for heaven; there is room for everyone, except those false prophets and those believers who are false to themselves. Even our Most Beloved, in Bukhari's hadith 1:38, said that religion should not be burdensome and you should not be an extremist. Look, I pray at least five times each day, but I realize not every believer has five prayers a day in him. Perhaps some would be much better people with three prayers, or even two! How can I fault that? Allah probably does not care! If we love Him and are happy with ourselves and our families, He is happy with us. Don't believe anything those other nitwits say—how in hell do they know? They bloody well don't!

The Restless Wind and Shifting Sands

Mani: I still think I should spend more time worshipping Allah.

Modi: Sometimes, Mani, I think of you not as skin and bones but as bricks and mortar. Even Allah's Prophet (peace be upon him) said in Bukhari 1:41 not to over-tax yourself with prayers because you just can't keep it up. Whatever you can do on a regular basis is best for you.

Radi: Mani is much closer to me than you think.

Modi: But all brick walls crack somewhere. No matter, I can see by the sun that it is time to think about prayers and lunch. My throat is dry, and I need some liquid patience. What do I need to do to get a drink around here, turn Christian?

Radi: No, just go to one of the cafés and ask for "Saudi coffee."

Modi: How did you know about that?

Radi: (blushes) I heard about it accidentally.

Modi: Right.

Mani: What on earth is Saudi coffee? (Modi and Radi laugh at him)

Harry J. Sweeney

Conversation 26: A Highjacked Religion?

Modi: Mani, you look very pensive this morning.

Mani: I have a problem understanding something.

Modi: What is it you do not understand?

Mani: What does it mean when the Americans say our religion was hijacked?

Modi: The Americans do not quite understand Islam and our scriptures. They believe that some unscrupulous extremists have pushed everyone else away from the pulpit and the mosque and are misinterpreting our scriptures.

Radi: I have listened to both Mainstream and Radicals and find they are not misquoting or misinterpreting anything. On the contrary, they are quoting exactly from the texts. Actually, they *must* quote directly because the people know these texts also and would know if something was not exactly as written.

Modi: Exactly. The Americans find it hard to believe that our scriptures would say such things as "Kill them wherever you find them." They do not understand that in Qur'an 2:191 the targets of the wrath are those Meccans who did not accept Islam and drove the believers out of Mecca. In the Qur'an 9:5, of course, the targets became those who left the faith. That verse goes on to tell the believers to let them alone if they rejoin the community and pay the tax.

Mani: I remember those ayats. Therefore, you are saying that the Americans hear or read our imams quoting from our scriptures and they say something has to be wrong, that our scriptures really do not say those things, when indeed they do.

Radi: Those people must be stupid.

The Restless Wind and Shifting Sands

Modi: The people are not stupid, Radi. They are not taught in school all the things they need to know to understand the world they live in. The children of Christians and Jews are taught to despise Christianity and Judaism. Some American public schools actually teach Muslim subjects and Islam appreciation.

Mani: That's nice.

Modi: Now what, pray tell, would happen if a new imam began preaching in a madrassa or a Mosque and told the students not to believe the scriptures or follow the religious traditions?

Radi: I would slice off his head, quickly

Mani: He would not last until the next class.

Modi: Our religion is protected everywhere. The smallest insult is met with outrageous wrath and violence, even death. The other religions are open for criticism, which means we can insult them as much as we want.

Radi: That is as it should be. We are the premier religion.

Modi: Not on your tintype, old pal. The premier religions are those faiths whose adherents are robust enough in their faiths to laugh at or at least walk away from the worst insults with no thoughts of retaliation. Their faith is not at all threatened by adversity.

Mani: What the hell is Radi's tintype? Look, you have him looking all over himself, trying to find it.

Modi: If I say Radi is an idiot and he is your friend, what do you think I mean? Have I truly insulted him?

Mani: Not really. We are three very good friends, and we take a lot from each other—and incidentally we expect to take a lot from each other and accept minor name-calling as friendly gibes. As I recall, Radi

Harry J. Sweeney

threatens to behead you at least once every day. He is still looking for his tintype.

Modi: Christians and Jews tell jokes about one another all the time and many times repeat jokes about themselves. I have seen very silly jokes about Moses on American TV, and no one seems to care. The Christians have witnessed some very improper images of Christ and of His Mother, Mary—very indecent stuff. Apparently the only concern from the Christians is that public funds were used to pay the artists.

Radi: That is showing disrespect for the religion. Hey! What is my tintype?

Modi: It's an old and rediscovered photographic process (ferrotype). When one says "not on your tintype" you assume you are holding your own photo in your hand, thus the expression could simply mean "not on your life." Radi, religions are supposed to survive people poking fun at them or even badly insulting them. Religion, remember, is tolerance and patience. Religion has to be bigger than disrespect or insults. If not, one could naturally suspect a lack of confidence in itself.

Radi: Insult my religion, and I will kill you—it is my duty to do so.

Modi: I know, Radi, I know. That is the problem. Your religion should be able to withstand scrutiny, insults, and even condemnation. By showing anger and violence, Radi, you are saying your religion is not strong enough to ignore those things.

Mani: Modi, Radi has it right. It is his duty to do something about any insult to our Most Beloved, Allah, or the religion. It is written.

Modi: I know. You are referring to Sura 33, specifically Ayat 57. I keep looking at that sura repeatedly with wonder. There are times when I do not feel comfortable quoting from it.

Radi: What is wrong with you? You are now insulting our sacred documents. I should remove your head.

The Restless Wind and Shifting Sands

Modi: Radi, what I said was I am not comfortable with it. Many people have died because of that ayat, and I am not at all convinced that such general killing was intended. Allah loves His people, and He is merciful. To ask a question about an ayat or a complete sura could not possibly cause Allah to blink an eyelid. Don't you ever look at Allah like a kind, old grandfather who takes you on his knee and explains how things work?

Mani: Don't say things like that; that is terrible—insulting.

Modi: Allah knows what is in my heart and understands my quandary. You do not understand. If Allah wanted me punished, there are millions of stars that could fall on me, thousands of thunderbolts that could rip me apart, and untold numbers of other accidents that could befall me. What you can do to me in this life is like a pebble on the beach to what Allah could do without lifting a finger. Therefore, one wonders how we humans dare to consider killing a person because *we think* he insulted Allah or the Prophet.

Radi: If I think so, he did. I will kill him.

Modi: Mani, I think Radi just insulted Allah. Should we kill him?

Mani: I think he did also. Well, we don't want to, but it is our duty.

Radi: Now wait a minute. I did not do anything.

Modi: But we think you did, Radi. Can we borrow your knife?

Radi: You can't do this to me!

Modi: If I call down the street that Radi insulted Allah, what would happen? Would they ask questions, or would they run down here with their knives bare?

Mani: Modi, you made your point.

Harry J. Sweeney

Modi: Hopefully. However, this is only Monday. By Tuesday I will have to start all over again.

Radi: He is going to die today, now.

Mani: I thought you learned your lesson.

Radi: This time he's insulting me!

The Restless Wind and Shifting Sands

Conversation 27: The Coalition versus Al-Qaida

Mani: Modi, Radi and I were just talking about you. You are a little late this morning.

Modi: Yes, I know. I was up late. My new job sent me on assignment.

Mani: That's right. You are working for one of the new newspapers now. Is it a tough job?

Modi: Sometimes just getting to where I must be is tough. Last night I was able to cover some negotiations between the coalition and one of the tribes. I had to travel with the coalition vehicles, though, thanks to Radi's friends.

Radi: What are the tribes doing negotiating with the coalition? That is treason. They should all be beheaded.

Modi: Radi, the tribes have complained repeatedly to al-Qaida people that they are tired of the indiscriminate bombings and shootings. Too many of their people have died or been maimed. It was bad enough when they were targeted by the Shiite militias; however, it was more than they could take to be targeted by Sunnis also. They have had enough of phony war.

Radi: They should be thankful. Those who died. . . .

Modi: Yes, Radi, we know. They are martyrs according to you. I am tired of hearing it.

Mani: But it is true, Modi. What Radi says is true.

Modi: You don't know that. Even if what is written is true or ever was true, remember, martyrdom counts only if you are fighting in the way of Allah and only for love of Him. If rewards or fame is any part of it, it is not martyrdom—it is suicide. Suicide means eternal torments.

Harry J. Sweeney

Radi: You are casting shadows on all of our martyrs; men who gave up their lives for Allah. You should die.

Modi: Martyrs? You mean kids who didn't really know what anything meant. I am sure that many a young Ali would think twice about martyrdom if he realized that he wouldn't be playing with his pal Ahmad anymore or seeing his parents. There are too many of our children lying there rotting in graves, thanks to you guys, and they had not even begun to live. You abused their trust in you.

Radi: Today you will lose your head. You are speaking against our religion.

Mani: You are going too far, Modi. Tell me, what were the negotiations about?

Modi: Religion should not be about killing our kids. The coalition is providing arms, ammunition, RPGs, and other benefits to those tribes who have asked for the means to defend themselves against al-Qaida. They have seen that the new government cannot or will not protect them and suspect that a predominantly Shiite power would not be very interested in protecting Sunnis. Of course, even though they specified defense against al-Qaida, we know that they need protection from the Shiite militias also. I believe Muqtada as-Sadr already got the message and gave orders to pull back.

Mani: I can understand that they need to protect themselves from Shiites, but. . . .

Modi: Don't bother to tell me that fighting al-Qaida is fighting one's own people.

Radi: It is. Are you going to tell me something different?

Modi: Not exactly. I will ask that you remember that when our Most Beloved in Yathrib heard about a rich caravan on its way to Mecca, to

The Restless Wind and Shifting Sands

further enrich the Meccans, he did not hesitate to attack it. And were they not his own people?

Mani: That situation was different. The Meccans were causing us harm.

Modi: I just finished saying that al-Qaida was indiscriminately killing tribesmen. Isn't that harm? Look, you two, al-Qaida attacked the coalition and it got its clock cleaned. So, they looked around for some softer targets and decided that they would destroy the new government a different way. No one looked forward to joining them for an attack on coalition troops; the people knew better and really did not have anything against the troops to begin with. Most of the people see them every day, and many take comfort from just seeing their patrols. When attacking government buildings became too dangerous, AQ went after people like you and me.

Radi: What is this about cleaning clocks? What are you talking about?

Mani: Radi, I have heard that one. It means you were beaten badly.

Radi: I have not heard the troops really beat up al-Qaida.

Modi: Who was supposed to carry the story? Would it be Al-Jazeera, the *New York Times*, or the *Washington Post*? How about that white-haired fool who brazenly ran for the U. S. presidency?

Mani: You keep telling us things like that. Do you watch Fox and CNN every day?

Modi: You bet, whenever we have electricity. Now listen to this. Do you think that the coalition is losing the fight here and is almost beaten? Do you see the troops slinking around, looking demoralized? When shot at, do they run away?

Radi: I would like to say yes, but for some reason Allah has not yet

Harry J. Sweeney

favored us with a way to defeat them. But He will. He will. I will be drenched in their blood.

Modi: It would more likely be your own. Would you believe that the American press and the dolts on the Left running for president all think the coalition is losing badly and need to be rescued as quickly as possible?

Mani: You must be kidding. What have they been smoking, some of the Afghanistan stuff?

Radi: Aha! Allah is taking a hand and covering the eyes of the press and all the candidates, making them believe all is lost and making them want to run home in disgrace. That is how our Most Beloved and Abu Bakr escaped from Mecca right through the Meccan soldiers searching for them. No one saw them.

Mani: Yes, yes. I am glad Radi said that. It certainly makes sense to me. Allah is covering the eyes of the American press and the president wannabes. I will say a special prayer praising Allah and thanking Him for His help.

Modi: If you want to keep thinking that way, fine. Now let's say just for sake of argument that Allah is not covering their eyes. Perhaps He is preparing something else more dramatic.

Radi: Oh? What?

Modi: It doesn't matter. Just suppose that Allah is not helping us right now for whatever reason. You know Allah knows all things and can do what He wants.

Mani: I pity the Americans having to put up with people and companies like that. Maliki here is bad enough.

Modi: Yes, Al-Maliki is not the best we can do. But in all fairness, remember, people have been killed just for belonging to the government.

The Restless Wind and Shifting Sands

Moreover, how long has it been since being in power did not mean getting everything you can get? We have never really been nationalists before the removal of Saddam. Some of us are just learning, but others are screaming and yelling that we must not be nationalists. We must be believers first and kill all the unbelievers. Those people are not part of the solution; they are a big part of the problem. There is nothing wrong with being a nationalist; it is not a curse. You simply love the land and people where you were born and want to preserve your way of life.

Radi: But Modi, Allah has said kill them wherever you find them. We find them here and must kill them.

Mani: What Radi says is true! Allah has told us we have a duty to do that.

Modi: Allah's words were exhortations to the believers fighting to build their religion in the seventh century against overwhelming odds. Allah has never mentioned the coalition. As far as being anti-believer is concerned, the coalition has Believers among them. However, never forget that they rid us of Saddam Hussein and his insane sons. Saddam has killed more believers than the coalition. Now the coalition is arming believers. They are arming tribal believers with modern arms to help them protect themselves. Do you know what that means? It means we are not their enemies and they know it! Al-Qaida has become a common enemy, the same as the Shiite militias.

Mani: That makes sense also. The government cannot protect us because it is too weak.

Modi: Now, Mani, where does that leave the coalition?

Mani: Allah, help us. (Looks skyward) Allah, help me for saying this. If the coalition departed, Modi, all of you moderates will be killed—perhaps everyone who ever voted with their purple fingers. And many of us mainstream will be killed. Only those who supported the jihad will be safe from the murderous Salafists. Those Kurds who could not escape into Turkey will be killed. The Salafist/Wahhabis will probably

Harry J. Sweeney

overthrow the Saudi royalists, despite American protection and perhaps deny oil to the West. I know they will deny it to the Americans. Europe now is almost a believer continent.

Modi: Have you considered that Iran might take a hand in Saudi Arabia and elsewhere? We would have a huge Sunni-Shiite war, unless we both joined forces to fight the Americans. That is what I am afraid will happen. Radi, you and Mani will never see your grandchildren.

Radi: That would be wonderful. I will leave this awful life and spend eternity in paradise.

Mani: Yes, Modi. That would be a good thing. I too long for paradise.

Modi: But what about your families? What about the people of Iraq? What about all of the innocent people of the world? What about living in peace and friendship?

Mani: Remember, Modi, only believers can be innocent!

Radi: Yes, and it is also written: Don't take Jews and Christians for your friends.

Modi: I am certain that there are millions of wonderful, innocent people in this world that love Allah or their God as much as we love Allah. In fact, Mani, many coalition young men have died for you—so that you could have a better life with a government of your own to look out for you. They rid you of Saddam Hussein and are trying to rid you of al-Qaida and other would-be butchers! Would you have done the same for them or anyone else?

Radi: We would be martyrs for our faith.

Modi: Yes, as long as you thought it guaranteed entering paradise. Coalition troops did not need that for their inspiration. Their lives are important to them. Their families and homes are important. They do not care about a quick trip to paradise and leaving the world behind.

The Restless Wind and Shifting Sands

Those troops gave up all of that to help you live yours in peace and freedom. They gave up the future they wanted because you were important to them also.

Mani: Perhaps I will think about that at noon prayer.

Radi: Bah. Who asked them? They all deserve to die. They should all burn forever.

Modi: I will say a prayer for you, Radi.

Radi: Why? So I will agree with you?

Modi: No, so that you will take a *ghusl* (full bath) one of these days.

Radi: (Starts to chase Modi) You son-of-Satan, I am going to bloody my knife today.

Harry J. Sweeney

Conversation 28: Killing Insurgents in Iraq, Killing babies in America

Modi: Good morning, all. Hope everyone had a good night's sleep.

Mani: You are bright and chipper. It must be Radi's turn to buy breakfast.

Radi: Oh no, it isn't. It's your turn, Mani. Why so happy looking, Modi? I know a few imams who would torture you just to find out what your sin was.

Modi: I found a good friend working for the newspaper who has a great head for history. He showed me a few things about research.

Radi: Good. Perhaps he will show you how everything that is happening today is simply the seventh century all over again.

Modi: Actually, he disagrees with that to a certain extent. He notes that many of the imams who have studied the past as if it were the only aspect of life worth knowing, think only in terms of the past. They relate only to the past for explanations and answers. It is as if the seventh century was only last week. They are too limited to be effective to anyone but others of the same genre.

Radi: All of the imams I respect tell me that everything must be observed and analyzed through the prism of seventh-century Islam. The only things new are the weapons. Everything else is exactly the same. Our scriptures are as alive today as they were when our Most Beloved first committed them to memory.

Mani: I agree with Radi completely.

Modi: If the Americans believed that way, they would not be the country they are. The people can listen to their political imams and see there is no logic behind what they say. Some dummies, of course, are in lockstep with their political imams and cannot see the logic or the reality that belie the words. For the most part, the Americans have some idea of logic and reality and reject many notions.

Mani: Can you explain that?

Modi: Well, the researcher showed me the other day just how bad and dumb a certain political imam was. Remember that white-haired twit we discussed the other day?

Mani: Yes, the whiner.

Modi: Well, when the Khmer Rouge was marching into Cambodia with murder in their hearts and on their lips, old White-Hair rejected the plea for arms and military aid to defend their country. One would have guessed his philosophy sounded something like *Peace through genocide*. And what happened was atrocious.

Mani: By Allah, he could not see the coming "killing fields?" He would not even consider defending them just in case?[22]

Modi: Some would say people of that persuasion are just insufferable bores who go through life pooh-poohing the analyses of better people.

Radi: Our people are better than that. Certainly, we look at everything through the seventh-century prism; however, our fighters are down-to-earth people who know whom to fear and whom not to fear. When we lie, we don't lie to our people, we lie to the enemy, and there are good reasons for telling the lie.

Mani: Radi is right, Modi. Our fighters know the truth and fight superior odds anyway, with hopes that our dedication and fierceness will overcome technology and numbers. There is a difference between being crazy and being stupid. Sometimes we pick out the strongest point and attack it simply because we think that perhaps the enemy is lax there, thinking that we would not be crazy enough to attack there.

---

22   *Voting to Kill*, by Jim Geraghty, page 57.

Harry J. Sweeney

Modi: Sometimes that is a smart tactic, not a crazy one. Our Most Beloved said more than once that war is deceit.

Radi: It seems to me that you are coming closer to our side, Modi.

Modi: Which side is that, Radi?

Radi: The true side of Islam, the path of our Most Beloved.

Modi: Our Most Beloved showed us more than one path. We can choose which path to follow, the path of peaceful existence, or the path to war. Remember, our Most Beloved walked the path of peace first.

Mani: Yes, Modi, that's right. He chose only the path of war when the armies of Mecca sent their power against him and tried to kill him and destroy Islam.

Modi: I am so glad that you said that. Suppose it became clear, regardless of who is saying what, that the Western powers, even America, were not trying to kill us and not trying to destroy Islam?

Radi: That is a lie, and you know it is.

Mani: It certainly appears that Americans are trying to kill us and want to destroy Islam.

Modi: I showed you more than once that the Americans do not even understand Islam. They have no clue that it is anything more than a religion. They do not know our Most Beloved or our scriptures. Americans respect religion and bend over backwards to accommodate it. They seem to hate only their own religions.

Mani: Why would they hate their own religions?

Modi: Because no Jewish or Christian religion would go along with killing their babies and giving its blessing to widespread adultery, unchecked fornication, and different lifestyles.

The Restless Wind and Shifting Sands

Mani: But our religion would be even stricter on those issues. In fact, we would kill the perpetrators quickly! Trials, why would we need trials? And as for alternate lifestyles, would those people not be the first ones killed under our religion?

Radi: Don't those baby-killers in America know all of this?

Modi: No. In the words of one of my grandsons, "Them stupid."

Radi: I do not understand any of this. I only see the Americans attacking our lands.

Modi: I know this, Radi. You are looking through the wrong prism. Just ask yourself, Radi, what are the troops actually doing?

Radi: They are killing our people. They kill men women and children indiscriminately.

Modi: Radi, our kids would not be crowding around the Americans for treats if what you said were true. Our people would not be going about their business in the midst of a patrol if they feared the Americans as killers of Arabs. Some troopers have knocked down doors and taken some people away. However, the doors have been repaired, and most of the people returned. The neighbors all knew who al-Qaida were, and why they didn't return.

Mani: I do not like interrupting your speech; however, I think it is time we vacated the area quickly and got breakfast somewhere.

Modi: (Looks around) Why? What is going on?

Radi: Don't you hear that? There is an American patrol in the neighborhood.

Modi: But I already told you, you have nothing to fear from the American patrols. They are not looking for trouble.

Harry J. Sweeney

Mani: I understand that. Nevertheless, you never know when Radi's friends decide to make themselves martyrs and get us caught in the crossfire.

Radi: I am going to decapitate both you guys. But I can wait until after breakfast.

The Restless Wind and Shifting Sands

Conversation 29: We are not threatened by non-believers.

Mani: I have not seen Modi today. I hope you didn't do anything to him.

Radi: I thought about it, but I had other things to do. (He snickers.)

Mani: I do not understand Modi sometimes. At times, he seems as strong in his religion as we are, but some of his ideas are truly *radical*.

Radi: His vision seems colored by too many ideas that do not come from the scriptures. Our scriptures are black and white, and that is how our thinking should be. He is a modernist who has accepted the stupid idea that non-believers have rights. Because he is in error, he puts other people of other religions on a par with us, Allah's chosen people. He thinks Christians and Jews are equal to us.

Mani: That is nonsense. Anyone familiar with the sharia knows that you are enjoined from treating non-believers as you must treat believers—that is almost blasphemy. With very few exceptions, the fate of any non-believer in our hands is up to us—enslave him or kill him—but a believer must never be hurt or killed unless for just cause. Suffice to say that a non-believer never has just cause to hurt or kill a believer.

Radi: I remember specifically an issue from long ago about a Muslim on a mission to Mecca who accidentally met a clansman. I do not have to tell you that our first duty is to the family, but the family's first duty is to the tribe. Islam is the only concept that can transcend family and tribe. The clansman, a one-eyed shepherd, had no animosity toward the Muslim and was no threat to him. However, the shepherd could not see how he could ever become a follower. As the shepherd slept, the follower killed him by driving the tip of his bow down through the clansman's good eye, into his brain. The follower killed other non-followers during the mission and related them all to our Most Beloved, who laughed and enjoyed the stories.[23]

---

23   Tabari 1440.

Harry J. Sweeney

Mani: The Prophet did not ask about killing the clansman?

Radi: No.

Mani: I would say that shows the sharia[24] to be correct. If a clansman is an unbeliever and can be killed without question, a foreigner or stranger who is not a believer would have no rights whatsoever under the laws of our religion.

Modi: I heard all of that. It was very interesting.

Mani: Radi is correct in what he says; he is backed up by scriptures.

Modi: I can readily say that, according to the scriptures, Radi is indeed correct.

Radi: I never thought I'd hear you say that.

Modi: I have a question about the scriptures.

Mani: Oh, oh! Modi is going to start something now.

Modi: Do you both want these scriptures to be correct as of now?

Radi: Of course we do. They are the holy words of Allah.

Modi: Not really. You were repeating a story—a hadith—told by Tabari. Not everything has the force of holy writ.

Radi: What does that mean?

Modi: It means Allah did not write the hadiths. Men wrote the hadiths based on stories told by others, and other men drew from these stories theories of law as well as of religion. What I say, and I told you more than once before, is that we live in a different world with wholly different people.

---

24   Reliance of the Traveller, Sacred Law of Islam, o1.2(2), page 584.

The Restless Wind and Shifting Sands

Mani: You are wrong, Modi. It is still the same world.

Modi: Mani, the Meccan polytheists are gone; there is one religion in Arabia. Islam is not besieged by anyone. We are in a world in which everyone, except us, declares that everyone should live and let live. Hold on; let me change that a little. Even some of us, quite a lot of us, in fact, agree among ourselves that everyone should live and let live.

Radi: I do not hear that from believers!

Modi: You are not listening. I have to admit that many people who believe what I said are intimidated by the threats and the killings that your friends have served up as a daily religious rite. The fact that the scriptures appear to validate these threats and killings in no way excuses them. We are not threatened by non-believers. We moderate and mainstream believers are threatened and killed by minor sects of believers, whose goal is to exercise dominance over all of us, trying to strip us of the free will that Allah had given us.

Radi: That is heresy. . . .

Modi: I expected you to use that word, Radi. I also expected you to reach for that knife, as you did. But let us simply clear away this fog of religious zeal and look at only one problem: the rest of the world, the non-believers, are not attacking us; in fact, the United Nations forbids any nation from discriminating against any other nation because of religion. If all other historical or geographical problems were called off, everything would be quiet. We would find ourselves more at odds with other Muslim nations than with the rest of the world. Even during the problems with Saddam Hussein, almost all of Europe stood against the United States to prevent the American attack. Of course, European greed was involved, but all of those Western countries still stood with us.

Mani: I had never thought of that.

Radi: I don't believe any of it.

Harry J. Sweeney

Modi: Radi, you *cannot* believe any of it. You have that seventh-century prism that does not allow you to see things as they are. Let me ask you, would you like to have peace in the world with all humanity at peace with everyone else, like one big, happy family?

Radi: Only if *Allahu Akbar* rings from every corner of the globe and the entire world is ruled by the sharia.

Modi: That is what I thought. Radi, you and I are believers, but we stand against each other as enemies. We are enemies only in your mind because I do not think as you do and I am willing to live in peace with you and also with the rest of the world.

Radi: That too is heresy. Do not take. . . .

Modi: I already know what the Qur'an says about taking Jews and Christians for friends. That may have been correct then, but the Prophet was telling Muslims not to try to ally themselves with other tribes (Christians or Jews) to survive a Meccan victory. He was not trying to make a social statement. I often wonder what would have happened if the Yathrib Jewish scholars had been more accommodating to our Most Beloved. Alas, they did not understand his status as a Jewish prophet more knowledgeable about their Torah than they.[25] Oh, well. I already pointed out that Christian nations have stood with us against the United States. You may not know it, but the Jews sent doctors and medical supplies to support us against the Serbs. And don't bother telling me that Allah spread his hands and forced these people to do those things against their wills. I am tired of hearing it.

Radi: I am a little tired of hearing you deride our religion. In any case, arguing is finished for today. I can hear Bilal calling us to prayer.

Modi: Radi, can we truly do our ablutions in a friendly manner and seriously pray together?

---

25   *Mohammed and the Unbelievers*, Center for the Study of Political Islam, pp. 51-55

The Restless Wind and Shifting Sands

Radi: As long as I'm not paying for lunch—and you don't push me in the water trough again.

Modi: You dip. (Grabs Radi's hat and runs off with it with Radi close behind).

Mani: Friends? Enemies? I hope I never find out.

Harry J. Sweeney

Conversation 30: Apostasy and Martyrdom

Radi: Here comes Modi—and he is smiling from ear to ear again.

Mani: Rats! We're in for another fight.

Modi: Good morning. You both look so glum; you must have seen the news also.

Mani: I am afraid to ask. What news?

Modi: Times Online's headline was "Young Muslims Begin Dangerous Fight for the Right to Abandon Faith." A group of Muslim youths are getting together to formulate ways to facilitate leaving their religion.

Mani: Allah preserve us! That is terrible!

Radi: Yes, it is terrible. What is going on there?

Modi: Putting myself in their heads, I can understand what they have been going through. Now take the Brits, for example. Arab boys see Brit boys and girls doing things together, having fun together, going on picnics, dates, dancing, holding hands and the Arab boys are not allowed to even look at a female. I believe that borders on the intolerable. It is a natural thing in Europe but outrageous to us.

Radi: Those Brit kids ought to be killed.

Modi: For what? For enjoying each other's presence? They see someone they like, and they spend time with that person, getting to know him or her better. They visit each other's homes and even take meals together. They meet each other's parents and siblings. It is real friendship.

Radi: And that leads to terrible sin.

Modi: What would that terrible sin be, Radi? That they might have a child together? Sure, it is not proper, but it happens. But not everyone is weak and unrestrained; moreover, they are all taught about birth control. But which is worse, bringing another baby into the world, or walking into a train station with a bomb and killing 100 people by blowing them to bits?

Radi: How can you even make such a comparison? There is nothing wrong with blowing Christians and Jews to bits.

Modi: Somehow, I knew you were going to say that. But getting back to your terrible sinners. Dating does not always lead to sex and pregnancy. After a few months or a year, the boy and girl may lose interest in each other and go on to other boys and girls. And the young Arab girls in their black or gray *abaya*s are looking at Brit girls in their colorful outfits and cannot help feeling a little envious, no matter what they say. I can't help thinking of all the school parties that the Muslims are not allowed to attend! Wow! The Brits are a very social nation and like their parties and other pleasant events. Can you imagine a social event in Riyadh? Boring. The only way to survive such an event is to down a few martinis or some scotch, but unfortunately, alcohol is also forbidden.

Mani: You are criticizing our religion. I won't be able to stop Radi if he starts to boil. You know what he is like. He will have your head on his front gate.

Modi: But what about you, Mani. Does such talk make your blood boil also? Do you believe I should be killed for expressing these opinions? It is an important question, Mani. Perhaps it is the most important question this year.

Mani: I don't know, Modi. I do not like hearing what you say, but I am not horrified as Radi is. I just want peace and quiet.

Modi: Radi and his friends will give you peace and quiet. But what about your kids? If your son came to you and told you very quietly and very seriously that he wanted to change his religion, would you hate him enough to kill him?

Harry J. Sweeney

Mani: (Looks at Radi) I don't know.

Modi: You had better begin thinking about it now. And try not to let the crazy knife-wielders influence you. Make up your own mind. The world is changing whether we all like it or not. Remember, a few years ago, the word "apostate" (*murtadd*) would stop people in their tracks. Today one finds it in Muslim newspapers everywhere. It has already been brought up to the United Nations as a right of everyone to change his or her religion without sanctions.

Radi: We must double our efforts to rule the world! We must kill these people who are hurting Islam. Kill them all!

Modi: Radi, a nice, young Arab girl sees a nice, young Christian boy and wants to get to know him and be close to him because she likes him and feels comfortable with him. Perhaps he feels the same about her. There is nothing wrong with that, you twit! How is that hurting Islam?

Radi: Everything is wrong with that! The penalty is at least 50 lashes, maybe more. It should be much more for girls speaking with boys.

Modi: For what? Just because it brings a penalty doesn't make it wrong!

Radi: For just thinking about each other!

Modi: I guess you are for building that sidewalk for females in Riyadh to ensure that men and women, no matter how old, cannot even walk on the same sidewalk.

Radi: I agree with that. Men and women should never be together if it can be avoided.

Modi: Have you ever wondered if that isn't our big problem here?

Mani: How do you figure that?

The Restless Wind and Shifting Sands

Modi: Young men are products of nature, and they want and need female companionship. If they do not get it, they become frustrated and have to have some other outlet.

Radi: Their outlet is prayer and worshipping Allah.

Modi: Their outlet is strapping on a homicide belt and blowing themselves to bits to get a chance at those 72 virgins. He needs female attention, and he will go to great lengths if he has to.

Mani: Our martyrs are holy people. You are insulting them.

Modi: Right, Mani. Tell me you know exactly why they strapped on those belts. You cannot.

Mani: Neither can you.

Modi: But I have a reasonable and logical idea, Mani. For a young man to kill himself when he is filled with all the bloom of life and love requires a much bigger reason—and you gave it to him: 72 virgins. He only wanted a little slice of paradise, but he was too poor to marry, and the penalty for sneaking around was too much.

Radi: I am not married, and I am not strapping on the belt.

Modi: But you tell us, Radi, how many sinners you and your friends have ambushed. How much blood have you had to wipe off your knife?

Radi: What has that to do with anything? I am simply taking Allah's vengeance.

Modi: And who asked you to take the vengeance? Allah? I thought that your priorities will change when you met someone soft and nice.

Mani: Speaking of soft and nice, the little restaurant has made those

Harry J. Sweeney

French croissants again, and I am hungry. I am paying today. (Modi laughs so hard he can't speak)

Radi: Maybe he needs some croissants and some "Saudi coffee." (Modi laughs even harder)

Mani: We may have to carry him. Look, he can't even walk. What on earth is Saudi coffee?

Radi: Hmm. Better slap him and bring him out of it; a crowd is forming. They'll think he already has had too much Saudi coffee. (Modi laughs even harder, and his two friends help him walk to the restaurant, mindful of the stares around them)

CHAPTER 4

<u>Conversation 31: What happened to the 72 virgins?</u>

Mani: What on earth are we doing in this hot desert at midnight? Are we nuts? I should be home in bed, snoring.

Modi: We are waiting for al-Qaida. Remember, a relative asked family and friends to help defend against an expected attack on their village. We just volunteered to help. How could we refuse?

Mani: I sure wish Radi were here. Why isn't he taking part?

Modi: Al-Qaida is not his enemy. He identifies with both AQ and the Taliban. He thinks our new government is evil.

Mani: But you did ask Radi, didn't you?

Modi: I could not do so. If I had explained what we needed to do and where we would be, he might let his buddies know about it, and they would turn the tables on us.

Mani: But would he really and truly do that if he knew we were going to be here?

Modi: Would you take the chance?

Mani: What is that over to the left? Something is moving.

Modi: I see it. Ah, it is only a truck. I hear the motor now. I do not see anything behind it. Perhaps the AQ are not coming tonight.

Mani: It's early yet. Modi, if we are involved in some shooting and get killed, are we martyrs?

Harry J. Sweeney

Modi: We will have the same claim to martyrdom as those walking into a kid's school with a homicide vest. Perhaps we have a better claim. It is not the group or the nation that Allah sides with. Allah loves us all, the saints and the sinners. Allah gives us intellect and free will; He lets us choose what to believe and what to follow. If you truly believe that you are fighting for love of Him, you are indeed a martyr. It does not matter what side you are on or what religion you profess. Many coalition soldiers were killed to help us. If Allah is all knowing and fair, the coalition troops can be martyrs also.

Mani: Are you saying that the Americans can go to paradise to enjoy those 72 houris?

Modi: I cannot give you my opinion until you let me know what your definition is of the houris.

Mani: Why, virgins, of course. That is what is written.

Modi: Mani, I hate to say this; however, scholars have been whispering about that translation for centuries. Almost everyone wants the translation to be virgins, but the most likely translation is White Raisins. The Torah discusses the identical situation, but the Torah talks about paradise and grapes.[26]

---

26   See Ibn Warraq (pseudonym): *What the Koran really says*, Amherst, NY, 2002, Prometheus Books, p. 84 (Syriac "white raisins" of "crystal clarity," per Christoph Luxenberg (pseudonym) in correcting Suras XLIV.54 and LII.20); Alexander Stille: "Scholars scrutinize the Koran's origin: A promise of moist virgins or dried fruit?" *New York Times* (and *International Herald Tribune*), March 4, 2002 (http://www.corkscrew-balloon.com/02/03/1bkk/04b.html); (anonymous :) "Virgins? What virgins? *The Guardian*, January 12, 2002: "In Syriac, the word *hur* is a feminine plural adjective meaning 'white', with the word "raisin" understood implicitly. Similarly, the immortal, pearl-like ephebes or youths of suras such as LXXVI.19 are really a misreading of a Syriac expression meaning 'chilled raisins (or drinks)' that the just will have the pleasure of tasting in contrast to the boiling drinks promised the unfaithful and damned."   http://www/guardian.co.uk/saturday_review/story/0,3605,631332,00. html; http://syrcom.cua.edu/Hugoye/Vol6No1/HV6N1PRPhenixHorn.html; and

The Restless Wind and Shifting Sands

Mani: What! (He jumps to his feet.)

Modi: Hey, get down, and for Allah's sake, shush. You will get us killed.

Mani: You are fooling with me. You can't be serious!

Modi: Call my bluff. When you see AQ coming over the ridge, run over to them and start shooting.

Mani: How could anyone make such a mistake?

Modi: When Abu Bakr's scholars began putting all those ayats together, some were written down on banana leaves. The Arabic they used at that time did not have the extra marks we use today. Without those marks to indicate vowels, one word, for example, could be BAN, BIN, or BUN. If a dot were missing, the BAN word could be BAB, NAB, NAN, TAB, BAT, NAT, and on and on. Even now, if you forget a mark or misplace one, it is not that easy to determine what the word is. Back then, memory was considered more reliable than writing for that reason. Don't fault the people trying to do the right thing; they had a very difficult, almost impossible task. Virgins and raisins are not that far apart in our writing.

Mani: You are making me ill.

Modi: Well, cut off the talk and keep watching the road.

Mani: Should we have something bigger than these Kalashnikovs?

Modi: Well, personally, I'd like to have a field piece on one side and a tank on the other. Some of the others have RPGs and some light machineguns. I just hope AQ does not bring any heavy stuff with

---

Nicholas D. Kristof: "Martyrs, virgins and grapes," *The New York Times*, August 4, 2004, http://nytimes.com/2004/08/04/opinion/04krist.html.

Harry J. Sweeney

them. They usually travel light so that they can travel fast, strike, and get out. They may have some grenades.

Mani: Someone's coming up behind us. (He redirects his AK.)

Fighter: I brought some coffee. It may be a long night. I also brought some water and a basin for ablutions.

Modi: Thank you (*shukran*) for that; both are welcome. Is there any sign of al-Qaida? (pours water from the pitcher over right hand, then left, washing to the elbow)

Fighter: Nothing so far. We sent out some people in different directions. They saw nothing. They are Bedouins who know this desert. If al-Qaida were there, they would know.

Mani: How many people are defending? Modi, would you save some of the water for me?

Fighter: We have not finished counting, but we expect about 200. It is many more than we anticipated. Fortunately, quite a few brought their personal Kalashnikovs. I would guess that a lot of people have had it with al-Qaida here. I have some more people to see. May Allah protect both of you.

Mani: What you told Radi the other day appears to be correct. Al-Qaida is not so popular here anymore. Why is that?

Modi: Too many failures and then killing other Sunnis to make their points. (He washes face, neck, and ears; with wet hands, wipes head and forehead. Sniffs some water from his hands and exhales it.)

Mani: What do we do if they don't come tonight? (Takes pitcher from Modi and begins his own ablutions.)

Modi: That depends. Would you like to make some good money?

The Restless Wind and Shifting Sands

Mani: (Perks up) Doing what?

Modi: I talked to our hosts before we came out here to watch. It seems they have a Shiite trans-shipment place staked out. They need a few good fighters to raid the place.

Mani: Oh, yeah? What's there? (He starts to remove his shoes, but Modi stops him.)

Modi: Remember, you washed your feet this morning and you wore shoes and socks, so you need only rub wet hands over your shoes as if you were actually washing your feet.

Mani: I will take your word for it. Modi, good grief! We were talking and I forgot the ablution prayers. Does that invalidate my ablutions?

Modi: An imam told us that we could even skip ablutions if we expected trouble straight away. Look, Mani, you are protecting Islam from the insurgents.

Mani: Strange. They say they are fighting jihad. But tell me what is at the place we are to raid.

Modi: Guns, ammo, RPGs, grenades, explosives. We will see lots of supplies.

Mani: I can guess it is from Iran, but who is supposed to get it all?

Modi: We are.

Mani: What?

Modi: Yep. However, we are not going to let them distribute it to us; we are going to take it from them and then turn anyone involved, especially Iranians, over to the government. We will pass out the arms to our own people, including a few Baathists on our side who know

Harry J. Sweeney

what they are doing and who want to help keep this country unified and free of the Taliban and Wahhabis.

Mani: You talked me into it. You are a devious salesman. OK, I am in, you SOB, even though I know that you are going to get me killed—with nothing more to look forward to than GRAPES! I guess we are ready for the early evening prayers.

Modi: Louie, something tells me this is the beginning of. . . .

Mani: Shut up, you damned fool! (They both laugh)

Modi: Shh! Did I just hear an RPG launch? (Explosion)

Mani: Look! They are shooting up on the right.

Modi: Look straight ahead. Here they come. (Mani and Modi begin shooting.)

The Restless Wind and Shifting Sands

<u>Conversation 32: Fighting in Anbar; Obligation only to tribe and family</u>

Mani: Shall we mention last night at Anbar to Radi? It may start a fight if he knew we fought against al-Qaida.

Modi: I would not say anything. Perhaps he will bring it up and have something interesting to say.

Mani: I really tasted fear there for a while, but it went away when those bullets started whizzing past. I couldn't hear anything after the first few shots.

Modi: I know how that goes. Carry a few spent bullets with you next time and stick them in your ears, point out. That will help. According to the sheikh, we stopped al-Qaida, and they lost a few fighters. We suffered a few wounded, but nothing serious. I guess we surprised them. They will not be surprised next time. I tried to give my AK back, but they told me to hang onto it. They may call us back. Besides the other raid they discussed, they want to build a border militia to plug the foreign-fighters gap. I wish someone would cut off funds to those insurgents.

Mani: I wonder if the same people are funding our militias. I am hanging onto my AK also. I could not dedicate enough time for a militia. I can barely afford the time here with the family. I think that is definitely a no-go. Oh! Here comes Radi.

Modi: I see him. I have that newspaper job, so I cannot spare the time either.

Radi: Good morning. Are we on for coffee?

Modi: We were just heading that way. What's new?

Radi: You are usually the one with news. What is going on?

Harry J. Sweeney

Modi: I visited some relatives last night and did not listen to any news or read anything. I had to visit; I had not done so for months.

Radi: I understand. I heard that one of the villages in Anbar was attacked by Baathists last night and al-Qaida had to come to the rescue. (Modi and Mani look at each other knowingly. Radi had it turned around)

Modi: Did you get any details on that attack?

Radi: I did not get anything yet, other than that summary.

Mani: I suppose we should check into that. It is not like the Baathists to attack villages in Anbar. Radi, do you have a cousin or someone there?

Radi: Actually, Modi, I do not. However, I could have had cousins on either side. I have loads of relatives. I am constantly ducking marriage with cousins.

Mani: I can understand that. I think everyone has relatives on both sides of that street. Radi, did you ever join al-Qaida?

Radi: I thought about it. It takes a while for everyone to be checked out. You have to be a pure enough believer to join their ranks. They have a long line of wannabes.

Modi: And to be pure enough means you either have to be crazy enough or stupid enough.

Mani: You are not being nice, Modi. AQ ranks have many dedicated believers just like you and me. With AQ, though, I am a Salafist, so I am halfway there already.

Modi: Sorry, Radi. I become a little rattled when I see what AQ and others are doing to my country. I feel like joining the fray also but not on the side of AQ.

The Restless Wind and Shifting Sands

Radi: If you are not on the side of AQ, you are fighting against Allah!

Modi: B/S, Radi. Allah does not take sides.

Radi: Are you really saying that we are not his chosen people?

Modi: What? How would I know that? Nobody knows. Those who do are lying to themselves. Perhaps we were at one time, but we have been killing our own people and others for decades, centuries, for almost no reason. We kill our children to gain a tactical advantage and many times we fail to gain the advantage. A terrible waste! No one but stupid leaders would want to sign treaties with us; it is obvious that treaties and negotiations mean nothing. We are at war with the entire world, we say; however, all the so-called enemies want us to do is cut out all the B/S and take our places in a peaceful world. We seem to be fighting a war with partners who are trying to help us.

Mani: Radi, if you had tribal relatives in Anbar and AQ were attacking the village, would you help them?

Radi: If they insisted, I would have to go. Remember. It is always my cousin and I against the world. But I could not fight against AQ. They are my friends.

Modi: But the people in Anbar would be your tribesmen. What about my cousin and me against my friend?

Radi: Now you are confusing me. I am a pure believer; I fight for Allah against the enemies of Allah, whoever they may be.

Mani: If I helped relatives in Anbar against AQ, would I be an enemy of Allah?

Radi: I will have to think about that. You have an obligation to your tribe and to your family; however, you also have an obligation to Allah to be the best believer possible—al-Qaida brings with them the purest form of Islam. To fight against pure Islam has to be against Allah.

Harry J. Sweeney

Modi: Well, Radi, what if we do not believe that AQ's or the Taliban's versions are pure? What if they are just mean-spirited sadists taking advantage of our laws to torture and kill?

Radi: What? Allah would not allow it!

Modi: Whenever you consider society, Radi, society stands alone. You must not allow religion to enter into it directly. You cannot postulate yourself what Allah wants in any situation, so you cannot use it as evidence of anything. You must not put yourself in His shoes because you are not God to juggle millions of esoteric facts in a second to decide what is right. You can only use logic, reality, and social and cultural data to make such decisions. For example, I am sure that our most caring and merciful Lord wants us to be happy in our religion, not suffering under the yoke of mental and physical slavery. AQ and the Taliban bring only slavery, suffering, and death. We saw that happening in Afghanistan and that is what they promise here. That, Radi, is evil and sinful. If you truly are for Allah, you must never help AQ! You must fight them!

Radi: You cannot be right. Allah requires strict obedience!

Mani: That is an interpretation, Radi, of imams who want power over us to direct our lives. There should be no compulsion in religion. No one should ever step between Allah and us. Besides, Radi, how would they know? They are not walking in His footsteps.

Modi: Do not forget, Radi, many of those imams have no right to guide people. Many are uneducated and simply self-serving. Some are sadists who like nothing better than to uncover some offense, no matter how trivial, that gives them the opportunity to punish someone. They have no idea what our scriptures say and probably never will know. Radi, you would be shocked to learn how many of our people, even some imams, do not know very much about the Qur'an or Ahadith. If they did not live in a Muslim country where they hear something every day, they would know very, very little. You know, Radi, the Muslims living in the West do not hear what we hear on loudspeakers, radio, TV, and

The Restless Wind and Shifting Sands

on the street every day. Some do not go to mosque, either because there are none nearby or because they have gotten out of the habit. Those deprived Muslims are still good, honest people—the West cannot be all that bad!

Mani: Many of the names of Allah include the Compassionate, the Merciful, the All Knowing, the All Forgiving, the Wise, and the Generous, among others. People are human, the All Knowing knows this and He knows that humans are frail and sometimes give in to some minor temptations. If He really wanted you to punish people who you believe have sinned, where is the compassion, the all forgiving, the mercy, and the generosity?

Radi: When he is punished, he is no longer a sinner.

Modi: He is no longer a person. Allah now has one fewer person to love and worship Him. You have robbed Him of a worshipper as you have robbed his children of a father and his wife of a husband. You have robbed a tribe of a member, weakening that tribe by one person. You have robbed his friends and his work. You have robbed the local shops of a customer. You robbed Allah and all of these others for what? Sin had nothing to do with it. You did it to satiate your own blood lust.

Mani: Radi, it seems to me that you are guilty of more than the sinners you punish.

Radi: I know you are both wrong, but my head hurts. I need some coffee.

Mani: Modi, it would seem you get the last word.

Modi: Donuts?

Harry J. Sweeney

<u>Conversation 33: Iran and Iraq</u>

Modi: That was some operation last night, Mani.

Mani: I could not figure out what I was doing. It was all manual labor. We were just transferring crates from one warehouse to another. I should have left my AK-47 home. I thought we were on a raid.

Modi: We were. It just so happens that three warehouses were involved on one side and two on the other. The Iranians separated the material so that if the coalition bombed one site, they still had 66 percent left.

Mani: I do not understand why it was not guarded.

Modi: It was. The Iranians are not the only group that can infiltrate. We even conned some of their guards to help us load. Iran wants their people to train us in guerilla warfare. I have an idea they just learned a lesson from us instead. How can you train the people who invented it?

Mani: That is another problem for me. I do not understand the Iran-Sunni connection. I thought they hated us as we hated them. It has been a blood-feud for over a thousand years.

Modi: I keep telling you, our Most Beloved said that war is deception. What is more deceiving than arming an enemy? You heard often that the enemy of my enemy is my friend.

Mani: Yes, I am aware of that. I am still a little shaky on why we stole it if they were giving it to us anyway.

Modi: It is a matter of sovereignty. If Iran gave it, Iran wants us dependent on their largesse. We would become pawns. By confiscating it, we show them that once the material is on our land it is ours and thank you very much for delivering it. By the way, our people did turn over a bunch of Iranian technicians to the government. That will certainly tighten some Iranian jaws.

The Restless Wind and Shifting Sands

Mani: So, Iran may not give us any more arms or equipment.

Modi: That is where you are wrong. Iran wants the Iraq war as muddied as possible so that they can find an opening to move in. They will do whatever it takes, no matter how bad it tastes, to muddy those waters.

Mani: They believe that Iraq will oblige them by allowing them to do that?

Modi: It is their error. However, they believe that by sending in Hizbullah—and they think Hizbullah cannot be defeated—they can simply plant their flag on Iraqi soil after that.

Mani: If Iran and Iraq fight each other, which one is fighting in the way of Allah?

Radi: Good morning, friends. Mani, I can hardly wait for Modi's answer to your question.

Modi: Neither. To fight in the way of Allah, you must be defending yourself and Islam from an enemy or enemies wanting to destroy the religion. If a Western power becomes peeved because we are blowing up its embassies, for example, and our reasons for such destruction are not in defense of Islam as a religion, anyone could readily argue that we are not fighting in the way of Allah. Try to convince me Saddam was trying to annex Kuwait for Allah's cause and not his own.

Radi: Don't change the subject! The Americans *are* trying to destroy Islam as a religion!

Modi: I hope Allah forgives you for your muddled thoughts. Americans could care less about our religion! They did not like attacks on their embassies and the attacks on their World Trade Center. That is common with Americans—they don't like being attacked.

Mani: But bin Laden attacked America for many reasons, including

Harry J. Sweeney

the fact that American troops were on Arabian soil. Our Most Beloved said on his deathbed that there should not be two religions in Arabia.

Modi: But he did not say that people from other faiths could not visit Arabia. The Americans protected Arabia from its enemies and from other states that would attack Arabia and secure not only Arabia's oil, but more importantly for us, it would also wrest from Arabia's protective hands the Kaaba! I would say that America is defending Islam, not attacking it. Almost any nation in the Middle East has the power to seize Arabia—if the Americans were to leave. Most assuredly, the primary goal would be to acquire the power of oil, not to secure the Kaaba. Saudi oil would make any wannabe a bigger player in world politics. Bin Laden is wrong; he should stick to business. He is on shaky ground when he speaks of politics or religion.

Mani: How can he be on shaky ground when Zawahiri is coaching him?

Radi: Dr. Zawahiri is an expert scholar on our scriptures.

Modi: That good doctor is one of the Brotherhood nuts. He should get an award for overacting. Dr. Z (Modi smiles) always reminds me of the lovable American character Yosemite Sam. Yosemite is always first to come to the rescue, verbose and loud, but he always misses one of the main points and comes to the wrong conclusion. Nevertheless, he was very popular. One of the unfortunate aspects of our scriptures, like almost all other scriptures, is that you can lay out the most evil scenario and find verses to support it. You can actually get things backwards.

Mani: You said that more than once before; however, I still don't understand that concept.

Modi: In the seventh century, whenever certain ayats (verses) were finally written down, words usually had one specific meaning. With the passage of time, however, almost all the meanings could be expanded or changed because the words now had alternate meanings. Sure, the scriptures have remained unchanged, but language has changed.

The Restless Wind and Shifting Sands

Judging from the content of the scriptures, perhaps it is not exactly a bad thing that they are now not as clear as they were when they were accepted as official verses.

Radi: Our imams know the original meanings and are careful to lead us in the right direction.

Modi: You know how I feel about some of the imams, Radi. Some of those guys do not know the scriptures and listen to people like Zawahiri—who has more than one ax to grind. If he is against a certain idea, he believes everyone else should be against it also.

Mani: When I listen to him, he makes sense.

Modi: Of course he does. You want him to make sense. He speaks with a backdrop of our ayats that can be interpreted to agree with what he says. Zawahiri knows that most Arabs feel guilty that they are not stricter in their religion. He is a snake-oil salesman.

Radi: I thought he was a doctor.

Mani: Radi, a snake-oil salesman is a smooth talker trained to convince people to take a certain action despite their better judgment. Usually, only rubes or dummies fall for that junk.

Radi: I guess snake-oil salesmen should all be killed.

Mani: Why? They are only making a living. Allah help the innocent or stupid dolt who spends his dinars for that swill. However, perhaps that is not kind of me to say that. I am just angry that we have so many stupid people in this country who do not know anything and don't want to know anything.

Modi: Radi, if everyone with whom you disagreed were killed, there would be very few people left on earth.

Radi: Hey, that is a great idea. How do we go about it?

Harry J. Sweeney

Modi: Forget it. You are too eager. Let's go get some breakfast.

Radi: I am for that.

Mani: Radi, what is that you tossed away?

Radi: Just some fluid to clean my blade.

Modi: (Reaches on the ground and reads the label) It's a bottle of snake oil!

Mani: Radi, sometimes you really disappoint me!

Radi: Oh, yeah? Well what are friends for?

The Restless Wind and Shifting Sands

Conversation 34: Wahhabis

Mani: Modi, where were you last night? I thought we were going to your cousins' together.

Modi: I am sorry about that. I was on my way but was stopped by the boss. I had to write two articles for the newspaper. Did you guys have some fun?

Mani: There was lots of shooting, and people died out there.

Modi: Wow! That's not good. What happened?

Mani: We were on our way to that Anbar village where we stored the new IEDs (improvised exploding devices) we stole from the Iranians, and the driver took a wrong turn. We thought we were entering a friendly village, but it turned out to be another training camp for foreign fighters and insurgents.

Modi: At Anbar? That is very strange.

Mani: It gets stranger. The instructors at the camp were themselves trained in North Korea. The students were from everywhere, even the UK.

Modi: Now I wish I had been there. You had a fire fight?

Mani: Very briefly. We went through the guard posts without knowing they were there, and they started calling for us to give them the password. None of them really wanted to start shooting, so we jumped off the lorries and tried to talk to them. Other guards showed up, concluded we were not part of their organization, and started firing. When they started running at us, shooting, we hit the dirt quickly, and only their friends were hit.

Modi: I am glad. Nobody else came out to challenge?

Harry J. Sweeney

Mani: An instructor came out with one of those old Soviet Makarovs, but one of our drivers took it away from him before he could rack the slide. He could have done some damage had it been an AK. When one of your cousins asked him about the Makarov, he said he picked it up in North Korea. That started an entirely new line of questions.

Modi: I guess so. How were they, as far as religion was concerned?

Mani: Typical Wahhabi trainees but not yet confirmed killers. Because of that, we had an easy time with them. There were so many, though, that Baghdad had to send two lorries to cart them away.

Modi: The government has to curb Wahhabism and Salafism. This business about not recognizing any laws or rules after the death of our Most Beloved is turning this country into a war zone within a war zone.

Mani: Modi, we cannot fault them for their beliefs.

Modi: We certainly can. The Muslim *umma* approved those laws and rules, and we were able to live and prosper. During the time of the Ottomans, those Wahhabis continued to be a thorn in the side of the *umma*. The caliph in Turkey had to send in troops to teach them a lesson once.

Mani: I remember the history lesson. For some time then it looked as if the House of Saud were finished, but they hung on for dear life until the British came along and gave them legitimacy.

Radi: Good morning. Are we in the middle of something?

Modi: We were talking about how the Ottomans crushed the House of Saud once, but the British rescued them from oblivion.

Radi: That is a lie. The Western powers launched a sneak attack against the Ottoman Empire.

The Restless Wind and Shifting Sands

Modi: Oh, yes. I forgot. They sent dive-bombers to strike the Turkish naval base at Pearl Harbor. (Mani tries vainly to suppress laughter)

Radi: What?

Mani: Radi, Modi is ridiculing your selected interpretation of history. I have to agree with Modi.

Radi: I know the truth! You are just repeating Western lies. The Western powers tried for years to destroy Islam as a religion. . . .

Modi: (Interrupting Radi) Radi, please don't insult our intelligence. We are friends here. We need to talk these out among ourselves and come to some kind of an understanding.

Radi: No, we do not. I have my truth. You have your lies. I am not Wahhabi, but I agree with the Salafists. They know the truth.

Modi: Radi, you know that Mani and I love you like a brother. We do not care what you believe. We argue with you because we want you to know that you are worth saving. People all over Iraq and elsewhere believe different things, most of which are of no interest to anyone. But the Salafists are busybodies that have to know everything that is going on and are going crazy over things that mean little or nothing. The Salafists, especially the Wahhabis, do not hesitate to kill their countrymen and others simply because of minor religious differences.

Radi: Yes. There are differences, and there should not be. People should conform to our way of worshipping Allah, or they should die, every one of those heretics!

Mani: Modi, you are wasting your time with him.

Radi: Mani, if you so-called mainstream Muslims don't come back into line with the real Islam, Allah will come down on you on the Day of Judgment, flinging you into the everlasting flames to writhe and scream forever.

Harry J. Sweeney

Mani: Radi, you cannot possibly know what you are saying. Modi and I do not condemn you for believing what you do. We are both trying to give you something else to think about. We both think about what you say; it is time you thought about what we say.

Radi: Allah will damn you both to the fire!

Modi: Well, Mani, I guess you have your answer.

Mani: I guess I do. How are we ever going to get anywhere ever if people like Radi are simply incapable of replacing their worn baggage with more pleasant-looking ones, easier to handle—with wheels even? Then we are looking at years of misery, gloom, and violent deaths.

Radi: (Looks around, confused) What baggage?

Modi: (Laughing) Mani, Why do we put up with him?

Mani: Because he is so cute. Look at those bedroom eyes.

Modi: Look out! He's pulled his knife. (They both run.)

Radi: I will kill you Sons of Satan!

The Restless Wind and Shifting Sands

<u>Conversation 35: President Ahmadinejad, Iran, and Europe.</u>

Modi: I guess you all saw or heard President Ahmadinejad in the United States.

Radi: I was expecting any minute for an RPG or roadside bomb to destroy his limousine. Nothing happened!

Mani: They do not have those types of attacks in the United States. "Jady" was welcome there. They did not even abbreviate his name.

Radi: They don't have politics in America?

Mani: Of course, but RPGs and bombs are not part of it.

Radi: Politics there must be terribly boring.

Modi: I wouldn't say they're boring. They have only two main parties, but they are as far apart as possible without shooting each other.

Radi: I know about that; they are funny; especially those two senators from that northern state. They remind me of some funny films I saw of Laurel and Hardy.

Mani: Did you notice "Jady's" use of deceit as a tactic at that university?

Radi: You bet! I was proud of him. Can you imagine, though, no homosexuals in Iran? Ha! Some of those chaps hold hands and kiss more than our guys do.

Modi: I would bet more than a few Iranian women would love to scratch his eyes out after his comments about all their freedoms.

Mani: Most of the Americans will dismiss his talk and dismiss him as a dolt. Even the host at the university denounced him.

Harry J. Sweeney

Modi: Yes, you are right. Sadly enough, I remember that some upstanding Americans were greeted with violence and were not allowed to speak. Yet "Dirty Jady" was treated with dignity. Calling him a few names does not rise to the level of what happened to those upstanding Americans.

Mani: There is just no telling about Americans.

Modi: Some people, Mani, even some Americans do not subscribe to Freedom of Speech if the speech does not agree with their views.

Radi: I noticed that also. I cannot figure out whether to hate them or love them. They always seem to be on our side, but they kill their babies and send their daughters out looking like prostitutes.

Modi: I know. Some of those Americans love their porn. No wonder their minds are all screwed up.

Radi: It is better for us, so I cannot complain. Without them, we would have an even harder time fighting their armies.

Mani: We also have Iran to thank for their training and their newer weapons. I heard on the news, though, that Iran is getting a little angry about losing some of their people over here.

Radi: Well, too bad! I love getting their weapons and their training, but I still hate them.

Modi: This hatred between the Shiites and Sunnis has been going on for too long—1,327 years, when our beloved Ali ibn Hussein was murdered on the site of Karbala.

Mani: It is still in my mind and in my heart. He was leading a procession to protest the unholy perfidies of the caliphate at the time. The soldiers of the caliph, as usual, beheaded all of the men, despite the status of some of them as relatives of the Prophet.

The Restless Wind and Shifting Sands

Radi was about to say something, but Modi stopped him.

Modi: We already know what you think, Radi, but sometimes you must learn to shut up when you are among friends.

Radi: The Shiites would have forced priesthood on us.

Modi: Who the hell cares? Is that any worse than the mess we have today?

Mani: Modi has told us time after time, Radi, that many of our imams are not a problem when they are leading us in prayers, but when some of them have the temerity to mount the pulpit and try to explain our religion to us, their lack of education and lack of wisdom shows. They incite the people who are as dumb as they are and foment too much trouble.

Radi: You people who do not join the jihad are the troublemakers. Because we are not all united in an all-out fight against the infidels, we do not have the power yet to take America and then the rest of the world. I must add, if you don't think we can do that, remember, we are pretty close to owning Europe as we speak.

Mani: I don't know about that, Mani. The newspapers are reporting more than just a few anti-Islam laws in Europe.

Radi: You are reading rumors. Some of our friends among the Europeans—useful idiots, Lenin called them--foolish as they are, will never allow the Europeans to defend themselves from us.

Modi: Not all European leaders are like that now, Radi. Europe again is changing.

Radi: Well, we will always have London.

Mani: Not so fast. Many of the polls show that the young Brit Muslims would rather see themselves more as Brits than Muslims. The British

Harry J. Sweeney

as a people now are getting a little tired of bombs and shootings. They welcome the comments and activities of the youngsters.

Radi: All of that will change when we toss the Americans out of Iraq and Afghanistan.

Mani: I am not so sure you can do that. The Americans are tough and smart.

Radi: Both governments, Iraq and Afghanistan need better auditing and are close to folding. Afghanistan may fold first. The next martyr may do the job. Many of the people surrounding Karzai are closer to Iran than to the Americans. The Americans are the key players there. They must win.

Mani: That is right, Modi. Do not forget, the Northern Alliance that helped the Americans win over the Taliban had always been hand-in-glove with Iran. You must also remember that the Constitution of Afghanistan is also based on the sharia, not on the American Constitution.

Modi: Radi, if the Americans did lose Afghanistan, it may be controlled by Iran and not the Taliban. The Taliban may be destroyed—the usual fate of your so-called useful idiots.

Radi: What did you call me?

Modi: Oh hell, not again. Radi, take that knife and. . . .

Mani: Calm down, Modi. Listen, Bilal calls.

Radi: Yes. Let us put all of our disputes aside for a little while.

Modi: Allah will bless both of you for your concern.

Radi: Ah, nuts!

The Restless Wind and Shifting Sands

Mani: What is the matter now, Radi?

Radi: Just as the adhan sounds, nature calls!
Mani and Modi laugh because upon wakening, Radi had to do a *ghusl*, a full-body wash. Ordinarily, for the next prayer, Radi would need only a partial wash (*wudu*); however, since he had a nature problem, he now has to take the time to do a full *ghusl* again.

Radi: (Running) I will get you guys for laughing. This is not funny!

Harry J. Sweeney

Conversation 36: Ahmadinejad, Oriana Fallaci, End of Days.

Mani: Modi, did you hear about President "Jady's" (Mahmoud Ahmadinejad's) speech at the UN the other day?

Modi: Oh, yes. But the electricity was off for a while, and I missed the beginning. Since I missed the beginning, I thought all of his ranting and raving was a self-confession.

Mani laughs so hard he bumps into Radi, almost knocking him down.

Radi: The president was ranting about the Western nations, especially America.

Modi: I know that now. However, it certainly appeared to me to be a world-class confession of his own crimes.

Mani: (Finds it hard to stop laughing) Modi, you need to curb your comments; you get too funny.

Radi: I do not think he's funny.

Modi: You don't think anything's funny. You remind me of the Ayatollah Khomeini.

Radi: Life is too serious for levity or laughter.

Modi: The ayatollah said something just like that. As I recall, the only person who ever struck him funny was the late Oriana Fallaci. However, the believers in Denmark, Italy, and other European cities had a big price on her head—and I mean *head*. They didn't think she was funny either.

Mani: I remember something about that. What did she do that was so evil?

The Restless Wind and Shifting Sands

Modi: Nothing evil. She wrote two books about the attitude and the actions of our believers who immigrated to Europe and trashed many of the places where they settled. She also complained about the eagerness of the national officials to accommodate the believers at the expense of the citizens. It is something akin to the way the American administration is treating illegal aliens at the expense of their own American workers.

Mani: I saw some of that on CNN. It was sandwiched somewhere between some stupid half-dressed female urchin and some judge giving bail to an illegal alien murderer. I have problems understanding American news programs. Out of ten minutes, they gave about a minute to the bail problem and the rest of the time to the urchin.

Radi: The Americans are all messed up and will have to deal with the flames after the Day of Judgment.

Modi: I wish you would get real. The Americans are not the Meccans of the seventh century, and we are not raiding their caravans and making deals with other tribes against them. We are in the twenty-first century now. Everything has changed. Get over it!

Radi: You are wrong, Modi. I told you before that the Americans are the polytheists—they worship their saints, Jesus Christ, and his mother.[27] They say there is only one God, but they worship more than one. We must kill them wherever we find them.[28]

---

27   Qur'an 4:171 "O People of the Scripture, do not commit excess in your religion or say about Allah except the truth. The Messiah, Jesus, the son of Mary, was but a messenger of Allah and His word which He directed to Mary and a soul [created at a command] from Him. So believe in Allah and His messengers. And do not say, 'Three'; desist - it is better for you. Indeed, Allah is but one God. Exalted is He above having a son. To Him belongs whatever is in the heavens and whatever is on the earth. And sufficient is Allah as Disposer of affairs."

28   Qur'an 2:191 "And kill them wherever you overtake them and expel them from wherever they have expelled you, and fitnah (disbelief) is worse than killing. And do not fight them at al-Masjid al-Ḥarâm (the Sacred Mosque in the vicinity of Mecca) until they fight you there. But if they fight you, then kill them. Such is the recompense of the disbelievers."

Harry J. Sweeney

Mani: Whatever your opinion is of the Americans, Radi, they have helped us here in Iraq. They have not tried to steal our oil, and they have given us the opportunity to vote our own people into the government. Except for the problem at Abu Ghraib, that was more hilarious than anything else, and even after a few unfortunate incidents during firefights with people firing at them, they have not tried to intimidate us or exploit us.

Radi: You are wrong, Mani. They tried to set up their own style of government that will endeavor to make us more like they are.

Modi: That statement is rubbish, Radi. How about keeping this subject on a higher level than that? Besides, we were talking about your buddy Ahmadinejad, President Jady!

Mani: Radi, I can hardly wait to hear your analysis of his reference to the Mahdi. I noticed he did not specifically mention the Twelfth Imam, but he had a reference to him.

Radi: I do not see anything wrong with his reminding everyone of the end of days. Perhaps he has the foresight to see the coming of the Mahdi. The Mahdi and Jesus will appear right before the Judgment. Not long after that, we will see who is flung into the fire and who sees paradise and the virgins. (Notices Mani laughing) What are you laughing at now?

Mani: Modi and I had a minor argument about that. Apparently, we are not the only ones arguing about what one sees after death or martyrdom. You say it is paradise with Fair-Skinned Virgins. Modi has it on good authority that it is a garden with lots of White Grapes.[29]

Radi: (Turns red with anger) Today you definitely will die, Modi. You dare to challenge the word of Allah, the All-Knowing?

Modi: It is a translation, Radi. It is someone's translation of what he thought he read or heard. We do not know exactly what was said;

---

29   See Conversation 31, note 21.

only what was written on banana leaves or plantain leaves. The early believers who were tasked with assembling the Qur'an, Allah bless their efforts and give them peace, had an almost impossible task. Our Arabic writing, given to us by Christian monks, had not been perfected until much later; it was not as reliable as it is now. Remember, the imams always said that in those days memorization was always superior to writing. Nonetheless, it should also be taken into consideration that many of our blessed people who memorized parts of the Qur'an had been exposed to terribly violent battles and arduous campaigns before they were called upon to regurgitate what they had committed to memory. Some of these people were also rather long of tooth, and memories could not always be verified. The ancient one may have had a choice between paradise and garden (in the Torah, it is garden) and between virgins and white grapes. I am not even going to ask you, Radi, which translation you would have given.

Radi: Prepare to die!

Mani: Radi, you will have to take Modi's head off some other time. I am starved and am ready for breakfast. I would not be able to enjoy my food if Modi's head was rolling around somewhere up the street.

The three friends forget their arguments and amiably saunter down the pothole-marked road toward the restaurant.

Harry J. Sweeney

Conversation 37: Afghanistan

Mani: I see that another patrol was ambushed again in Afghanistan. It seems to be almost as bad there as here.

Modi: It would seem so. Remember, though, that Gulbuddin Hikmatyar is back in the country. During the anti-Soviet campaign, he considered it important to own the night and eliminate patrols during the day. He always led a superior fighting force.

Radi: I have heard that he and the Taliban have merged and that the new insurgency is much more powerful than before.

Modi: I would agree that together they might be numerically superior to just the Taliban alone; however, his HIG (*Hizb-i Islami Gulbuddin*) still hates the Taliban from the old days. I do not see them merging or even fighting together if they can avoid it. Nonetheless, I agree that if the coalition forces do not know they are fighting two groups instead of one they are in for a surprise.

Mani: How does the HIG stack up to the Taliban?

Modi: They will always be inferior in number. The Taliban will always be able to recruit more people. I am surprised that the HIG still exists. It was a larger group once, but many of the secondary leaders opposed Hikmatyar and took advantage of the government's offer of amnesty.

Mani: Is that the Hizb-i Islami Kabul (HIK)?

Radi: I have heard of them. They are a treasonous rabble.

Modi: As usual, Radi, you are off the mark. The HIK leadership simply decided to work for a form of democracy within the government. Actually, although they have the same root name, Hizb-i Islami (Islamic Party), the Kabul group is now a recognized and accepted political party, while the Gulbuddin group has been identified as a terrorist group.

The Restless Wind and Shifting Sands

Radi: I understand, though, that the cooperation of the Taliban and HIG make them very powerful. I know that the Americans there are taking a beating.

Modi: Not to worry, Radi. The HIG depend too much on their leader. They love him and support him; however, if something should happen to him, they will disappear. It is he, not the Taliban, who understands what it takes to fight the Americans. He studied the Vietnam War very closely and actively fought the Soviet military machine. The Taliban are learning by watching how his group operates. He is probably smarter than anyone they know.

Mani: I do not understand how he can do all that; he hates the Taliban more than he hates the government. He has many of his friends in government.

Modi: Mani, he was defeated by the Taliban, thanks only to the post-Soviet government that would not support him against those idiot students. Many of those people went to the Northern Alliance, which in turn defeated the Taliban after 9/11 with American help. He wanted an Islamic nation, similar to Iran but without the mullahs. He was not fond of Wahhabis, and his relations with al-Qaida and the Taliban naturally will be strained. He does not like Iran, though Iran hosted him when he was on the run. He certainly does not like Karzai.

Radi: Ha! So, the Americans are close to losing in Afghanistan!

Modi: I cannot agree with that assessment. HIG loses important commanders frequently. Those people cannot be replaced. Some are saying that Hikmatyar himself is doing some of the killings because of the appeal of new amnesty offers. Some of those people are simply tired of fighting. They want to spend time with their grandchildren, so the amnesty appeals to them.

Mani: You are saying that he is losing important people he cannot replace and that he has only his original followers and cannot recruit

Harry J. Sweeney

more. Moreover, if something happens to him, poof! They are all gone.

Modi: That is about it. Additionally, without Hikmatyar the Taliban has no alternative but to rely on Iran for brains and military support.

Radi: After what you said, even you must admit that it is much more important that all believers stand up and join jihad or they will be hypocrites, hated and warned by Allah.[30] Modi, you are called by Allah to jihad, and you know it.

Modi: My jihad, Radi, is making myself a stronger and better believer. That, my friend, is what is known as the "Greater Jihad"!

Mani: I do believe he has you there, Radi. You and I know that fighting, even in the way of Allah, is the minor jihad.

Radi: You are both saying nothing. Know you that the lame, the blind, and the sick can be excused from jihad, but those who join jihad God will admit to Gardens through which rivers flow. He who turns his back on Allah and jihad will be punished with a grievous penalty.

Mani: Note, Modi, he talked about Gardens and not paradise and he said nothing about the virgins.

Radi: Both of you will lose your heads today.

Modi: Radi, you must heed what I am saying. As believers, we can choose the government we want, as long as it does not disregard the true laws of Islam. The government that we chose here in Iraq is one that will fairly and equally serve both Sunnis and Shiites. The insurgents, including al-Qaida are fighting against that government. Although they try to sell us on the idea that they are trying to establish a strict, Islamic government, we do not really know this because deception is

---

30   Qur'an 63:7 "They (the hypocrites) are the ones who say, 'Spend nothing on those who are with God's Apostle, to the end that they may disperse.' But to God belong the treasures of the heaven and the earth; but the Hypocrites understand not."

The Restless Wind and Shifting Sands

no longer just a tactic of war, it has become a tradition of Arabs to get their way.

Mani: Be careful, Modi, Radi is getting mad.

Modi: Remember, Radi, if you insist on helping to wage war against Allah or hindering His works and continue to sow mischief throughout the land, your punishment is execution, crucifixion, or having a hand and foot cut off from opposite sides, or exile. And it may not be your choice. Besides that, your punishment in this life will be followed by a heavier punishment in the next.

Mani: Uh oh! I have never seen his face so scarlet.

Radi: I will talk that one over with my imam.

Modi: Please, Radi, try somebody other than that nitwit you have been following. Two weeks ago, someone told him a joke about a Syrian naval vessel falling off the edge of the ocean, and he did not know it was a joke.

Radi: Well, what was so funny about that?

Mani: Modi, Radi got you that time.

Modi: OK, he got me. I am buying breakfast.

Harry J. Sweeney

<u>Conversation 38: That old-time religion.</u>

Modi: Good morning, Mani. I see you found the right coffee shop.

Mani: Hi. What is on for this morning?

Modi: Radi wanted to discuss again the reasons why the people of Mecca rejected our Most Beloved prophet.

Mani: Be careful how you explain it to him; you know how excited he gets.

Modi: I know. Here he comes now.

Radi: Good morning all. Modi, if you do not mind, I want to get right to the issue.

Modi: Fine. How do you want to start?

Radi: Did our prophet have Allah's messages or not?

Modi: He said very clearly that he was Allah's messenger (*rasul Allah*) and that he repeated the messages that Allah had the Angel Gabriel give to him. As he recited the messages, he ensured that he was speaking for Allah.

Radi: Then why were the messages not accepted?

Modi: They were accepted from some of the people but mostly from the immediate family of the prophet and his personal friends. Others did not accept the messages for a variety of reasons.

Mani: I guess the chief reason was that it would be a complete change in religion for the people of Mecca. They were quite accustomed to dealing with their gods. After all, these gods could be seen and were not at all as fearsome as the single God that our Most Beloved talked about.

The Restless Wind and Shifting Sands

Modi: Not only that, but also the Meccans did a good business and wanted to have a good time with their money. They were not interested in anyone telling them they could not drink spirits and whoop it up after a good business week.

Mani: And do not forget that the Meccans were also making a good income from the pilgrims that visited the Kaaba. If Muhammad had in mind to destroy the idols, as he did, the Meccans would lose a fortune from those visitors.

Modi: But I have to tell you, Radi, that there was something about the prophet that the Meccans did not like. He was not the only monotheist prophet in town. There were others who were more successful than he, though their respective numbers of followers were not really impressive. They claimed that their kinsman actually insulted their gods, and they could not accept that. In addition, he was an orphan and not very well liked. A messenger of Allah in their eyes had to be someone they could look up to, as they looked up to others of his clan.

Mani: Even his marriage to Khadija, Radi, was held against him. Generally, the Arabs looked for the youngest virgins to marry, whereas Muhammad's first marriage was to a widow 15 years his senior. Of course, she was wealthy and had a good business; however, the age differential was still important to the Meccans.

Radi: Did Muhammad not understand the reasons for their reluctance?

Modi: He did read the anger and the lack of respect in their voices, Radi.

Mani: Some people actually threw things at him, and he came home looking pretty bad one night. He had been accosted and throttled.

Radi: Is that why he sent some of the followers to Ethiopia?

Modi: Yes. Abu Bakr, his best friend went also. Since the Christian king there seemed friendly toward Muslims, he thought it might be a safe place for a base. Unfortunately, it was too far away. He tried a few places closer, but people were just not interested in having him around. If it had not been for his kinsman and Abu Bakr, he might have been banished from Mecca forever. As it was, he was asked to leave the city.

Mani: But fortunately for him some Jews from Yathrib heard him preach outside Mecca, and he sounded fine to them. They had both Jewish tribes and Arab tribes in Yathrib and nobody could get along because there was no trust there, and no mediator. They needed a person wise enough to settle disputes equitably—a mediator of sorts. And he needed a safe place to settle his few followers while he was developing his religion.

Modi: But when his tribesman and other Meccans discovered he was leaving Mecca for a competitor city, Yathrib, they were angrier still—angry enough to murder him.

Mani: They set out to do just that, but with a little stealth he was able to outwit them and hide out with Abu Bakr until it was safe to travel.

Modi: It was after that, Radi, the Prophet changed toward the Meccans; they had become not just people unwilling to make a change in religion, they had also become deniers of the word of Allah, enemies who drove the Muslims from their homes and their families.

Mani: In Yathrib, fortunately for our Most Beloved, the local Arabs flocked to his cause. They had heard the Jews talk about a prophet with whom they had talked in Mecca.

Modi: And they wanted to get on his good side before the Jews monopolized him. However, the Muslim numbers continued to grow in Yathrib, and the prophet found himself quickly obliged to assume more authority than he expected.

Mani: Instead of a preacher of a new religion, Radi, he found himself as the chief executive of a growing city.

The Restless Wind and Shifting Sands

Modi: He was not prepared for this task, Radi, but if you read the Qur'an verses of the time he was learning as he went from one crisis to another He continued to resolve disputes between the tribes, but also he had to resolve the dispute between his Muslims and everyone else.

Mani: He now had to establish a manner of social norms for his followers.

Modi: Yes, Radi, and a very close study of our scriptures of the time shows what a very hard time he had trying to establish rules for living with each other.

Mani: Meanwhile, the families of his Meccan followers were bringing their families from Mecca, and after that, after his social programs were discussed, more people left Mecca for this new way of life in a city now called Medina (*al-Madinat an-Nabî*, 'the Prophet's City').

Radi: And all this time, his family and others in Mecca were at war with him.

Modi: No, Radi. To be perfectly frank, the Meccans did not have much to do with the Muslims until they began to interfere with their trade. Once their trade was interrupted and their income threatened, that forced the Meccans to do something about it, though they went about it with a great deal of reluctance that turned into failure.

Mani: (Laughs) The Meccans found it hard to deal with Muhammad's idea of warfare.

Radi: I am glad that I asked about all of this. My friends had a completely different story.

Modi: No doubt. Can't you develop a new set of friendships? Don't you know anyone a little more knowledgeable?

Radi: I have you guys.

Harry J. Sweeney

Mani: Then what do you need with the others.

Radi: I don't know. I guess I am just used to them.

Modi: I need some "Saudi coffee."

Mani: Me too. I think I need a "double", whatever on earth Saudi coffee is.

The Restless Wind and Shifting Sands

<u>Conversation 39: What could be better than killing people for offenses against Allah?</u>

Mani: Modi, have you seen Radi this morning?

Modi: No. Is he still playing executioner with those friends of his? If so, he may sleep late.

Mani: Aha! He will miss prayers. We can chide him for that. Missing prayer brings on a death penalty.[31] I was reading over the law last night, and I saw it. That surprised me. I must be more observant about the time.

Modi: We cannot chide him too much. If he were out all night killing people that have been denounced as heretics, blasphemers, apostates, or whatever, assuredly he would not miss Isha, the Evening Prayer, but if he slept at all, he might miss the Early Morning Prayer. If you look at the next subparagraph to what you read last night, you will see that Radi would have an excuse for missing it.[32] If he is awakened by sunlight, he knows he is too late. He might even forget to make it up.

Mani: Of course, we are only speculating. He may have gotten a job somewhere.

Modi: Pardon my laughter. Do they have jobs for throat-cutting specialists?

Mani: (Suppresses his laughter) Modi, you can be cruel sometimes.

---

31   Sacred Law (*Reliance of the Traveller*) f1.4 "A Muslim who holds the prayer to be obligatory but through lack of concern neglects to perform it until its proper time is over has not committed unbelief." [See W18.0 for related arguments.] "Rather, he is executed, washed, prayed over, and buried in a Muslim cemetery." [It is not obligatory that he is asked to repent, in which case he is not executed.]

32   Ibid. F1.5 "No one has an excuse to delay the prayer beyond its time except: (1) someone asleep,   (2) someone who forgot it, (3) or someone who delayed it to combine two prayers during a journey."[Discussion also found in F15.12 et al.]

Harry J. Sweeney

Modi: (Very serious) But everyone survives my cruelty. I choose my words to hurt people who hurt others with more than words.

Radi: Good morning, friends. What are we discussing today?

Mani: I guess it is hurting people with words.

Radi: Ha! Is that ever a waste of time! If you want to hurt someone, use a stout stick or a sharp knife.

Modi: Radi, I know about the knife. What's the stick for?

Radi: For women. You know yourself you must beat them occasionally.[33]

Mani: The Qur'an is talking about married men beating their wives, Radi. You are not married, so it lets you out.

Radi: If I see a woman doing something she should not do, I can beat her on the spot.

Mani: You are referring to the Taliban and the Saudi Ethics Police, or whatever they call themselves now. You have not been appointed as a policeman here.

Modi: Yes, Radi. You beat some woman in Iraq, and her husband or brothers will be coming after you. They will not be pleased.

Radi: After me? I would be sought for doing my duty?

---

33   Qur'an 4:34 "Men are in charge of women by [right of] what Allah has given one over the other and what they spend [for maintenance] from their wealth. So righteous women are devoutly obedient, guarding in [the husband's] absence what Allah would have them guard. But those [wives] from whom you fear arrogance - [first] advise them, [then if they persist] forsake them in bed, and [finally] strike them. But if they obey you [once more], seek no means against them. Indeed, Allah is ever Exalted and Grand."

The Restless Wind and Shifting Sands

Mani: They may not consider it your duty and bring you up on charges, seeking retaliation. [34]

Radi: I will have to check on that a little closer.

Mani: Yes, Radi, you may have people looking for you.

Radi: (Laughs) I might at that. I must be on my guard.

Modi: You know, Radi, our new laws do not allow you to run around with that pack of wolves, killing people because you heard they were violating some religious law.

Radi: Our religious obligations are sacred and transcend those of the government.

Mani: Not anymore, Radi. In and around Baghdad, people are complying with those new laws. The only exceptions are al-Qaida and a few insurgent groups that are considered outlaws anyway. Compliance is spreading into the outer districts. You can complain about the unfairness of it all from your jail cell.

Modi: Mani is right. You may have to find something better to do.

Radi: What could be better than killing people for offenses against Allah? I can lift up my heart to Allah and rejoice when my hands are covered in honest blood.

Modi: I believe there is a better word for that, Radi. The short term is "murderer." The longer term is "psychogenetic killer."

Radi: I think I have been insulted. Mani, what did he say?

Mani: I think Modi is wrong. He said in effect that you have become psychotic because of mental conflicts. That can't be right.

---

34   Sacred Law (*Reliance*) o3.1 [et al.] "Retaliation is obligatory when there is an intentional injury against life or limb."

177

Harry J. Sweeney

Radi: Thanks, Mani, for coming to my defense. You are a good friend.

Mani: You are welcome, Radi. However, I have not finished my analysis yet.

Modi: I can hardly wait.

Radi: Modi, let my good friend Mani speak! He will tell you I am not psychotic.

Modi: On the contrary, Radi. You are indeed psychotic but not because of mental conflicts. You are psychotic because of mental deficiency. You have a one-track mind, going the wrong way, and the track is not finished yet.

Radi: I don't know what any of that means, but you two are now on my doomed list.

Modi: Well, before you put us on your dumb list, Radi, look at the time.

Radi: That is DOOMED list, you heathen! You will die for your last insults. You too, Mani.

Mani: Fine, Radi, but you will have to defer all executions until later. It is time to answer Bilal and see to our ablutions.

Modi: And, Radi, please don't break wind until after prayers.

Radi: Ooops! I am afraid it is too late.

Modi and Mani laugh; they both called him a heathen and shook their heads.

The Restless Wind and Shifting Sands

Conversation 40: Hamas-Iraqi versus al-Qaida

Mani: Good morning, Modi. I like my new job.

Modi: I thought you would. There is not much to it.

Mani: Well, I am guarding tons of munitions, and I am just a little apprehensive. A lot could happen.

Modi: Not to worry. You have a good group behind you. It is Hamas-Iraqi. Not even al-Qaida wants to take them on with a level playing field.

Mani: I thought they fought on the side of AQ?

Modi: They did. You know, a few of us Sunnis answered some hard questions truthfully and determined that we are in real trouble whenever the coalition leaves. You see, we want the democracy; we just want to ensure that we are not departing from the religion. We are not looking for the religion of the Wahhabis and Salafists. We are looking for a comfortable and merciful view of life and death. We want an end to the killings and the bickering. So now Hamas-Iraqi is working with the coalition instead of against it.

Mani: What? Am I working for the coalition?

Modi: The way things are now, Mani, if you are not with al-Qaida, not with Iran, and not in training at one of the camps in Lebanon, Syria, or Pakistan, you are with the coalition.

Mani: It is going to take me a while to reconcile myself with that news.

Radi: What news are you talking about?

Mani: Modi and I were talking about Hamas-Iraqi taking on al-Qaida.

Harry J. Sweeney

Radi: I saw that in the press. I had to look closely to make sure it wasn't Modi writing it.

Modi: You seem to be taking it in stride. I thought you would be quite angry about that.

Radi: I do not like the idea. I am more concerned with maintaining the strictness of our faith. If we are all as fervent as we are supposed to be, it would not matter what type of government we have. If the group that fights is not Salafist, it is not fighting in the way of Allah; thus I will not support it, and Allah will strike them dead.

Modi: Just who do you suppose should be the authority on how fervent a believer should be?

Radi: It would have to be the most fervent of the sects, as long as they were Salafists. Anyone less would weaken the religion.

Mani: What is this "weaken the religion" idea?

Radi: After the death of our Most Beloved, peace be upon him, our religion underwent a terrible upheaval, and whenever the smoke cleared and the caliphate came under control of caliphs who were not rightly guided, they simply were not strict enough, and the people were descending into the horrors of laxity. For centuries, the religion became weaker and immoral. Once they became lax in their religious duties, the laxity permeated everything.

Modi: Laxity? What you are trying to say and doing it so badly, Radi, is very important. Our religion was undergoing the same growing pains that other religions had undergone. We were not sliding into laxity but adjusting ourselves and our beliefs to a less rigid and more flexible system, similar to that of Christianity and Judaism. Rigidity and inflexibility should never be norms when dealing with humans.

Mani: Modi, if Allah established the rules, how can we dare change anything?

The Restless Wind and Shifting Sands

Modi: That is the radical viewpoint, Mani. We all fervently believe that Allah is the author of the Qur'an. Because we do, no change can ever be suggested, let alone started. The Qur'an, of course, is not the total religion. The hadiths and the detailed life of Muhammad may be just as important in the lives of the faithful. What our Most Beloved has said in his lifetime the faithful hear almost every day in one way or another—in the mosque or on the street. I know I do not have to remind you that we are constantly told that our Most Beloved led a perfect life and we must emulate him in all things.

Radi: Modi, you have that correct. You surprise me.

Modi: Radi, the idea you just do not seem to get is that the world has changed. Everything has changed, including the way we look at everything. The world has moved on. Christians have changed, and so have Jews. We have many more people in the world, and there are more important questions than what our imams are discussing with us. We cannot keep fighting against the Meccan polytheists and the Yathrib Jews! They are all gone.

Mani: What type of questions do you mean?

Modi: One might better solve the problem of how we help establish peace in the world without trying to destroy every other nation and religion and enslave everyone except our believers. We could also ask how we might get together with the rest of the world and find cures for diseases and more food for the starving. When our people were starving in some places, the West rushed in with food and medicine. What did we ever do for them? Christians and Jews have helped us everywhere. Look at what they did for us in Bosnia, for example.

Radi: Allah made them. . . .

Modi: I hate to stop you, but I know you are going to ask us to believe something that we have tossed out a long time ago as rubbish. Allah did not send any angels down to blow dust in the West's eyes to make them do what they did. Look, whenever we discuss what people do,

Harry J. Sweeney

you must assume people are doing it for a reason. If you continue to believe that our God actually creates miracles to make Western people do things to help us, you lose sight of humanity. Loving and serving Allah is only part of the equation, Radi. It is just as important to love and help our fellow man. Religion is part of life; it is certainly not the whole of life. If so, there would be no sense in being born on earth to enjoy earth's fruits and the comforts and joys of earth's humanity. Many people here hate Jews, and they never even saw or met one.

Radi: You are the one who missed the point, Modi. Loving and serving Allah and taking the entire world for Allah is all there is.

Modi: You and people like you are the problem; you have no understanding of your own religion; you need to go beyond your rituals, your seventh-century rulings, and your complete disdain for everyone not a believer. A non-believer to your group should be more than just an animal.

Mani: I can understand that, Radi. Do you still call Jews and Christians apes and pigs?

Radi: Of course we do. That is what they are.

Modi: Would you say, Radi, that apes and pigs make good believers?

Radi: Why would you ask such a question? Apes and pigs do not make good anything.

Modi: Well, Radi, why do we recruit new believers from the apes and pigs?

Mani: I saw that one coming, Modi. You need to be more subtle.

Modi: With Radi?

Radi: I know what you two are saying. Of course, Allah gives them the

The Restless Wind and Shifting Sands

gift of faith, and when they accept His gift, he changes them from apes and pigs into good believers.

Modi: I guess there is no convincing you that there is more to life than dreamt of in your philosophy. You cannot enjoy life, you long for death, and it is necessary that you ruin it for everyone else.

Radi: There is only our religion. Nothing else matters. We are not here to enjoy life. We are here to suffer through it and hope that it comes to an end quickly. Kill me now and make me a martyr!

Mani: I guess that means you don't want to join us for lunch then.

Radi: Hey! I didn't say that. Who is buying?

CHAPTER 5

Conversation 41: The Women's Viewpoint

Let us stray just a little and taking a brief look at the distaff side of the Modi, Mani, and Radi discussions with Modi's wife Hayat, Mani's wife Barma, and Radi's fiancée, Zaina.

Hayat: I am glad that you dropped over today. Modi's parents will be here later and I have to make a meal with which I am not familiar.

Barma: Oh, OK. And they are from where?

Hayat: They were from Egypt. But I have no idea what dishes to prepare for Egyptians.

Barma: That is not a problem. I can do a couple of Egyptian dishes just to spice things up. They also would like most of the things we like anyway.

Hayat: I hope I have the ingredients here.

Barma: No problem; their meals are relatively simple. Not to worry.

Hayat: Someone is coming in the gate. It must be Zaina. She is helpful, too. She told me yesterday she knew of a special dish.

Zaina: Hi, everyone. Hayat, I took the liberty of putting that dish together for you. Where do you want it?

Hayat: I'll take care of it. How is that husband-to-be of yours doing?

Zaina: Don't ask. We are no closer to getting married than we were last year. He is impossible. I have no idea why I like him.

The Restless Wind and Shifting Sands

Hayat: I can tell you that, from what I have seen, love is not only blind, it's stupid. You must have a death wish. Modi tells me how he is.

Barma: Oh, yes. He has Mani scared to death with that big knife.

Zaina: (Laughs) That knife is not his. He borrowed it from our kitchen. He said he knew a good friend with a better wheel that sharpened knives like a razor. He just never brought it back.

Hayat: Well what about all that crazy stuff he does at night?

Zaina: He just goes along with some friends of his, but they won't let him go along all the time because he talks too much.

Barma: Oh, yes. Mani would agree with that. Mani has heard all those nasty arguments between Modi and him. Mani does not know which of the two to rely on. The three are such friends that Mani does not want to offend either of the others; however, the subject matter is too important to ignore. Modi and Radi are exact opposites in their views on Islam.

Hayat: I for one am glad that Modi is the way he is. He lives exactly the way he explains his view of religion. We talk a lot, and he asks me all the time what I need for the house. I have the freedom to leave the house whenever I want. He just asks that I be careful of the old beards and take someone else with me to avoid any talk. He would like to visit another country so that we can pack some of our conservative clothing and do things together—a little recreation—a little privacy.

Barma: Modi did say something like that to Mani. Unfortunately, Radi heard part of it, Mani said, and raised a big fuss about how the Qur'an, the sira, and the hadiths lay out exactly how a man must act with his wife. Modi, spoke up, as usual, and told Radi something about the relationship of a man and his wife needing to rise above the pettiness of the old beards and truly to be none of their business.

Zaina: Oh, I remember that one. Radi went berserk because Modi

Harry J. Sweeney

said that the relationship between a man and his wife was between them and Allah. I wanted to tell Radi that I did not intend to be very strict about all those stupid taboos but not after he pitched a fit about Modi.

Hayat: Oh, I can just hear Radi now on that one. Modi said the same thing about prayers. He always prayed, but if he had to go somewhere and help a friend in an emergency, he considered it more important than prayer. He feels Allah would agree with that.

Zaina: Oh, yes. Radi yelled for a half hour while my parents were trying to eat. They almost asked him to leave. My parents were from the old school also and feel about the same as he does. However, they do not talk about it and do not force their views on me.

Hayat: Won't Radi? He is fire and brimstone and off-with-their-heads when arguing with Modi. He is one of the younger "old beards."

Zaina: Well, don't tell anyone I told you, but I stopped his harangue one evening and told him in front of my parents that I will be faithful and as obedient as I believe a wife should be. However, I told him if he raises his hand to me or scolds me in front of someone else, I will divorce him just that quick and make him eat the dowry.

Barma: Knowing Radi, I know he did not like the part about your not returning the dowry.

Hayat: I can see why Radi has not gotten married yet. He is afraid of you. He could not show off to others just how much of a lord and master he is in the house. Where did you get the idea you could divorce him? That is not part of the sharia.

Zaina: The new national laws allow it and although the sharia specifies that it is valid from a husband, it does not specify that it is *invalid* from a wife. Well, it is my life as well as his. You know, I told him that as soon as the wedding is over I am going to sign a paper that says, "I divorce you if you raise your hand to me or humiliate me."

The Restless Wind and Shifting Sands

Barma: You can do that?

Zaina: Well, it is a conditional divorce. If he can do it to me, I would suppose I can do it to him. And if he ever does, it becomes a legal divorce. The imam has to try to get us back together and talk about it, but it is a divorce as valid as if I had said, "I divorce you" three times in front of him.

Hayat: Zaina, I am not at all sure you are right. I hope so.

Barma: Does he show visible signs that he loves you?

Zaina: Yes, that is why I can get away with all of that. Believe me; I am very glad that my parents are as conservative as they are. Otherwise, we would have been in a lot of trouble. It will not be too long before I let him know when the wedding will be.

Hayat: (Laughs) Oh, he will love that. He will drive Modi and Mani up a wall for days. (Barma laughs)

Hayat: Is Radi really as conservative as he lets on?

Zaina: Oh, yes. He would no sooner miss or be late for a prayer than miss or be late for a meal. (Everyone laughs.)

Barma: How does he feel about Mani not always siding with him?

Zaina: He says that Modi confuses him from time to time, but when push comes to shove, when the insurgents win, he will remember the fundamentals quickly. Mani has been trained well and will never push aside the scriptures.

Hayat: That is exactly what Modi fears. He is so afraid that we will languish under a totalitarian regime and that all of the mainstreamers will do nothing to stop it.

Zaina: I won't say this to Radi, but we women need to put together

Harry J. Sweeney

some kind of movement and roust some of these kitchen shadows out of their houses and into our own organization. We need to show them how to dress and put those *abaya*s and *chador*s in some dusty closet. One of these days, just for the sake of mischief, I will warn my folks first, and then when Radi shows up, I will come downstairs in a miniskirt and sheer blouse. If he does not faint dead away, he will want to get married *toute de suite*.

As far as men are concerned, the men will always find themselves in plural organizations. There must be at least 50 different organizations here for them. We need only one. I have to have a name that will tell who we are and who we want to be and at the same time will immediately grab everyone's attention.

Hayat: I know. How about "The Playmate Club"? (Laughter)

The Restless Wind and Shifting Sands

<u>Conversation 42: Ancient Chinese Strategies in Iraq.</u>

Mani: Morning, Modi. I saw on al-Jazeera this morning that some of the American generals want to claim victory here.

Modi: Hi, Mani. That is not only premature, it is falling into the Fifteenth or Sixteenth Strategy; I forget which.

Radi: Ha, Modi. It is Strategy 15, *Lure the Tiger down the Mountain.*[35] I think the coalition should declare retreat. Good move.

Mani: I don't get it. What are you two talking about?

Modi: *The 36 Chinese Strategies*, Mani; we use them here, and they were almost always used by rebels or insurgents against superior forces. The fifteenth was an easy one. The Mongol cavalry forces were great at attacking forces in the field but not in defensive positions. So they would make an ineffective attack and allow themselves to be driven off. Directly afterward, they would retreat in disorder, as if they were beaten.

Mani: What good would that do?

Radi: Heh, heh. They would pretend to be beaten. Remember, they were good at fighting forces in the field, not behind walls. By looking as if they were beaten and running away, the defending enemy general would order an attack against them—outside the walls.

Mani: I see. At some point, the Mongol cavalry would reorganize and attack the forces that were now in the field.

Modi: Exactly. The Mongols that "escaped" to the right or left would now ride back, join up with each other, and become an anvil. The Mongols in front of the defenders would turn and become the hammer.

---

35   *The Thirty-Six Strategies of Ancient China*, Stefan H. Verstappen, p. 71. China Books & Periodicals, South San Francisco, CA 94080, Second Printing 2004.

Harry J. Sweeney

The plan on paper looks almost like a *fleur-de-lis*. The defenders would be surrounded and easily defeated.

Radi: And what is even better, when the armies are defeated, the country itself becomes vulnerable. Heh, heh. Pillage and murder. Slaves!

Mani: How do we know all of this good information?

Modi: Mao Tse-tung wrote his *Six Principles of Guerrilla Warfare*, based on the *36 strategies*. Che Guevara in Cuba knew Mao's *principles* and incorporated them into his *Guerrilla Warfare*. The Viet Minh used a version of the *strategies* against the French and against the Americans.

Mani: I see. The *36 principles* are something like a handbook on how to fight the Americans.

Modi: You can call it that. Of course, it has to be translated into some kind of action. That means some folks have to sit and think.

Radi: And that means that some people sit and drink tea or coffee while people like me have all the fun, lopping off heads.

Mani: Did our Most Beloved use that ruse to win?

Modi: In a sense, it was used against him. In the Battle of Uhud, the archers were carrying the day against the Meccans, though others were fighting as well. However, the archers were keeping the Meccans from flanking the Muslims. The Meccans either by tactic or necessity appeared to be beaten and left their positions, abandoning their private property in full view of the archers.

Mani: I do remember that. When the archers left their positions to grab for the abandoned spoils of war, Khalid ibn al-Walid led an attack that flanked the Muslims and won the battle.[36]

Radi: Modi, you left out something important. Our valiant fighters

36 Mohammed and the Unbelievers, Center for the Study of Political Islam, pp. 83, 84.

The Restless Wind and Shifting Sands

after that were vulnerable to be surrounded and to be killed, probably ending the religion right there. However, Allah put fear into the Meccan hearts, and they turned their mounts toward home and ran away as fast as they could go, declaring victory.[37]

Mani: I understand. The Muslim fighters were left to fight another day and finally defeat the Meccans. Allah definitely looked after us.

Modi: Mani, you simply cannot constantly look for miracles from Allah whenever something good happens to us. The armies of Medina trained and were equipped to fight. They were told that winning a battle would make them rich and if they were killed in battle their families would get their share and they would go to paradise immediately. That was a powerful incentive to fight at the time.

Radi: Radi, it is not true that the men fought for paradise. They fought for love of Allah and for love of Islam.

Modi: Radi, during the Battle of Badr, Muhammad said, "By Allah, every man who is slain this day by fighting with courage and advancing not retreating will enter paradise." One of his fighters, who had stopped to eat, turned to our Most Beloved and said, "You mean there is nothing between paradise and me but being killed by the Quraysh?" With that, he threw away his food, grabbed his sword, and sped off to be killed.[38]

Mani: Why are you and Radi always in dispute? You both tell the same story, but you both give different details.

Radi: The devil is in Modi's details. One of these days, I will separate his head from his neck.

Modi: Unlike Radi, Mani, I do not believe that Allah directly helps or directly hinders us. Our Most Beloved was a great general and indeed a very lucky one. The Meccans were poorly led and had no real stomach

---

37   Ibid.

38   Ibid., 66.

Harry J. Sweeney

for fighting once it got beyond a certain degree of violence. Our people came on like screaming banshees because they knew they personally could not lose; the ones still alive were victorious and rich. The dead, however, were on their way to paradise. For the Meccans, their deaths left their families destitute and neither honor nor paradise for them. The Muslims did not need a host of angels fighting with them; they had powerful incentives.

Radi: Everything you say is heresy. You should be reported to the authorities and whipped within an inch of your life. You are distorting what is in the Qur'an.

Modi: I do not know why you would call it heresy, Radi. If you really studied our scriptures, you would read what was said at Badr, and you would see how we lost at Uhud. It does not take a scholar to get to the truth of each battle. Give anyone a great incentive to risk his life, and he will do so.

Radi: See, there you go again. I am definitely going to let the imams know that you are spreading untrue rumors about our history.

Mani: And just when do you plan to do this horrible thing?

Radi: Probably after lunch today? Who is buying?

Modi: It is your turn again, but again I'll buy.

Radi: Then I guess I will wait until tomorrow to turn you in.

Modi: What a pal.

The Restless Wind and Shifting Sands

<u>Conversation 43: Iraqis fight Al-Qaida, Laugh at Abu Ghraib.</u>

Modi: Are you OK, Mani? That mortar was too close. It must have been an 81 mm.

Mani: It was indeed close. I can hardly hear. Everything is OK though. Are you sure that wasn't a bomb?

Modi: It seemed like it. But it was definitely an 81 mm mortar instead of the 60 mm. Al-Qaida is getting serious about pounding us.

Mani: Do our folks have a plan here, or are they calling in a coalition air strike, or what? These AQ fighters are tough.

Modi: It seems like a good plan to me. We are to keep pressure on them as long as possible to hold them here. We've been here an hour, and I think they have been wearing us down with those 81s. Group 2 will begin pressuring them from the rear, and Group 3 from the left. They will lob in high explosives. We then must back up and search for tunnel entrances.

Mani: Is that a Group 2 mortar I just heard?

Modi: I hope so. Yep, it landed inside the village. When six mortars begin lobbing, they are finished. I hear two more pops. Now we should search for tunnel entrances.

The next day. . . .

Modi: We did well last night, Mani. We closed down another AQ village, and you found that tunnel entrance.

Mani: Just luck. I almost stumbled into it.

Modi: But luck never happens until you do what it takes to get there.

Harry J. Sweeney

Mani: I am just glad that some of those chaps surrendered. I had hoped they would not fight to the death. Anyway, we can take a few days off.

Modi: Those AQ people are bad news. They did not leave too many fighters above ground to try to hold us off while the others got away. If you hadn't found that tunnel, taking the compound would have been for nothing. We took many prisoners. You may get a bonus for finding it.

Radi: Good morning, you two. You look like cats that ate a canary. What is going on?

Mani: We heard another AQ camp was taken last night. They captured another leader and lots of fighters.

Radi: Probably just another coalition rumor. How can they say they captured this person or that? We all know they fight to the death.

Modi: Not this time, Radi. Quite a few fighters were rounded up.

Radi: Bah! It was probably a ruse. Wait and see. Al-Qaida will strike tomorrow and blow something up that was important.

Modi: Yeah, probably another girls' school.

Mani: They are getting pretty good at girls' schools. Or is that the Taliban?

Radi: You are insulting AQ fighters and their supporters. They are fighting in the way of Allah.

Modi: I am not going to keep telling you how I feel about that. This war and AQ has nothing to do with our religion. Radi, how many mosques have been destroyed by the coalition? How many imams were kidnapped or killed by the coalition? How many Qur'ans have been destroyed?

The Restless Wind and Shifting Sands

Radi: Well, what about Abu Ghraib?

Mani: (Laughs) Anyone who looks at that seriously is a moron! So what if a couple of strong, brave, fierce fighters found themselves in embarrassing positions? How many graves had to be dug as a result? On the scale of things that happened in Iraq, especially by Saddam yesterday and by al-Qaida and the Mahdi army today, Abu Ghraib was not even a wart on some American senator's red nose.

Modi: Mani's right. When looked at alongside what Zarqawi has done to innocent Iraqi people, AG does not rise to sticking your thumb on your nose and waving your fingers. No prudent Iraqi I know even considers Abu Ghraib as anything to think about and every one of us was shocked, shocked when the Americans themselves made such a big deal out of it. Somebody there is not right in the head.

Radi: You are asking for it. Meanwhile, we will continue to fight, and with Allah's help, we will win here and everywhere. Even now the European governments are considering the sharia.

Modi: Considering but not buying, Radi. Why would any European who has no death wish want a legal system that protects only Muslims?

Radi: It is simply acknowledging that we are superior to them; that's all. You must remember that we are the chosen people of Allah.

Modi: For the chosen people of Allah, we have not done very well for ourselves. If you look at our living standards and our economy—even with all of our oil—we look impoverished compared to Europe and America. And speaking of America, the believers that live there are quite happy to be there. And even the Muslim residents of Israel are rebelling against a plan to transfer ownership of those parts of Israel to the Palestinian Authority, making them Palestinian Arabs instead of Israeli Arabs.

Mani: I remember. None of the Arab residents of Israel voted in the

Harry J. Sweeney

Palestinian elections for fear of jeopardizing their status as residents of Israel.[39]

Radi: You two are in a conspiracy to commit heresy and blasphemy. How can you turn against Allah as you are doing and deny Him the world that He created?

Modi: Radi, nothing anywhere says that He created the world specifically for us. I love my religion, but I see nothing written anywhere that says that we who are supposed to be His chosen people have any moral authority to make war on other nations now—nations that are not a danger to Islam—and take what belongs to them.

Radi: You forget, Allah wants to hear *"Allahu Akbar"* ring out from every corner of the world.

Modi: Those are the Ayatollah Khomeini's words, Radi. We are responsible for bringing the Qur'an and the Sharia to the world. We are not truly responsible for shoving it down everyone's throats. There should be no compulsion in religion.

Radi: What about Sura 2, ayats 190 and 193?[40] They tell us to convert the world to Islam and keep fighting until we are successful.

Modi: I know it has been interpreted that way, but only by radicals who themselves want to see a Muslim world no matter what it costs. You are talking about hundreds of millions of people—men, women, and children. Is having everybody Muslim really worth all of those lives lost?

Radi: Of course I do. It is well worth that and more if that is what it takes.

---

39   http://www.danielpipes.org/article/2534.
40   Sura 2:190 Fight in the way of Allah those who fight you but do not transgress. Indeed. Allah does not like transgressors. 2:193 Fight them until there is no [more] fitnah and [until] worship is for Allah. But if they cease, then there is to be no aggression except against the oppressors.

The Restless Wind and Shifting Sands

Mani: Radi, you are a sadist!

Radi: I thought I was a Salafist!

Modi: You're a nitwit! Now let's go eat.

Harry J. Sweeney

Conversation 44: The wives discuss their husbands.

Hayat (wife of Modi): Good morning, Barma. I thought I would drop in and say hello. Modi is sleeping in for a while.

Barma (wife of Mani): Hi, Hayat. Come right in. Mani is asleep also. Our husbands were with Hamas-Iraqi again, fighting al-Qaida.

Hayat: Shhh. Don't say that too loud. Modi says there are too many ears on our streets.

Barma: I think there are too many mouths too. Sit now and have some coffee. I made fresh pastries.

Hayat: Your pastries are too nice, Barma; one look and my teeth start decaying.

Barma: (Laughs) Honestly, Hayat, you and Modi must have gone to the same school. You both have wonderful comments.

Hayat: Modi gets his naturally. I have to think about mine.

Barma: There's the door. Zaina said she would drop in also.

Zaina (fiancée of Radi): Morning all. Barma, you made those pastries again. How nice.

Barma: Help yourself. Did Modi and Radi really have a fight a couple of days ago?

Zaina: Not according to Radi. You know how they are. Radi is really very uptight about our scriptures and will not give an inch. If a person is tired and does only seven *raka*s instead of eight because he forgot, Radi becomes furious. If someone does not start his *Isha* prayer until 1 minute after midnight, Radi wants to kill him.

The Restless Wind and Shifting Sands

Hayat: I keep telling you, Zaina, you will have to rein him in. He will get himself killed if he keeps erupting like that. He has Modi worried.

Zaina: I know. You and I know that our scriptures do not leave much room for error. I love praying to Allah, and five times per day does not bother me in the least. However, some of our neighbors with husbands out of work, their in-laws living with them, and babies of their own should have a dispensation or something. I know one of my neighbors may be going to the hospital with a stroke from too much work.

Hayat: Modi says that taking care of babies is truly God's work and should be counted as prayers when you are up all night tending to a baby in pain. He thinks the same about caring for elderly parents.

Barma: I do not agree with that. I think we women should go say our prayers and let our husbands deal with the sick babies. (They all laugh.)

Zaina: Some Christians say that they live their lives so that everything they do is a prayer of one sort or another.

Hayat: I can understand that. I guess if you have your own farm and are alone most of the time it is easy to communicate with Allah and offer to him whatever work you have to do anyway. I would think it is healthier than smoking or chewing tobacco.

Barma: If you communicate with Allah by yourself too much and people see you talking away with no one there, you do get quite a reputation.

Zaina: Yes. Like Radi. (Laughter) Seriously though, Radi is not a bad sort. He thinks the world of Modi and Mani. He is honestly afraid that Modi, at least, is headed for the fires of hell. Radi believes he is doing everything he can to save him. You should hear him at prayer.

Hayat: Modi seems to understand that. At the same time, Modi sees

Harry J. Sweeney

Radi as a product of some unfortunate interpretation and is trying to convince him to simmer down and enjoy life.

Zaina: Unfortunately, Hayat, "enjoy life" is a term that sets him off. Modi probably has told you how he feels about that.

Hayat: Oh, yes. "Life is only temporary. This life is a test. It is a favor to us if we are killed young. Living too long is terrible. . . ." I think I have heard it all. I feel sorry for him.

Barma: I feel bad about it also. Each of us has our own form of enjoyment. Is Radi not in his own way enjoying life? Does he not enjoy being with Modi and Mani, ranting about all the sinners who should be killed one way or another?

Hayat: Barma, I think you have something there. Modi may not have thought that Radi in his own way was enjoying life. If Radi would miss those scenarios if for some reason they were stopped, we could say he was finding enjoyment in them.

Barma: Therefore, if Modi would say he agrees with Radi and ceases talking as a moderate for a while, Radi might calm down and become less of a tyrant.

Zaina: That is where you are wrong. If Modi started taking his side, Radi would then go to the next level and rave even more about how things should be. I don't know how many levels there are, but I am not willing to find out. (Laughter)

Barma: I guess that we should leave things as they are. Modi and Mani certainly do not need to be taken to the next level, whatever that is. (Laughter)

Zaina: By the way, Radi knows about Modi and Mani fighting for Hamas-Iraqi out of town. Obviously, they were trying to keep it from him.

The Restless Wind and Shifting Sands

Hayat: Yes. They just did not want their heated discussions to lead to all-out war. They have been talking around it.

Zaina: That is what I was thinking. He did not feel so bad about their hiding that information after I shared that with him.

Barma: Good for you. We have to avoid any situations that would lead to their not talking to each other.

Zaina: I do not think Radi would go that far. (Laughter) He loves to talk.

Hayat: I asked Modi if he shouldn't let Radi know that a great many of our people only go through the motions here; they love the basics of their religion, but they are tired of the imams and the purists always stirring everybody up for unnecessary jihad.

Zaina: I think that would only stir Radi up more. He might go on a tirade.

Hayat: Modi says the same thing. Any new updates on when you two will be getting married?

Barma: Yes. We are just dying to hear about your coming wedding.

Zaina: It will be whenever he runs out of excuses. (Laughter)

Hayat: What is his excuse this time?

Zaina: He says he wants a peaceful wedding without explosions and burp guns going off and spoiling our wedding.

Barma: That won't happen for a long time.

Hayat: That is the worst delaying tactic I have ever heard.

Harry J. Sweeney

Zaina: I know. He thought he had me on that one, but I think I may have changed his mind.

Hayat: I can hardly wait. What did you tell him?

Zaina: I said I could not control the IEDs, the RPGs, or the AKs, but he has to remember I control the S.E.X. (Laughter)

The Restless Wind and Shifting Sands

<u>Conversation 45: The Scandal—Muhammad and Zainab</u>

Mani: Good morning, Modi. Nice morning.

Modi: That it is. Look, there is Radi bright and early.

Radi: Good morning all. It is a beautiful day.

Modi: Radi says it is a beautiful day. What are you up to, Radi?

Radi: Just remarking, Modi. I have a question to ask you.

Modi: If it is not a loaded one, I will try to answer.

Radi: Some believers said that they were having a problem with one of the marriages of our Most Beloved. I knew that one of his wives was named Zainab but did not know she was married to his son before our Most Beloved married her. Those believers need to know why it could not be considered sacrilegious.

Modi: Radi, the short answer is that Zaid, the first husband of Zainab, was our Most Beloved's adopted son. He was from a Christian tribe, carried off and sold into slavery. Khadija made a present of him to our Most Beloved, who adopted him as his son. He was not a blood relative, so his wife would not be a blood relative. Zainab's marriage to Zaid and her subsequent marriage to Muhammad were both sanctioned by verses in the Qur'an, 33:36-38.

Mani: I do not completely understand why our Most Beloved would create such consternation about a marriage when he had so many from which to choose. Was he that infatuated with her?

Modi: It was Muhammad who first decided that she should wed Zaid. The son did not like her very well, nor was she agreeable to marrying him. She was Hashemite and socially was his better. Our Most Beloved wanted the marriage for some reason and said that it was revealed to him that they should marry. Neither one would violate Allah's wishes.

203

Harry J. Sweeney

Radi: Since everyone knew that Zaid was his adopted son, what caused all of the problems? I understand there was quite a scandal at the time.

Modi: A scandal there was. It was a scandal at the worst of times. The Battle of the Trench was about to begin and the Hypocrites were verbally abusing our Most Beloved, and to top everything else off, his wives were the subject of some scandalous talk of their own. It is all covered in Sura 33.

Mani: But why should that marriage be a scandal? I still do not understand it.

Modi: Mani and Radi, Islam and the laws of Islam were extant in Medina, the City of the Prophet. However, tradition was still strong, as it was in Mecca. Traditionally, an adopted son was considered a blood relative and that interfered with the Islamic laws of inheritance and social standing. There were many complaints that adopted sons were given inheritances that rightfully belonged to others, for example.

Mani: So it was necessary for Islam to show the supremacy of its laws over tradition.

Modi: Exactly. Since this one tradition had been particularly annoying, it became necessary for our Most Beloved to show the significance of the law. First, he captured everyone's attention by marrying his son's divorced wife. Many people were having fits about that. After he was finally challenged on it, he showed everyone that he had received a revelation from Allah, instructing him to marry Zainab, in Qur'an 33:37, 38.

Radi: So all those people who were so concerned about our Most Beloved doing something wrong should have just trusted him. How could they mistrust him, since Allah trusted him to be His Messenger?

Mani: Exactly, Radi. How could he do anything wrong?

The Restless Wind and Shifting Sands

Radi: You said something about the wives also being involved in a scandal?

Modi: There was not much to that, Radi. First, the wives were complaining that there were not enough household funds. Actually, our Most Beloved had no income at that time. Allah advised the wives it was not in their best interests to complain but to be patient. Muhammad could divorce them all and find more suitable wives if they want. They were also reminded to be more prudent in their attire. That revelation is shown in Qur'an 33:28-35, 59. Radi, they were not ordered to be as covered up as the Wahhabis want, but just to dress carefully. I think the Wahhabis go too far.

Radi: We could argue about that, but go on. I think we should hear the rest of it.

Modi: Radi, remember that the Hypocrites were criticizing our Most Beloved something fierce. It is almost as bad as the American senators criticizing their president about us—also in the middle of a war. It was outrageous!

Radi: Ha! I remember that one senator. I thought he would have apoplexy every time he tried to say something bad about his president. Nothing he said made any sense. He was funny.

Mani: So that gives us some idea of the abuse that our Most Beloved had to endure while he was trying to protect the people and to save Islam.

Modi: You are right, Mani. It is bad enough to try to organize defenses, listen to suggestions, worry about income, and try to soothe the feelings of your wives. To do all this and then suffer the slings and arrows of outrageous kibitzers is more than most leaders can bear.

Radi: I can agree with that. Surely our Most Beloved was a great man.

Modi: You are right. In fact, Allah had revealed to him two verses that

Harry J. Sweeney

warned the people that He is not pleased about any of them insulting His Messenger and that he had an unpleasant punishment awaiting them for that. The verses are in Qur'an 33:56, 57.

Mani: It was only fair to warn them.

Modi: It was fair at the time, Mani. However, those ayats had unintended consequences down through the ages.

Radi: How could a statement from Allah have consequences that were not intended? Allah knows everything and is all merciful.

Modi: Radi, you will have to think a little about this. Every religion should allow criticism and reply to it. No religion or state should ever punish an outsider because he or she does not like that religion or state. Because of ayat 33:57, several people have been killed in different parts of the world for insulting Islam, Muhammad, or Muslims in general. That is wrong! We all know the greatness of our religion and of our Prophet, but the unbelievers do not know any of this. If Americans can stand whiners burning their flag and waving nasty placards and banners while marching up and down their streets, we can ignore a few dumb insults or questions without getting excited.

Mani: Those people should be punished for insulting our Most Beloved.

Modi: When you said Pope Benedict is a criminal several months ago, should you be killed for that statement? Radi insults the pope, Christianity in general, Jews—oh, how he insults and threatens Jews. Should he be killed for those statements?

Mani: I should say not! They are true statements, not insults.

Modi: True to you, maybe, but not true to Pope Benedict or the Christians. Pope Benedict is a friend to some of our imams.

Radi: Those imams should be shot! They are heretics!

The Restless Wind and Shifting Sands

Modi: There, Radi. Under the interpretations that the Islamic judges promulgated after the Danish Cartoons—CARTOONS, by heavens!—you have insulted Islam and Muslims. I have every right to kill you for that!

Radi: What?

Modi: Give me your knife!

Radi: What? (Modi reaches into Radi's pocket and retrieves Radi's knife) Now, off with your head. (Both start running.)

Mani: Since you are heading in that direction, swing by my house. Barma has lunch waiting.

Harry J. Sweeney

Conversation 46: On Reading the Qur'an.

In a restaurant in Baghdad.

Modi: I have always liked this restaurant; it has a quiet location. Radi, you have something on your mind. You look worried.

Radi: Good morning, Modi. I will order coffee for everyone. The reason for my concern is that I have a visitor from Holland at my house. He is a cousin on my father's side, a believer, of course, but he knows very little about our faith.

Mani: Do not the Muslims in Holland have mosques? I read somewhere they have some very large ones there.

Radi: They do; however, when he goes to mosque, he does not understand what the imams are saying. Somehow, as a child, he missed quite a lot. My cousin was attending a British school because his father was working in a place too far from a Muslim school. There were other Muslims in the schools, so he figured it was OK to have his son there.

Modi: Your cousin could have been taught at home. It would not be that difficult.

Radi: I agree; however, my cousin's mother was not a believer and could not teach him the religion. His father, besides working, went to night school to improve himself. Well, he improved himself and now has less time than before to teach my cousin. He tried tutors, but the tutors either were wrapped up in politics or were too strict.

Mani: So, he was sent to you.

Radi: Yes, he was. He is still asleep. He is tired from his trip.

Modi: Radi, I get the idea that he wants to learn the basics of his religion so that he can understand what is going on in the world, and he can go on from there if he wants.

The Restless Wind and Shifting Sands

Radi: That sounds right. He says that he has read the Qur'an from cover to cover twice but has not really learned anything from it.

Modi: I fully understand his dilemma. My advice is that he should start with the sira, the life of our Most Beloved. I would not advise just any sira, but one that provides the Qur'anic references and Ahadith references as part of the historical flow.

Mani: Oh, yes. Since he probably speaks better Dutch than Arabic, Modi and I suggest the one from America, *Mohammed and the Unbelievers, A Political Life*, by the Center for the Study of Political Islam. I don't know if it is printed in Dutch yet; however, it should be by now. Just as Modi says, as the story of our Most Beloved progresses, the Qur'anic and Ahadith references are right there. It is awesome.

Radi: Why did it not help just to read the Qur'an? He could get a book on the hadiths also, could he not?

Modi: Radi, there are thousands of individual hadiths. You know that. In addition, reading the Qur'an? That is not for a beginner; he could not get much if anything out of such reading.

Mani: Modi is right. The Qur'an is not organized chronologically. It is organized according to the length of the suras, except for the first one. Once your cousin goes through the sira once or twice, only then does the Qur'an begin to make sense. It is possible then to refer to the Qur'an for further reading on certain issues of interest. When your cousin begins to do that, he is on the verge of becoming a scholar.

Radi: I do not know if he wants to go that far.

Modi: Perhaps not. However, if he follows those guidelines, there is no reason why he could not become a recognized scholar. Look, Maududi and Qutb were recognized scholars. Neither of them do anything for me because both of them had an agenda; their vision was not the vision of the common people who simply wanted to live, let live, and bring up their kids like everyone else in the world.

Harry J. Sweeney

Mani: Remember, Radi, Qutb wrote what is supposed to be his greatest works while awaiting execution by Nasser. He smuggled it out of jail.

Modi: We could use new scholars with a fresh approach to Islam and the world. Some scholars had a rough life and a violent death; others went mad. Some were so engrossed in words on paper that they missed what life was about. Those are scholars, not philosophers. The scholars taught not only a religion, but ideology as well, as if the two could never be separated. They taught how wonderful death could be, but they did not teach the rudiments of enjoying life and being thankful for life's little pleasures. We have had enough of the old-fashioned, long-bearded scholars who celebrated death instead of life.

Radi: It is not proper even to consider reforming our religion. That is a death penalty.

Modi: We are not talking about reform. We are talking about new scholars with a fresh approach to translating what is already there. For example, we were discussing the thirty-third sura yesterday. Every time I go through that sura, my heart starts palpitating as if there were something there that I missed. Perhaps a new scholar with a fresh outlook can review Sura 33 and find what I cannot see.

Mani: I believe that philosophers look at what the scholars have done and also look at life and then try to put the two together so that people in general have a reliable guide to take them through life as happily and productively as possible while still giving Allah His due.

Radi: Oh! I can understand that.

Mani: So, Radi, you can tell your cousin to put his Qur'an away for a little while and get himself a sira that has all the elements we discussed. After that, he will know how to read the Qur'an.

Modi: That is right. If he has a computer, even in Holland he can get free downloads of the Ahadith from different Web sites. He really

The Restless Wind and Shifting Sands

needs to have Bukhari, Muslim, Malik, and Dawud. That collection totals about 18,000.

Radi: Are you kidding. He can get that for nothing?

Modi: You bet.

Radi: Perhaps I should get a computer.

Mani: Oh, yes, Radi. You could enroll in Islam 101.

Radi: Do they actually have that, Mani, or are you just kidding me?

Modi: Yes, Radi, they have it. It is www.islam101.com . Perhaps you should get a computer and go through some of those sites. It may make a better person of you.

Radi: Will it make a better believer of me?

Mani: Radi, Modi told you a few times before that it is not the religion but the person. If in your heart you are a good person, of course you will be a good believer. However, even mean, evil people will find enough in our scriptures to justify their malevolence.

Modi: That is why we need more scholars, Radi. Remember what our wives do each spring? They open all the doors and windows, shake all the rugs and carpets, and sweep the house like crazy. It seems as if they are moving all the stale air out and bringing in new air. Perhaps they know something we missed.

Radi: This coffee is good. We need to come here more often. Thank you, my friends. I think my cousin will become a good believer by taking your advice. Even if he doesn't, at least he will know something about his religion. Perhaps non-Muslims, especially Americans, would understand us better if they took some time to do that.

Modi, Mani: Amen.

Harry J. Sweeney

Modi: It does not take much work, Radi. The sira is interesting. It is so much better than going through life—and wars—having to depend upon politicians who do not know what they should know and cannot explain what is going on. Politicians have agendas too—and they will not tell you anything that interferes with their agenda, even if it is something you really must know.

Mani: Because they cannot explain—because they do not know—they lie! The more they lie, the worse things become.

Radi: You mean the politicians will not take a few hours to read a book? They would rather be uninformed and ignorant than to find out the truth?

Mani: Go figure.

The Restless Wind and Shifting Sands

<u>Conversation 47: The United States and the First Barbary Pirates.</u>

Radi: Modi, I hate to say this, but you were right about history.

Mani: Allah be praised! Just what did Modi tell you, Radi?

Radi: He told me a few things about history's repeating itself unless we continually look at the past to get a better handle on the present. My imam's brother is a teacher. He told me that when he was a lad he had heard stories about what Modi told me.

Mani: Modi, what did you tell him?

Modi: I simply mentioned that the Middle East has always been important to the Americans, even before their Constitution.[41]   In fact, we Arabs were the reason for the individual states' finally getting together and creating their Constitution and the reason for their finally—against much objection—building their own navy[42].

Radi: What is really strange—and funny—is that the people in the Northeast were against creating a navy. They were afraid their European friends would be offended if they built a navy to protect their commerce.[43] At the time, it seemed as if George Washington and Thomas Jefferson were the only two people who believed the Americans had the stomach to defend themselves. Remember, this was after a hard-fought war for their independence from Great Britain!

Modi: And how about this one: Jefferson suggested to the Europeans that instead of paying all that annual tribute money to our Barbary pirates, the Americans should build a fleet and combine with Europe's great navies to suppress the terrorism on the Mediterranean. Europe, especially France, refused. The excuse they gave was that it was more

---

41   Power, Faith, and Fantasy, by Michael B. Orem, W.W. Norton & Company, NY, NY, pp 20-22.

42   Ibid., pp 29-32.

43   Ibid., pp 34, 35.

213

Harry J. Sweeney

cost-effective to pay extortion. We found out much later that the Europeans simply were afraid of us.[44]

Radi: In the end, America had to create its Constitution, strengthen its federal government, build a navy, and attack our Arab terrorists and the states sponsoring them.

Mani: I have not heard or read any of those stories.

Modi: Don't feel bad; neither have many Americans. They know that their American squadrons finally won but only after we handed them their tail feathers dozens of times and made them pay millions to get their sailors back. The Americans won because they had to put together a larger force to fight the British for the second time. One could also say that they beat the British at sea using the same tactics we used on the Yankee squadrons in the Mediterranean Sea.[45]

Mani: (Laughs) This stuff is great. For once, I am glad Radi brought something up to discuss. I have to get some of these books to read.

Modi: You will have to learn a Western language, Mani. Thanks to our Salafist friends, we do not have many books available that are not strictly religious. As you know, some of the imams constantly say not to read. How many times have you heard, "If it agrees with the Qur'an, you should already know it; if it does not agree with the Qur'an, you should not read it."

Radi: I agree with that.

Modi: But if you agreed with that wholeheartedly, Radi, you would not want to know the things I just shared with you. You must have *some* doubt.

Radi: Those things were only tidbits, Modi. I already have forgotten

---

44   Ibid., pp 18, 19, 24, 25, 75.
45   Ibid., pp 69-75.

The Restless Wind and Shifting Sands

them. The only important knowledge is in the Qur'an and the hadiths. It is only important that we all fear Allah and worship Him properly.

Mani: Isn't it important that Allah loves us? Has that gotten lost somewhere in our faith? How can He be all merciful and all forgiving if He does not love us?

Modi: Radi, Mani has very good points there. You need to give those things some more thought. I bring up my kids to love Allah, and I most assuredly tell them that Allah loves us in return. I let them know that even if we sometimes go astray Allah in His mercy gives us whatever help we need to return to Him. When we do return to Him and he sees in our hearts that we are really sorry to have strayed, then He forgives us.

Radi: You have been raised in our faith; you know that Allah has already chosen our paths. . .

Modi: Pardon the interruption, Radi, but I really do not want to hear that stuff again. We are not predestined for paradise or the fire, and we do have choices in our lives.

Mani: I thought the only way out of the scheduled path was to become a martyr.

Modi: Many imams and others want us to think that way, especially when they are recruiting for suicide bombers. Allah has told us that life is much too precious to waste. When a person is fighting a truly religious war but is killed in the course of fighting, that person is a martyr. In this war of insurgency, which is not a religious war, very unscrupulous commanders are wasting our youth by inducing them to commit suicide to gain a tactical advantage—and sometimes to retaliate against someone or some group. That is not right; it is not Islam.

Radi: You have it wrong. You should lose your head. It is a religious war, pure and simple!

Harry J. Sweeney

Modi: One would think that the tenets of Islam would be that we wait and support a new democratic government that promises peace and freedom. If in the course of events the government begins to issue rules against our religion, we can think in terms of jihad.

Mani: By Allah, Radi, I think Modi may be right on that issue. People are dying, and they do not know why. Our children—our future—are being wasted by blowing themselves apart for nothing! Radi, can't your friends stop this mess?

Radi: You not only refuse to fight in the way of Allah, you also insult the martyrs and our holy fighters. This blade I am unsheathing will be the sword of Allah, and I will remove your heads as our Most Beloved removed the heads of the treasonous 800 Banu Quraiza!

Modi: Put that thing away, Radi! If you want to discuss the Banu Quraiza, we will talk about killing all the men and many boys from an entire tribe of Jews, and enslaving their women. It was all because the Jews would not abandon their religion, nor would they fight on the Sabbath to defend themselves. I am surprised you even mentioned it.

Mani: Of all the great things accomplished during the creation of our beloved Islam, the one image that I cannot erase from my mind is the "old married woman," twelve-year-old Aisha, our Most Beloved's wife, allowed to watch the ghastly executions that lasted far into the night.

Radi: You will both be thrown into the fire and will suffer throughout eternity! You will not be able to cry in anguish because your heads will be elsewhere, eaten by dogs.

Mani: Modi, I think I may be losing my appetite.

Modi: Yes, me too. I think that the "eaten by dogs" thing did it.

Radi: Hey, wait a minute! That new restaurant opens today.

The Restless Wind and Shifting Sands

Mani: What do you think, Modi? Can we get our appetite back before we get there?

Modi: I doubt it. That last outburst was rather gross.

Radi: Please fellows! I'm hungry, and it's Mani's turn.

Mani: Allah be praised! He said, "Please." Did you hear that?

Modi: I certainly did. Make him say, "Pretty please."

Radi: Why you. . . . (Chases them, brandishing his knife.)

Harry J. Sweeney

Conversation 48: People of Anbar versus Al-Qaida

Mani: Modi, I am glad that we were able to help this Anbar village against al-Qaida, but I still do not understand what was going on. It was quite a fight!

Modi: Al-Qaida had abducted three Christians who were working with the construction crew and were planning to decapitate them.

Mani: Were they proselytizing among us here?

Modi: Oh, no. They were not. They were wearing Christian symbols. I understand that a few people here gave them some friendly advice about that, but they were hardheaded about advertising who they were.

Mani: They had every right to wear their religious symbols.

Modi: Of course they did. To be sure, we have every right to go swimming in the ocean. But tell me, Mani, would you push that right by jumping in among sharks?

Mani: That is a silly question. I would consider that stupid.

Modi: Al-Qaida prides itself on being strict within the confines of the Qur'an, but in this case they have departed considerably. If you are familiar with Sura 5, Ayat 2, it says in part, "And do not let your hatred of a people for having obstructed you from *al-Masjid al-Haram* (Sacred Mosque, the Grand Mosque at Mecca) lead you to transgress. And cooperate in righteousness and piety, but do not cooperate in sin and aggression."

Mani: That is very powerful, Modi. It tells AQ that not only must they not let their hatred for Christians or others lead believers to abduct and kill them, but also if the Christians were helping our people create something helpful, believers are obliged to join in and help. Allah help us. If that ayat becomes widely known, AQ will go crazy.

The Restless Wind and Shifting Sands

Modi: Allah had followed up with His Qur'an 5:8, which says in part, "Do not let the hatred of a people prevent you from being just. Be just; that is nearer to righteousness. And fear Allah; indeed Allah is acquainted with what you do."

Mani: You are right about that. Allah is telling them not only are they not to transgress against those Christians, but also He is ordering them to be just with them. He also reminds them that He is watching. I believe those AQ fighters are in trouble.

Modi: Can you think of something else it means?

Mani: (Thinks; then snaps his fingers) Yes! It means no martyrdom for them if they are fighting Christians out of hatred and not out of necessity. I love this, Modi; however, I am not going to be the one to spread that news.

Modi: We should not have to do this. The imams are obliged to call the people's attention to these commands from Allah.

Mani: You can bet your boots that many will not do so. We may be obliged to remind them somehow.

The next day, in Baghdad:

Radi: I did not see you yesterday. What happened?

Mani: We visited my relatives again.

Radi: The ones in Anbar? Did you join the militia there?

Modi: Bite your tongue, Radi! We were the militia.

Radi: Yeah, right. That will be the day, when you two pick up AKs

Harry J. Sweeney

and go plowing into al-Qaida fighters like the one who made our Most Beloved laugh.[46] (Radi grins.)

Mani: If you want to discuss Anbar, Radi, my relatives have told us quite a bit about who is fighting al-Qaida. It is not only Hamas-Iraqi, but also every man who can find a weapon.

Modi: Mani is telling the truth. The people in that province and in Baghdad are tired of AQ's anti-Islamic policies!

Radi: What? You cannot be serious! Al-Qaida is the epitome of the believer! I wish I could be as fervent a Salafist as they are. They are my heroes.

Modi: Do not ever wish you could be stricter than they in their faith, Radi. Indeed, you are strict enough now. It is not the strictness in their religion that pleases Allah about people. It is the love in their hearts.

Mani: Yes, Radi, it is not only love of Allah, but also love of one's fellow man.

Radi: You two must stay away from Anbar. You are learning the wrong stuff. Allah is going to remember you on Judgment Day. He may even strike you now with a mighty punishment.

Mani: I believe that Allah is looking at us with a gleam in His eye because we will not abandon a friend to the errors of fanaticism.

Radi: I should draw my knife now and reduce the heads on the street by two. Allah would see my righteous deed and provide me with a great reward.

Modi: You might be in for a great reward whenever you are married. You must remember that Allah knows what is in your heart. Until you

---

46   Ishaq's *Sira*, margin note 445 (I445) is a reference to the Battle of Badr.

The Restless Wind and Shifting Sands

are married, I am certain that what is in your mind every day is not pleasant to him.

Radi: That is between Allah and me.

Mani: Radi, you have turned people in, perhaps helped get them killed, because you believed that they committed some kind of sin.

Radi: That is what we are supposed to do to sinners.

Mani: In that case, Modi and I must turn you in for all of those impure thoughts you have because you are not married.

Modi: Yes, Radi, we saw you ogling that poor woman in the brown *abaya* at the market last week.

Radi: Aha! You are making fun of our religion again. Allah may punish me for not acting in His stead to punish you.

Mani: You are a real piece of work, Radi.

Radi: You be very careful. Allah may inflict a very, very nasty punishment on you both.

(Modi and Mani look up in the sky, act as if they found nothing, and shrug their shoulders. Suddenly, Mani's eyes and mouth open wide as if he thought of something.)

Mani: Radi is right! I see the punishment now.

Modi: What is it?

Mani: (Laughs, then points to Radi. Mani and Modi begin running.)

Harry J. Sweeney

Radi: Wait a minute! What is the punish-. . . .(He catches on and starts after them, faking rage.)

[Note: The theme of "Justice" was adapted from Islam 101, Web site address: www.islam101.com/rights/hrM2.htm . The verse translations were quoted from the Noble Qur'an.]

The Restless Wind and Shifting Sands

Conversation 49: Muhammad at Yathrib; On robbing caravans.

Modi and Mani are on a hill overlooking a road in Anbar Province, Iraq.

Mani: How many times has our Most Beloved lain like this in Arabia, awaiting the Meccan polytheists?

Modi: Quite a few times. He did so even when he was not certain that the Meccans would come at all. He was a good general. He shared the boredom and the misery as well as the excitement, the danger, and the profits.

Mani: I never quite understood the stories told about his robbing caravans. Is not that like highway robbery or piracy?

Modi: It was a different time, Mani, and different circumstances. The Jews of Yathrib invited him to be a judge and settle disputes among the tribes of Jews and Arabs in and around their city.

Mani: Yes, I remember that.

Modi: That was only the starting point. The more disputes came his way, the more he discerned their needs to be greater than they thought. The residents of Yathrib needed a complete government with laws that regulated their commerce and their daily affairs.

Mani: I see. Since the Messenger was in the process of developing and teaching the new religion, he was the obvious person to become the new leader. Since the disputes brought to him were in the commercial and daily affairs area anyway, his decisions in early cases could conceivably have taken on the force of law if applied to ensuing cases.

Modi: You are right. It would be *stare decisis*,[47] pure and simple.

---

47 "Let the decision stand." Decisions made in early cases also should stand in similar cases.

Harry J. Sweeney

However, the problem with Yathrib was that the Messenger was spread very thin and could not give full attention to each of his tasks.

Mani: Are you saying that he made mistakes or was not up to the job?

Modi: By no means am I saying that. Nonetheless, I have a suspicion that many laws would be different had he the time to reflect and the time to teach the people about fairness and propriety.

Mani: I suspect that you are saying that the unfortunate war with the Meccans had a deleterious effect on his time—and perhaps on his patience.

Modi: I would think it would if he were an ordinary man like you and me. Our Most Beloved seems to have been an extraordinary person, and he took on an enormous job in Yathrib. One of the problems that he did not anticipate was that when the families of the believers followed them to Yathrib, now Medina, and more Arabs fled Mecca to join him, they swelled the ranks of the believers. Muhammad had not the food or the funds to house them and feed them.

Mani: Are you saying that he just turned to caravan robbing to feed his people?

Modi: It was not that simple. Since the Prophet and his followers were forced to leave Mecca and relocate elsewhere, a *de facto* state of war existed between the two factions. The believers considered the Meccans at fault in their dire predicament and that anything that happened to the Meccans as a result was deserved. You and I both know that there are no kept secrets in the Middle East, except from Europeans and Americans. It was the same back in the seventh century. Muhammad discovered the Meccan plan for a rich caravan from Syria, which was expected to pass near Medina on its return trip to Mecca. The Prophet let his followers know that he planned to attack the caravan.

Mani: Did the Meccans know about Muhammad's plan?

The Restless Wind and Shifting Sands

Modi: The Meccans knew before the caravan left Syria. No secret is safe, remember? And they knew they had to protect this caravan. It consisted of about one thousand camels with valuable merchandise, accompanied by only forty armed riders. The Meccans consequently assembled a powerful force to protect the caravan and defeat the believers.

Mani: You have a strange look on your face. You are holding something back. Out with it, Modi.

Modi: You are too sharp for me, Mani. (Smiles sheepishly) What the Meccans did not know was that the caravan was not Muhammad's primary objective. He was trying to lure the Meccan forces out in the field. Medina lived under the threat of a Meccan invasion, but the two sides had not yet met in open combat. When finally they did meet, the Meccans had to contend with Abu Bakr's forces on one side and Umar's on the other. However, the believers were very poorly armed and greatly outnumbered. Nonetheless, our fighters believed in their Prophet and knew in their hearts that no matter what happened they personally could not lose. If they survived, there would be spoils to divide evenly; if they did not survive, their families would be given their share, and they themselves would go directly to paradise.

Mani: And the Meccans fought with the fear of dying while we fought welcoming death.

Modi: Yes, it made a huge difference. And the spoils made a difference in the morale of the believers. Their ranks swelled even more.

Mani: Did that not happen at Badr?

Modi: Yep. And that changed the course of the entire world.

The following day in Baghdad:

Radi: Good morning, you two. The news is not good.

Harry J. Sweeney

Mani: Why not? Did the Iranians lose more missiles or something?

Radi: Besides that, al-Qaida lost more men last night in Anbar.

Modi: Serves them right for trying to attack a small village.

Radi: The people fighting al-Qaida do not know what they are doing.

Mani: They seem to be winning the battles. They must know something.

Radi: They are on the wrong side. They should be fighting with AQ, not against it.

Mani: Radi does not get the picture yet. Radi, AQ is fighting the villagers and has been for some time. How can the villagers be on the wrong side when they are on their own side? They are protecting themselves.

Radi: But the government is weak and no longer credible.

Modi: You dummy! We know that. Nonetheless, it is our government; the only one we have. If we can stop the nonsense and establish peace, we can fix anything that needs fixing. Your friends are not solving anything; they are the problem.

Radi: But the prime minister is Shiite, most of his cabinet is Shiite, he has many Iranian friends, they are all Shiite, and his stooge, Muqtada as-Sadr is Shiite. Even the great Al Sistani is Shiite.

Mani: Modi, do you think Radi is into something?

Modi: Mani, look at that face! He does have a worried look.

Mani: He is just impatient. It is lunchtime, and it is your turn to buy.

The Restless Wind and Shifting Sands

Modi: When is it ever his turn to buy?

Mani: In the evening during Ramadan, when everything is free—if you know the right families.

Harry J. Sweeney

Conversation 50: On Palestine.

Modi: Radi, I hear you and your imam had a falling out.

Radi: Yes, that is right. I think he is becoming addled.

Mani: I thought you liked him; he was really a puritan Salafist. I went to his sermon only once, and he scared me something fierce.

Radi: But now he is getting soft. Old Ayman was drunk again last week. He already had been to see the magistrate four times. On the fourth time, they gave him eighty lashes.[48] This is the second time he has been drunk since then, but the imam does not take it seriously. The last time they took pity on him because of his age.

Modi: Radi, Ayman is pretty old, and his latest wife is an old sourpuss. She is always complaining, and I was told she could not cook worth a hoot.

Mani: The poor chap has so many grandchildren that he doesn't know all their names anymore. If anyone deserves to be drunk, he does.

Radi: Our Most Beloved had said that if someone is drunk the fourth time, kill him.[49]

Modi: Radi, have a heart! Do you remember that wedding feast we attended last year? That evening, you were three-sheets-to-the-wind with a fair breeze.

Mani: Yeah, I remember that too, Radi. And the next morning you were on a rolling deck all day. (Modi laughs.)

---

48   Dawud, Book 38, 4473: "Abu Bakr gave forty lashes for drinking wine, and then Umar in the beginning of his Caliphate inflicted forty stripes and at the end of his Caliphate he inflicted eighty stripes. Uthman inflicted punishments, eighty and forty stripes, and finally Mu'awiyah established eighty stripes."

49   Ibid., 4469: Narrated Abu Hurayrah: "The Prophet [pbuh] said: 'If he is intoxicated, flog him: again if he is intoxicated, flog him; again if he is intoxicated, flog him. If he does it a fourth time, kill him.'" See also 4466, 4467, 4470.

The Restless Wind and Shifting Sands

Radi: (Embarrassed) I was not drunk, just festive.

Modi: Radi, you had a good reason for being drunk. You needed some time away from your head lopping and hate speeches.

Mani: Take it easy on Ayman. He needs some time away from reality.

Modi: You are not an imam or anything, Radi. Why are you always so concerned about punishing people?

Radi: If the imams or the magistrates do not do their jobs, or if the sin happens elsewhere, it is the task of the family or the tribe to take action.

Mani: Of course, it is tradition; however, we are now a nation of laws. We must leave everything to the authorities.

Modi: Radi, perhaps we need to tell you, no one gets retirement pay for being a vigilante. (Mani laughs.)

Radi: You two are heaping verbal abuse upon me today. Calumny is a sin and Allah warned about that in the Book.[50] If I remember correctly, that should be worth about eighty stripes apiece.[51]

Modi: You certainly are a real buddy, Radi old pal. I feel obligated to tell you, though, that you would have a hard time providing evidence of calumny.

---

50   Qur'an 33:58 "And as for those who malign believing men and believing women without their having done any wrong – they surely burden themselves with the guilt of calumny, and [thus] with a flagrant sin."

51   Dawud: Book 38, 4452: Narrated 'Abdullah ibn 'Abbas: "A man of Bakr ibn Layth came to the Prophet [pbuh] and made confession four times that he had committed fornication with a woman, so he had a hundred lashes administered to him. The man had not been married. He then asked him to produce proof against the woman, and she said: I swear by Allah, Apostle of Allah, that he has lied. Then he was given the punishment of eighty lashes of falsehood."

Harry J. Sweeney

Mani: Yes, Radi. We are your friends, and we are trying to bring you back to the straight and narrow. However, you refuse to listen to the voices of moderation and adhere only to the bellowing of the fanatics.

Radi: My ears listen only to the teachings of the Qur'an, and I obey only the sharia.

Modi: Your ears listen only to the voices that narrow the meanings of the verses. Surely, they ascribe hatred meant for the polytheists who denied you access to the *Masjid al-Haram* (Grand Mosque) by unfair extension to the People of the Book, who deny you nothing that is rightfully yours.

Radi: Another lie. What about Palestine?

Mani: What about claiming ownership of an area that nobody wanted until the Jews returned to reoccupy it? A land whose name, I might add, we cannot even pronounce."

Modi: Don't get me started on Palestine, Radi. I have had enough, and the entire Middle East has had enough of the lies, the destruction, and the killing, all because the Jews were returned a very small portion of the land that had been their homeland since antiquity and had been nothing but a garbage dump ever since. Just do not bring it up!

Mani: As a matter of fact, Radi, if you really want to make an ownership claim to Palestine, take it up with the King of Jordan. As soon as the land was offered to the Jews, King Abdullah seized most of it and left only 25 percent to be divided up between the Jews and some Arabs who wanted to live there.

Modi: Or you could sue the Brits. They are the ones who did not have the guts to say no to Abdullah. They were in charge at the time and did not do their job.

Radi: All of these things are lies. We have always had Palestine as a homeland.

The Restless Wind and Shifting Sands

Mani: Radi, remember, you get eighty lashes for lying. If you don't get them here, Allah will have someone waiting.

Radi: You are the ones telling the lies.

Modi: Would you want to make a wager on that?

Radi: What kind of wager?

Modi: At Judgment Day, we will go before Allah. If my lies are more numerous than yours, I will take on the punishment for both of us. However, if yours are more numerous than mine, you take on my punishment as well as yours. With Allah as judge, it has to be fair.

Radi: I am not going to make such a wager. After all, I am allowed to lie any time it advances the interest of my religion.

Mani: Only when you cannot advance it any other way, Radi. You are not going to get a pass on lying when you would be better off telling the truth.

Modi: I think some of Radi's friends, the politicians, seem to lie even when it is not in their best interest.

Mani: I noticed that. I guess they have to keep in practice.

Modi: I don't think politicians need the practice. But getting back to Ayman, Radi, I thought I read in the newspapers that Ayman did get another eighty stripes recently.

Radi: I know. I saw that, but it wasn't fair. A few others and I complained that he should have been whipped. But they gave him only ten lashes.

Mani: Yeah, Radi, but they used eight twigs to do it. Eight times ten is eighty!
(Mani and Modi laugh; Radi shakes his head.)

Harry J. Sweeney

Radi: I hear the *adhan*. It is time for the noon prayer.

Mani: Yes. It is nice to pray among friends.

CHAPTER 6

Conversation 51: Reform—A capital offense!

Mani: Modi, I keep hearing rumors about more reformers. I thought that reforming the religion was a thing of the past. So many people have been killed for even bringing the subject up; I had to look around to see who was in earshot before I spoke of it.

Modi: You are right to do that. There are many people whose only contribution to Islam is a sharp tongue and a sharp knife; they are ready to pounce on anything that does not literally agree with what they believe is the only truth. Besides, it is the sharia they are protecting. Without the sharia, these male chauvinists would not be in power five minutes.

Radi: Modi, you and Mani should know there is only one truth and it is written in al-Kitab, the Qur'an. It is the literal word of Allah. Anyone who defies or seeks to change one word of His exact truth should be killed.

Modi: Is that to teach him a lesson, Radi? Why should the old beards kill anyone for *suggesting* change? If they are dead, what about the lessons they learned? Are they afraid that someone may find something to end their ridiculous power? If that is the aim of the reformers, they are going about it the wrong way. Islam as a religion is not the problem. The political ideology and the social ideology enforced by the sharia could be reviewed, but not the religion. If the sharia is suspended or repealed for something more akin to the UN Declaration of Human Rights, it really would be a religion of peace, according to the Europeans—but they do not even agree with each other.

Radi: Infidel, you and others like you must be taught a lesson. The lesson is simply a reminder that you are not dealing with an earthly person; you are dealing with Allah.

Harry J. Sweeney

Modi: Radi, I am trying to deal with understanding in general. I am not equipped to speak directly to Allah, none of us are. .

Radi: We have the word of our Prophet that the words of Allah were revealed to him over a twenty-two year period.

Mani: Modi, Sura 17, ayats 105 through 111 give Allah's description of His revealing the Qur'an to Muhammad step-by-step over the years. I am surprised that you did not know that.

Modi: Actually, Mani, I do know it; however, I needed to know whether or not Radi was aware of it. I see by his answer that he was not. I had a sudden thought that confused me. What if after all this time, the UN decided that the world should have only one religion—ours? What would we argue about?

Mani: I guess the world would be at peace. We would not be fighting any of these religious wars against Israel and the West.

Modi: You do not think that even with a Muslim Israel, the Arabs who call themselves Palestinians would abandon the fight? You don't think other Arab nations would still want to attack the al-Saud for control of our holy places? What about Iran? Would Iran abandon its dream of being the supreme power in this region?

Radi: We were talking about something else, Modi.

Mani: What would a reformer change, if it were not the Qur'an?

Modi: I would think that a reformer would cherish the Qur'an, but would create another companion document that agrees with al-Kitab, but provides a modern version that everyone can read and understand. We need to allow the individual believer to read the original word of Allah as they do today, but also to refer to the modern version for practical use. The document should discourage abusing our faith by the unlawful or inadvertent attributing of seventh century problems on the part of the Meccan polytheists and Yathrib/Medina Jews, to any group or nation today. Our most beloved pardoned and made peace with the people of Mecca; so should we make peace with the rest of humanity today. We must not hate people today for something others did in another time and place.

Mani: That is a thought, Modi; however, I would leave that type of thinking to the *ulama*. They are better equipped to deal with those questions. I do not like it when plain people speak of change. They usually do not have enough learning to matter.

Radi: No! There is no room for that type of thinking. You should both bite the blade and be buried separately from your heads! Just say NO to any reform.

Modi: We also need an internal policy discussion about what constitutes a capital crime. Perhaps the *ulama* might consider alternative penalties or none for changing one's religion. I would also suggest we look again at honor killings. We could also clear up female circumcision once and for all.

Mani: I would not push things. Nonetheless, I would say that it would be important to create a law that prevents people from taking capital punishment into their own hands. We should leave the matter of punishment to law enforcement and the courts.

Modi: That is a good one, Mani. Yes, outlaw vigilantism! And make all citizens equal, men, women, and non-Muslims, in our courts.

Radi: I am going to report both of you to the imam! I never hear such trash before! You are both guilty of blasphemy and apostasy (draws his knife).

Modi: That is fine, Radi, you do that. But before you go, let me tell you this. We are here in the street, talking about what a reformer is and what he would probably think about. Please remember, we said that our basic documents, especially the Qur'an, would remain unchanged and revered as they are now. What are you going to tell the imam?

Harry J. Sweeney

Radi: I will say you are reformers. That is all I need to say. They will come after you and lop off both heads before you can say another word.

Mani: Won't they ask us if your charge against us is true?

Radi: Of course not. Why should they? All they need to hear is the word reformer and your goose is cooked. They are not going to wait for any conversation.

Modi: Don't you see how that endangers you, Radi? You are in a very vulnerable spot.

Radi: (Frowns and looks worried) I don't know how that would ever concern me. I am a pure Salafist and love my religion. You are the criminals!

Mani: How many people have a grudge against you, Radi?

Modi: Yes. You told us that you have lopped off many a head, but the relatives could not exact retaliation because of a technical righteousness on your part.

Radi: That is right. They sinned and I lopped.

Modi: How long will it take for at least one of those many relatives to get the idea that all they need to do is accuse you of something, just to retaliate?

Radi: Why would anyone believe that? Everyone knows I am the righteous arm of Allah.

Mani: You told us if you called us reformers, they would not give us a chance to defend ourselves; they would simply kill us because someone said we were reformers.

Radi: Yes, so? Uh…oh. I see what you mean.

The Restless Wind and Shifting Sands

Modi: Aha! Things do not look so rosy the way they are, do they?

Mani: You have a married sister, Radi. Suppose her daughter, your niece that you dote on so much, were to say to her father that she could not stand the ugly kid he picked out for her—and you thought the choice was deplorable—and your brother-in-law, whom you never liked, decides to stone her. What would you do?

Radi: That is not fair. You are talking about someone dear to me and bringing up a situation I could do nothing about; it is righteous on his part.

Modi: You would not try to stop him from killing his daughter?

Radi: No. He has every right to kill his children if they do not obey him.

Modi: Well, Mani, if that is the way he thinks; he has gotten too dangerous for us.

Mani: Yep. Let's swing by the imam's house and swear out a complaint that Radi is a reformer.

Radi: What? You can't do that. That is not right.

Mani: So what? There are many things that are not right here. What is only one more?

Radi: I will remind them that I am the righteous one!

Mani: They won't bother to ask.

Modi: I think Radi is worried.

Mani: But is he learning anything?

Radi: What are you scheming now?

Harry J. Sweeney

Modi: We have decided to go through with it, but first there is prayer, then lunch—and you are buying, by the way—and I hope that we can remember to see the imam after all that.

Radi: I smell a rat.

Mani: I bet it is a strong odor.

Modi: Yeah, Radi, time for your full body ablution.

Radi: I will not get mad. I will not get mad. I will not... (grits his teeth and gives chase)

The Restless Wind and Shifting Sands

Conversation 52: On Aisha

Radi: Modi, do you remember my cousin from Holland?

Modi: Oh, yes. Nice person. Did he get home all right?

Radi: Yes, he had no problems at all. Thanks to you, he is interested in our history. He sent a letter.

Mani: Aha! What does he want to know?

Radi: He is interested in Aisha. Apparently, he takes some abuse from some infidels calling our Most Beloved some nasty names.

Modi: I guess we had better give him some answers then. I suppose his first question is how old she was when our Most Beloved married her. Most people, believers as well, put her age at nine at marriage. However, they don't really know. No one knows the exact birth date. We do accept age nine though, as her age at marriage.

Mani: I understand that she was betrothed to someone else earlier. She could have been married earlier than she was to our Great Founder.

Modi: I have to look it up, but I believe that her father, Abu Bakr wanted her married before they migrated to Ethiopia. They were escaping from Meccan pressure and Abu Bakr did not believe she was up to such an arduous journey. Therefore, the answer is yes. It is possible that Aisha could have been married two years sooner.

Radi: So, originally she could have been married at seven years.

Modi: Yes, maybe younger. But as far as her actual marriage is concerned, she could have been anywhere between nine and thirteen. Others say she could have been older; however, Aisha herself says she was nine. That is good enough for me. She was betrothed to her only husband directly after the infidel Jubayr refused the marriage prior to

Harry J. Sweeney

the Muslim journey to Ethiopia. However, the marriage to our Most Beloved never took place until after the Hijira, when she settled in Medina.

Mani: I wish we had better records from back then. It is not good to need specific information and not have it; or to have conflicts even in written records.

Modi: I feel that way about many documents during that period.

Radi: I know what you are saying, Modi, but Allah has seen to it that the documents that we cherish were collected and compiled the way He wanted it.

Modi: You need not answer, Radi, although it would be nice to know how everyone knew Allah's plans for collecting and arranging everything.

Mani: Don't mind Modi, Radi. What else does he want to know?

Radi: What about the charge of adultery against her?

Modi: I can actually make short work of that one. Aisha was accompanying her husband on a trip with several others. She had received a necklace as a gift, but lost it. Her search took her out of camp and when she returned, everyone was gone. She had to wait there alone for a few hours before another believer showed up and took her to rejoin the caravan.

Mani: Oh! I bet that went over well with everyone.

Modi: You bet. She was alone with another man not her husband for almost a day. Some tongues were wagging eight-to-the-bar. Voices were bouncing around her husband's head about divorce and punishment, despite the fact that everyone close to her swore that she would never do anything wrong.

The Restless Wind and Shifting Sands

Radi: What happened? I think I know, but I want to be sure.

Modi: Well, talk about a *deus-ex-machina*[52] ending, it was revealed by Allah in Qur'an 24:11 that Aisha was innocent. Those who had spoken against her received forty lashes.

Mani: Ooops! I guess that taught them something.

Radi: I do not understand the comment you made about our Most Beloved's receiving the revelation from Allah confirming Aisha's innocence.

Modi: Well, you just look at that situation, Radi. Suppose your fiancée were gone from your sight and her parents' sight for a day or so, and then she showed up in some man's car. Just what would you say to her?

Radi: Nothing. I would never see her again. Besides, her parents would kill her.

Mani: Would you not wait to hear her explanation?

Radi: Not on your tintype, Mani.

Modi: (laughs) He's been waiting for weeks to say that.

Mani: You and her parents would just abandon her to a stoning, despite how devoted she has been to you all this time?

Radi: Of course. There is no explaining a situation like that.

---

52   Referring to Greek plays in which the god or gods are lowered onto the stage by means of a crane or other machine, to untangle an impossible situation for the hero and save the day. It is used today to describe an artificial or improbable ending.

Harry J. Sweeney

Modi: But that was the situation that Aisha was confronting so long ago. You would not have believed Aisha.

Mani: You would have gotten forty lashes, Radi.

Modi: Perhaps your fiancée fainted, someone took her to the hospital, and it was a doctor who brought her home.

Radi: Well, Modi, if it were something like that.

Mani: But you folks would not have waited for the reason.

Modi: Look at it this way, if someone ran up at the last moment and showed everyone she was unconscious in a hospital for half a day, what would you call it?

Radi: A lie?

Mani: Radi, Modi is trying to get you to say it is a miracle.

Radi: Oh.

Modi: What I was trying to say, Radi, was that the revelation exonerating Aisha was a miracle. But you would not have believed it.

Radi: I would believe if our Most Beloved said it.

Mani: Radi, you only want to avoid those forty lashes.

Radi: If I were traveling with our Most Beloved, I would think differently than if I were standing around with you two.

Mani: That sounds like bigotry to me. Modi, I think Radi does not believe in miracles.

Modi: I want to believe in miracles, but Radi is not cooperative.

The Restless Wind and Shifting Sands

Radi: What have miracles to do with me?

Modi: Nothing, so far. But if you ever pay for a meal...

Mani: Now that would be a miracle.

Harry J. Sweeney

<u>Conversation 53: Qur'an sura 33; the Islam Ideology.</u>

Mani: Radi is in a good mood today.

Modi: Good morning. I hope your nephew appreciated all that information you sent him.

Radi: He certainly did appreciate it. He said it disarmed a few of the religion's detractors.

Modi: I am glad to hear that. Nonetheless, one should leave another's religion alone. Having said that and knowing you were about to jump in with something horrible, let me add that a decent religion with confidence in itself should not worry about detractors.

Radi: Allah has not said we need NOT worry about detractors. Your favorite sura, 33, ayat 57 says,

"Indeed, those who abuse Allah and His Messenger - Allah has cursed them in this world and the Hereafter and prepared for them a humiliating punishment."

Following that ayat directly is ayat 58, which says,

"And those who annoy believing men and women undeservedly, they bear the crime of slander and plain sin."

Mani: Radi is right, Modi. Detractors of the religion deserve anything they get.

Modi: That is not quite right, Mani. You cannot kill someone just because he or she said something about your religion. I can remember recently that you excoriated both Jews and Christians and they did not pick up axes or picks and kill you and your kids.

Radi: Oh yes, they did. Remember the little Palestinian boy who was killed by Israelis while he hid behind his father.

The Restless Wind and Shifting Sands

Modi: You jerk! You know very well that the video already has been discredited. Even the cameraman laughed when they confronted him with the truth.

Mani: It does not matter, Modi. People should not discredit our religion.

Modi: Let me put it to you this way, Mani. It is rude and beneath anyone's dignity to criticize another person's religion. Nonetheless, you must take into consideration that our religion is a little different from other religions. Our religion is not only a religion, like Judaism or Christianity, but also an ideology like Capitalism or Socialism. So, if someone says Communism stinks—you might remember that Qutb said something like that—who cares? A little later, Nikita Khrushchev said something similar about Capitalism. Nobody really cared what he said. Was Communism or Capitalism hurt by either person's words? No.
What about someone saying Islam is evil? Are they really talking about Islam as a religion? I doubt it; it would not make sense. However saying it about an ideology does make sense. For example, Radi, I for one do not appreciate your interpretation of our ideology. It not only makes me sick, it puts me in a position in which I cannot defend against what is being said.

Mani: You are confusing me, Modi. Our religion is still our religion and nobody should insult us. If they are insulting Radi, they are insulting me also.

Radi: See, Modi. You just do not get it.

Modi: Mani, let us say that Smith is a Marxist and Brown is a Capitalist. They are both Christians; even if only one acts like a Christian (I cannot understand how Christians can be Marxists). Now look at Radi. As far as religion goes, he follows Islam. You know what? Nobody cares that he is a Muslim. I am also a Muslim and I follow an ideology that says I believe in live-and-let-live. Some people call that the ideology of a "moderate." Now, here is the deal: nobody cares about me; I am

Harry J. Sweeney

accepted and not challenged because I fit in with the rest of the world. They need not worry about me. Getting back to Radi, people do not care that he is a Muslim, but he is also a radical extremist that believes everyone not a Muslim should be killed.

Mani: I see. The John Smiths of the world worry about Radi because he thinks all John Smiths should be killed.

Modi: Yes. They have a right to worry.

Radi: Anyone who loves life more than death should die!

Modi: See, now he has me worried.

Mani: But how about me? Why should the John Smiths of the world worry about me?

Modi: Because you will not choose sides and stick with the side you choose, Mani. You outnumber both of us. If you decide at the last minute to join my side, the John Smiths can breathe easier. However, if at the last minute you jump aboard Radi's kill-them-all express, you could upset everybody. The John Smith's really do not want to fight another war. They prefer to be left in peace. Radi has no right to say what he says and his buddies have no right to kill anyone simply because they are not Muslims.

Mani: I hate to disagree with you, but Radi is right. I myself would not want to kill anyone, or even fight a war. I prefer to live and let live, just as you do. However, we do have the right to kill the unbelievers simply because they are unbelievers.

Modi: With your last sentence, Mani, you told John Smith you do not really want to kill him; however, you also told him you have every right to do so. If he had any sense at all, he should get you first.

Mani: Ha! With his government the way it is? We could walk right in there and take over. We just have to tell them we are the new lobby for

The Restless Wind and Shifting Sands

the immigrants. They will do anything we say. One of us could dress up like a bishop and tell everybody to lineup for holy Kool-Aid.

Modi: You nut!

Radi: What is Mani talking about?

Modi: I don't know; something he saw on TV, I guess.

Harry J. Sweeney

Conversation 54: Waterboarding!

Modi: Radi, what on earth are you so happy about?

Radi: Hi, Modi. Have you seen the CNN reports about the American version of waterboarding?

Mani: Waterboarding? What is that? Is it waterskiing with a 2 x 4 or something?

Radi: (Laughs) No. It is the American idea of torture.

Modi: Oh, yes. I did hear about that. Torture? I do not think so.

Radi: Well, I happen to know that some of our groups have some very mild methods of torture. The believers who want sinners to admit their guilt sometimes drive toothpicks or even brads under fingernails. Anything less than that could not be torture.

Mani: Ooh! That has to be painful. Is waterboarding painful?

Radi: Ha! No, it is not painful. It just gives a sensation of drowning,

Mani: And the Americans consider that torture?

Modi: Not all of them. They are in the minority.

Radi: The one I like to watch is taking pliers and slowly pulling out the fingernails. Our insurgents like that one because sometimes they get information before the first fingernail is completely out.

Mani: Don't say that. My nails hurt just hearing about it. You like to watch stuff like that?

Radi: Yep. But it is not half as much fun as taking a finger joint off each time a prisoner refuses to answer. They really yell, but usually they

The Restless Wind and Shifting Sands

admit their sins after the second or third finger is removed. Some use a sharp knife, but I have seen others use a hammer and a wood chisel.

Mani: They use a wood chisel?

Radi: Yes. I understand that they put a narrow chisel where they want to cut and....

Modi: I do not want to hear the rest, Radi. That is sick. You say we are using such drastic torture techniques to force prisoners into confessing crimes against us as well as giving information?

Radi: It's not all that bad. After they admit they are committing crimes, we administer antiseptics and bandage their wounds.

Mani: Then what do you do?

Radi: Well, then we kill them.

Modi: Oh, I see. You very mercifully end their misery.

Radi: Yes, that is right.

Mani: Do you use waterboarding at all?

Radi: No. However, I guess we might consider it if we needed to question some little kids.

Modi: My, how merciful we are. Do we have any videos to send the Americans? It would make waterboarding look like tea and cookies. I bet the people we torture would rather have waterboarding.

Radi: So much for our mild forms of torture. We do have more reliable and more painful forms of torture.

Mani: I do not think I want to hear about them.

Harry J. Sweeney

Modi: What could be more painful than having a finger joint cut off with a wood chisel?

Radi: Well, a popular form of torture here is to have a prisoner's hands tied behind him, with a rope tied to the wrists and pulled through a pulley in the ceiling until the prisoner is a few feet off the ground. I understand the pain in the shoulder sockets induces a great deal of screaming. Of course, we also have whipping with metal-tipped whips, electrodes in effective places, teeth extractions, truncheons, and fists.

Mani: I would really hate to see your variation on waterboarding.

Radi: It is simple. We hang the prisoner by the feet and let him down slowly into a large bucket filled with water. He drowns, we revive him, and we drown him again. It is effective. The problem we have with that form is that sometimes we cannot revive him.

Mani: Oh, that is too bad. You miss out on all that fun.

Radi: You are critical of torture, Mani, but how else do we get important information that the prisoner does not want to give up?

Mani: You do not think waterboarding will do it?

Radi: Why bother when we have other, more effective methods. I heard that in Zanzibar, it was not unusual to force kerosene down a prisoner's throat and insert a fuse in his stomach.

Mani feels sick and turns away.

Radi: Mani looks a little green. Is he sick?

Modi: No, Radi, he is not the one who is sick. You brought up the subject of waterboarding, and we should have stayed with that subject.

Radi: Bah. How can the Americans say that waterboarding is even in the torture category? It is almost a kid's game.

The Restless Wind and Shifting Sands

Modi: Well, we had a discussion once before about the Americans not growing up and still thinking like kids.

Radi: Yes. I remember that. Do you remember those American commercials that were in that video I received from my cousin? Do those leftist Americans really long for the Walgreen town of Perfect? That seems rather farfetched.

Modi: It is not far off the mark. It is not even clear to some leftist Americans what the goal is; but what is very clear is what they do not want and will not accept. They do not want life the way it is with everyone free to think and live as they please, limited only by law and their economic conditions. However, they are two-faced. On one hand, they do not want violent, hateful murderers killed; however, on the other hand, they think nothing of killing their own innocent babies. That is as bad as these idiot insurgents conning our kids into being suicide bombers.

Radi: Their kids are their future. They do not see anything wrong with killing them?

Modi: No. The desire of some Americans to kill the unborn is unusually strong; it affects everything they do in politics. They go berserk if they suspect a judicial candidate does not support killing the unborn.

Mani: Are we finished with the subject of torture?

Modi: Are you OK? We are finished with the subject. We are now discussing American abortions.

Mani: Allah be merciful! Modi, if that is not a terrible form of torture, what else could be? What a shame.

Radi: Oh, I don't know about that. If they keep that up, there won't be any more Americans.

Harry J. Sweeney

Modi: Now I am getting sick. We may have to forget about lunch.

Radi: Now that is real torture.

Mani: Bilal is calling.

The Restless Wind and Shifting Sands

<u>Conversation 55: Unemployment and Marriage.</u>

Again, I am departing from the usual dialogues in order to present a look at the lives of other people, fictitious, of course, in the world of Islam. Abdul-Samad is an Iraqi lad of 18, and Masoud, 19, also an Iraqi, is his best friend. They are both unemployed and have been looking for work for weeks.

Abdul-Samad: Masoud, what shall we do today?

Masoud: What did we do yesterday?

Abdul-Samad: We looked for jobs. We did not find any.

Masoud: There is so much construction going on, somebody must have openings. There must be something soon.

Abdul-Samad: You would think so. My older brother is the only one working in our family. He wants to marry, but he cannot because all his money goes to us.

Masoud: I would like to get married also, but I am broke with no job. I saw the sweetest girl in the world.

Abdul-Samad: How could you possibly know anything about her?

Masoud: I saw her face while she was in the market. It was angelic. And when she spoke, it was like hearing the angels sing. I saw her pick up some vegetables and her hands looked soft and delicate. I know I am in love with her.

Abdul-Samad: But she might be betrothed to someone else.

Masoud: I thought of that and asked around. Nobody seems to know. I saw where she lived and heard her name, Falak. She is my star. I asked father to find out about Star, but he said better to forget about her until I find work.

253

Harry J. Sweeney

Abdul-Samad: Has she noticed you?

Masoud: Are you kidding? How can anyone tell? If she so much as smiled at me or even acknowledged my presence, it would be the whip for her.

Abdul-Samad: Yes, where is my head? My sister likes a boy who lives down the street, but she cannot tell anyone. I know about it because every time the boy is within view, I look for her and find her gazing at him with those cow eyes of hers. I want so much to tell him, but our whole family would be dishonored and one of us would have to be publicly whipped. Father told older brother that he was going to ask around to marry her off. He said. "It is not right that one son should carry such a burden when I, his father, can find a husband for her."

Masoud: Your sister is such a good person, Abdul-Samad, that she deserves a good match, not just any old husband. That is not right. What kind of person does he consider acceptable? She should have a husband who will be kind to her.

Abdul-Samad: He does not care a whit about that. He would like a match with a shopkeeper or a vegetable seller. He would like to pick up a job out of it or at least see some free vegetables occasionally. He needs to see some profit from giving up his daughter. Of course, his priority is just losing the expense of feeding her.

Masoud: Abdul-Samad, I feel so badly about that, if I could, I would marry her just to keep her happy.

Abdul-Samad: But what about your Star?

Masoud: I feel bad about Falak also. What am I going to do? I have to find a job. Maybe I should join the police or the army.

Abdul-Samad: A few months ago, I would have gotten excited and suggested that you forget about such nonsense. But now, after the Americans finally became serious about our security, I have changed

The Restless Wind and Shifting Sands

my mind. Joining the army might be a good idea. It is just that the government is so untrustworthy.

Masoud: You don't think I know that? Every government is dishonest to some extent. One of the arguments I had with myself about being a policeman was, do I have to be dishonest too? If all of the people in my squad are on the take, must I follow their lead? If I do not, will they find a way to do something to me?

Abdul-Samad: I can see how that could be a problem for you. You are an honest person. Would military service be any different?

Masoud: I would think so. Soldiers generally do not come into contact with civilians. The chief enemies of the soldier are the officers who want quick promotions, and the politicians who think they are all worthless pawns. I really feel bad about the American troops here. It is so obvious that they are here for the best of reasons and they have the greatest of intentions to help us. However, I have watched CNN until I was sick, seeing brave American soldiers treated like tennis balls. Some people in the American congress should be taken to task!

Abdul-Samad: Hopefully, it will not be so bad in our army. Perhaps we will learn something from the American mistakes.

Masoud: Government leaders never seem to learn from the mistakes of others. They make the same mistakes continuously. Remember, you can tell an insane person if he does exactly the same thing over and over again, always looking for a different result.

Abdul-Samad: You are becoming cynical. Nonetheless, I find myself agreeing with you. Am I to assume then that you will try to enlist in the army?

Masoud: Yes. I will go there as soon as they open. If they will not take me, I will have to try the police.

Abdul-Samad: I will accompany you. You know what? If they take

255

you, I will enlist also. You can forget the police, though. You know, we could share a house.

Masoud: I would be proud and happy to have you with me. If they take me, Abdul-Samad, I will make you my brother-in-law.

Abdul-Samad: But your great love is your Star!

Masoud: She was until you mentioned your sister. Falak then became great love number 2. I could not stand it if your father traded your little sister for vegetables. Little sisters must be worth more than a basket of vegetables.

Abdul-Samad: Masoud, I was thinking that if my little sister were given a raw deal, I would go to the Brigade and be a martyr. As I thought more about it, I know my family would be given a lot of money, but my life would be wasted on blowing up something or somebody that would hurt our people instead of help.

Masoud: You are right about that. Those martyrs did more damage to their people and their country and did very little to the enemy.

Abdul-Samad: And then people started realizing that the Americans were not the enemy. Al-Qaida and the foreign fighters were the enemies. If I were to be a martyr, I would have to go after some radical Saudis— however; there is no money in it to help my family or my sister.

Masoud: Abdul-Samad, future brother-in-law I hope, let us go down and enlist together. If they won't take us, we will become unpaid martyrs and blow up some extremist-owned building or group.

Abdul-Samad: Where would we get the bombs?

Masoud: I don't know. What a fix we are in. We can't even blow ourselves up without money. The army better take us. The army has to take us.

The Restless Wind and Shifting Sands

Abdul-Samad: If they take us, Masoud, I will run directly home and tell father to hell with his damned vegetables, I found a good man to marry little sister, and I will move out also. The family will not have me for an expense. I will live with my brother-in-law and share his expenses. Masoud, something tells me this is the beginning of a beautiful friendship.

Masoud: What?

Abdul-Samad: Nothing. I just heard that somewhere.

Harry J. Sweeney

Conversation 56: The Qur'an and women's fashions.

Mani: Modi, did you replace your computer yet? Are you back on the Internet?

Modi: No, I have not had the funds. I use the computer at work, but only for business. What is up?

Mani: Radi has been raising cane the last few days about Holland again. His nephew says that the stores there created brand new lines of fashions for Muslim women. He has a page from one of the catalogs and will not let me see it. It is not only Holland that is having new fashions.

Modi: (Laughs) That is no surprise. Last year I saw a story on some obscure channel that mentioned such a phenomenon. When I saw some of the apparel, I thought they were gorgeous. They were using all colors of the rainbow—I could hardly believe my eyes when I actually saw a miniskirt in Campbell plaid. If Radi has something like that, he will go on for days.

Mani: That is what his neighbors are saying. He will not show them the page either.

Modi: That is a shame, Mani. Radi is such a decent sort otherwise; however, those nuts he pals around with outside the mosque are not funny. It is strange how just a few people can drive the rest of us insane by their ignorance.

Mani: But Modi, Radi really is correct. Women are supposed to keep themselves fully covered and unobtrusive. You know about Ayat 24:30.

Modi: Mani, I am surprised at that. I would bet our Most Beloved would be also. In the Qur'an, only verses 24:31 and 33:59 refer to women dressing modestly. Verse 24:30 was addressed to men. Women wore protective headscarves in those days, so that 24:31 simply advises

The Restless Wind and Shifting Sands

them to cover their chests with it if they need to for modesty's sake. Both verses 30 and 31 said guard your private parts, and generally, people do that; it is not necessarily a problem. However, 31 also added a warning for the women not to stamp their feet to make their "adornment" jingle. I guess some men are turned on by the sound of gold or silver. There is nothing in the Qur'an about hijabs or *niqabs*. I believe, old chap, that such cover-ups are traditions from our Bedouin days.

Mani: I know I read that verse repeatedly, but I never got that idea from it. Whenever you recite it, I do not get the idea that women are supposed to wear that ugly headgear.

Modi: The most radical of translations of verse 33:59 only tells females that they should adjust part of their outer garments so that they can be recognized as women and not be abused. It also reminds everyone that Allah is always forgiving and merciful. Now, what does that tell you?

Mani: I have not heard anything in your recitation that talked about abayas, chadors, hijabs, or black-only.

Modi: Mani, you said it all. Women have been cheated for years. They were forced into ultra-conservative vanity rules that did not exist, except in the minds of some folks that could only think in black-and-white. They were cheated out of the fun of walking by a group of men and seeing their appreciative stares. Gone are the days when some Nomad sheik would come galloping into a village to scoop up a young woman he had admired from afar.

Mani: Modi, I feel sad at the thought that many women were severely punished and even killed because they were breaking rules that did not exist.

Modi: That by itself is a good reason for our looking at the verses again and making a more realistic determination of what Allah was saying to us. The fact that He reminded us that He is always forgiving and merciful should tell us that He knows we are human and like to show off on occasion.

Harry J. Sweeney

Mani: I certainly wish I could get hold of that catalog page from our pal Radi.

Modi: I will try to get my newspaper office to consider an article about the new fashions. Come to think of it, if they agree to print an article like that, complete with photographs, it might brighten this place up a little.

Mani: Al-Qaida will go nuts if women all of a sudden began to dress as they do in parts of Lebanon.

Modi: To hell with al-Qaida! They were never our friends. They are only prudes who think they know the Words of Allah, but they do not. They only know the words that others made up, spinning the meanings as they went along with some outrageous agenda.

Radi: I heard that. Who do you think you are, insulting our friends and heroes like that?

Modi: Hello, Radi. I thought you were still running around your neighborhood, poking holes in the air.

Radi: That was very funny. One of these nights, my friends and I will pay you a visit. You have been insulting Allah, Muhammad, the Qur'an, and the hadiths.

Modi: Don't forget the Dalai Lama. I must have insulted him somehow, since I seem to have insulted everyone else.

Radi: I have told you time and time again I was not going to put up with your air of moderation. The Qur'an is sacred just as it is and nobody better ever change one letter of it. It is Allah's gift to us.

Modi: You do not even know the Qur'an, Radi. I have heard you recite it two or three times. It is obvious you have no idea what you are saying.

The Restless Wind and Shifting Sands

Radi: (Reveals his knife.) I will have your head for that.

Mani: Modi, why don't you apologize or something?

Modi: I should apologize to Radi? Why should I? People like Radi are the source of many of our troubles. He thinks he knows everything and he knows nothing. He is too busy defending nonsense instead of taking the time to really read and discuss the things he should know.

Mani: But Radi studied the Qur'an just as you did, Modi.

Modi: Not quite. There is a difference between studying to know the way Allah wanted things and researching to find little tidbits, which when taken out of context can be used as a weapon against our people. Why is he so dead set against the new colorful dresses, chic jackets, and great looking shoes? Because he is an ignorant prude who sees evil everywhere he looks. Radi, it is time for you to grow up. I am sure your fiancée will look great in some of those new dresses.

Radi: What?

Modi: You saw the photos from the catalog. That one dress, the black one with the gold trim and the style of the Cossack; can't you just see Zaina with that dress and the red jacket and the gold buttons? The dress came just above the knee and the black leather boots really set the whole package off. Try to visualize Zaina in that outfit.

Mani: Oh, yes, Radi. I bet Zaina would be a knockout in that outfit. (Radi, still holding his knife, is in deep thought).

Modi: Can't you just see her with just a little Egyptian eyeliner and just a hint of lip rouge? Why, she would be the most beautiful vision in all of Baghdad. (Radi continues to stare into space).

Mani: (Cautiously backs up, away from Radi) Yes, yes. That black dress and red jacket would set off her dark eyes. What a wonderful vision she

Harry J. Sweeney

would be, arm and arm with you. (He hurriedly walks away, unnoticed by Radi).

Modi: (Walks quietly away while he speaks) I just cannot think of a lovelier vision than Zaina with large, golden earrings set off by her jet-black hair. Oh, what a picture she makes.

Radi: Hey, do you guys think I should buy…where are you? (Modi and Mani are nowhere in sight. Passers-by wonder to whom he is speaking. He shakes his fist): I am going to get you sons of snakes! Hey, why are you looking at me like that? I am not crazy!

The Restless Wind and Shifting Sands

Conversation 57: "Is not your wife your tilth (tilled land)?"

Mani: Modi, I see Radi coming this way. He looks very serious. Could he be mad about our leaving him in the middle of the street, talking to himself?

Modi: Well, these long beards have long memories also. They never forget anything—even if they did not know it in the first place. If one of the pseudo-intellectual imams told them a story, no matter how bizarre it was, they would remember it as if it happened.

Mani: That does not seem very bright.

Modi: It is their way of knowing their religion; it is blind faith. Radi, Allah bless him, makes lots of leaps of faith. The seventh century is as recent to him as last week's film—and just as fictional.

Radi: My fiancée wants to get married soon. She says she is getting tired of waiting.

Modi: Why you old rascal. Have you two been…ah…naughty?

Radi: I resent that, Modi. Be serious. I am in a tight spot here.

Mani: What could be happening to put you in a tight spot?

Radi: Well, we had a discussion about marriage. When I mentioned that my wife must be mine from the top of her head to the bottoms of her feet, she laughed at me. I told her it was from the Qur'an, and that made her laugh more.

Modi: It was a decision by Sheik Abd al-Wakil Durud, Radi; however, it is mentioned in the law.[53] You could tell her that—and then duck!

Radi: I also told her that she is obliged to drop everything and let me

---

53   Reliance of the Traveller, m5.4, page 526.

263

Harry J. Sweeney

enjoy her anytime I want. Is not your wife your tilth? And can't you sow your tilth anytime you want?

Modi: (Modi and Mani both laugh) In theory Radi, you are right. It is in the Qur'an[54]. But if you read the law[55], there are a few conditions you must observe. I am afraid that one of them is: "Not tonight, I have a headache". Look in m5.1 (c) of the law.

(Mani is on the ground, laughing)

Radi: Why is Mani laughing so hard?

Modi: Because we have all been there, Radi, Now it is your turn.

Radi: I don't think it is funny; I am trying to understand why Zaina threw me out and told me not to come back until I knew my place.

(Modi and Mani begin laughing all over again)

Modi: Radi, your place is definitely with Zaina. She is some woman! You must stop believing what your old-beard friends have been telling you. They do not know how things work—only how they want them to work. If you can borrow a copy of the law, you will find that Zaina has just as much right to you as you have to her.[56]

Mani: Yes, Radi. You have an obligation to please her as often as it takes for her not to want to stray.

Radi: What? What kind of nonsense is that?

Modi: Mani is right. It is in the law. If Zaina asks and you decline without sufficient reason, you are breaking the law.

Mani: Yes. And you like to go after people who break the law.

---

54   Qur'an 2:23
55   Reliance of the Traveller, m5.1, page 524
56   Reliance of the Traveller, m5.2, page 526

The Restless Wind and Shifting Sands

Modi: And who will be coming after you?

Mani: Will Zaina ever let him out to play?

Radi: Maybe I should not marry.

Modi: There will come a time, Radi, that you will regret that so badly you will hate yourself. Remember, no matter where you look in our scriptures, men are strongly urged to marry.

Mani: I can assure you, Radi, that marrying was the best thing I ever did. My wife and I do not agree on everything, but we are very happy with each other.

Modi: You are not happy the way you are, Radi. I can see that every day. You are looking for refuge among those long-beards you call friends. They are already married, so they can go home to their wives and enjoy their children. You cannot.

Radi: How do you know I am not happy; you cannot read my mind.

Modi: We can hear it in your voice and see the emptiness in your eyes.

Radi: Baa. You do not know what you are saying.

Mani: Just think, you will be side-by-side with beautiful Zaina.

Radi: I can't argue with that.

Modi: I remember that Zaina was a darn good cook, too. Many people would be coming to your nightly spread during Ramadan.

Mani: Yeah, Modi. I guess Radi will become famous for his Ramadan meals.

Radi: That would be nice.

Harry J. Sweeney

Mani: Modi, if he and Zaina want lots of kids, the kids will have to support them in their old age.

Radi: What? Say that again.

Modi: Mani is right. The more kids you and Zaina have, the more people will be supporting you in your old age.

Radi: Oh! Hmm. You say they must do that?

Modi: Radi, it is definitely in the law[57]. If they did not support you, they would be in moral, ethical, and legal trouble.

Radi: Oh my. They would have to support me. How soon could I start having kids?

Mani and Modi look at each other and laugh

Modi: It takes nine months from the date you start. And you can start the night you get married.

Radi: If I get married today, it means I can start tonight?

Modi: Yes. But you would have to hurry; Zaina might change her mind.

Radi: She can do that?

Mani: When was the last time you talked to her?

Radi: About an hour ago.

Modi: Oops. You had better show us your heels; if you do not pop the question quickly, you may not be able to start on those kids tonight. (Radi starts running down the street) See ya, Radi.

---

57   Ibid., m12.1, et al., pages 547-549

The Restless Wind and Shifting Sands

Mani: Poor Zaina. Wait until she gets hold of him.

Modi: Oh yeah? Wait until she gets hold of us.

Harry J. Sweeney

Conversation 58: Young Muhammad

Radi: Modi, why do some of our detractors continue to call our Most Beloved a camel driver?

Modi: Probably because he was a camel driver, Radi.

Radi: Why you blasphemous infidel, where's my knife? I will cut you in two for your insults.

Mani: Radi, don't be so belligerent. Modi is right.

Radi: What? You too? Blood will be running this morning.

Modi: Radi, you know that Muhammad's father, Abdullah died before Muhammad was born. When he was five, his mother died. His grandfather raised him for a while and then he died. His uncle, Abu Talib, took on the task of raising him. Abu Talib was a prosperous trader. If the boy Muhammad stayed with him, he would pull his weight as everyone else did.

Mani: Abu Talib took him on trade excursions to Syria and other places to teach him the business. He started from the ground up, as camel-driver. That is where his detractors got the idea.

Modi: But Radi, our Most Beloved was good at it and learned quite a lot. He was able to make trips alone and deal with the merchants everywhere to bring profits home to his uncle.

Radi: So, he was a lowly camel-driver?

Modi: What is lowly about it? That is what he learned to do and he did it and did it well. When you are good at what you do, there is nothing lowly about it.

Mani: Modi is right. It is too bad that so many of us today have no sense of self-actualization, no will to be good at something. It is a

268

The Restless Wind and Shifting Sands

shame. My grandfather used to make trade baskets to hold the supplies on the camels. Everyone bought from him because he made baskets better than anyone else did and they lasted longer.

Modi: I remember him, a nice man. His baskets indeed were superior. But he could not keep up with demand.

Mani: He did not want to hire others because he saw their work. They did not have the patience that he had. He died a poor man, but local caravan people still use his baskets. The used ones cost more than the newer ones sold by others.

Radi: What has that got to do with our Most Beloved?

Modi: Radi, our Most Beloved became so well known for his competence and his honesty that the rich widow Khadija employed him to do her trading.

Mani: As time went on, she had to promote him because he was making her wealthier. Finally, she brought up the idea of marriage. Although she was older than he, she became everything to him. He also became wealthy and could have had other wives, but he never took a second wife as long as Khadija was alive.

Modi: Yes, Radi, the story of our Most Beloved and his Khadija was quite a love story. You simply must read about his life. There are many books on that subject[58]. Even André Servier's *La Psychologie du Musulman*[59] provides some interesting information, even though the author was not a fan of Islam.

Mani: I read Monsieur Servier's version and found it to be anti-Islam.

---

58   Recommended are "Mohammed and the Unbelievers, Center for the Study of Political Islam —based on the Sirat of Ishaq, and Muhammedanism by (Sir) H.A.R. Gibb.

59   English translation of the book has its own website and free downloads. http://musulmanbook.blogspot.com/2005/11/read-this-first-about-book-islam-and.html

Harry J. Sweeney

Modi: Monsieur Servier drew correctly from the early Western view of Islam. The people of the West do not think as we do in the East; what we consider normal, they consider outrageous. Look at this current business about the British teacher in the Sudan.

Mani: You mean the business about the teddy bear? What is the big deal? She was only sentenced to forty lashes. It could have been more,

Modi: See? You say it is no big deal, but to the West it is a very big deal to whip a woman, especially if she is innocent.

Radi: What does innocence have to do with anything? If she could not produce a sufficient number of witnesses; she is guilty.

Modi: If you had a son and wanted to honor our Most Beloved, what name would you give him?

Radi: That is a stupid question. I would name him Muhammad. That would be in honor of our wonderful Prophet.

Modi: Following that logic, if a child had a favorite teddy bear and wanted to honor our Most Beloved, what name would he choose?

Radi: I see your point. It is honoring the Prophet, not equating him with an animal or a stuffed toy.

Modi: Now you got it. But it goes farther than that. Now listen closely to this nuance. In the classroom was a very popular boy by the name of Muhammad. The kiddies named the teddy bear after that boy.

Radi: Oh! (He makes a strange face.) Allah forbid, everybody was wrong!

Modi: Not quite. Everyone but the kiddies and teacher were wrong. The teacher deserved accolades for being positive and allowing the kiddies to cross cultures and religions to come to a decision. If she

The Restless Wind and Shifting Sands

decides to quit and return to the United Kingdom, we are the losers. We must draw a line between the paranoia of the old beards, along with the pettifogging busybodies who are on the alert for any possibility of evil intent, and the rest of the people who have more to do than look for dirt on the bottom of your shoes.

Radi: Why are you looking at me so intently? I am not an old beard.

Mani: Not yet, Radi. However, those nasties that you run around with will surely turn you into one.

Modi: Please, Radi. If I have to beg an old friend, I beg you to read about your religion. The old beards do not know and cannot teach you anything but hate. Hatred and death, that pair of ghouls do not become our religion. With just another look at what is written, we will find the warmth of the sun and the smile of a happy child.

Mani: Yes, Radi. I had a cousin who was a happy, bubbling toddler who was into everything and loved life while his mother was still in charge of him. When his father took over, he became morose and ill tempered. He hated people he did not even know. At last, life itself meant so little to him; he just killed himself without seeking martyrdom. That father of his cursed him for depriving him of all that martyr money.

Radi: The father was right cursing him. He could have received a great deal of money for that.

Modi: Radi, what are we going to do with you. We tell you stories and you get the wrong message.

Mani: Maybe you have to tell him what the message is before you tell the story.

Modi: I don't think Radi is that dumb!

Radi: I did like the one you told about the three bears.

Harry J. Sweeney

Modi: You did?

Radi: Yeah. That golden haired infidel sure got to eat a lot of food.

The Restless Wind and Shifting Sands

Conversation 59: Ahmadiyya Movement

Mani: Modi, I have an eerie feeling something is not right.

Modi: I know just how you feel. It took me a few weeks to adapt.

Mani: Adapt to what?

Modi: For example, when I did my ablutions early this morning, I had running water. I did not have to fill a pot yesterday and keep it for later ablutions. I did not spill water all over me because of a bomb blast down the street. All of my windowpanes are still there from last week.

Mani: I see. As we look up the street, many of the holes have been filled in and we do not have to avoid some of the holes in the rain.

Modi: Yes, you are right about that. I will never forget Radi stepping in a puddle and almost disappearing from sight. He would have drowned if we did not know he was with us. Of course, he was shocked and thrashing around as if he were in the ocean.

Mani: He is a piece of work. Not to change the subject, but I keep hearing that the new Iranian explosive devices are devastating. However, I have not heard any since that first one. What is going on?

Modi: You mean what is not going on? One thing, between us and the Americans, AQ had their behinds handed to them. They not only have to lick their wounds and reorganize, they need resuscitation.

Mani: I heard that al-Qaida was coming back.

Modi: Right, they were trying to, but a few of the Sheikhs were tired of dealing with them. They told the Americans that they would turn them over on one condition–they wanted them first. The Americans only said that if they found a certain American congressman with them, the U.S. Marines want to talk with him–as soon as possible.

273

Harry J. Sweeney

Radi: I hear that al-Qaida is coming back in force.

Modi: Well, you can sit up and wait for them tonight. Take a pillow and some water for early ablutions.

Mani: Radi, you may as well stay home.

Radi: Things are getting a little monotonous. Even my friends find nothing to do anymore. They don't bother to patrol the streets looking for sinners.

Modi: Things are changing. People are catching on to the new Qur'anic movement and seem to like it. It works for them.

Radi: What? A new movement? Reformers?

Modi: Actually not. They are studying the Qur'an and find it expedient to have a working group stay with it, re-writing some of the rules as they go along. They say they are not reforming the religion, just reviving it, something akin to what the Americans do every so often.

Radi: Revive the religion? I am not sure I like that. There is only one way to deal with a sinner. You cut off his head.

Modi: Cutting off someone's head means that a wife loses and husband, kids lose a father, and the Muslim community loses the *zakat* payments. Radi, one of the first rules of the movement is cutting out the violence. Their tolerance clause, in fact, accepts other religions and faiths and recognizes the freedom of people to choose the faith they want. What is wrong with the theme: "Love everyone, hate no one"?

Radi: Oh, Allah, what have they done?

Mani: They have erased the idea of apostasy, that's what they have done. Radi, it is a good thing to do. Too many people were being killed for nothing. You remember the Egyptian scholar who was chased down

The Restless Wind and Shifting Sands

the street with his father shooting at him—all because he changed his religion?

Modi: Yes Radi, now try to think. People got sick of al-Qaida, women are tossing their chadors for the new look in abayas that do not hide the female form. In some places, Lebanon for one, you can now buy miniskirts and sheer blouses. I believe that people simply became tired and offended by the stonings and the hangings for no reason. There is a new wind in Iraq and elsewhere that very well may be the death knell for barbarism and radicalism.

Mani: No! People like Radi we will have with us always. If Lebanon falls to the *Hizbullah*, it will be back to the *chador* and *hijab*.

Modi: Perhaps. Under this new movement, if it catches on in other places as well, it will make Islam an even greater religion than it was.

Radi: Oh yeah? Does it have a name?

Modi: It certainly has a name, The Lahore Ahmadiyya movement.[60]

Radi: We will kill all of those people in the movement. We will again show everyone that there is only one Islam and it will be controlled by the Salafists and the Wahhabis, the only pure ones faithful to the Qur'an as it is written.

Mani: Just like that?

Radi: Of course just like that! We will not accept for one second any idea or thought that even appears to conflict with exactly how the Qur'an was written centuries ago.

Modi: You for one have no idea how the Qur'an was originally written. Have you ever tried to write Arabic on a banana leaf? Have you ever seen written Arabic in its original form? Arabic writing was so inexact;

---

60   http://www.kalima.ae/eng/titles/to-be-translated.php

Harry J. Sweeney

memory was accepted as the most accurate record. Caliphs Abu Bakr and Uthman collected individual verses from the memory of people who had been through terrible battles with the Meccans and others for years. Some, such as Abu Bakr, had to leave Mecca for Ethiopia in fear of their lives, then return years later to relocate to Medina for many more years. Some then returned to Mecca much later to be reunited with their families at last. Just how much would half of these people remember after all of that time, upheaval, and fighting? Something may have been lost—and what if the lost information was important?

Radi: Allah made certain that all of the verses were found and translated correctly. It is one of the miracles of the Qur'an.

Modi: Miracles? Radi, we can't do that with our computers. Couldn't somebody with an agenda change a word or even a sentence to give himself an edge or get himself out of hot water? Look! I have never really understood the 72-virgins idea; it is beyond me. Why not just white grapes? How can one understand you cannot touch a woman not your wife (and you can only have four of those), then you commit suicide (also forbidden) and finally you expect Allah to reward you with 72 virgins you are not allowed to touch? I don't understand.

Radi: You forget, Allah can do anything he wants. What about those women your right hand possesses? You do not know everything, Modi. Nobody said you must understand everything.

Modi: Right, Radi. How many times have you known Him to do something bizarre—out of the ordinary? Now sit back in comfort and watch the Iraqi Government issue work itself out. Perhaps we will see just who it is Allah wants to win. Perhaps you are wondering why He just does not spread His hands out and say He too is tired of all this mess in the Middle East and say "Let there be an end to this nonsense." When will you ever learn that God does not take a hand in the daily affairs of men, that He lets them work things out themselves?

Radi: Modi, you were told when you were a child that Allah works in His own time and in His own way.

The Restless Wind and Shifting Sands

Modi: Yes, Radi, I remember that. And I also remember that some people sit around for decades just waiting for something to happen, a Messiah or a Mahdi to finally come along and chase away all of the bad guys. However, we do not have the luxury of waiting that long for a savior anymore.

Radi: I sense you are going to blaspheme again. Why is time so critical suddenly?

Mani: Well, we have an asteroid bearing down on us that can blow us to smithereens. Don't you read the papers?

Radi: Why doesn't somebody tell me these things?

Mani: The miracle is that your parents kept you, Radi.

Radi: What?! (Gives chase—toward the coffee shop)

Harry J. Sweeney

Conversation 60: Prayer Times

Mani and Modi are helping local militia in al-Habbariyah, Karbala.

Mani: It is getting a little boring here, tonight. Nothing is going on. It must be after midnight. Your cousins are doing pretty well here; they have lots of business. Modi.

Modi: This area does get a little boring at night. Once we did have a really hot time here, though. Nobody will ever forget it.

Mani: Oh? When was that?

Modi: It was in the year 680. The Caliph attacked a caravan of relatives of the Prophet; Hussein ibn Ali was murdered.

Mani: Modi, you rascal. You keep doing that to me. That happened more than 1,300 years ago.

Modi: But to the Shiites, that event is more like two weeks ago.

Mani: Yeah. I don't think they ever forget. I am sleepy already. What time is *Fajr*?

Modi: Early Morning Prayer will be 5:31 AM. The newspaper said *Zuhr* or Early Afternoon Prayer will be 12:02 PM, but I do not think that is right. I would wait until at least 12:05. As you know, we call *Zawaal* Noontime, but it actually occurs right after noon and prayers are prohibited at noon exactly. The sun does not enter *Zawaal* for a minute-and-a-half and another 60 seconds is added for one other calculation you do not want to know about.

Mani: What are you talking about? I have not understood anything you said.

Modi: In Early Afternoon Prayer calculation, anyone doing it must always add a minimum of 2.5 minutes after 12:00 to begin the prayer.

The Restless Wind and Shifting Sands

That is the technical minimum. Many scholars prefer adding another 2.5 minutes to be correct. Therefore, I always say 12:05 should be the earliest for the *Zuhr*.

Mani: I will take your word for that, although sometimes I think you are bonkers. Come to think of it, the newspaper said *Zuhr* was 12:02 yesterday also. I remember that because I almost had no time to do anything between *Zuhr* and *'Asr* which was 2:47 PM.

Modi: You had 2 hours and 43 minutes before Late Afternoon Prayer; that was time enough for the cinema.

Mani: Just about. Remember you have to add ablutions into the calculations before each prayer. And if you have to do a full body wash, that is even more time. You cannot put anything off or the prayer will not count; you have to make it up.

Modi: Nobody said it was easy to be a believer. Remember, though, you do not need to do ablutions unless they are needed. Look at all the good credit you are piling up for judgment day.

Mani: Modi, look over there with your binoculars. It looks as if some of our guys are up and running.

Modi: I do not know where they are running yet. Oh, that is it! It looks as if some fighters were trying to infiltrate and our guys spotted them. (Explosions!) There go our mortars. I also see a group of guys farther out. They will flank the infiltrators.

Mani: Well, a little excitement, anyway. (Looks around.) Do you see anyone around here?

Modi: Not really. We planned it so that the farther out from the center, the closer together the pickets were established. If they tried to infiltrate, we wanted them to try on our terms, not theirs.

Mani: Why are they trying to infiltrate?

Harry J. Sweeney

Modi: They need a victory so badly, even getting past our pickets to blow up a truck or tool shed will be celebrated like a Philadelphia touchdown.

Mani: What's a Phila-something touchdown?

Modi: A flashy score near the end of a game they can't win. Never mind, it is not important.

Mani: Getting back to the prayer times. Why can't we just have standard prayer times every day instead of having to look them up all the time?

Modi: For any important matters, Mani, we must use sacred time to be accurate. Our Most Beloved had a timekeeper in Medina to monitor this sacred time for the umma (community). It is evident that he wanted to maintain accurate times for prayer, Ramadan, Hajj, etc., according the Allah's schedule, the lunar calendar. Since lunar times are not consistent with our standard times, we must tweak our schedules every day to be accurate.

Mani: I guess we will always have to do that tweaking.

Modi: Yes. Our Most Beloved thought it important that we do it this way. It is nice to know that we always run on accurate time.

Mani: I certainly would like to have more than a couple of hours between prayers in the afternoon.

Modi: That is the reason for breaking up the day like that, Mani. It is to keep people like you out of trouble.

Mani: Does any other organization control anyone's time that closely.

Modi: One that I can think of, US Marine Basic Training.

Mani: You are impossible.

The Restless Wind and Shifting Sands

Modi: Right now, I would settle for impassible.

Mani: Hey, Modi, look at that (points to the moon).

Modi: (looks to where Mani is pointing). What are you pointing at?

Mani: The moon is telling us it is time for coffee.

Friendly fighter: Coffee anyone? I brought some.

Modi: You saw this guy coming, Mani. (They both laugh.)

Mani: I am going to look up Prayer in the law, now that you convinced me that there is a lot to know.

Modi: That is a good idea. I have to warn you, you will have to look through 119 pages, not including funeral prayers.

Mani: Well, Modi, if you make a mistake in some places, the least you will undergo is embarrassment. Depending upon where you are praying, making mistakes can be very unpleasant.

Modi: Yes, in some places form is more importance than substance. You could be in serious trouble just for adding a special prayer to our Most Beloved, to Hussein ibn Ali, or to anyone else you respect that has passed on.

Mani: Modi, you have convinced me. I am going to buy one of those Prayer Time Watches. I do not want to hear they are inaccurate! Okay, I see that smirk. I will stay with the newspapers. Go to sleep. I will wake you when the SUN comes up.

CHAPTER 7

Conversation 61: Turkey and American Democrats

Mani: Hi, Modi. Are you ready for a coffee break?

Modi: You bet. The usual place?

Mani: That is fine with me. What is going on with the Americans and Turkey? I thought they were fast friends.

Modi: They were, since World War I. It seems that the Turks were part of the Central Powers, and when Germany went berserk with their submarines, the U. S. president, Woodrow Wilson, leader of the Democrats, was forced to declare war on the Central Powers—except for Turkey.

Radi: Good morning. You were saying, Modi?

Modi: The Democrats, as usual, were trying to stay out of the war, even though their bosom buddies, Europe, wanted them in to help. Remember now how the one party was condemning President Bush for acting without Europe? They forget that the president invited Europe to jump in. When Democrat Wilson declared against the Central Powers without Turkey, Europe went nuts. They had their hands full and needed help with Turkey.

Radi: Aha! The Americans were scared out of their wits by Turkey, a Muslim power.

Modi: Actually, you are partially right, Radi. One party was afraid of any country in the Middle East. Even when Turkey committed genocide against the Armenians, the Yanks were up and screaming for the Wilson administration to declare war, but they refused—and they had people on the spot providing reports of the atrocities in progress against men,

The Restless Wind and Shifting Sands

women, and children. Whole villages were slaughtered, and the United States was seen by the world as cowardly because Wilson continued to say no, just as they do now with respect to Darfur. But the United Nations refuses to take a hand in Darfur.

Radi: Ha! It is right, though, that the Arab-speaking Janjaweed make short work of the Christians there. I hope they kill them all. They had their chances to convert to Islam! Now they will all burn in hell forever. Behead them all!

Mani: As the King of Spain said to Hugo Chávez, Radi, "Shut up!"

Modi: Besides being generally afraid of the Middle East, Wilson also relied on what his State Department was telling him. They were afraid that all the time and work they spent in Turkey and the Middle East would go to waste if the U.S. declared war on Turkey. And of all people from whom to take advice, the Democrats listened to the American missionaries on the scene. They failed to convert Muslims in the Middle East, but at least the Christians succeeded in building and running schools.

Mani: It seemed as if the Democrats and the president were listening only to the people who told them what they wanted to hear.

Modi: You could say that. They are still doing it. The American people wanted war with Turkey at the time and so did the newspapers and Theodore Roosevelt, the former president. The Democrats simply ignored the people. Just as Iran has never forgiven the American administration for the Muhammad Mossadegh affair, many European states have not forgiven them for not declaring war on Turkey.

Mani: Did America take part in the peace talks at Versailles?

Modi: Yes and no. Nobody listened to Wilson, and they told him what he could do with his Fourteen Points. Because he did not declare war on Turkey, he could not prevent the Europeans from cutting up the Muslim nations into the mosaic the Europeans wanted. And he could

Harry J. Sweeney

not prevent the Europeans from laying the economic and political groundwork that gave rise to Hitler.

Mani: I now understand the phrase, "a coward dies a thousand deaths, and a hero dies but once." America is dying the death of a thousand cuts now because of one political party's refusal to do something heroic. Instead, they did not take a stand to prevent a massacre of the Armenians and in so obviously leaving the Ottoman Empire out of their declaration of war against the Central Powers. These failures caused the horrible deaths of more than a million Armenians; it caused crises in the Middle East thereafter, and indirectly resulted in the rise of Nazism.

Modi: You are right. Admiral Lord Nelson once said that "England expects every man to do his duty." It is a simple statement but very direct and very effective. It would be a good rule for the world for every person to do what he is supposed to do, the way he is supposed to do it. We cannot refuse to do something simply because we are having a bad day or because it is difficult or because no one else seems to care. You know, the Democrats tried to bring the original Armenian massacres up again in congress. Those unwary folks must not know it was a trap! They did not know that once the story was out, the entire world would know what fools they were back then.

Mani: Modi, as hard as life always was for our Most Beloved, he always did what Allah had in mind for him to do. Nowhere in the Qur'an do I read that Allah admonished him for not doing what he was supposed to do.

Modi: Remember, He did admonish him for taking the easy way out in order to save some lives and make things easier for his people.[61] Our Most Beloved learned that one has to do the right thing no matter who it hurts and how much one has to lose.

------

61   Then Gabriel came to the apostle and said, "What have you done, Muhammad? You have read to these people something I did not bring you from God and you have said what He did not say to you." (Ibn Ishaq, p. 166).

The Restless Wind and Shifting Sands

Radi: How dare you say such things about our Most Beloved? Our Most Beloved was perfect in every way! His is the only life that must be emulated by all of us.

Modi: "There are more things in heaven and earth, Horatio, than are dreamt of in your philosophy." I trust you have heard of Shakespeare's Hamlet?

Radi: Why are you calling me Horatio? What are you talking about?

Mani: You ignorant nut!

Modi: Radi, if you would cooperate, we would all go to a respected imam and be his student for a week to learn our religion the way it should be learned.

Radi: Ha! You want to brainwash me. I have already learned my religion from someone well known and respected for his knowledge.

Mani: You were? Who was that?

Radi: Ali ibn Nadr al-Baghdadi taught me.

Modi: You must be kidding, Radi. He was a thief and murderer. He was hanged five years ago by his village. He was also a spy for Saddam.

Radi: He was a reformed thief.

Modi: Yeah, reformed after they cut off a hand and foot!

Radi: But he knew his religion well.

Modi: He hussled food and drinks. He would tell anybody anything they wanted to hear, as long as they paid. Oh, Radi, you really do need to see a real imam. You paid that one-hand, one-foot, lying creep to make you into a monster?

Harry J. Sweeney

Mani: Yes, Radi. I think you should join us in our quest for advanced knowledge.

Radi: On one condition.

Radi, Modi, and Mani (together): YOU PAY!

The Restless Wind and Shifting Sands

Conversation 62: Female Genital Mutilation

Mani: Modi, I have an important question for you. My cousin has a little daughter, and it is their tribe's tradition to seek a betrothal before age twelve. The last three attempts were affirmative; however, in each case they would not agree unless the girl was circumcised. They said she was not pure for marriage until circumcised.

Modi: I take it from what you have said that the girl was not circumcised.

Mani: Right. Her tribe does not do that.

Modi: But if her tribe does not do that, is she marrying outside the tribe? Is she marrying a non-relative?

Mani: Yes. The tribe has been bereft of men since so many had been killed, joined the insurgents, or emigrated to Europe. There are some families with sons in Europe that have asked for brides, but there is no interest in one so young because of European marriage laws.

Modi: I have news for you and for them, Mani. Those marriage laws are almost universal now. Very few countries today allow marriages for girls under 18.

Radi: We should wipe those infidels out and replace all their laws with the sharia. I know how to deal with them.

Modi: Good morning to you too, Radi. Glad to see you are alive and chipper. Perhaps chipper is not the right word. Mani, what you are talking about is called female genital mutilation (FGM). There are three different forms of FGM, not any of them of any benefit to anyone, least of all the person undergoing the procedure.

Radi: You must mean female circumcision, Modi. It is commanded by the Qur'an, and you MUST do it to all females.

Harry J. Sweeney

Modi: See what we are up against, Mani? Radi, No such command is in the Qur'an, and it is not approved in any way by our religion. I happen to have an idea where the notion came from; however, you will not find it in the Qur'an.

Radi: Ha! Our Most Beloved said to a midwife not to cut too deep because it will be better for the husband. I remember it from the Qur'an.

Modi: You have it wrong again. First, it was not from the Qur'an, but from the hadiths of Dawud, number 5251. Second, as Dawud himself admits, it is a very weak hadith because of authentication, and it cannot be used as a source of law. Besides, even if it were truly authenticated, though it was not prohibited by our Most Beloved, it certainly was not encouraged.

Radi: You must have it wrong. The Qur'an says that circumcising women makes them pure, more loyal to their husbands, better looking, and it calms them down and lets them tend to their duties.

Mani: You are a male chauvinist, you know that? Everything for you and nothing for them. Why don't you ask females what they think? They are the ones who must endure that barbarous procedure.

Radi: Who cares what they think? We have been given the strength and intelligence to rule over women.

Modi: Radi, none of what you say about FGM is true. FGM actually predates Islam and is a practice from the days of chaos and immorality. Many of the early Muslims discovered it during their escape to Ethiopia in the seventh century. Men were afraid then that when they reached old age, since they married younger women and girls, they would not be able to match their wives' sex drives.[62] Well too bad for those "dirty old men." Nevertheless, most Muslims do not practice this so-called rite of passage for females. I certainly would not want any daughter

---

62   http://www.minaret.org/fgm-pamphlet.htm, by Imad-ad-Dean Ahmad, Ph.D.

The Restless Wind and Shifting Sands

of mine to undergo such a monstrous, unnecessary ritual. And if any person suggested I do it, I will punch out his lights.

Mani: Radi, how can any father or mother do such a terrible thing to their little girls?

Radi: Because it is their duty! Their daughters must be pure for marriage.

Mani: How about their sons?

Radi: Yes, the girls must be pure to marry our sons! We do not want our sons to be marrying just anybody. Those fine specimens of humanity are too gullible to choose right. We must choose for them to ensure they are getting the best women from their own families.

Modi: Eventually, Radi, we will all be inbred and running around like jackasses.

Mani: Some of our sons are already doing that. We have a wonderful opportunity in Europe to have our sons choose European wives. That definitely brings in newer blood and will strengthen our bloodlines.

Modi: Not quite, Mani. We allow our sons to marry European women, and most of them convert to Islam. But we do not allow our daughters to marry European men; in fact, we kill them even if they only talk about it.

Radi: European men should not have control over Muslim women. Besides, the man should control the religion, not the wife.

Mani: Male chauvinist! What a dolt.

Modi: The old beards back here said the same thing about jobs. They said that Muslims must not work for non-Muslim masters. Why do those jerks think Muslims went to Europe and America? They wanted freedom and jobs. They did not care about who owned the businesses;

Harry J. Sweeney

of course the Europeans were the bosses—it was Europe! The people who believe these stupid busybodies here had to go on welfare, which gave the people of Europe the wrong impression. I for one am glad the authorities threw a lot of them back.

Mani: I can see that. It is good that some of our people are getting ahead. Even the United Kingdom, I read, is opening up new opportunities for education and business ownership. In addition, Scotland is looking for about 30,000 new workers.

Modi: See, Radi, when they shut down people like you, everybody starts moving ahead. You folks are the bottlenecks.

Radi: Oh, yeah? We are going to slice your neck and put your head in a bottle.

Mani: Careful, Radi, it is Modi's turn to buy lunch today.

Modi: And we have a new restaurant opening near your place.

Radi: You know what? I hear the *adhan*, Bilal is calling.

Mani: We have to hurry a little to complete *wudu* first.

The Restless Wind and Shifting Sands

<u>Conversation 63: Honor Killing</u>

Mani: Modi, did you go down to Basra to see the handover from the British to our own army and police forces?

Modi: No. I feel a little ambivalent about it. In one sense, I am pleased that the British are going, but in another sense, I don't know if our army and police forces are ready for the task without help. Remember, the Iraqi government has a history of imperfection.

Radi: It will now make it very easy for our insurgents to attack your so-called forces and take Basra back for Allah.

Modi: Allah has nothing to do with this, Radi. This matter is strictly a nationalist affair. It is bad enough that we have to muddle through managing that area without you nitwits upsetting everything again.

Radi: Ha! This is now the first step in taking Iraq back! We will remove the heads of all who get in our way. They will spend eternity in the fiery pit, and we will laugh. We will kill everyone not with us!

Mani: Radi, doesn't your country mean anything to you?

Radi: The entire world means something to me. It belongs to Allah and all who are not believers do not belong in it, except as slaves. We will take it back for its rightful owner—Allah. Taking Basra back is the first step.

Modi: You do not have Basra yet. We do not know whether our army and police forces are up to the task of defending it, but we will see. Perhaps the people will help as they did in Anbar.

Radi: Bah! Al-Qaida and others simply left Iraq because we knew the U.S. forces would run away and we could walk right back in and start killing all the officials and the people who supported them. Every finger that touched the purple will be cut off before the head is removed from the shoulders.

Harry J. Sweeney

Modi: You are not telling the truth about al-Qaida, and you know and I know that the American forces do not run. The American politicians are what always worry us.

Radi: It does not matter who is in power there. We have Allah on our side, along with squadrons of angels.

Mani: You just keep on believing that, Radi. (To Modi, quietly) He has a point, Modi. After all, squadrons of angels did help defeat the Meccans.

Modi: Oh, come on, Mani! You can't believe that! The squadrons of angels, Mani, were the exhortations of our Most Beloved and the power of faith. The believers had faith that if they were killed in battle they would go to paradise immediately and their families would be given their share of the booty from the raids or the battles. The Meccans fought well, but they were not foolhardy—they believed they had but one life and were not going to waste it by fighting wildly.

Radi: None of that matters now, even though you are wrong. You will see us take back this entire country for Allah.

Modi: If you take it back, it will not be for Allah; it will be for Iran.

Radi: What? How can you say that? We fight for Allah! No infidels will survive our onslaught!

Modi: You may think you are. Where did you get the weapons? Iran. Where do you get the roadside bombs? Iran. Where do the fighters go to escape the Americans? Iran. When you look at so-called foreign fighters, who are they? Hizbullah. Look around the entire area of Basra, Radi, and tell me whom you see. Iran wants Iraq, and they were the ones bankrolling the antigovernment fighters. Can't you see that?

Radi: None of that means anything! (He is now red faced with anger) We will take back this entire world for Allah! *We* will remember people

The Restless Wind and Shifting Sands

like you who try to stand in Allah's way. You will burn in hell for all eternity!

Modi: You say "we". Do you have a frog in your pocket or something? Radi, you and your kind do not do anything but ruin and destroy. Your kind does not build much at all—and those places you do put up are drab, unimaginative, and crude. With the exception of some oil-rich monarchs, tyrants, and cronies, the people's lives have not improved since the seventh century.

Radi: See how you think? You act as if life is permanent. It is not! In fact, it is best if you can leave this earth as soon as possible.

Modi: You are so wrapped up in killing and death; you have no sense for living and enjoying life. You do not love your fellow man; you hate him and are suspicious of every word, action, and motive. What other type of nation would even consider building separate sidewalks to segregate women from men? Just this morning Fox News reported a Pakistani living in Canada strangled his 16-year-old daughter to death for not wearing her headscarf to school. Her brother set up the killing. What kind of hatred does a man have who can look his young daughter in the eyes and strangle her to death? Radi, that is monstrous! And what brother would hate his sister enough to deliver her into the hands of the killer? Radi, you know that the hijab is not required by the Qur'an.

Radi: See, you do not understand! He proved his love for Allah and His laws, as Abraham had shown his love. Satan caused his daughter to remove her hijab on the way to school. Her father was right to kill her for sinning and causing dishonor to his family! If he had other daughters, he would let them watch their sister being killed so violently; they would now know not to sin. Her brother was heroic in bringing his sister to her rightful death!

Modi: Ninety-nine percent of this world would not agree with you, Radi. Daughters are precious. Sons are precious. Life is precious. I say again, the hijab is not required by the Qur'an. The daughter was killed, strangled for nothing!

Radi: Bah! I kill and kill and die for Allah! *Allahu Akbar*!

Mani: I am not sure that Radi is wrong.

Modi: Not you too, Mani! You had better make up your mind. Remember, Radi says that the people who are not 100 percent with the radicals are against them and deserve to die just like the infidels. I would rather die for something I believed strongly than for something I didn't.

Mani: I for one would never hurt my daughter, but how can I condemn that other father for doing what he believed was right? You say it is not in the Qur'an; how many of our people really know the Qur'an? He did what he believed was right!

Modi: You yourself and anyone who has a family and wants to have a family must determine for themselves what is right and what is wrong, no matter what anyone said 1400 years ago in a different world. Look into the faces of your family when you ask that question. Go outside your home and look up and down the street at your neighbors. Do they deserve to die because of what someone believes someone else meant 1400 years ago when language was not as advanced as it is now?

Mani: Say what you want. I believe in the Qur'an, the hadiths, and the sharia. You know that the Qur'an was given to Muhammad by Allah to present to all mankind. Everyone in this world is now responsible for knowing the Qur'an and for keeping its commandments. Sharia must now be global law everywhere. I feel that I must become more pious. Yes, Modi, perhaps we must all become more pious. Are you ready for lunch, Radi?

The Restless Wind and Shifting Sands

Conversation 64: Honor Killing

Again, we change the pace a little and present another matter that now has come much closer to home—honor killing. We looked at an honor killing in Canada in Conversation 63.

On June 11, 2007, the Associated Press, London reported the conviction of a Kurdish father for strangling his daughter with a bootlace. She found her arranged marriage abusive.

On March 2, 2005, Der Spiegel International Online reported the honor killing by their families of six Muslim women living in Berlin over a four-month period. They were living like Germans.

Reports submitted to the United Nations Commission on Human Rights show that honor killings have occurred in Bangladesh, Great Britain, Brazil, Ecuador, Egypt, India, Israel, Italy, Jordan, Pakistan, Morocco, Sweden, Turkey, and Uganda. In countries not submitting reports to the UN, the practice was condoned under the rule of the fundamentalist Taliban government in Afghanistan and has been reported in Iraq and Iran." (*National Geographic News*, 2/12/2002)

It seems that every year women are killed by their families for actions on their part that would not be surprising or even noted in the West. If anything, many of the actions would be subjects of love stories in books or films. This is the West, however, and we have already "been there and done that," learned from it, and left it all behind us. We have learned that life is precious, so precious that it requires a Titanic-sized reason to take it.

In the West, we recognize that each individual is different, even among our own children. Parents have discovered that planning for their children does not always work; some of them march to a different drummer. How many times has a son or daughter whose enviable admission to a medical school was assured, announced at the last minute that he or she was more interested in law enforcement or fire safety? How many graduating attorneys who were already nominated

Harry J. Sweeney

for a vice presidency of dad's firm declined that invitation in order to work as a civil rights advocate or public defender?

While in the West the individual is responsible only for himself and his own actions, the East sees things quite differently. In the East, the family gives birth to the individual and thus becomes responsible for that individual from birth to death. In the West, if a person finds his daughter having trysts with the boy next door, either the parents force the two to marry or try to keep them apart--case closed. In post-1960 America, some parents seem to have no obligation to do anything about it except keep them supplied with condoms and hope they make use of them. In the East, however, the family's honor is at stake and cannot be restored without proper punishment applied. Even if a family might otherwise be lenient for some reason, the daughter is no longer considered marriageable and would be an economic drain on family resources. The usual solution is death by stoning. There is now another alternative. In some places the daughter can restore her honor and her family's honor by volunteering as a homicide bomber. One could be excused for entertaining the thought that such a ruling appears to be more tactical than compassionate.

No matter what the parents or husbands say about the murders, we cannot buy their excuse that it is a matter of religion. The tradition of killing women in the Middle East was in existence long before Islam came along. In Arab families, innocent female babies were slaughtered simply because of the *possibility* that someday they *might* bring dishonor to the family. Some years ago in Pakistan a father had his older daughter stoned to death for running away with her boyfriend. The father, whose honor was now restored with that daughter's death, then stabbed his younger daughter to death because he did not want her to ever stain his honor as her sister did.

Whenever the family or village takes such action against a female, sometimes there is no record of the event. The family can also erase the name from family records. The infant, girl, or woman killed then seems never to have existed. If authorities do discover the killing, bribes often can solve the problem. When bribes do not solve the problem, as in some countries, the father or brother, whoever was responsible, may serve only six months in jail. Even though Islam expresses the importance and the reverence of its women, too many men still hold the notion of ownership of their women, and still do not hesitate to simply dispose of them whenever a problem occurs.

The late Dr. Raphael Patai, cultural anthropologist, in his book *The Arab Mind*, notes that, "While honor in its non-sexual, general connotation is termed '*sharaf*', the specific kind of honor that is connected with women and depends on their proper conduct is called '*ird*'. *Sharaf* is something flexible: depending on a man's behavior, way of talking and acting, his *sharaf* can be acquired, augmented, diminished, lost, regained, and so on. In contrast, *ird* is a rigid concept: every woman has her ascribed *ird*; she is born with it and grows up with it; she cannot augment it because it is something absolute; but it is her duty to preserve it. A sexual offense on her part, however slight, causes her <u>ird</u> to be lost, and it can never be regained." Even if a woman is attacked and raped, in many circles her *ird* has been lost and can never be regained. The woman would be killed.

"A man can diminish or lose his *sharaf* by showing a lack of bravery or courage, or by lack of hospitality or generosity." However, he himself would be dishonored, but his dishonor would not be shared by others of the family. A woman's loss of *ird*, however, would destroy the *sharaf* of all of the men in her family. One can see that the core of *sharaf* is the protection of the *ird* of one's female family members. That protection is the obligation of her own family, not her husband. If a woman cheats on her husband, for example, it is the duty of her own family to put her to death because their honor was besmirched, not the husband's. Under the school of thought of the Bedouin, allowing the husband to put their daughter (his wife) to death would give too much power to an outsider, weakening the family's control of its members.

Remember, the family of the Bedouin is a team. When the tribe is on the move, the several families make up a much bigger team. When each

Harry J. Sweeney

cooperates, the tribe has its honor intact. One female who is out of line affects the team; and a team without honor affects the tribe. A tribe without honor can be attacked and the men killed by a larger tribe or a coalition of smaller ones. Therefore, to restore honor to the family and to the tribe, it is a necessity that any woman out of line be killed as quickly as possible. It is the basis of the tradition that still exists today.

Whenever a Western state welcomes immigrants from the Middle East, it is incumbent on state officials to know what they are doing. The Middle East immigrants are mostly Muslims. Muslims have their own ideas of how things should be, how states should be run, and how people should act with one another. Normally, all of those Eastern ideas conflict with ours in the West. It does not take a brain surgeon to know that bringing together hundreds of thousands or millions of people into a country with serious culture and religious differences is asking for serious trouble—as some have already discovered. Of course, there are always those who discover nothing that conflicts with their own agenda or their adopted doctrine. Those agents of the state must be replaced with honest, knowledgeable administrators. Nonetheless, agents of the state must know the culture and the religion of each substantial group in that state, especially the newcomers and the states with whom they are in conflict. One would justifiably believe that any state welcoming new visitors with a culture and religion distinctly different or even inimical to those already in the state would be equipped in advance to solve the various problems, which for the most part are predictable in those situations. Melanie Phillips, Bruce Bawer, Bat Ye'or, and Oriana Fallaci all condemned European states and the United Kingdom for their ignorance and denial with respect to their inability to solve problems between their immigrants and their citizens and between the immigrants and the law. Many of these recurring problems still remain unresolved.

It is also necessary for the people in each state that welcomes immigrants or is in conflict with states with inimical cultures or religions, to know something about the culture and religion of the other peoples and states and not to rely on rumors or sound bites from others who do

The Restless Wind and Shifting Sands

not know or have self-serving agendas. Learning should be a womb-to-tomb activity. In this information age of ours, what you do not know can ruin your plans, your economic well-being, and your health. It is not too late to learn something new every day. What you learn today, may turn out to be important to you tomorrow.

Harry J. Sweeney

Conversation 65: Sharia Funding and Zakat

Radi: Good morning, Modi and Mani. Ah, it is a beautiful morning, isn't it?

Mani: Modi, if Radi is that pleasant, I smell a rat.

Modi: I refuse to elucidate on that remark. On the other hand, I have to agree that when Radi looks happy, somebody is dead, dying, or being tortured.

Radi: That is not a nice thing to say about an old friend, Modi. However, I understand you do not like my opinions on how to treat sinners. Kill them all for Allah, along with the nonbelievers, the infidels.

Mani: What if the rest of the world suddenly developed some brains, Radi, saw you radicals for what you really are, and decided to put you out of business?

Radi: No chance of that. Have you seen the latest copy of the *August Review*? It appears that the West has already lost. The global bankers have embraced Islam.

Mani: What? That does not make sense? Why should they?

Modi: It was bound to happen. There is a lot of money, especially oil money in the Middle East; however, there is also *zakat* money rolling in from all over the world. Remember, Mani, if you consider 2.5 percent of the assets of more than one billion people—and counting; annually, that is not just big bucks. That is world-class finance pouring through banks to be redistributed to the needy and to others.

Radi: But the best part, Modi, is that the loans and the investments, insurance, and other financial services will be available only wherever sharia law is in effect.

The Restless Wind and Shifting Sands

Mani: Why would that be so important, Radi? The West will always have its own funding.

Modi: The Salafists, Mani, are planning on global bankers slowly becoming the source of funds. When you cannot get funds anywhere else and the need is critical, interest-free loans look pretty good.

Mani: The West would not trade their freedoms for money; I can't see the Americans ever accepting sharia law.

Radi: Ha! Americans get hungry just like everyone else.

Modi: It is not the American people, Mani. Look at their leadership; some of those people are dumb as rocks. Some banker will give them a song and dance about interest-free loans and the possibility of campaign funds, and they will get in line.

Mani: But what about the people?

Modi: One naive group of people will believe anything the pseudo-intellectuals tell them. That should be about half the country. A part of the stronger but less numerous groups will want to fight, but they will not have the votes to avoid a change in law. A sizable number of Yuppies in both groups will not care, as long as they can watch sports, drive fast cars, and kill any babies they produce. Remember, these funds are not available unless the sharia is in force.

Radi: Yes, Mani, just watch how many American politicians will turn down free campaign funds. And American business will turn against the people in an instant when they smell global cash and interest-free loans.

Modi: Yes, Mani, Radi is right about that. Look at the politicians and the global businesses that have already turned against the American worker. They sent the $20-to-$50-per-hour jobs here and to India, Pakistan, Africa, and just about everywhere they could. Those jobs were replaced with minimum-wage jobs, and the president is bragging

Harry J. Sweeney

about the new jobs. Wouldn't you think those people would hesitate to sell them out again?

Radi: America may become a Muslim country whether it wants to or not. Hah! I will be glad to see that day.

Mani: We are trying here to smooth out the sharia, Modi. It is too barbaric! Many people have seen the other side of the coin and want to taste some of the freedoms the rest of the world enjoys.

Modi: Now listen. People who know, have learned what it is all about. You and I know because we are here, and that is our religion. However, the rest of the world has something better. We cannot change because the old beards here will not let loose their control and they threaten to kill anyone who even speaks of reform. They will kill anyone, anyone who even looks as if they want reform. That is not the type of law we want. You had to have noticed that many, many of our people were quite happy about emigrating away from strict laws with vigilantes enforcing them.

Radi: That is the law with regard to reform, Modi. It is the best law for anyone. We do not want to coddle thieves, murderers, rapists, and other criminals as they do in Europe and America. They are garbage and should not live. If they murder someone, who cares why they did it? The parents or other family members should then kill the murderer.

Mani: The murderer then becomes a victim to his family members, and they in turn will go after his killers.

Radi: No, Mani. It doesn't work that way. When your relative is murdered, you let the others know your intentions. The sharia lets you know whether you are entitled to retaliation or not according to circumstances. If you are so entitled, the man to be legally killed can either be killed without consequences, or he can pay a wrongful death indemnity and escape his execution. But you have to get to him first.

Modi: The *August Review* is right in accusing global bankers of being

The Restless Wind and Shifting Sands

amoral when it comes to money. It is now best that American workers and thinkers and others begin learning about Islam; they may be the only ones to know. The leaders do not seem to know about Islam; neither do the media. You know, many Americans seem to be in denial about almost everything.

Mani: Wouldn't it be too hard and time consuming for Americans to learn about our religion, Modi? I agree that they should know something about it; it has already come to their shores.

Modi: From what I've seen, Mani, it would be easier than reading the agreement on some of this new software I just bought.

Mani: Those software agreements are something else; they are almost as bad as those home owners' association agreements. My cousin in Maryland still cannot figure his agreement out, and he is an attorney.

Modi: Well, as Muslims know, you cannot just pick up a Qur'an cold turkey and begin reading. That will not work. You must first read the life of Muhammad, especially one that contains references to specific verses in the Qur'an. I would call that a gateway to the Qur'an.

Radi: Bah!

Mani: Radi does not believe you need a gateway.

Modi: Ha! He has been trying to read it for 10 years and still doesn't get it. That is why he gets those dumb friends of his to read it to him; however, they do not read it to him, they just recite what they heard on the street.

Radi: I will have you know I will soon be a reciter!

Modi: Oh yes, a reciter of menus.

Radi: I will have your head for that. (Gives chase)

Harry J. Sweeney

Conversation 66: HIV

Radi: Good morning, Modi and Mani.

Mani: Good morning, Radi. You are not ranting and raving this morning. I am afraid to ask why.

Radi: As you know, the Sunni and Shiite scholars have been meeting this week and have agreed that our tacit cease-fire should be formalized. They also want our prime minister and our president to visit Iran and propose to the Iranians that they continue to keep hands off Iraq and perhaps sign a nonaggression treaty.

Modi: That seems to be very good news, but I would not get my hopes up about Iran. It is great news that this cease-fire between Sunnis and Shiites can work itself into a permanent way of life.

Mani: It would be even better if we could drop the enmity between us and begin to assimilate with each other. I know that our families could all use some new blood, especially if some new brains come with it. The tradition of marrying only related people is getting too old.

Modi: The families in Europe are getting new blood. The women have told their suitors they cannot marry non-Muslims, so some of the men are converting.

Radi: You are right about that. However, as soon as those Europeans find out about praying five times per day, arising before dawn, along with ablutions and the *zakat*, they convert back. I wish I were there; I could kill many apostates.

Modi: You cannot kill apostates in European countries, Radi. It is against their laws.

Radi: It does not matter. It is against the national law in Muslim countries also, just to appease the United Nations, but once it is done,

The Restless Wind and Shifting Sands

nobody presses it because the sharia says there will be no consequences for it. So the laws overlook the killing or give a slap on the wrist.

Mani: Yes, Modi, a law is only as good as how rigidly it is enforced.

Modi: I am certain that the Europeans will be very rigid about killing apostates. They are already tightening up on honor killings.

Radi: That is terrible. There is nothing wrong with honor killings.

Modi: We will talk about that crime later, Radi. You know that in America there are no real problems about honor killings, except with the newcomers there. Some Muslim women seem to gravitate to American non-believers without insisting on converting. I have a third cousin who married a Texan. She said life is exciting.

Radi: It is your duty to go there and kill her, Modi.

Modi: You can forget that, Radi. I think what she did was her choice and nobody else's business. Good for her!

Radi: Next you will be saying that Americans should come here for wives and husbands.

Mani: What is wrong with that, Radi?

Radi: Bringing all those bad traditions with them: drugs, abortion, hard porn, free sex, homosexuality, HIV. We do not need any of that junk.

Mani: Oh, I agree with that. However, if you must know, the people to whom you refer are not the military. They are the antimilitary crowd. I like the idea of American military being here and helping us—saving us, actually. However, the American soldiers leave all the other stuff at home.

Modi: You do not seem to understand. It is a matter of freedom. You

Harry J. Sweeney

have the freedom to choose whether you want to use drugs, watch hard porn, or engage in free sex.

Radi: Why would anyone choose HIV?

Modi: They do not choose HIV, stupid! It is a disease passed on to them by someone else.

Mani: Passed on to them having free sex, Modi?

Modi: Well, yes. That is usually the way. Some people get it from unfortunate transfusions.

Radi: Modi, how does the HIV get into the transfusion blood?

Modi: I guess the wrong people give blood and the blood banks may not analyze it as strictly as they should.

Mani: Aha! What about children seeing all that porn around.

Modi: I imagine the Americans have laws about that.

Radi: Laws or not, we do not want any of those "freedoms" over here. If that is part of democracy, they can have it.

Mani: Radi is right about that. All of that garbage does not belong here or anywhere for that matter.

Modi: Well, I certainly do not like that part of America. I do not know how many Americans object to it. I would bet about half or more of the Americans hate it also.

Radi: Then why is it allowed? Who wants it?

Modi: The San Francisco – New York Axis of evil wants it. They could not live without drugs, porn, free sex, and abortion. From what I see, they are the ones who want non-traditional marriages. It seems to

The Restless Wind and Shifting Sands

me that when they foster abortions and childless marriages, they are longing for extinction.

Radi: If half of the Americans do not want that mess, why don't they just kill the ones who do? They are heading for extinction anyway.

Modi: Well, Radi, why don't we in Iraq just kill all the radicals? It is the same difference.

Mani: It is more likely that the radicals here will kill all of the moderates. I think it would be the same in America, but the moderates there have all the guns.

Radi: Aha! Then if that were the case, if the guys in America just got rid of the porn lovers, the rest of the world would not hate America as they do.

Modi: That's a thought. Next time I speak to an American I will tell him. However, I would have to tell the Europeans also. That is where the American softies got all this junk, trying to emulate their European heroes. The "rest of the world" that would change their minds would only be third world countries, certainly not Europe.

Harry J. Sweeney

Conversation 67: "Kill them wherever you find them!"

Radi: Peace be with you, Modi.

Modi: And with you peace, my friend.

Radi: We have had a few arguments last year.

Modi: Of course, Radi. We look at things differently. You are strict about each word of the Qur'an and I am not. It is good, very good if you knew the Qur'an, Radi, but you seem to know only selected ayats. You use those selected verses to threaten any person, group, or nation that does not completely agree with you.

Radi: That is where you are wrong, Modi. Everyone in my family has learned to recite the Qur'an.

Mani: Good morning, everyone.

Radi and Modi: *Marhaban to you too*, Mani.

Mani: Hello to you, too. I know that Radi's family members are all reciters, Modi.

Modi: That is fine; however, reciting and understanding are two different things and they are worlds apart. Take for instance all those great kids you see in the news videos of the Pakistani madrassas. Do you think for one moment, the poor students in those schools know what they are saying?

Radi: Why wouldn't they?

Modi: For one thing, it is not their language! They are memorizing in Arabic, but their own language is either Pashtu or Urdu, among the 300 languages spoken there. Did you know that the national language of Pakistan is English?

308

The Restless Wind and Shifting Sands

Radi: What? You are kidding! I thought they spoke Arabic.

Modi: Very few speak Arabic as a native language, but many can recite the 114 suras of the Qur'an in Arabic. Now one can truly understand what a tasking those children have, memorizing 114 chapters of the Qur'an in a language they do not know.

Mani: Modi, I am astounded. Is that not a terrible waste of time if they truly do not know what they are saying?

Modi: I can understand that many lessons about other important subjects could be taught in that period—including the Qur'an and the hadiths.

Radi: I would like to teach the Qur'an to young minds.

Modi: Radi, you do not know the Qur'an; you would only teach those warlike phrases you like to amplify, and strut around like a veteran warrior, waving an imaginary sword at an imaginary enemy. The West laughs at people like that, but many of our people are not educated enough to know one should not take them seriously.

Mani: I have studied the Qur'an extensively and I do not find fault with what Radi says. He has always quoted it correctly.

Modi: I can attest to his quoting it correctly. That is not the point. I will give you an example, he is always yelling, "Kill them wherever you find them." He uses that phrase to justify killing Westerners and anyone who does not agree with him.

Radi: Well, that is the way it is.

Modi: Not quite. The first use of that term was in the Qur'an 2:191, which was preceded by 2:190: "And Fight in God's cause against those who wage war against you, but do not commit aggression—for verily God does not love aggressors." The ayat 2:191 continues, "And slay them wherever you may come upon them, and drive them away from

Harry J. Sweeney

wherever they drove you away—for oppression is worse than killing.[63] And fight not against them near the Inviolable House of Worship (Mecca), unless they fight against you there first; but if they fight against you, slay them: such shall be the recompense of those who deny the truth (Meccans). Sura 9:5 uses the terms also; however, it is the same usage as 2:191.

Mani: Did you forget Qur'an 4:89, Modi?

Modi: I was saving it for last. It does not differ very much from the others, except that it was much clearer that the infidels were the Meccans.[64] In fact, one of the conditions that allowed the believers to take Meccans for their allies again was "...if they forsake the domain of evil." That meant if the Meccans followed the hijira and left Mecca for Medina.

Radi: Mani, I think Modi is making that up.

Mani: Well, Radi, it is easy enough to check—go look in your Qur'an.

Radi: Perhaps later; I would have to go through my ablutions to open al-Kitab, just as I do for prayer. Perhaps I will do so after Noon Prayer.

Mani: I cannot believe Radi. He will not look up your answers because he does not want to go through the motions to open the Qur'an.

Modi: I can understand. Too bad, we are not allowed to have "working copies."

---

63   Muhammad Asad's notes on page 51 of his *Message of the Qur'an* assures us that the injunction "slay them wherever you come upon them" is valid only in the context of hostilities already in progress, on the understanding that "those who wage war against you" are aggressors or oppressors. Asad hints that it must be a war in God's cause, not necessarily a war against another Muslim state, or against a Western power assisting a Muslim state.

64   Ibid, page 139, notes 108 and 109

The Restless Wind and Shifting Sands

Mani: I do not completely understand the difference between us about the Qur'an. You are always so levelheaded, but Radi and I seem to agree on one aspect and you do not.

Modi: I will try to make it simple. If the Qur'an talks about killing people wherever you find them, and then identifies the fact that killing them only means in a de facto war—not one in which your imagination makes you think someone is oppressing you—and they are truly the aggressors, like Saddam Hussein against Kuwait, those people you can fight. But the fight has to be God's war, in which the aggressor is trying to kill all of the Muslims, for example. It does not include a war in which a coalition is trying to help a Muslim country recover from a past tyrant and now fighting against insurgents.

You also must understand that, as Muhammad Asad points out, the "them" in "kill them wherever you find them" has been unarguably pointed out as Meccans and no one else. While you can extend the idea of the defensive war beyond the confines of the seventh century, according to Asad, it would not be proper to extend the seventh century "infidels" or "polytheists" or "hypocrites", etc., beyond that period.

Mani: I think I understand now. Radi is saying that when the Qur'an says "kill them" it means if you see an American tourist walking down the street in Cairo, minding his own business, you can walk right up to him and slit his throat.

Radi: Yep! The Qur'an spells it out that way. "…wherever you find them."

Mani: But you say, Modi that the Qur'an is only talking about the seventh century enemies in those particular ayats.

Modi: That is right. Do you think for one minute that Allah, a merciful and forgiving God, wants us running around with swords, killing everyone?

Radi: Yep! That is what he wants! Isn't that right, Mani?

311

Harry J. Sweeney

Mani: I do not know. I will have to think about it and ask an imam.

Modi: If you were to be in a position where you had to make that decision in a second because things are happening, Mani, what would you decide? Remember, you only have a second.

Mani: It depends. If Radi is right beside me and he starts hacking away at non-Muslims, I would have to join him, I guess. I have never heard an imam say what you have said to me. I am not sure you are right.

Modi: You only can take one road or the other, Mani. We have come to a fork in the road and you can take the road to war and bloodshed with Radi or you can take the road to peace with me. One way or the other you must go. Which road do you take?

Mani: I do not know. I like you both.

Modi: It is not about friends, it is about killing non-Muslims or leaving them alone. Which road will you take?

Mani: I just do not know, now let me alone.

Modi: Sometimes, Mani, you are more dangerous than Radi. We know what he will do if we turn our back on him. He is committed, you are not. You will have to choose, sooner or later.

The Restless Wind and Shifting Sands

Conversation 68: Muhammad's Early Life.

Radi: Hello, peace be upon you.

Modi: And with you, peace.

Mani: Good morning.

Radi: Modi, some people tell me you know something about our history. I have heard that since our Most Beloved was orphaned at a young age, he was given to a Bedouin clan. That does not sound right to me.

Modi: It is partly true, Radi. His father, Abdullah, died while out of town on business well before he was born. His mother, Amina was a young bride and missed her new husband terribly. After her baby was born, in 570, the child was given to a Bedouin family to be raised in the desert.

Mani: Good grief, Modi. Why did his mother do that?

Modi: It was not just her, Mani, his grandfather, Abdel[65] Muttalib, had been looking after Amina, and now was looking after both mother and son. It was the custom of Arab nobility and others to send their babies out to be raised by Bedouin families because the atmosphere in the city was not good for them. They expected the babies to be strong and healthy when they returned 5-10 years later. This became a cottage industry among the Bedouins.

Radi: Amina was away from her son that long?

Modi: Yes and no. When he reached two years old, Halimah, the Bedouin, brought him back according to the contract; however, there was a growing epidemic in the city and Amina asked her to take him

---

65   His name was Shaybah, the nephew of al-Muttalib; people mistook him for a slave, hence the name Abdel. Even when people learned who he was, the name stuck.

Harry J. Sweeney

back to the Banu Sa'd for another few years. Halimah finally returned him to his mother when he was five. Amina died a year later.

Mani: Is that when he was orphaned, with no mother or father?

Modi: No, the lad was never orphaned. When the grandfather, Abdel Muttalib was pushing seventy-nine, he secured a promise from his son, Abu Talib, to take care of his nephew after the old man passed on. The uncle tried to live up to his promise, but he was the poorest of the old man's sons and had a hard time making ends meet.

Radi: Why did Abdel Muttalib give the young Muhammad to the poorest of his sons and not one of the richer ones?

Modi: Actually, none of his sons were rich. The clan had a reversal of fortune after the old man died and actually lost their leadership position in Mecca. To answer your main question, though, Abu Talib was the kindest—the only son who volunteered to look after their nephew.

Mani: How bad was that?

Modi: Their sub-clan, the Banu Hashim, lost almost everything; their children had to work to support the clan. The Banu Ummayah gained the leadership; it was a much larger clan.

Radi: Did Muhammad do something to take revenge?

Modi: No, Radi. One sub-tribe did not attack the other, although there was much of that going on at that time with major clans. To be sure, between the two Quraish sub-clans, it was an economic disaster for one and an economic coup for the other. The tribe did not go out of existence; everyone just had to work harder.

Mani: What happened then?

Modi: You know the rest of the story. Muhammad even went on caravans with his uncle and sometimes led the caravans. He was eventually hired

The Restless Wind and Shifting Sands

by the rich widow, Khadija, to lead her trade caravans. He added to her fortunes and they married. He never took a second wife while Khadija was alive. That was unusual for a rich Arab merchant who could have as many wives as he wanted.

Mani: Do you know anything about the Kaaba's history?

Modi: You probably know most of its history from the imams, but the Kaaba predates our religion considerably. Remember, Mecca became an international crossroads as well as the "Mecca" of idolatry before it was named. The Kaaba was a source of income from pilgrims traveling from all over. In fact, it was such a lucrative income that a Kaaba without the icons or statues is still a source of income. Although there are no idols to venerate when things are good, or to kick when things are bad, nevertheless, the pilgrims are involved with the same traditional activities and observances as those pilgrims that visited the Kaaba before the capture of Mecca.

Radi: What about the attack on the Kaaba by a foreign army, when God himself struck the foreign army?

Modi: Radi, King Dhu Nuwas from Yemen was bored with the little icons and statues, so he converted to Judaism in the sixth century. At about the same time, a fervent Christian named Quaymiyun, converted the Arabs of Najran to Christianity. The Yemen king was so furious about the expanding Christianity; he assembled an army and executed everyone that would not convert to Judaism.

Radi: Hey, I like his style, but not his religion.

Modi: The survivors appealed to Emperor Justinian, who suggested that his Abyssinian allies, who were Christians, take care of the problem.

Mani: But the Abyssinians were friends of the Muslims.

Modi: That came later. Meanwhile, the Abyssinian general, Abrahah, conquered Yemen and afterwards, Christianity spread again. While he

Harry J. Sweeney

was cleaning up Yemen, he heard about the Kaaba and decided while he was in the neighborhood; he should destroy the pagan temple.

Radi: Did he have a large army. The Kaaba was never destroyed that way.

Modi: His army was so large, that after Abrahah let the Meccans know he was only after the Kaaba, not the people, the Quraish leader of Mecca, Abdel Muttalib, our Most Beloved's grandfather, decided to leave the city. But his daughter-in-law, pregnant with Muhammad decided to stay in the city. Traveling was too dangerous for her and Abrahah said he would not harm the people.

Mani: What happened? Did Abrahah attack?

Modi: He wanted to attack; however, he called it off. While legend has it that God defeated Abrahah's army, the more plausible opinion is that his army was living off the land and the cities and was visited with viruses that defied the medicines of the day. Even Abrahah himself succumbed.

Radi: I prefer to think it was Allah and his angels.

Modi: Well, at least it was not screaming barbarians, swinging swords and cutting off people's heads.

Radi: You are blaspheming again.

Modi: Radi, you were such a joy, listening to the story for all this time without going nuts and bringing up blasphemy or apostasy. It was a pleasure to answer the questions and tell the story.

Radi: You were the one who mentioned sword-swinging barbarians.

Modi: Oh, was that your mating call?

Radi: I am going to remove your head.

The Restless Wind and Shifting Sands

Mani: Radi, shh! Do you hear that?

Radi: What?

Mani: Someone's cutting into a loaf of bread.

Radi: Sniffs the air. Where?

Modi: Radi, you are a nut! Look, Afternoon Prayer is not until 2:49 today, so we have time to eat before ablutions. I am buying.

Radi: Last one to the restaurant is a polytheist.

Mani: You rejecter-of-the-truth!

Adapted from the book "Muhammad" by Yahiya Emerick, Chapters 1, 2; Alpha Books, Critical Lives Series (Penguin Group)

Harry J. Sweeney

Conversation 69: On reading Qur'an Sura 2.

Radi: A friend is trying to learn the Qur'an. I told him just to read it and Allah will make things clear to him. He read the second sura[66] three times and still cannot make sense of it.

Modi: The second sura, "al Baqarah"[67] is the longest sura in the Qur'an. I cannot blame him for not understanding it right away.

Radi: Why is it so long?

Modi: Because ayats were added to it as time went by. If you remember the first sura, al Fatihah[68], it was revealed in Mecca and ended with a prayer asking for guidance to the straight path. Although Sura 2 was revealed later, in Medina, it provides that guidance mentioned in Sura 1.

Mani: I was always wondering about that myself.

Modi: Most of the second sura was revealed during the first two years in Medina. However, the rest of the ayats were revealed in later periods, but they were related to the guidance in this sura, so that is why they are there.

Radi: I do not understand why Allah organized the Qur'an as He did. It is so difficult to understand.

Mani: You are not alone. We could have had a little tweaking done to help, but those headhunters of yours, Radi, would not let anybody change anything.

Radi: Why were so many subjects put into that one chapter?

---

66 A sura is a chapter in the Qur'an. An ayat is a verse inside a sura
67 The Cow, named for one of the subjects in the sura, ayats 67-73
68 The Opening. It is the opening sura of the Qur'an.

318

The Restless Wind and Shifting Sands

Modi: Others have said it was because when the sura was started, many subjects had to be discussed lightly, but no one anticipated the numbers of Muslims that would crowd Medina so soon after the hijira. When the spoils were divided after the Battle of Badr, Medina's population grew considerably.

Mani: I see. It was very important that more details were added quickly so that the people would know how to live in peace with each other.

Modi: Right. It was also important to know how to go to war and win against overwhelming odds.

Mani: You mean that since many of our guiding principles were being established during that period in Medina, other ayats that were revealed later had to go back to that second sura, even though they were revealed after many more suras were revealed?

Modi: Yes. That sura was significantly expanded. Look, remember that our Most Beloved tried to explain to the Jews that they used to be Muslims in the beginning, but they "strayed away through centuries of degeneration". When they were told about it and given a chance to redeem themselves, they clung to their wickedness and joined those who would try to crush Islam. They inexplicably dropped the name of Muslim and called themselves Jews. The people had to know about the Jews so they would understand why some Jewish tribes were banished and others were attacked.

Mani: Too bad all those arguments about the Jews were not given their own sura. It would have made things a little clearer. Sura 2 would not have been so crowded.

Modi: For a while there, it appeared that the Jewish tribes were pleased with Muhammad's work and cooperated with him. The breach came when he visited their place of worship and announced that he was the new Jewish Prophet. The Jews, some of whom had been studying and

Harry J. Sweeney

researching for decades, greeted that in several different ways, none of them pleasing to Muhammad. They just did not accept him as a Jewish prophet. It is said that they might have been afraid that a close study would show some of their scriptures were changed.

Mani: So, that is the source of the many ayats in that sura, castigating the Jews quite bitterly. I guess it was important to let the people know about the Jews right away.

Modi: Some of the ire was directed at the *munafiqin* (hypocrites). Those were the Muslims who were like some American senators to a moderate president. The less they knew, the more sullenly and loudly they knew it. You may remember they were particularly annoying right before the Battle of the Trench. The people had to learn about them also.

Mani: What kind of guidance was in Sura 2?

Modi: Of course, I do not have al Kitab with me to try to give you a list, but I will do what I can. He divided mankind into three main groups: Believers, Disbelievers, and Hypocrites. Allah invited mankind to accept the guidance, just as Allah had invited Adam and Eve to do so. The Jews were invited to take part in Islam, but they refused, so Allah had quite a lot to say about that. Allah also changed the qibla from Jerusalem to Mecca[69].

Modi (takes a breath): The details on prayers, fasting, the zakat[70], the Haj[71] and jihad all found their way into the sura, as did drinking and gambling. The formal prayers, salat, are very important in Islam, even though arising before dawn to begin the first prayer is hard to take at times. It was necessary that the people knew as soon as possible the

---

69   Qibla--the direction that should be faced when a Muslim prays. Most mosques build a niche in a wall to indicate the qibla. The qibla plays an important part in everyday ceremonies. The qibla was changed from Jerusalem to Mecca after the arguments between the Jews and Muhammad began.

70 Poor Tax: 2.5 percent of one's capital annually.

71 Pilgrimages to Mecca.

The Restless Wind and Shifting Sands

right way to do things. Did you know, Radi that your prayers mean nothing without the ablutions first?

Radi: That is quite a lot of guidance for that period.

Modi: People needed a set of laws to live by, and they had to be based upon the principles laid down in Medina. Muhammad did not write the sharia, but it is based on the Qur'an, the hadiths, the sira, and centuries of study, analysis, and debate.

Radi: Debate?

Mani: Yes, Radi. Nothing is supposed to be set in stone, although sometimes it looks like it.

Modi: Allah also revealed in that sura that he wanted everyone to spend in the way of Allah and not horde wealth. He did not want just a few wealthy people cornering the markets and getting wealthier while others starved. It was fine if people bought things that made life easy for them, as long as they did not drink, gamble, and abuse others. Lending money at high interest rates was one way of abusing your fellow believers and He was not going to allow anyone to do that.

Mani: I read Sayyid Qutb's book, *Social Justice in Islam*. One would think that he had the Qur'an open beside him as he wrote.

Modi: Well, what do you think, Radi? Do you have enough information to give to your friend about learning the Qur'an?

Radi: I think I do for the second sura, but I know he will have to do as you suggested last week. He should use the sira as a guide to reading the Qur'an.

Modi: He can always look around for the Maududi work, *Towards*

Harry J. Sweeney

Understanding the Qur'an in several volumes. Fortunately, they are not too expensive. They are out of print, so he can only find them used.

Mani: I used to have an imam explain things to me, but the imams are too busy now with larger congregations and so many things going on. In some mosques, they do not allow the non-radicals to speak, especially if the building was financed with money from certain places. Now I find that some of these imams are getting confused because the people turned against al-Qaida and the other insurgents.

Modi: Yes, I know. We may see a different world before long. Our planet is getting smaller, because we have more people. Except for some dumb holdouts, people want more freedom to think and act for themselves. I saw some statistics showing 40 percent of young Muslims in Europe are not practicing their religion. Waking up for prayer before dawn after a night on the town does not compute, I guess.

Mani: I agree. One of these days, our women are going to get together, turn on some of these old beards, and they are going to discover what "getting stoned" really means. I know they are really looking at some sharia pages.

Radi: Well, I don't agree. I love this religion and it should not change at all.

Modi: Very well, Radi. You keep that thought; however, our *ulama* must do more work to expose other religions that bring harm to our neighbors. Once a religion brings harm to innocent people, it can become a cult and must be suppressed. Remember that.

Radi: There is nothing wrong with my religion. I will kill the first person who does not agree.

Mani: Radi is always a case in point, Modi.

Radi: What does that mean?

The Restless Wind and Shifting Sands

Mani: It means when there is nothing more to be said, you are still saying it.

Partially adapted from Maududi's introduction to Sura 2 of *The Noble Qur'an*, download version (imaanstar.com)

Harry J. Sweeney

Conversation 70: On Reading Sura 3.

Mani: Modi, Sura 3 is the second longest in the Qur'an. Is it that long because more ayats were added, as you said about Sura 2?

Modi: Basically, yes; however, it has its own distinct rationale. Remember that the second sura warned the believers of the trials and the tribulations that awaited them.

Radi: Yes, I remember that. Some of the believers showed great determination and belief in our Prophet. When one new believer was assured what awaited him as a martyr, he took off like a banshee and waded into those Meccans with his sword swinging like crazy.

Modi: In the second sura, Allah reminded the believers what could happen when they listened to His Messenger. However, He had to remind them that there are still armies of enemies that are arrayed against them. Therefore, they dare not let down their guard or listen to the hypocrites who would lead them astray.

Mani: Well, they did so well at Badr, perhaps just complimenting the believers would have been enough. They were greatly outnumbered and still came out victorious.

Modi: Unfortunately the Meccans were not the only ones against the believers. Medina was just a very small puddle in the great desert of enemies against Islam. They found that out in the Battle of Uhud. Not only did they lose the battle by not doing what they were told, they almost lost their Prophet as well.

Radi: They lost only because 300 hypocrites pulled out of the marching formations and returned to Medina.

Modi: It was not only that, Radi. I mentioned a few weeks ago that the archers were told not to move from their positions no matter what happened. However, the Meccans set a trap by pretending to pull out and leaving their belongings for the taking. Well, the archers

The Restless Wind and Shifting Sands

deserted their posts to claim the loot, and then the Meccans charged Muhammad's position and almost killed him. He was wounded.

Radi: Did he kill the archers? I would have.

Modi: Why would he do that? The Muslims had not been a community very long and were also relatively inexperienced in conducting warfare.

Mani: So they needed training in accepting their leaders' orders and in believing in what they are doing.

Modi: That is right. Besides that, they were cautioned to learn all about Christians and Jews, knowing their strengths as well as their weaknesses and knowing their arguments as well. The unbelievers should be defeated wherever they are met, not just on the battlefield.

Mani: Do you see what Allah was doing, Radi? He was teaching the believers that if they studied and believed the available Qur'an revelations they would grow stronger in their faith. As Muslims strong in their faith and believing in their leadership, they need never fear following Muhammad into future battles.

Radi: I understand that. But the Jews were still interfering and should have all been killed right away.

Modi: We would like to get away from killing. And for Allah's sake, stop dreaming up excuses for punishing people. If a person believes only one tenth of what his religion teaches, so what? He is still a believer and may improve in time. Why punish him or her? When it comes to the Jews, for instance, I do not know how the battle at Badr would have come out without Jewish fighters and Jewish support.

Mani: I don't know about the Jewish contribution, but about punishing people, you are right. That is what the second sura is all about. Allah is teaching Muslims how to be better. He is showing them how much better things will be if they learn more and have faith. He is not warning

Harry J. Sweeney

them that He will kill them for not learning. However, He is warning them that if they just give up and join the opposition against Him they will know His anger.

Modi: You know, Allah in this sura also gave the Jews still another opportunity to return to their original teaching, walk away from their perfidies and their false pride, and again be the Muslims that they should be. He explained what happens either way. The Jews continued to deny His prophethood, continued to ignore his blandishments and warnings, and even allied themselves with those who would destroy Islam and kill Muslims.

Radi: We should kill them all.

Modi: I tell you again; those Jews were either killed or at any rate died more than 1,300 years ago, thirteen centuries. The Jews that are alive today are far removed from the Jews of Arabia. Did not Allah and Muhammad forgive the polytheists in Mecca? Not all the Meccans were convinced they should convert to Islam.

Mani: I agree with Modi, Radi. When a person needs help in his religion, don't kill him; help him. You may be nurturing a future scholar or martyr.

Radi: I never thought of that.

Modi: Radi, that includes people who are leaving the religion. A person may be leaving as an apostate; however, that same person may gain more knowledge and understanding, see the light, and become a wonderful teacher for others.

Radi: But the sharia tells us that apostates are subject to death by anyone with access to him. The sharia also tells us that his killing will be without consequences.

Modi: I know all of this, Radi. You need to understand that there were reasons in the seventh century for killing apostates. They were also traitors and were working with the polytheists and others to hurt Islam. Apostates are no longer a danger to us, and we must believe there will be a time when they return much wiser.

Radi: Why didn't Allah bring this information up in the Qur'an that someday that may all change?

Mani: Perhaps, Radi, Allah left it up to us to use our heads and make those determinations for ourselves. We are not stupid, Radi. Allah knows that and perhaps wants us to think beyond what He has given us as a start.

Radi: I must disagree. I will follow only what has been written. I will kill anyone leaving the religion and anyone who I suspect even thinks of changing the Qur'an.

Modi: What about a supplement to the Qur'an, Radi?

Radi: It should be met with instant death.

Modi: Are you certain you want to go that far?

Radi: Yes, I am certain. Anyone writing and distributing a supplement to our glorious Qur'an should die.

Modi: You mean people like Ishaq, Bukhari, Malik, Maududi and Qutb? They all wrote supplements to the Qur'an. Books, essays, hadiths, and other supplements.

Radi: Oops. I did not mean those people.

Modi: Then why will some supplements be acceptable and others not?

Mani: I think Radi has no answer. He does not know.

Modi: Then perhaps there should be an end to killing people for

Harry J. Sweeney

reasons that are unknown or not understood. Far more people are killed in the name of the Qur'an for reasons not really understood. It is bad enough that ignorant thugs do it; however, the "believers" that use subterfuge to goad others into doing these murders "for the love of Allah" are the real villains. Allah knows what is in our hearts and will drag those demons on their faces and fling them into the fire very early on judgment day.

Radi: Uh, can we talk about this over coffee or something?

Partially adapted from Maududi's Introduction to Sura 3, online version of the Noble Qur'an.

CHAPTER 8

Conversation 71: On Reading Sura 4a

Mani: I again read Sura Four last night and found it much more interesting than my previous readings. You really must consider that the people were adapting to a new religion while in the middle of a war to defend that religion. If you don't keep it in mind, it will not make sense.

Modi: Bravo! That is exactly right. The Battle of Uhud was behind them and they were still reeling from that setback. Many of the believers were disheartened. The Battle of Badr showed how good they can be, achieving victory when it seemed impossible. And Uhud showed how bad things can be if they failed to follow all of their instructions.

Mani: It was a particularly bad time for widows and orphans. There were so many that Allah had to allow men to have more than one wife; otherwise, women and children would be homeless with no means of support. Allah also had to instruct new stepfathers on safeguarding the inheritances of the orphans and enjoin them from robbing or cheating them. That way, the fighters knew that their kids were cared for if they, the fathers, were martyred and the mother remarried.

Radi: See, Allah looks after us and expects us to follow His instructions to the letter. When He says that apostates and heretics must be killed, we must do that quickly.

Mani: I have to agree with Radi. I cannot see why you are against killing apostates, Modi.

Modi: You said it yourself, Mani. These laws were promulgated at a time when the people were not used to their new religion and during a

Harry J. Sweeney

time of war when they were being persecuted by the Meccans, and when tribes of Jews were defying their treaties, according to the Prophet.

Mani: You are saying that in order to preserve the religion, it was necessary at that time to kill traitors.

Modi: What else could be done with them? There were no prisons. The only magistrate was Muhammad; and his time was taken up fighting, preparing to fight, and trying to run a new government with untrained people. What could you do with traitors while they were awaiting trials that might be very long in coming?

Mani: I can understand that. He did not have any help in conducting government affairs; he had to manage everything himself. He also had to figure out how to deal with Muslim hypocrites and the Jewish tribes aiding the Meccans.

Modi: Exactly. You can add that he had to develop a penal code and develop religious rites and rules for moral conduct. The penal code, the sharia, was adapted by principles laid down in the Qur'an, after much debate over the meaning of each word. And despite all of these other tasks, Muhammad and Allah had to motivate the believers to do more, learn more, and put aside their fears of combat. If they did not overcome their powerful enemies first, Allah would be obliged to rely on others, and they would no longer be His chosen people.

Radi: That had to motivate them. To no longer be His chosen people would be hard to take.

Modi: Thankfully, Allah also decided to make the religion travel-friendly and warrior-friendly by allowing the believers to "clean" themselves with pure earth when water was not available for their ablutions. The believers were also cautioned to be generous and kind to neighboring communities.

Mani: I noticed those ayats. In one sense, it helped to consolidate the

The Restless Wind and Shifting Sands

communities and unify the people, and in another sense, it helped to propagate the new religion.

Modi: Remember, new members were very important. New members meant more fighters and more income through the zakat. It also meant more tradesmen and agricultural workers. Believers who were still living in Mecca were asked to relocate to Medina whenever they could do so.

Radi: Many new laws were also given to us about family life.

Modi: That is right, Radi. Allah and Muhammad made justice a big part of family life. By so doing, they showed non-believers a much superior religious philosophy and a more peaceful family life.

Mani: But Modi, why are some wives treated so unfairly now? It seems that honor killings now are threatening our reputation in Europe, Canada, and America.

Modi: Honor killings are not Islamic. They predate Islam, but many of our people do not understand the difference between our religion and our traditions. Our leaders still have to address strongly these inhumane practices. You are right to bring them up.

Mani: Perhaps we could get our government to spend the money for Public Relations work that includes documentary films and TV programs. We could put notices in newspapers and magazines. And we can teach the new generation in schools.

Modi: Whatever we do about Honor Killings, we had better start doing it now!

Radi: Don't you dare! Honor Killings are right and appropriate. People must be killed when they commit sin! Families cannot live in their communities without honor.

Harry J. Sweeney

Mani: If you were killed the first time you sinned, Radi, how many years would it have cost you so far?

Modi: I don't think Radi can count that high.

Radi: I can so. (Modi and Mani laugh at his answer)

Mani: What about verses 4:157 and 4:158 that rattled a few Christians? When you put them both together, they conflict greatly with the book. In Q4:156, Allah notes that Jews boasted of having slain "Jesus Christ, the son of Mary who claimed to be an apostle of God." Qur'an 4:157 states,

"However, they did not slay him, but it only seemed to them [as if it had been] so;[72] and verily, those who hold conflicting views thereon are indeed confused, having no [real] knowledge thereof, and following mere conjecture. For a certainty, they did not slay him. God raised him unto Himself[73] –and God is indeed wise."

Radi: I bet that showed the Christians something.

Modi: That is a part of the Qur'an that I never understood. When one considers all of the virtues of Allah, some of the ayats concerning Jews and Christians do not appear to coincide with His very nature. There are so many ways that ideas can be conveyed without calling good people of other religions fools or liars. Of course, I know I am not supposed to have the intelligence necessary to understand God.

Radi: At last you said something sensible.

Mani: Modi, you were just playing with another ayat from this sura,

---

72   Muhammad Asad in his note 171 (<u>Message of the Qur'an</u>) indicates that the Qur'an categorically denies the   Crucifixion as another fanciful legend surrounding Christ.

73 In his note 172, Asad explains the passage to mean that God honored him; He did not raise him physically up to Heaven.

The Restless Wind and Shifting Sands

number 82, I am surprised at you; and I expected Radi to call you on it.

Modi: You mean,

"Will they not, then, try to understand this Qur'an? Had it issued from any but God, they surely would have found in it many an inner contradiction."[74]

Mani: I seem to recall...

Modi: I would not go into what you are thinking with our f-r-i-e-n-d around.

Radi: Hey, wise guy! I know my name when it is spelled. (Modi and Mani laugh)

Mani: Radi, you know that Modi is doing you a favor by having these last three talks with you.

Radi: What is that supposed to mean?

Mani: Modi knows you need to know at least the gist of what al-Kitab is about, but he knows you will not be able to get much out of it without some help.

Radi: I see. So he is just giving me an outline of what the verses are talking about.

Mani: I read it myself a few times, but could not understand it until Modi showed me a few things.

Modi: Well, someone showed me; I just passed it on.

---

74 Muhammad Asad's note 97 assures us that the Qur'an is free of all inner contradictions—in spite of its having been revealed over a period of twenty-three years. He states it could only have been created by a supra-human source.

Harry J. Sweeney

Mani: Anyone know the *zuhr* time today? I forgot to check the newspaper.

Modi: According to the internet, Islamic Finder, zuhr is 12:12, asr is 2:58, maghrib is 5:17 and isha is 6.39.

Radi: Where did you get those times?

Modi: I just clicked on the Islamic Finder website, selected the country, then the city and it gave me a chart for the entire week. I could have selected a chart for the entire month. Well, pals, we do not have time to have lunch first, so off to *wudu* (pre-prayer ablutions). Except for you, Radi; you need a full body wash.

Radi: (Red-faced): I need a *ghusl?* Oh, you heard it, eh?

Mani: Yeah, and my nose detected it.

Radi: You guys are mean.

The Restless Wind and Shifting Sands

<u>Conversation 72: On Reading Sura 5; Killing Apostates</u>

Mani: I tried to read Sura 5 for three days. I knew what the verses mean, but I did not quite get the context. I seemed to be missing something.

Modi: In order to make sense out of the sura, you must realize that it was revealed after the Treaty of Hudaibiyya. That treaty cast a giant shadow over the entire sura.

Radi: There is nothing wrong with that treaty; it was a great victory.

Modi: I did not say there was anything wrong with the treaty—yet. If you remember, Radi, in the year 6 of the Hijira, Muhammad had either exiled or eliminated the tribes in and around Medina whom he did not trust. It included the hapless Banu Quraiza.

Radi: Ha! They surrendered to Muhammad and he decapitated all the men. I wish I had been there to help.

Mani: Perhaps I could wish that for you too.

Radi: You could?

Modi: Yes. I think seeing 800 men decapitated like that would be too much for even you, Radi. It included many unfortunate male children also, who were just old enough to have some pubic hair starting. The women and girls went into slavery. Radi, you would have to feel something after experiencing all that unnecessary death.

Mani: Radi is just posturing. I always feel bad just thinking of it. All of those people getting into line to have their heads sliced off. And the children, how horrified they must have been!

Radi: Forget that trash! As far as Muhammad could see at the time, Mecca had to be next; there was no city left he needed to take.

Harry J. Sweeney

Mani: That is when he gathered a force to gain entrance to Mecca for the lesser pilgrimage, Umrah. I bet that shook up the Meccans.

Modi: Yes, indeed. The Meccans still had an effective army, but they were losing the trade caravans and could not protect them and protect Mecca also.

Mani: So that is why the Meccans were eager to conclude a treaty. They were losing money and losing fighters.

Modi: The Meccans needed a breather, so they proposed that the Muslims could begin their pilgrimages to the Kaaba the following year. In addition, both sides pledged to cease hostilities for a ten year period.

Radi: Heh, heh. What a brilliant general! For the next eighteen months, Mecca took its breather while Muhammad built up his forces. He had no intention of waiting ten years to take Mecca. When he felt strong enough, Muhammad started again for Mecca with a large army to invade the city in defiance of the treaty.

Mani: That is when the Meccan leader went to Muhammad to try to call off the attack.

Radi: The leader's daughter tried that first and the believers just captured her. When her father showed up, he and his daughter were threatened with decapitation if they did not convert.

Modi: You are only partly right. Abu Sufyan's daughter, Ramlah was Muhammad's wife since the second year of the Hijira. About Abu Sufyan, however, even though his safety was guaranteed by Muhammad, Abu Sufyan indeed was threatened by decapitation if he did not convert. Guarantees were not always sacrosanct in that era.

Mani: After Abu Sufyan converted, Modi, he traveled to Mecca and assured the Meccans that the Muslims were ten thousand strong and

The Restless Wind and Shifting Sands

they were inviting a blood bath if they did not convert to Islam. So, the Muslims strolled into Mecca triumphantly.

Modi: Thus, when Yassir Arafat had returned from signing a treaty with the Jews, he assured everyone it was another Treaty of Hudaibiyya. It turned the catcalling into cheers. Some of the Jewish diplomats understood, but none of the Americans.

Radi: Yeah, I remember that. That was another brilliant move. When you cannot beat the enemy, sign a treaty with him. Then, when he is enjoying the peace, you build up your army to attack him.

Mani: I understand now. The rest of the sura was the believers consolidating their position by expanding and enforcing the laws they worked on in Medina, building mosques, and creating new laws for trade and commerce.

"O you who have believed, do not violate the rights of Allah or [the sanctity of] the sacred month or [neglect the marking of] the sacrificial animals and garlanding [them] or [violate the safety of] those coming to the Sacred House seeking bounty from their Lord and [His] approval. But when you come out of iúram (state of pilgrimage), then [you may] hunt. And do not let the hatred of a people for having obstructed you from al-Masjid al-haram (Mecca) lead you to transgress. And cooperate in righteousness and piety, but do not cooperate in sin and aggression. And fear Allah; indeed, Allah is severe in penalty." **Qur'an 5:2.**

Modi: You are right. They were building a new civilization and culture with the Qur'an, the hadiths, and their past history as the foundation documents. The Muslim state would now dominate every aspect of Muslim life in Arabia.

Mani: That is why I saw ayats insisting upon justice and guarding against the sinful administrations of their predecessors.

Modi: You should have noticed also that Allah stressed that the people pay strict attention to their Prophet and remain obedient to him and

Harry J. Sweeney

Allah. He laid out the case that if they did not obey the Prophet in all things, they could not save themselves from ghastly punishments.

"Allah has promised those who believe and do righteous deeds [that] for them there is forgiveness and great reward." 5:9. "But those who disbelieve and deny Our signs - those are the companions of Hellfire." 5:10.

Radi: Yes, and I am one of those punishments. See? I told you guys that Allah wants all these sinners purged from the face of the earth.

Modi: Down boy. You may interpret the ayats so, Radi; however, others do not interpret them the same way. You and people like you never have been commissioned as judge and jury over people.

Mani: I believe that, Radi. We have the sharia all right, but you are not the one to implement it. As Modi said, you and your cronies have no such credentials.

Radi: I need no badges to do Allah's work!

Modi: Nice try, Radi. However, the new Constitution that is still getting attention calls for a police force, judges, and juries. It will not be long before they will be adding in statutes against so-called religious executions. Vigilantes will be banned. Outlawed!

Radi: They said they will make no laws that conflict with the sharia or the Qur'an.

Modi: The Qur'an is not violated by such statutes.

Radi: What about killing infidels wherever you find them?

Mani: I guess you will need a time machine to take you back to Medina prior to 632. You could join with our Prophet and kill all the infidels and polytheists you can catch.

The Restless Wind and Shifting Sands

Radi: I think I have you on this one, though. What about killing apostates? If a person is a Muslim or was a Muslim, no matter the reason, and now professes not to be a Muslim, he is an apostate. The Sacred Law, o1.2 states that even "A Christian or a Jewish subject of an Islamic State" may kill an apostate from Islam without consequences.

Modi: If you look further into Book O, Radi, you will find that o8.3 states that only the caliph or his representative may kill an apostate. If someone else kills him, the killer is disciplined. And still further, o25.1 and Qur'an 4:59 orders believers to obey Allah and obey the Prophet and those of authority over you.

Mani: And from what I understand, Radi, not having a caliph does not give you the right to set yourself up as one. Wherever you are in a Muslim state, that state is your authority. You may kill an apostate and get away with it sometimes only because the state decides to take no action.

Modi: Mani is right. However, I am certain that once the police force is trained, they will arrest you and take you before a magistrate, who incidentally can be accepted as a representative of a caliph. You could be imprisoned for a long time, especially if the chap you killed is someone important.

Radi: I am not going to like these new rules.

Mani: Look how many people do not like your rules!

Modi: I have also been advised that people who have taken the law into their hands in these matters will not be given amnesty!

Radi: That is unfair! That is a change in the rule.

Mani: No way, Radi. The only change is now they are going after people who have been implementing their own rules.

Modi: Yours did not agree with Q 4:59, Radi.

Harry J. Sweeney

Radi: That is beside the point.

Modi: That is the point. Get it through your thick head—no amnesty, ever! Justice as well as law and order cry out continuously, no amnesty! And that includes amnesty with any other name.

Radi: Aaaargh! You guys also make me so…hungry!

The Restless Wind and Shifting Sands

<u>Conversation 73: On Reading Sura 6</u>

Radi: I have been studying Sura 6, Modi, and found it much easier than the others so far. I read it the first time without Maududi's introduction and thought I understood most of it; however, after I read Maududi, I found I had not understood it, and the introduction cleared it up.

Mani: I had the same experience, Radi.

Modi: Only the introduction warns you that you are reading the first Meccan Sura in the Qur'an, other than The Opening, and a sura revealed during the final year of Muhammad.

Radi: I did not understand, though, why Allah chose again to remind us He is the only God and to worship anyone or anything else is *shirk*, a grievous sin.

Mani: Hmm. That is close to what I was thinking. Suras 2 through 4 gave us a very good hint as to what was in store for us if we did not give Him His due.

Radi: I believe that it is Sura 6, ayat 32, that you thought should be reworded, Modi. Quote:

"And the life of this world is nothing but play and amusement. But far better is the house in the Hereafter for those who are al-Mutaqûn (the pious). Will you not then understand?"

Modi: I am surprised you remembered that, Radi. You are right. That ayat and others like it have been worded in such a way as to trash the only world we know and glorify the world we know not.

Mani: Why is that a problem?

Modi: Many people shrug off this life and dream only of the next. People should spend this life enjoying what Allah has given them in

Harry J. Sweeney

this life, the earth, the animals, the rain, rivers, and other people. They should also use their heads for thinking and improving themselves. Remember the first words of the verse: "And the life of this world is nothing but play and amusement." It is play and amusement for whom? Say that to some folks I know and they will be very, very upset.

Radi: I especially enjoy other people. Heh, heh.

Modi: Life should be pleasant, filled with the laughter of children and grandchildren, not dark and gloomy, filled with slavery, destruction, hatred, and violent death.

Mani: Look how many ayats followed that one, describing the retribution for sin. In ayat 43, Q6:43 to you, Radi, Satan was brought up. I always considered that *Shaitan* was an early Christian invention to give them a more powerful epithet to hurl at one another.[75]

Radi: You will sing another tune when you meet up with Him, Mani.

Mani: No thanks, having you for a friend is quite enough.

Modi: I read ayat 137 first in the Noble Qur'an of the Saudis, and I thought I knew the tradition to which the ayat referred but was not sure. I switched to the Glorious Qur'an of Pickthall, and it was much clearer. However, the *Message of the Qur'an* of Asad not only cleared it up, but the reference note (123)[76] was outstanding. Q6:140 agrees with his reference note, calling such parents "ignorant." Ayat 151 of this sura also shows Allah's great displeasure about Arabs killing their

---

75   *The Origin of Satan*, by Elaine Pagels.

76   Note 123: "This is a reference to the custom prevalent among the pre-Islamic Arabs of burying alive some of their unwanted children, mainly girls, and also to the occasional offering of a boy-child in sacrifice to one or another of their idols. Apart from this historical reference, the above Qur'an verse seems to point out, by implication, the psychological fact that an attribution of divinity to anyone or anything but God brings with it an ever-growing dependence on all kinds of imaginary powers which must be "propitiated" by formal and often absurd and cruel rites: and this, in turn, leads to the loss of all spiritual freedom and to moral self-destruction." Muhammad Asad.

The Restless Wind and Shifting Sands

children. Three times in one sura Allah condemns the practice of honor killing!

Mani: Is ayat Q6:137 the one about burying baby girls alive? Tradition often is ignorance carried forward without question by uneducated people. Can you imagine burying your baby girl alive for any damned reason? I have a very playful daughter who is the delight of my life. When I watch her at play, I see Allah's most beautiful gift to a father and mother. And when she looks at me and smiles, that is itself paradise! If ever I would want time to stand still, it is only when I hold her and hear her laughter.

Radi: You will have to find a good husband for her. Oh!

(Mani punches Radi and knocks him down.)

Radi: What is the matter with you? Are you crazy?

Mani: When I talk about my beautiful baby girl, Radi, I do not want to hear anything about finding husbands, arranging marriages, honor killings, or anything else in that dirty mind of yours. When I speak beautiful words about my baby girl, you had better just listen and say nothing.

(Modi helps Radi to his feet. Radi rubs his jaw. He opens his mouth to speak, but Modi clamps his hand over his mouth.)

Modi: Just listen for a while, Radi. Do not say anything.

Mani: I heard you say many times a certain sentence and ran into it only last night in this sura, ayat 144:

"And who could be more wicked than he who, without any (real) knowledge, attributes his own lying inventions to God, and thus leads people astray. Behold, God does not grace (such) evildoing folk with His guidance."

Harry J. Sweeney

Modi: Yes. How many imams are simply making up rules or rearranging the wording on ayats or leaving words out of ayats to fit a personal, political, or tactical agenda that they consider holy? God never said what they are imputing to Him. Surely that would rate a very special place in hell.

Mani: Radi is still quiet. I think Q6:144 makes him feel ill.

Modi: I believe that you should let him be for a while, now that he is quiet. However, you should be glad that he is quiet this time. Something may be getting through to him.

Radi: I heard my name mentioned. I did not realize that honor killings were so evil. I thought Allah commanded that they be done.

Modi: Good for you, Radi. You are joining the human race.

Radi: Who's ahead?

Mani: Not the humans, that is for sure.

Radi: There is one ayat in this sura that tells me that I am right in punishing people who sin. It is Q6:157:

"We shall requite those who turn away from Our messages in disdain with evil suffering for having thus turned away."

Wouldn't you say that the verse gives me the right to torture the fool before I lop off his head?

Modi: The ayat does not say that a believer must punish those who turn away from "Our messages with evil suffering for having thus turned away." It says "We will", meaning Allah will see to it. If you suddenly were given superhuman sight and you saw one of God's angels about to smite an evildoer, would you interfere and try to smite the evildoer first?

The Restless Wind and Shifting Sands

Radi: Of course not. I would honor the angel's presence and his task.

Modi: Then, Radi, when you see an evildoer, just presume that he soon will meet such an angel whose task it is to smite him. Therefore, if you plan to do it yourself, you are only interfering with Allah's work. Then go on about your business and be pleased with yourself because Allah sees all and knows our hidden thoughts.

Radi: That is something to think about.

Mani: I left my slip of paper at home. What are the prayer times today?

Modi: Well, you already know that *Fajr* was 4:34 AM. *Zuhr* will be at 11:52 PM, *Asr* at 3:14 PM, *Maghrib* at 5:57 PM and *Isha* will be at 7:09 PM.[77]

Mani: I am amazed at your memory. How can you just rattle those times off like that?

Modi: There is a neighborhood message board behind you. The times are posted there.

Mani: Looks as if we just have time for *wudu*; oops, Bilal has started to call.

Radi: Mani, I apologize for getting you upset.

Mani: Please, do not apologize. We Arabs have an image to maintain.

---

77   The prayer times for October 1, 2009. http://www.islamicity.com/Prayer-Times/nprayvb4.asp?daylgt=N&stdate=&endate=&dstgroup=0&citydisplay=Baghdad&statedisplay=Baghdad&countrydisplay=Iraq&zipdisplay=n%2Fa&searchmode=ByCityID&city=Baghdad&gmt=3&latd=033&latm=20.3&latS=N&longd=044&longm=23.63&longW=E&id=2476526&zipcode=&intvl=0&rad1=2&Month7=10&Year7=2009&MonthQ=1&YearQ=0&YearY=0&hm7=9&hy7=1430&calculate=Calculate+Prayer+Times+for+Baghdad%2C+Baghdad%2C+Iraq

Harry J. Sweeney

Radi: OK, to hell with you then. I will not bother to clean my knife to kill you.

Mani: That's better. Apology accepted.

[This conversation was partially adapted from Maududi's Introduction to Sura 6]

The Restless Wind and Shifting Sands

<u>Conversation 74: On Understanding Sura 6</u>

Mani: Good morning, Modi: I went through Sura 6 the last two nights. It seems to me that Allah was still vexed at the Meccans.

Modi: Remember, this chapter, along with Sura 5, was released during the last year of Muhammad's life. You recall that the Meccans were forced to convert to what they called "Muhammad's religion," but many Meccans still bristled at the situation. They did their best to ignore him.

Mani: They ignored him even though they knew that Allah was behind him?

Modi: As authoritative as Muhammad and Islam was in Medina, Modi, it was not the same in Mecca. Remember, the Meccans set out to kill him more than once when he lived there. That is the main reason for his escape to Yathrib. It was life or death for him. Even after all this time, the people of Mecca were still not too sure Allah was actually behind him.

Mani: I noticed that Allah stopped addressing the believers and turned to the Jews again in this sura.

Modi: The Jews first lost their assets, then their homes, and finally their lives. They were trying to follow the commandments in their Torah, all 613 of them, minus a few that pertain only to Israel. Jewish scholars, who loved every word of the Torah and spent lifetimes studying less than a paragraph, were accused of changing the commandments and debasing the religion. I have to believe that someone changed the texts, but if it were not the scholars who loved every sacred letter of the scriptures, who could it have been? Who could have corrupted the religion?

Mani: Allah revealed to Muhammad that the scriptures were changed and the religion thus corrupted. Our Most Beloved was angry with them in Medina for such corruption. Should Allah have revealed exactly who did it? That would have been important to know then and now.

Harry J. Sweeney

Modi: Allah does what He sees fit and does so in His own time, Mani. Muhammad also became angry because the scholars rejected his prophethood, and they told him straight on he did not know Hebrew scripture well enough to criticize anything. It was after that exchange that Allah began to reveal that Muhammad was right in what he said.

Radi: Muhammad knew Hebrew scripture better than the Jews, Modi; he told them that Allah had revealed their perfidies to him. He was right to go to them and tell them that he knew all about it. In ayat 7:35 and 7:36, Allah revealed:

"Oh children of Adam, if there come to you messengers from among you relating to you my verses, then whoever fears Allah and reforms—there will be no fear concerning them, nor will they grieve;" "but they who give the lie to Our messages and scorn them in their pride—these are destined to the fire, therein to abide."

Mani: It seems to me that Allah was giving the Jews a second chance to abandon what they were doing and follow the teachings of the Qur'an. Then they would be saved.

Modi: But Mani, that was your interpretation. You are a Muslim and not a Jewish scholar, one who had spent decades studying the Torah, trying to understand God's every word. Mani, Radi, with all that you know now and how you love Muhammad and the Qur'an, suppose a new prophet descended from Mt. Hira with good credentials and said that someone in our past screwed up and got everything wrong and that we must return to the Jewish Torah. How would you take that?

Radi: Terrible! How would we know he was a true prophet?

Modi: How did our fathers know who Muhammad was?

Radi: He waged war against the unbelievers and won against great odds.

The Restless Wind and Shifting Sands

Modi: And the Israelis on the first day of existence crushed seven Arab armies when the Arab armies had them outnumbered shamefully! Look we can argue all day on whether the Jews deserved the fulmination to which they have been subjected for centuries. We need to move on.

Mani: Ayat 7:172 seems to have gone in a different direction.

"And whenever thy Sustainer brings forth their offspring from the loins of the children of Adam, He [thus] calls upon them to bear witness about themselves: 'Am I not your sustainer?'—to which they answer: "Yea, indeed, we do bear witness thereto."

Radi: I have no idea what that means. (Mani nods his head in agreement).

Modi: I admit I had some problems with that ayat myself. Fortunately, Muhammad Asad addressed it.[78] He indicated that Allah has given all of us the innate ability to perceive the Supreme Being, so people who resist the messages are doing so for their own cynical reasons. They will pay dearly for such resistance.

Mani: But what about 7:199:

"Make due allowance for man's nature and enjoin the doing of what is right; and leave alone all those who choose to remain ignorant."

Modi: (laughs) That one seems to be a little different from 7:172 which you said previously. It warns not to expect too much from humanity; after all, men were created weak; therefore do not be too harsh with those who err. That sounds like something that could be addressed to you, Radi.

Radi: You made that up! (Mani shows him the ayat from his working Qur'an. He quickly covers it with the cloth again.)

---

78   *Message of the Qur'an*, Muhammad Asad, note 139, page 261.

Harry J. Sweeney

Modi: So it appears that trying to understand the Qur'an by simply reading it is asking for trouble.

Mani: I can see that. I really thought I knew it well, Modi, but I can see I did not. Even now, after all of this, I know I need to spend more time on it.

Modi: In all of this time we have reviewed only seven suras. The answer I seek is where these radical imams get the temerity to tell us that they know the Qur'an and where it tells them to kill Christians and Jews. It has been more than 1,300 years since problems had occurred with some Christians living in Arabia; those were only on the fringe of Christianity. And Palestine is really the only thorn in the side of the Arabs as far as Jews are concerned—Palestine and the state of Israel.

Mani: Well, there does seem to be a lot of bad blood between Christians and believers. Where did we get such enmity?

Modi: Remember the crusades?

Mani: Oh, yeah. I heard quite a few stories about them.

Modi: Again, Mani, it is too far in the past to be considered anything but ancient history. It should never factor into anything that goes on today. Nobody is trying to suppress our religion! Nobody cares what religion anybody follows—except us!

Radi: We are commanded very seriously never to rest until *"Allahu Akbar"* is heard from every corner of the earth.

Modi: I guess Radi just woke up. Radi, that expression is heard from almost every corner of the earth now. If you want, we could finance some trips for you to the North and South Poles to start some echoes there.

Radi: What?

The Restless Wind and Shifting Sands

Modi: Radi, Islam is just about in every country of the world, even Ireland. Scotland is advertising for more Muslim immigrants. What more do you want?

Mani: Well, what do we do now?

Modi: We need to keep studying and learn how to be as good as we are supposed to be. That, my friend, is true jihad; jihad does not include making war on poor, innocent tourists.

Mani: How will we know when we get to that point?

Modi: We will cover that a little later. Meanwhile, according to my watch, we should start walking toward the mosque for a little *wudu,* some prayer, and a good speaker.

Mani: Lunch, afterwards?

Modi: Who is buying?

Mani: Radi.

Radi: What? I just bought!

Mani: Yeah, two weeks ago.

Harry J. Sweeney

Conversation 75: "Strike from them every fingertip!"

Mani: Are you certain that we will be safe here in the open? There seems to be more traffic on that road down there than I would have guessed. Aren't we too close to Tikrit?

Modi: That is the Al-Haditha-to-Kirkuk road you are scanning. It does have lots of traffic. We are about 40 miles northwest of Tikrit, but it is off this road. Anything coming from Tikrit would come from that crossroads about 5 miles east of here; that traffic would be coming the other way.

Mani: I know Saddam is dead, but he still gives me chills to be so close to Tikrit.

Modi: Have some Saudi coffee. I put some in the flask to prevent chills.

Mani: Saudi coffee? What on earth is Saudi coffee? Do you drink some and turn into a toad or something?

Modi: It is just strong coffee. It is very strong. You can get it in almost any shop, but you have to ask.

Mani: I will wait. Modi, there is a lot of military traffic down there.

Modi: That is expected. About three years ago, some U.S. troops received a tip from locals about some bad stuff not too far from here. They found a cache of chemical agents, missiles, and two mobile laboratories. They were pretty excited about that. So, the military folks have been returning here on and off, to ensure that they don't miss anything. Recently, they found some cars that were being stuffed with explosives. The terrorists ran off before they could finish their tasks, leaving the almost-finished car-bombs.

Mani: What kind of chemical agents? I don't remember that.

The Restless Wind and Shifting Sands

Modi: GF nerve gas (Cyclosarin) for one. I don't know if they ever identified the other one. I never saw a follow-up to the story. Some of the missiles were surface to surface, others surface to air. You know about the three car-bombs, don't you?

Mani: That was on TV. So, it seems that the bad guys come way out here, build explosives into some cars, and drive them to wherever they want.

Modi: That is why they hired all of us. We just watch the traffic to see if there is anything unusual on or off the road. It is worth the money to have teams of spotters every two or three miles. I want to look at that old car. (Looks through binoculars)

Mani: Do you see anything unusual?

Modi: No. The driver is not too young and not too prosperous, so he fits the car he is driving. Wait! He has no passengers, and the sedan is big enough. I am going to call it in. It costs money enough to drive from Al-Haditha up here. He would have looked around for someone to help pay for petrol. (Modi speaks with someone on cell phone). Ha! The authorities will check it out. They said it could have been someone from the oil fields a few miles down the road. They are all over the place here anyway.

Mani: Will the headquarters people call you if they catch someone?

Modi: They may wait until we return to the unit. They do not want too much phone traffic. You can bet that al-Qaida monitors our traffic whenever they can. They do not have any FISA laws to keep them from finding what is on their enemies' minds. Remind me not to move to America; it is not safe there. They have unusual people who are deathly afraid of offending anyone, even their enemies. They would kill everyone in the country before letting them monitor enemy spy traffic. They seem to deny spies are already there, awaiting orders to attack one or more of their cities. Americans have done some good things for us.

Harry J. Sweeney

I would like to repay them by turning their Uriah Heeps over to Radi; I would tell him they are polytheists.

Mani: I bet Radi is fit to be tied. He was ready to take on Sura 9 today. I know he has been studying it.

Modi: Good for him. He is still pretty shaky with some of those verses, but he does not go off like a rocket any more. He is a little more careful about what he says.

Mani: That's what scares me. Usually we know what is on his mind. I would rather hear him yell he is coming for my head—then I know to run like crazy. This way, he may decide to burn my house down, and I would not know until I smelled smoke.

Modi: He was trained by the wrong imams. Remember when he was really hot about verse 8:12?

Mani: Let me see, 8:12:

*"**Remember when your Lord inspired to the angels. 'I am with you, so strengthen those who have believed. I will cast terror into the hearts of those who disbelieved, so strike [them] above the necks, and strike from them every fingertip.'"***

Yes, I remember he was going to sharpen his sword and sneak up on the soldiers one by one. He did not know why he had to cut off fingertips, though. He was dead certain that the ayat meant kill everyone not a Muslim.

Modi: Hold that thought! That was the Saudi translation. The other translations are close enough, and in any case it is not the translations that are so important. What is important is the entire thought. They recite only a small part of the text and make everyone think it means something terrible. I told Radi that Muhammad had a common problem with his troops. It was their first big battle—Badr. They were greatly outnumbered, and they had the jitters. The Meccans had

354

The Restless Wind and Shifting Sands

poisoned the nearby wells, but Allah saw to it that it rained enough to provide sufficient water and gave the army of believers the inner calm they needed. Mani, that one idea took three verses, 8:09 to 8:11 before He got to 8:12. They repeated only the middle verse.

Mani: So Allah only was reminding them that He was their strength and their salvation.

Modi: You are correct. The believers did not want to go. If Muhammad had not announced that those who died on the battlefield would be martyrs and go to paradise immediately, he would have had a few more problems.

Mani: I can imagine that. But continue with ayat 8:12.

Modi: That part of the verse that talked about striking the necks and the fingertips meant "destroy them utterly"[79] or something to that effect, like the American expression "let's go clean their clocks." He was not collecting fingertips. But Allah continued:

"This because they have cut themselves off from God and His Apostle -- verily God is severe in retribution. (8:13) This for you, O enemies of God! Taste it then and know that suffering through fire awaits those who deny the truth." (8:14)

Mani: So what Allah was really saying was, Don't be afraid of the Meccans. I am angry with them for turning away from Me, so I am not going to let them harm you. Now, go out and clean their clocks!

Modi: That is about it. A pep rally. When you put it all together, it is nothing at all, despite the terrible horror that some imams make out of it. And by the way, notice that by *unbelievers* He was not talking about Christians and Jews; He was talking about the Meccans who refused to believe Muhammad. Anyone who says that verse talks about Americans is sick!

---

79   *Message of the Qur'an*, Muhammad Asad, note 15, page 272.

Harry J. Sweeney

Mani: Wait, Modi. You recited a verse the other day about that from Sura 6.

Modi: (Narrows his eyes and thinks) Aha! Ayat 6:21,

"And who could be more wicked than he who attributes his own lying inventions to God or gives the lie to His messages? Verily, such evildoers will never attain to a happy state."

Mani: I am glad you remembered that one. Every time I want to tell Radi about it, I cannot think of it. He in turn should tell those ratty friends of his about that ayat. If they keep filling his head with their nonsense, they are responsible for whatever evil comes out of it.

Modi: Yes, I know. I was really worried about the statements of bin Laden and Zawahiri, but thanks to these people north and west of Baghdad, I can see that they have not lost faith and realize what those two liars are doing.

Mani: I have to admit, I was taken in also. I am always envious of those terrorists who seem to be so much stronger in their religion, and I always feel that I should do something grand to make up for my laxity. But as you say, they are not really stronger in their religion, they are simply following an agenda of bitterness, hatred, and violence, and they lie about the source.

Modi: That is their plan. They are like Ali Baba trying to open up secret passages in the minds of those who only think they have been lax. They want to exploit the false guilt and entice good people into doing something awful to make up for their imagined laxity. Good people always seem to think they are not good enough; that is what makes them vulnerable to con artists like Ayman and Osama. Allah will see to it on Judgment Day that bin Laden and Zawahiri are shown to be what they are, *ibaad ash-shaitaan*--servants of Satan. Their abode shall be the fire forever.

Mani: I really believe, Modi, that you should be a registered imam. You

The Restless Wind and Shifting Sands

truly are an imam. I do not know what kind of fool I would be without your wisdom.

Modi: Thank you for those kind words. Here, have some Saudi coffee.

Mani: Whoa! This stuff is outrageous (hic), but it warms me all over. What on earth is it?

Modi: Very strong coffee.

Mani: (sniffs the flask) It smells like something besides coffee.

Modi: Don't ask. Just enjoy. Take another swig—I mean sip.

Mani: On second thought, it is nice. I still can't tell what it is, but now I don't care.

Harry J. Sweeney

<u>Conversation 76: Discussing Sura 8.</u>

Radi: I am glad you two returned in good shape. I was worried about you.

Mani: Why should you be worried about us? We were with relatives and friends.

Radi: While you were gone, I managed to put a few other things aside and really studied Sura 8. To understand the sura, I discovered, it was necessary to know the problems Muhammad was having in Mecca with his own tribe, the Quraish.

Mani: It is a little hot. If we are going to discuss Chapter 8, let's sit under that tree. Muhammad said quite a lot to the Meccans that led them to believe that they were going to lose their income from the Kaaba. That was too much for them to handle. They were ready to murder him for that.

Radi: What I understand is that many of the Quraish were outraged when they heard about the "Night Journey to Jerusalem". If it had not been for Abu Bakr swearing that he believed that story, our prophet would have been targeted with more criticism.

Modi: You both seem to miss something even more important. When the Quraish discovered the followers of Muhammad were moving from Mecca to Medina in small groups, they decided that they had to put an end to Muhammad before he too escaped.

Radi: Yes. That is when they decided that the team of assassins should be made up of one member of each of the families of the Quraish, except Muhammad's family, to do the killing and avoid retaliation. They were willing to pay the blood money if it came to that.

Modi: Not only were they angry about Muhammad speaking against their gods and their way of life, they were also outraged that he would betray them by moving to Yathrib, their competitor city. That was like

The Restless Wind and Shifting Sands

joining the enemy then. Remember, your family first, then the tribe. There is no number three. Yathrib, on the other hand, welcomed him into their midst because of their feuding. They needed an arbitrator desperately.

Mani: And he told them up front that they would have to accept him as a prophet as well. But Modi, how did he obtain so much power there?

Modi: As soon as he began solving their feuding, he recognized that all the tribes needed new laws on dealing with each other and they needed a new social culture. Since he was in the process of developing the new religion, he saw that the new Muslims and the tribes of Yathrib needed the same instructions.

Radi: So, while he was expanding tasks to deal with the people of Yathrib, Arabs and Jews both, he was also attaining more and more power that went with those tasks.

Modi: Right. He was a referee, magistrate, lawgiver, mayor, and chief financial officer of Yathrib, soon to be renamed Medina (Madinat an-Nabi, City of the Prophet). However, that was not so important to him as defeating the Meccans and bringing his new religion to them.

Mani: What made him attack the Meccans while he was still under strength?

Modi: Many scholars look toward the idea that Muhammad needed a fight to cement his position a little better in Medina and to let the Meccans know that the Muslims were no pushovers. I doubt that this thinking was complete. Remember, more and more believer families were leaving Mecca and coming into Medina with little more than their clothes and a few other possessions.

Radi: I can see that. They needed help to settle in, not to mention food and shelter.

Harry J. Sweeney

Modi: Muhammad knew that there was a caravan on its way back from Syria with about $250,000 in trade goods. If he could attack and take that caravan, he could relieve the suffering of the new arrivals and also relieve a few other folks in Medina. At the same time, he could hurt the Quraish economically and politically.

Radi: Muhammad went out to meet the Meccans, outnumbered three to one.

Mani: Not quite, Radi. The leader of the caravan got word to the Meccan militia that the caravan was now safe, so everyone could go home. Many of them did go home. The militia were not professional fighters, and they were scrambled before they could get ready for battle or even alert their allies in the area. Others wanted to go home but were coerced or shamed into staying. By the time Muhammad's followers attacked, those followers were the superior force.

Modi: Sun Tzu said "There are battles that should not be fought and commands that should not be obeyed." Badr, for the Meccans, is one of those battles. They were not ready for it, they did not have the heart for it, and a large number simply went home, feeling that there was no longer any need for a battle. The Muslims won the battle and took many spoils of war home with them.

Mani: What is even more important, Modi, they were now a power in Arabia.

Modi: You are right about that. They went from a small religion in a state to the state itself. Of course, Muhammad gave all the credit to the thousand angels that Allah sent to help.

Radi: It also helped that the war booty was shared generously with the fighters who actually fought the battle. Wasn't that in the Qur'an, Sura 8, ayat 41?

"And know that anything you obtain of war booty—then indeed, for Allah is one fifth of it and for the Messenger and for [his] near

The Restless Wind and Shifting Sands

relatives and orphans, the needy, and the [stranded] traveler, if you have believed in Allah and in which We sent down to Our Servant on the day of criterion—the day when two armies met. And Allah, over all things, is competent."

Mani: That sounds a little cryptic to me.

Modi: The revelation is saying in only so many words that it is not really spoils of war because Allah caused the victory. He could very well have withheld the victory to teach them a lesson. It is His bounty and is allowing the fighters and family of martyrs to share in this bounty.

Radi: But what about the angels? Were angels there or not?

Modi: Remember Muhammad Asad's Note 14?[80] Angels never actually physically fought in any battle. Of course, one might agree that Muhammad's genius was worth more than a thousand angels in any battle.

Mani: Many imams are actually telling their pupils that angels fought in those battles and will help us against Western armies.

Modi: They should receive at least 100 stripes for each time they teach that nonsense. The same with the counselors who refuse to tell Muslim wannabes about what could happen if they become disillusioned by the religion and decide to leave it. Even the Catholics give their nuns a long opt-out period of time. Even afterwards, when they have been full-fledged nuns for years, they can quit without sanctions.

Radi: I believe in the angels. And you know how I feel about apostates.

Mani: Sometimes you think only with your knife.

Radi: Thou shalt not suffer an apostate to live.

---

80   *Message of the Qur'an*, Muhammad Asad, page 272.

Harry J. Sweeney

Mani: Radi, you got that one wrong. I do not know where you hear these things! It is, "Thou shalt not suffer a witch to live." And it is a Christian saying, not ours, you dimwatt.

Radi: Whatever. I thought it sounded appropriate.

Mani: You know, if we get ourselves up from under this tree, we might have time to get a bite to eat before Bilal calls us to prayer.

Modi: I don't know. We could give it a try.

Radi: I probably should go home first and do some chores.

Modi: Fine with me. I'm buying.

Radi: Aha! Where are we dining?

Mani: It figures.

[This conversation was partially adapted from Maududi's Introduction to Sura 8.]

The Restless Wind and Shifting Sands

<u>Conversation 77: Discussing the Sharia in London.</u>

Introducing three new characters, from London. They are good friends but do not always see things the same way. Yaman is an original immigrant from Morocco and quite moderate in his views, while Umran is a first-generation British-born extremist with many radical friends, and Martin is a second-generation British-born technician who is apolitical.

Umran: Ha! We are winning big battles now. Have you read the papers? We are going to be ruled here in the United Kingdom by the sharia.

Yaman: I did not come to this country to be ruled by the sharia. I came here to escape from the sharia and from people who love to abuse it. I came here to be British.

Martin: What is the sharia?

Umran: It is Islamic law, you fool. Hasn't your imam taught you anything?

Martin: What's an imam? I will have you know that I graduated from all the schools and have a good job. You seem to have lots of time on your hands. Do you have a job?

Umran: If you do not know what an imam is, you have left your religion! Your head should leave you and probably will soon enough. Of course I have work! I monitor our religion here and teach everyone what they should do about the British abuse of our religion.

Yaman: You are crazy. You are just now saying the Brits are giving us the sharia——and I say they are nuts for even thinking in those terms. And then you say they are abusing us. But you may be right at that; making us abide by the sharia is definitely abuse.

363

Harry J. Sweeney

Martin: The sharia, is that where they cut off your hooks if the peelers pinch you for nicking some bloke's wallet?

Yaman: What?

Martin: I said, doesn't the sharia call for cutting off hands and feet?

Yaman: Yes, it does but only for serious offenses. If you steal food to feed your family, they don't amputate.

Umran: Thank Allah for small favors! I heard about a robbery not too far from here and that is the excuse the bugger gave in court. The judge said you don't feed your family by stealing a truckload of bread.

Martin: Whoa! I am gobsmacked. You mean some bloody scroat wants to bring that bog stuff up here for the new mingers downtown?

Yaman: What?

Martin: You must learn English one of these days. I said some jerk wants to bring that absurd nonsense to jolly old England for the immigrants?

Yaman: The archbishop says Muslims could choose the legal system they want to be ruled under.

Umran: Yes. He said that there should be an end to the monopoly on British law by such things as British history, Christian ethics, English Common Law, and western civilization.[81]

Yaman: I cannot see how anyone who calls himself British could dare to bring in such medieval claptrap. That is brutish, not British.

Umran: You are insulting Islam! That is a crime here. You will go to jail.

---

81   SPECTATOR.CO.UK. "*Dhimmi*—or just dim?" Saturday, 9 February 2008.

The Restless Wind and Shifting Sands

Yaman: Now tell Martin here what the sharia would say about that?

Umran: Well, naturally you would be killed, perhaps beheaded.

Martin: For giving an opinion? Coo. That is slime.

Umran: Of course. It is a grave sin to have such opinions!

Martin: You barmy blokes are round the bloody bend.

Umran: What?

Yaman: I think he means you bloody fools are nuts! Martin, you could also be sentenced to death for insulting the Prophet, heresy, having sex with someone not your spouse, unless it is your slave, refusing to marry the person picked out for you, and several other things.

Martin: Those are just blow-offs.[82] What if one bloke kills another?

Yaman: That is the retaliation section. If one person kills your sister without a good reason, you can kill him if you can find him, or if you can't find him, you can kill his sister. Another alternative is accepting blood money for the killing. You may have to settle for half of what you would get if he killed your brother.

Martin: They think they can flog that to the local twits?

Yaman: They know they cannot convince the British people, they only have to sell it to the leadership, and they will make laws of it.

Umran: They should get used to the sharia as soon as possible. Once we convert the United Kingdom to a Muslim country, everyone will be under sharia law. Then many heads will roll. Many heads!

Yaman: I had that thought. And the first heads will be the British leaders who made all of this possible.

---

82   Petty, not worth thinking about.

Harry J. Sweeney

Umran: Yes. Isn't that hilarious?

Martin: Total pants, you wanker!

Umran, Yaman together: What?

Martin: You don't know Brits. They don't snocker well. You can bugger that stuff and hop it if it was up to them.

Yaman: I believe he is saying that the entire idea is terrible and the British people cannot be scammed. You are right, Martin, but remember that it is the leadership that is being fed this dog food.

Umran: What language is that?

Yaman: It is street-talk.

Umran: That language should be against the law. It is a code. Everyone speaking it is dangerous and should be beheaded.

Yaman: How dare you speak so ill of a country that takes you in and gives you a living wage until you find work—and you don't even look for work. When you came here, you were supposed to become British, not an extremist agitator.

Martin: You can take that load of cobblers and codswallop and bugger off before you come-a-cropper here, you gagging wanker. We believe in horses for courses, not your piddle dribble.

Umran : Pardon me for staring, but I have no idea are you saying?

Yaman: I am pretty sure he said you should pack up your bull crap and get lost before you get what is coming to you here. The Brits believe in letting people alone to get along with one another and they don't need the cow pies you peddle.

Umran: Why didn't he say that?

The Restless Wind and Shifting Sands

Yaman: I thought he did. Eloquently.

Umran (looks at his watch): It is time for *wudu*.

Yaman: I will show you. It is nearby. It is only a little mosque, temporary, but soon we will have the biggest in Europe right here in London. It will be seen all during the Olympics.

Umran: Isn't Martin coming along with us?

Yaman: He does not observe. He is happy the way he is and does not want to be bothered. He is really a decent person. I have a lot of respect for his ability and his advice.

Umran: Aha, a cultural believer. But he should be killed… (Yaman grabs his shirt collar and pulls him closer, nose to nose).

Yaman: Look, you sod, you had better cut the crap or by Allah I will clean your clock. I will pray with you because we are believers, but get it through your thick skull that Martin is a believer just as good as you or anyone else. He loves Allah his way. He does not need to visit a mosque or pray five times per day to be good in God's eyes or ours. And he does not believe in going around killing people for stupid reasons! (He lets go of the shirt; Umran runs away.)

Yaman: He is going the wrong way—he's heading for the synagogue.

Martin: He's in for a bit of fun; the Israelis are having a do there today.

Harry J. Sweeney

<u>Conversation 78: Discussion of Sura 9</u>.

Modi: Look at Al-Tabah, Sura 9, verse 38.

"O you who have attained the faith! What is amiss with you that, when you are called upon, "Go forth to war in God's cause," you cling to the earth? Would you comfort yourselves with the comforts of this worldly life in preference to the good of the life to come? But the enjoyment of life in this world is but a paltry thing when compared to the life to come."

Mani: Why are you starting that far into Sura 9? Radi and I both spent quite some time at the beginning.

Modi: I guessed that you would. But the verses 38 to 41 are really the theme for the sura. In one sense, it seems to be an extension of Sura 8; remember there is no "Bismillah" in the introduction. In another sense, however, it was revealed long after Sura 8.

Radi: I thought the chapter was going to talk about crushing the unbelievers who have already been given the opportunity to become believers. I was specifically looking at ayat 29:

"Fight against those who – despite having been vouchsafed [aforetime]—do not [truly] believe either in God or the Last Day, and do not consider forbidden that which God and His Apostle have forbidden, and do not follow the religion of truth [which God has enjoined upon them], till they agree to pay the exemption tax (jizya) with a willing hand, after having been humbled [in war]."

Modi: Radi, it already follows the other suras to date. Up to this time, Muhammad was concerned with the Meccans. The Meccans were bad enough, but now he was facing the possibility of battle with the Roman Empire. The Romans had just defeated the Persians and he thought they were now looking to wipe out the Muslims.

Mani: That is where the armies met at Mutah and our Muslim armies were handed a defeat.

The Restless Wind and Shifting Sands

Modi: That is correct; however, Islamic scholars always call it a victory. They do not seem to realize that our army would have been wiped out and the Roman armies would have continued to Medina if the Roman commander had not suspected Muhammad's usual trick of retreat and ambush. The Romans indeed beat the Muslims, no contest, but the Muslims conned the Romans away from total victory.

Radi: I believe it was a victory.

Modi: Radi, you may turn into a real loser if you continue to think that how you want things to end can by itself change the reality. Look at what Allah was saying in ayat 38; now listen to 39-41:

"If you do not go forth to war in God's cause, He will chastise you with a grievous chastisement, and place another people in your stead—whereas you shall in no wise harm Him: for, God has the power to will anything…

"Go forth to war, whether it be easy or difficult for you, and strive hard in God's cause with your possessions and your lives: this is for your own good – if you but knew it."

Mani: Our people must have been very upset to become acquainted with a revelation upbraiding them like that. Nonetheless, we must keep in mind that preparing for war against Romans is very serious.

Radi: (Bares his knife) Are you saying you doubt that Allah and his angels would bring us victory? Tell me.

Mani: Shut up and put your goat-sticker away, Radi. We are in an important discussion here. Just listen if you cannot contribute any wisdom.

Modi: I understand what you are saying, and it is very serious. It is also important, however, to remember that the sura only talks about Romans and Muslims and the 7th century. Look, Muhammad knew better than to send an inferior force against the Romans. When our army saw what they were facing, they wanted to wait and send for all available

Harry J. Sweeney

reinforcements—which probably would not have helped. Someone did not hear the order to hold fast and the troops continued marching against the Romans and were routed. We lost three commanders. One commander used up 9 swords in the battle.

Radi: Our armies went out again 30,000 strong to defeat the Romans at Tabuk, but the Romans retreated when they saw us.

Modi: Oh good grief! I do not know who told you that, Radi, but what was a major battle to us at Mutah, to the Romans was only a minor skirmish with bandits. The Romans did not retreat; they did not consider us a threat and did not even have any troops in the area because they had no reason for it. Radi, we were small fry to the Romans.

Mani: I could see a problem coming. The people were pushed to give up not only their lives, but their possessions again. In the old days, when they were fighting Meccans, the people would invest in our army and rake in profits on their investment. They were not so sure about investing in war with the Romans. They were not a gang of country bumpkins with little or no training. They were real power!

Radi: Ah, we could have defeated the Romans just as we can defeat the Americans.

Modi: Radi, here in Iraq, our several armies were defeated in less than a week. The much bragged-about Republican Guards did not want any part of the Americans; they hid their uniforms and took off. Even our big, brave, fight-to-the-death Saddam found himself a deep hole and dived into it.

Mani: Yes, Radi. You must see things as they are. You are leaving yourself vulnerable to those lying imams that would make you believe we have the power to fight the world and win.

Radi: Hah! So much you know. We are taking Europe without firing a shot.

The Restless Wind and Shifting Sands

Modi: I must admit that it looked like that for a while, but even The Netherlands and Denmark did a Charles Martel[83] on you. You will find that even European Muslims will not agree with you anymore. People like Holland's Geert Wilders are making the people of Europe look around and think.

Mani: Of course, the inept and disreputable United Nations is being pushed into rewriting Free Speech rules so that nobody can criticize Islam or Islamic attacks against individuals or nations. One of these days, whenever the U.S. leadership gets some guts, maybe they will ride these United Nations slugs out of town on a rail!

Modi: Naaah! They will never develop brains or guts. They will always be play-babies, easy prey for people like Radi. Can you imagine a group of people, charged with defending that great country, who are scared to death of even offending their enemies? What a bunch of ninnies.

Mani: I noticed, Modi, not to change the subject, that in our sura today, ayat 72, what Allah really has set aside for believers:

"God has promised the believers, both men and women – gardens through which running waters flow, therein to abide, and goodly dwellings in gardens of perpetual bliss: but God's acceptance is the greatest bliss of all – for this, this is the triumph supreme!"

Radi: Where are the virgins?

Modi: Shall we tell him, Mani?

Radi: Tell me what?

Mani: You know, Radi, that back through the centuries we were always saddled with translation problems.

Radi: What does that have to do with virgins?

---

83   Charles Martel, "The Hammer", stopped the Muslim invasion at Tours in 732.

Harry J. Sweeney

Mani: Well, we know you would love to be a martyr to get into paradise quickly.

Radi: So? If you cannot guarantee reaching paradise any other way, even by prayer and good works, why not hope for martyrdom?

Modi: I have some bad news for you, Radi. It is here in the newspaper.

Radi: Well, what does it say?

Modi: You will have to read it for yourself. It says the old translations about 72 virgins were incorrect.

Radi: Incorrect! (Mani and Modi start walking) Well, what do we get if we're martyred; let's see what it says... What? White Grapes?! Aaaargh!

(See conversation 36, note 1 for a discussion on white grapes/white raisins.)

The Restless Wind and Shifting Sands

<u>Conversation 79: Sura 9, predestination, martyrdom and white grapes.</u>

Mani: When we discussed that ninth sura the other day. I was wrapped up in such technical details I forgot to summarize.

Modi: You did not mention the fierce Battle of Hunayn.

Mani: Yes. You know, I saw one of the American John Wayne films at the American camp, *Fort Apache*, the film was called. I could almost swear it was the Battle of Hunayn rewritten to fit the American West. The Muslim army of 12,000 greatly outnumbered the force put together by the four clans led by the Hawazin, but they had to navigate through a narrow pass. Just as the Indians did in the film, the forces of the four clans occupied the high ground and rained stones, rocks, and almost an avalanche down upon the Muslims. Another raiding party was awaiting those Muslims who reached a point that was free of the death raining down upon them.

Modi: I can hardly blame the Muslims for panicking. One minute they are smug in their numbers, feeling themselves unbeatable, but the next minute they are running for their lives, not understanding what is happening.

Radi: You did not understand the story, Mani. Our Muslims did not flee in panic; they stood their ground and fought back fiercely.

Modi: You are too much a chauvinist, Radi. Our guys certainly did panic. It took Imam Ali all of his strength and courage to cut off the runaways and reassemble them to change their directions and fight. Even the Qur'an mentions it in sura 9:25:

"Now God has helped you in many battlefields, and, on the day of Hunayn, when ye prided yourselves on your numbers; but it availed you nothing; and the earth, with all its breadth, became too straight for you: then turned ye your backs in flight."

Harry J. Sweeney

Radi: That was in the Qur'an? I guess so, if you have the ayat number.

Mani: I guess the Prophet could have depended on you to stay on target that day, Radi.

Radi: Of course.

Mani: Much of the discourse in sura 9, Radi, had to do with Allah's and Muhammad's scorn, heaped not only upon the hypocrites who wanted to see Islam destroyed, but also upon the Muslims who grew rich under Islam but would not fight for Islam and Allah. Being rich, they felt themselves less obligated to go and fight or at least provide funds for both the Hunayn and Mutah battles. They certainly should have provided funds for the battle that if lost could have totally destroyed Islam, the battle against Roman legions at Tabuk. Fortunately, the Tabuk battle never materialized.

Radi: I can never understand why Allah doesn't simply snap his fingers and send all of those people to the everlasting fires.

Mani: Perhaps, Radi, Allah knows that, except for the hypocrites, the people who were lax about fighting had joined many other battles and were just tired of warfare. Those who fight have a right to grow weary of war, not those who sit at home and complain about the noise. The rich Muslims had an obligation to help however they could; after all, the fighting was for their religion and their new way of life. Muhammad had challenged us over and over again to spend in the way of Allah and not to hoard wealth.

Modi: Bravo, Mani. Your analyses are improving. Sura 9 is not the easiest to understand. The reason behind that is that the Qur'an is not the history of a tribe of people but the complete manual for living in peace or war, from before the rooster crows each day to midnight. It is more than a religious treatise but covers each phase of a person's life through childhood, marriage, and death. Not a breath should be

The Restless Wind and Shifting Sands

taken without clear knowledge that one proceeds in the footsteps of the Prophet.

Mani: Wait a second there, Modi. You make it seem robotic. We have free will, don't we?

Radi: Yes, Mani. Allah has given us free will to follow closely in Muhammad's footsteps or reside forever in the great fires. However, having said this, I recollect other words that dispute this sense. Allah knows before we are born what turns we make and why, and He has already selected through His grand plan who will see paradise and who will writhe in anguish forever.

Modi: I have seen that puzzle drive some to the brink of insanity, Radi. One must simply do one's best to stay on the straight and narrow, honoring Allah and His Apostle and doing good works—which sometimes might be against one's nature.

Mani: That puzzles me also. Several imams have reinforced the idea that no matter what I do, my fate is already decided. Even if I succeeded in being a good example for all, I may react to something that negates my good works and has already been planned to happen. Therefore I can never be certain in my mind that my purity of heart or valiant attempts to remain pure has earned me the right to paradise. Since purity and good works cannot guarantee paradise, that means only martyrdom can do so. But for martyrdom to fulfill its promise, it has to be pure and only for love of Allah; it cannot be motivated by any other considerations, or it has the opposite effect.

Modi: Oh, Mani, I feel so sorry for those brigade members that parade around in their white clothing, posing for pictures, and basking in their own heroism. And with the hundreds or even thousands of dollars they know will be coming to their parents, how could they bet eternity on the reasons for their pending martyrdom being 100 percent pure?

Radi: What are you talking about? A martyr goes to paradise

Harry J. Sweeney

immediately after passing from life to death. Of course, we disagree on whether we get virgins or (ugh) white grapes.

Mani: I wonder how many grapes it would take to make up for all those virgins.

Radi: (Shows his knife) Are you making fun of the Qur'an? I will have your head.

Modi: I thought you were going to talk to your imam about that translation problem, Radi.

Radi: I asked him about the white grapes, and he got angry and will not talk to me.

Mani: I wonder why that is, Radi.

Modi: Could it be that he feels he has been found out? He does not want to argue with someone who might really know something? Some imams will give the benefit of their "knowledge" only to those who know little. Of course, if they themselves are found out, they may be shunned or even beaten if it is determined they were purposely giving out wrong information about the religion.

Radi: You mentioned that a few days ago: Ayat 6:21,

"And who could be more wicked than he who attributes his own lying inventions to God or gives the lie to His messages? Verily, such evildoers will never attain to a happy state."

Modi: Very good, Radi. Perhaps we are getting closer with respect to the Qur'an.

Radi: I would not bet on that, Modi, knowing your views are not necessarily agreeing with them. You moderates make me sick, like the European wimps who give in to everything we want. It is hard for me to believe also that big, strong, virile America seems sometimes to be led by that man and woman team who sound as if they were playing a game..

Modi: Yes, I saw her on Al-Jazeera, making a fool of herself in Syria. I still am not really sure what she accomplished in Syria, if anything. I would have paid anything to be there if she were visiting the first President Assad. He could not stand insufferable people.

Radi: Wow, talk about me! You sure are unforgiving.

Modi: I just cannot stand little people in big countries with big responsibilities and little ability. The American people cannot possibly understand how much damage that man/woman team does to their reputation and standing. An old Asian statement promises that an army of sheep led by a lion is more to be feared than an army of lions led by sheep.

Mani: I just had a chance to look over some of the verses of Sura 9. Modi, it makes a difference to discuss or at least read introductions to the suras before reading the ayats themselves. I can now understand what Allah is saying. I was more than a little foggy before. This is great!

Modi: Super. Anybody ready for a late breakfast?

Radi: I am always up for a late breakfast. I have been thinking, Modi, these conversations deserve a better scenario. How about lining up a coffee house that will let us sit, talk, and drink coffee?

Mani: That is a good idea, Radi, glad I thought of it.

Radi: What?

Modi: Brilliant idea, Mani. You know which places we like. Why don't you ask a couple?

Harry J. Sweeney

Mani: I am pretty sure I can get Abu Nadir's place. He needs business and has good coffee.

Radi: Hey, it's not Mani's idea. What about me?

Modi: Oh, OK, Radi. You can come also; you can pay first.

Radi: What? You dogs! Where's my knife!!

The Restless Wind and Shifting Sands

Conversation 80: "They have little fighting credibility."

Mani: Did you see the newspaper article about how many Muslim countries want the United Nations to adopt an international law outlawing blasphemy against Islam, Muslims, the Qur'an, etc.?

Modi: Yes, I did. I am surprised they have not done it before now. They expect the Europeans to cave in to their demands and get behind the proposal—just to show they are not racists.

Mani: What does being called racists have to do with it?

Modi: Europeans in general are more afraid of being called racists than they are of putting their people at risk. Actually, it is not so much the people—the people are much better than their leaders—the leaders are the problem. Look at the Archbishop of Canterbury, for instance. It is unbelievable and shocking that he is suggesting adopting the sharia. And Livingstone? I just don't understand his attitude. He is just a little too obliging. I am suspicious.

Mani: Won't the Americans stiffen European spines a little?

Modi: (laughs) Not really. They have not yet been able to get them to look at sanctions for Iran. It would take someone they do not have now to get their attention and tell them to stand up and act like real people instead of Little Lord Fauntleroys. Americans only have one John Bolton, and it is just too bad that only one of the parties makes use of his skill and intelligence.

Mani: What if there is a leftist president and the Democrats retain congress?

Modi: In that case, I have an idea that there is such a stark difference between the two parties now we may find ourselves back in square one. We conceivably could lose what we have gained unless the present policies remain intact! It is a shame we have to start worrying all over again. The Americans have done wonders for us, despite all the terrible

Harry J. Sweeney

people against them. They are beautiful and brave. I love them. But America under the Democrats would be just different from Americans under the Republicans. I hope that they will not be like the Banu Quraiza, afraid unto death of offending someone.

Radi: Ha! I knew the Americans would surrender. They are all cowards!

Mani: You know better than that, Radi. You try to take on just one of those Yanks, even one with just fuzz on his face, and he will turn you every way but loose. I remember the words of Ishaq. Can you picture Americans accepting this fate as did the Quraiza?

"The (Quraiza) captives were taken into Medina, where they dug mass graves in the marketplace. It was a long day, but eight hundred Jews met their deaths that day. Muhammad and his twelve-year-old wife sat and watched the executions (beheadings) the entire day and into the night. The Apostle of Allah had every male Jew killed. For every Jewish male (child), pubic hair was a death sentence. If he had no pubic hair, then he would (escape death), then be raised as a Muslim."[84]

Modi: When I think of that, I just cannot put myself in the place of a young boy standing in the line that moved steadily forward in the blood-drenched trench, awaiting his turn to have his head cut off as the people far in front of him suffered that fate. Every death had its own sound, and it hurt him to hear it, as much as it hurt him to see it. There is no one to save him. No one cares that he is not guilty of anything and does not deserve this rotten fate. When will someone finally arise and say, "Enough!"? When will it ever be enough? No one that day said, "Enough."[85] The line continued to move forward. (Modi's eyes began to water as he spoke.) When it was his turn… (Modi could not continue.)

Radi: Why are you looking so glum, Modi. They were only Jews.

---

84   Mohammed and the Unbelievers: A Political Life, Center for the Study of Political Islam, page 102.

The Restless Wind and Shifting Sands

Mani: How can you be so indifferent to human tragedy because of their tribe or their religion? Someone else with a sickness has erased your humanity. Many of the surviving children of the Banu Quraiza were raised as Muslims, married, had children and their children had children, and on and on. You might be a descendant of one of those Jewish kids, Radi.

Radi: What? You say that again and you will taste my blade.

Modi: If you were a descendant of that tribe, Radi, you were lucky enough to be a descendant of one who lived that day. Now think! What if you would have been a descendant of the boy I talked about? You too would have been punished, and for something you were not even alive yet to do.

Radi: That is a terrible thought. You too should taste my blade.

Modi: I hope that you cannot do things like that, Radi. You know, the sharia is not all that popular in some Muslim areas. Many like the speed in which punishment is meted out to those who deserve it. The Europeans and some Americans are simply too squeamish about dealing with murderers and other predators. They do not like to punish people and make it very difficult to punish criminals.

Mani: Yes, they keep death-row inmates around almost forever, wasting their tax dollars by feeding them, clothing them, and entertaining them for years. After a while, they even let some go—to rob, rape, and kill again. I have seen videos of prisoners honing their fighting skills with professional strength-building equipment and boxing training. That, to me is neither punishing nor reforming them. It is just making them more efficient criminals.

Modi: I guess the West should determine guilt or innocence their own way; however, once guilt is determined, they should consider punishing them our way, with our speed.

Harry J. Sweeney

Radi: I like our laws better. When someone does something to you, you can retaliate in kind.

Mani: No, Radi. You leave the law and punishment to the professionals. We do not want our men retreating into the lawless human jungle again. We must move on. And as Modi said often enough, we cannot keep killing Americans; they are our best hope to escape from a culture of death. I want to live and enjoy my kids and my grandkids. I do not want anyone telling me I must put on a suicide vest and kill Jews.

Modi: Good for you, Mani. Look, Radi, we want to remain Muslims because we love Allah and want to serve him. We just do not want others who really do not know, trying to tell us how we must best serve Him. I am getting sick and tired of some of those single-minded, crotchety people.

Radi: Remember, Modi, all of those laws and instructions come from Allah. You must heed them under severe penalties.

Modi: Do you realize, Radi, that we must take the word of so many people who are always quick to tell us what is God's will? Do you also realize how many questions we may not ask? Normally, when one denies another's right to ask questions, it is because one either does not know the answer, or because one does not want others to know the answer.

Mani: Getting back to the Americans, do you really believe the one American political party is so different from the other?

Modi: Yes, Mani, decidedly. My impression is that one party generally sees things as they are but can never seem to explain it to others. The competing party always takes advantage of that shortcoming by painting colorful, if fanciful, mind pictures. While I see a lot of stern-faced politicians all over the world, in the USA I see children playing a game. Some seem to yell and scream and make up stories about the others to get them in trouble, just like spoiled brats. But the others are like professional victims; they either do not know what their

The Restless Wind and Shifting Sands

competitors are doing, or just do not consider what they are doing is important enough to fight about.

Mani: I have heard it all before. Some people do not want the world to be the way it is, and they believe they can change it. The more they try, the more people get hurt. They are in denial about hurting people. I guess you heard the old saying: to make an omelet you must break some eggs. That may be fine for omelets, but you never should think about people that way. Of course, they only treat their own citizens that way; they fawn over Europe and whine about how inferior their own culture is to everyone else's.

Radi: I look forward to having them build their own mass graves and...

Modi, **Mani**: Shut up, you moron!

Radi: Say what you want about me. I will see the Americans surrendering and paying the *jizya* tax to us, their superiors.

Modi: There are too many good people to stop that from happening, Radi.

Radi: Not that I can see of their Congress.

Mani: He has a point there, Modi.

Modi: I noticed. He should wear a different hat to hide it.

Radi: Have I been insulted, Mani?

Mani: What makes you think so?

Radi: He has a strange look on his face.

Mani: Maybe he's hungry.

Harry J. Sweeney

Radi: So am I, let's go eat. (Modi and Mani start running)

Mani: (Calls over his shoulder to Radi) Last one there pays.

Radi: Hey! That is not fair. (Runs after them)

CHAPTER 9

<u>Conversation 81: "It is an ideology and a bunch of outdated traditions."</u>

And now back to the Modi's kitchen, where Modi's wife Hayat is playing host to Mani's wife Barma and Radi's fiancée Zaina. They helped Hayat with some housework and helped prepare the midday meal for Modi and his two friends. They are having coffee.

Zaina: I really have to thank you two for showing me how to do some of these things. I thought years ago that I was happily missing all these things because my parents were rich and could afford to hire help. Now I have to learn how to do things because Radi and I will not be that well off.

Barma: We are glad to help, Zaina. Has Radi set a date yet?

Zaina: No, darn him. Your husbands almost got to him once, and he came running into the house breathless, saying we must get married right then! He was cackling something about having his children supporting him in his old age.

Hayat: Modi told me about it. That must have been hilarious. I can hardly keep from laughing just thinking about it. What did you say to him?

Zaina: When he said we had to get married just then, I asked, "Why? Are you pregnant?? Then he swore to me he wasn't. (The wives laugh at that.) I had to calm him down with some Saudi coffee.

Hayat: Modi tells me that Radi is getting a little extreme again.

Zaina: I know. I had to tell him I was not going to marry some cruel old fogy who might just murder our first born if she were a girl. That is

385

Harry J. Sweeney

not Islamic, and those other old fogies on high know that. They should be doing something about it.

Barma: Oh, God! As modern as we are becoming, we still have to live with those evil traditions. That tradition should have been scrapped long ago.

Hayat: Yes, along with the old fogies that believe we should continue living like that.

Zaina: You two lucked out with husbands. How on earth do they stay out of trouble with the self-righteous?

Hayat: Well, Modi avoids conversations with anyone he does not know. He is quite aware that all it takes is one word to the wrong person and he will get a nocturnal visitor with a sharp knife.

Barma: Horrors! Why can't somebody come along and grab these people between the legs and escort them to Abu Ghraib or someplace? This world has already had its fill of the foul-mouthed, mush-brained prigs who think they are the final world on the Qur'an.

Hayat: You are right about that. I suffered through their ranting in the Mosque and just wanted to rise and tell those mealy-mouthed woman-haters they are not the begin-all and the end-all of Islam. They are the monsters in what otherwise could be a beautiful and serene Islam; hopefully they will be so outed on the Day of Judgment. They are no better than serial killers.

Zaina: Of course, Hayat, you know you are talking about Radi's other friends.

Barma: (laughs) You bet I do. Are you going to take him in hand? Teach him *our* Islam?

Zaina: At least once per visit I tell him how I feel. I always find the words to call his friends some very choice names. I told him that he

The Restless Wind and Shifting Sands

was not going to restrict me to my house, no matter what he tells his friends. I am going to go where I want, cook what I want, and that twit better be ready to do what is right for me. I want to be able to love him with every fiber that is in me. I also want that love returned—our contract is not going to lease my body for whatever pittance the dowry represents. I do not need his friends or any imam telling me how to love a man. That reminds me, I told my parents what I was going to do one night to convince him, and they rushed upstairs so they would not see it.

Barma: Oh? What did you do?

Zaina: Radi was reading the daily paper downstairs, and I crept downstairs in one of my scanty Victoria Secret outfits--the one with the high, red boots. He did not see me at first because he was buried in the paper.

Hayat: What did he do when he looked up and saw you in that triple-x outfit?

Zaina: Well first, that paper ripped all the way down the crease. (They all laugh.) When he dropped the paper, I lounged across his lap and threw my arms around his neck.

Barma: What did he do then?

Zaina: Well, first he sweated bullets. After that, he looked to see if the curtains were drawn. I got the idea he was scared out of his wits. Then I planted a big kiss on him. He was all arms and legs with that. (laughter) I asked him if he liked me in that outfit, but he could not speak. So I said, "Okay, I won't wear it anymore." Then he really looked scared, and his eyes bulged. (laughter) I told him if he wanted me to be his little vixen and dress like that only for him, he will have to leave his hypocrisy at the door.

Hayat: What did he say to that?

Harry J. Sweeney

Zaina: He tried to say something, but he could only stutter. He sounded like a diesel truck. I don't think he has been right since. He wants to get married, but is afraid I am too much for his peace of mind.

Hayat: You are right, Zaina, and Radi is the lucky one. If more of our women would do something like that, set the theme, as it were, we could force our men to be more human.

Barma: Unfortunately, ladies, too many of our women have their husbands chosen by their fathers. Fathers are not all heart when it comes to their daughters and have no business choosing husbands for them. The poor dears do not even see their new husbands sometimes until the ceremony. And too often the husbands are not exactly "new". Can't you just see the fathers go purple if the bride turned to the husband and said something like, "Look, big boy, you are not exactly a prize bull, so let me give it to you straight. You and I are not going to play house until you understand that you get nothing out of this marriage unless you are ready to throw away your parents' ideas of what marriage is all about.'

Zaina: What on earth could happen to her?

Hayat: There is no doubt her father would cut her throat.

Zaina: What? He would murder her for that little speech?

Hayat: He would be outraged; she dishonored him. If she had a little sister, historically speaking, he would kill his other daughter as well so the second daughter could not dishonor him. What a ghoul!

Zaina: Oh my God! What kind of religion is this to some people?

Hayat: Modi told me that Islam is not just a religion, it is an ideology as well--and a bunch of outdated traditions.

Zaina: An ideology?

The Restless Wind and Shifting Sands

Hayat: Yep. He said it is the only religion with an army. They can put out a call and humiliate hundreds of thousands of fighters into joining or supporting a fray that does not really concern them. They have an army of Public Relations people and attorneys that force laws through in other countries that forbid people from even saying anything at all negative about us. Europe now has blasphemy laws, would you believe. Those countries must be nuts! They are also a government, a very inept government. A very inept, male-dominated government that really believes Allah is on its side. We are the chosen people, they keep saying in the Mosques. Bah.

Zaina: You don't believe we are the chosen people?

Hayat: Of course, I have to believe that. At the same time, I just look around. You have seen American modern kitchens on those Internet sites before they cut them off. After seeing what American woman have and the cars American men and women drive, tell me how we can be His chosen people? I just do not understand it is beyond me. Doesn't. Allah love everyone the same?

Barma: Are you arguing with the Qur'an, Hayat? It gives men lots of rights over us.

Hayat: No, Barma, I have a problem just with the people who act like it was written last week instead of the seventh century. Why do the imams not explain to us how the messages deal with issues when the woman has to work and there is no work for the man? Besides, they act as if we were at war with every non-Muslim on earth. From what I have seen on CNN, the Muslims who moved to Europe are not all remaining theologically orthodox. Some of the daughters are risking their lives by saying no to their fathers and running away with Europeans. Did you see that Muslim who was born in London asking on British TV what the sharia was? I bet those imams are livid.

Barma: I thought they had already taken Europe and made it a Muslim continent.

Harry J. Sweeney

Hayat: See how those hypocrites lie? Zaina, do not for any reason give in to Radi. You make that man of yours toe the mark. You make sure he knows who is boss once he steps foot in the house. Once he knows and acts accordingly, you two can have all the fun you want.

Barma: Yes, Zaina. Don't you ever take any guff from him. And you had better warn him not to bring any of his priggish friends around or you'll embarrass him royally. People like Radi cannot stand to be embarrassed. Zaina, you are such a decent woman, I do not understand how you can fall for a guy like that.

Zaina: Well, love is blind, I guess.

Hayat: Yeah. It is also stupid! (Laughter)

The Restless Wind and Shifting Sands

<u>Conversation 82: The Winchester and the Kalashnikov.</u>

Modi and Mani are again with Mani's cousins, in a village town east of Baghdad. They are on a hilltop guarding the entrance to the village. Radi is not with them because he prefers al-Qaida and insurgents.

Mani: These rifles are a little heavier than we had last time we were up here.

Modi: Last time you had a Chinese SKS, if I remember correctly. That one in your hands is a Winchester Model 70 with heavy barrel and a Leupold scope your cousins managed to procure from his US Army contacts. It is no different than the Remington you used once before—and you certainly impressed your cousins with your shooting then. You impressed me too—I was proud of you.

Mani: That was only because those people were trying to kill us. Why do I have this heavy thing now, and you have that lighter AK-47?

Modi: You are a better shot with a rifle than I. Therefore, whenever we get a target, you get to take the shot while I spot and protect you.

Mani: I have no idea what that means, Modi. I like the part about protecting me, but I am not sure I understand the situation.

Modi: Look, you are a better shot, so we don't waste time and ammunition when we have a target. I look over the situation while you settle in. Then I use my spotter scope here to allow you to set your scope for distance. You probably should set it now for about 500 meters. You can always change it. (Mani takes some time to set his scope)

Mani: Then what?

Modi: Then I let you know whether it is clear enough to take your shot. I am not going to let you shoot unless it is a clear shot and no more than a squad will be coming up here after us. A squad we can

Harry J. Sweeney

handle. Now we can relax for a few minutes. I will call in to let them know we will be taking five practice shots.

Mani: I said I would I would help out with guard duty, Modi; I did not really want to shoot anyone.

Modi: When it comes to al-Qaida and other terrorists, Mani, being passive means to surrender. If you do not take an active role, you are letting them control the situation. If you put them in control, they will kill you, passive or not.

Mani: Look, Modi, I volunteered here to help my relatives. I thought we would only call in and warn them of danger. I do not want to hurt anyone. I am not like Radi, ready to cut off someone's head at the slightest provocation.

Modi: Mani, Radi and his friends believe all of this garbage they are being told by those addle-headed imams who are still locked in the seventh century. They make him believe that if he does not start killing Jews, Christians, and even passive believers, Allah is going to punish him severely.

Mani: I know that ayat (verse), but I did not pay any attention to it. He was not talking to us. If I remember correctly, he said that to the Muslims who did not want to take part in the imagined battle with a Roman legion.

Modi: Right, good memory. But, Mani, you know that those hypocrites know it also. It is beyond belief they are in denial about that and sell that nonsense to people who are not knowledgeable about the Qur'an. If people insist they are too busy to learn something about the Qur'an, to make up their own mind, sooner or later they will become a victim of the prigs who will use it against them. But, hey, while it is quiet, let's try a shot so I can get an idea about where that rifle is shooting. Use that door on the abandoned hut as a target.

Mani: Right.

The Restless Wind and Shifting Sands

Modi: Good first shot! You hit the door, Mani. At this distance, that was a great shot. I would not change any setting. Try that same shot again. See that splash of green toward the bottom of the door? Try to hit it.

Mani: Like falling off a camel.

Modi: You nailed it again, Mani. You and the rifle could use a little polish, but no matter; you are good enough for what we are doing.

Mani: So, what do I do now?

Modi: Just relax. I am calling in to tell them practice is over. (speaks on the cell phone). Mani, I do not know where you practice, but your shooting was impressive.

Mani: It has to be this rifle. It is already set up well; I only had to re-set the scope. I guess I can shoot at doors all right, but I still do not know about people.

Modi: Mani, please listen to me. When dealing with al-Qaida and company, there is no such thing as a conscientious objector. You either fight or you give al-Qaida thugs the right to remove your head and your sons' heads, make your wife a slave, and marry off your toddler daughters. Now think about that. Is that what you want for your family?

Mani: Of course not. That is gross and makes me want to throw up.

Modi: Well, if you can't fight for your country, fight for your family-- your little daughter.

Mani: Why do these people make us change our ways?

Modi: Some of the real people are so ignorant about things they do not know they are being scammed by their own leaders. But it does not matter; they believe that Allah will curse them if they do not chop

Harry J. Sweeney

people like you into little pieces. Look at some of those people in Darfur. Their big thing is to cut your heart out and let you watch them munch on it as you slowly die. Someone told them the more they can make you hate them as you are dying, the better they will be in Allah's eyes.

Mani: These people, Modi, are so hateful, they fill me with revulsion.

Modi: Don't get angry, and don't hate. Just stay cool and accept the fact that we have people among us who have no conscience or soul; nothing keeps them from being monsters and sub-humans. In most cases, you can only kill them; otherwise, they would continue to be a weight around your neck, waiting for you to make a mistake or for some nitwit goodytwoshoes to pat them on the head and set them free.

Mani: It is hard for me to say that we are the same religion.

Modi: Well, we are. Our religion has a very large tent and accommodates grievous sinners as well as real, decent people. It is up to us and to our friends around the world to cut that cancer out. And we must do this before their lawyers push stupid countries into creating laws that give them the upper hand. The strange thing about laws is that the stupid, naïve countries create laws that prohibit us from defending ourselves. These so-called representatives, the professional lawmakers don't give a damn if the bad guys cut us to pieces. All they care about is safeguarding their precious paper laws.

(Mani, turns to his task and looks through his scope as he slowly turns the rifle)

Mani: If I see one of those ghouls in my sight this day, I am going to present him with a new orifice in his head.

Modi: I knew you could do it Mani. I knew you had it in you. You showed it.

The Restless Wind and Shifting Sands

Mani: Just how did I show it?

Modi: Radi said something about your daughter and you decked him. Not a second passed between his saying it and your punching him in the mouth. It is a shame we can't do that to all the people who need it.

Mani: You have that right.

Harry J. Sweeney

<u>Conversation 83: "If the Americans leave, most of us probably will die."</u>

Hayat, wife of Modi, Barma, wife of Mani, and Zaina, fiancée of Radi, are at in the kitchen at Mani's house, helping with dinner.

Barma: Where did the boys go? I heard you chase them out.

Hayat: They probably went down to the Mosque to see if anything is going on.

Zaina: They were all reading the newspaper. What else could be going on? (Barma and Hayat laugh at that)

Barma: The newspapers do not really report everything. They are getting to be like the ones in Europe and America; they don't report anything that conflicts with the policy or politics of the newspaper.

Zaina: What does that mean?

Hayat: It means they do not want to print stupid things that our people do, such as honor killings, or economic sacrifices. You know and I know those things go on all the time. A woman has a baby and it turns out to be a girl. If it is born at home, the father takes it out into the desert and buries it and nobody knows or cares. The tradition called for that kind of killing whenever traveling from one oasis to another. Some of these people still do it.

Zaina: But won't the neighbors know?

Hayat: The neighbors do the same things, most of them. There are some modern Iraqis that respect the national law and put the traditions aside. But they know that if the Americans leave and the ghoulish radicals return, they will be killed themselves for being "anti-religious".

Zaina: How is that anti-religious? That tradition is not sanctioned by our religion.

The Restless Wind and Shifting Sands

Hayat: I know; however, the extremists do not really know the difference. (Zaina looks at the ceiling and throws her hands up)

Barma: I know the frustration, Zaina. We must persevere in keeping our husbands free of those people and their insane ideas.

Zaina: The extremists must be Neanderthal.

Hayat: I was thinking Cro-Magnon. (They all laugh)

Barma: You see, Zaina, if the newspapers printed all that stuff about killing girl babies and circumcising females, some Americans will get the idea that we are uncivilized and will just lump us in with the rest of the world's barbarians and just abandon us.

Zaina: But the Americans kill their babies, don't they. Aren't they uncivilized?

Hayat: They kill them, but they are a little irrational about it. If it is even one day before it is born, they think it is okay to kill it. If they wait until it is born, it is then a crime. But they don't care if it is a boy or a girl; they just kill it because they do not want it.

Zaina: That is just as bad as our jerks burying the girl babies alive. Do they circumcise their girls too?

Barma: No, that is against the law there. That sounds strange: they will kill them but will not circumcise them. As soon as they get to school though, they seem to confuse them with respect to values and sexuality. In fact, they do that to boys and girls both.

Hayat: It is not as easy as that. In fact, it is downright confusing to us here. They talk to boys and girls in the early grades, showing them how to use condoms—that might be their morning class. In the afternoon, they have other classes that teach the boys how not to be so macho and the girls how to be more macho.

Harry J. Sweeney

Zaina: What the heck kind of country is that?

Barma: It is very confusing. Many people do not want the schools to teach their kids because they do not want their boys coming home confused about their role as males. They certainly don't want their girls planning to rob banks. But some of the states force the kids to go.

Zaina: Remind me never to immigrate to America, no matter how bad it gets here.

Barma: If the real Americans leave, most of us probably will die within the first few days. Well, Radi and I might survive, but if I do, Radi will make my life not worth living.

Hayat: How did you come to that conclusion?

Zaina: Radi is still a radical. He believes that nonsense that Zawahiri and Osama bin Stupid continually hand out. He says he would set the date if I would wear the abaya, hijab, and *niqab*. I told him to get lost.

Hayat: Good for you. It is bad enough that the *niqab* was yesterday's garb. Today it has no place in our society. It is a symbol of male supremacy. Whoever wears it serves notice to the world that she agrees with the concept that males have rights over her and she has none. She cannot even show her face in public without the mask.

Zaina: I know that; that is why I told Radi to get rid of his Neander...I mean Cro-Magnon ideas. I hate those damned abayas, and the chadors are worse; they make you look as if you're wearing a laundry bag. (Hayat and Barma laugh) Well, I have to admit that some of the new abayas are OK, and some of the thobes are adorable.

Hayat: Many of the women wear the old abayas and chadors because at first they thought it was a requirement of the religion. Their men do not tell them otherwise. It is not so much the husbands mind the other

The Restless Wind and Shifting Sands

men looking; they just don't want their wives to see other men could be interested.

Barma: Whenever women discover it is not required by the religion, they continue to wear them anyway; their husbands will not let them out of the house without them.

Zaina: We women will have to have a conference and require all women to attend. Of course, we need a safe place to stay when we finish deciding how life is going to be between men and women from now on. And if they bring up the idea of what the Holy Book says, we tell 'em, "You interpreted everything your way for almost 1300 years, now we re-interpret it our way for the next 1300 years." (Hayat and Barma laugh)

Hayat: You definitely will need a safe place to stay. You may have to go to America after all.

Zaina: How about California?

Barma: I am not sure that is part of America.

Harry J. Sweeney

<u>Conversation 84: The Hijab</u>

Mani: Modi, I saw your wife in the market yesterday.

Modi: Yes, she told me.

Mani: I hardly recognized her with that abaya and the black hijab.

Modi: We had relatives visiting for a few days. She did not know them, so she decided to be cautious.

Radi: She should be cautious all the time, Modi. Women are required by the Qur'an to wear the hijab

Modi: That is where you are wrong, Radi. I thought you knew everything.

Radi: It is in the Qur'an; I saw it.

Modi: Radi, the word hijab is in the Qur'an only four times. Each of those times the word did not mean an article of clothing, but a screen, a barrier, or a place of seclusion.

Radi: What? You are lying to me again.

Mani: No, Radi. I know about that also; my wife has told me often enough. Look, she told me so many times I know them from memory: Verses 7:46, 17:45, 19:17, and 42:51. In the first two, hijab meant barrier. In 19:17, describing Mary, our Mariam, hijab (hijaban) suggested a place of seclusion, a separation from others. Finally, and this is the closest we come to an article of clothing, in 42:51 it is said that "It is not given to mortal man that God should speak to him otherwise than through sudden inspiration (revelation) or [by a voice, as it were,] from behind a veil..."

Radi: You know I am going to look them up.

The Restless Wind and Shifting Sands

Modi: Radi, my al-Kitab (Qur'an) is on the table, under the cloth. You can look them up there.

Radi: I will wait until I am home. I do not feel like going through all the ablutions right now before opening your Qur'an.

Modi: You just went through your ablutions for morning prayer an hour ago. Why are you not still clean?

Mani: He probably broke wind again between the restaurant and here. (Both laugh)

Radi: I do not understand why al-Kitab does not mention the abaya or chador.

Mani: Umar wondered about that also, remember. He wanted Muhammad to publish a revelation much stricter on women's clothing. He was disappointed with that first one at Zainab's wedding.

Radi: But Modi, how could our holy Prophet even know what would be in any revelation?

Mani: Yeah. I had wondered what Umar was trying to suggest. Perhaps he thought Muhammad would suggest it to the angel Gabriel.

Radi: I doubt that he would do that. Muhammad received the revelations as Allah saw fit to pass them to him. He could never know what was to be revealed and he never asked for anything special. Of course, Allah always knew what was bothering him.

Modi: Yes, that seems to be the case. The prophet was annoyed at what he considered the rudeness of his wedding guests, and lo! He received a revelation ending that annoyance forever. Allah knew what was in his heart.

Mani: And he argued with his family and friends when Aisha was not in her enclosed Howdah, then showed up with a young Muslim

Harry J. Sweeney

soldier. That was a scandal until Muhammad went into his tent and had a revelation that she was innocent.

Radi: Allah knows all things and did not want His prophet hurt by punishing Aisha for something she did not do.

Modi: Radi, these things are not unknown. You already know about Zainab's wedding and you can read more details in Bukhari, 8.24.255 and 257. The Aisha scandal is well known and she herself has written about it. The revelation was in 24:11-20.

Radi: What are you trying to say about the revelations?

Mani: We are confirming that Allah knows what is in our hearts, Radi. We are just showing you that Allah's revelations arrived in the nick of time to lift our Most Beloved out of some pretty tight spots. In some cases, the revelations mentioned mere mortals by name.

Modi: Remember, we were discussing modesty among women. You insisted that the Qur'an ordered all women to wear the hijab. Our position is that al-Kitab only enjoined women–and men–to dress and act modestly. We showed you that whenever the word hijab was used in the book (Qur'an) it had nothing to do with a full body sheath, covering everything but the eyes.

Radi: But if you and your wives believe all of that, why don't they dress the way they want and just toss the veils and things?

Modi: Because some of your friends, Modi, would beat them unmercifully without even asking why they were wearing those other garments. They could break an arm or a leg or lose an eye. And these things would happen because people like you have your own idea of what the Holy Book means and you force those meanings on others who only want to live in peace.

Radi: I know what the Holy Book says.

Modi: The book is not written in your Arabic, Radi! There are also foreign words used whenever Arabic had no words for some meanings. You have not studied classical Arabic. You do not know what is in the Book; you cannot read it.

Radi: But my imam...

Modi: Your imam is an extremist radical, bent on destroying the planet if Islam cannot rule the world. He is a nut case, a fanatic. He is so far out even al-Qaida won't have him. Is that the kind of people you respect? You are my good friend, Radi, but your other friends will see the flames.

Mani: Unless you want to accompany him in the fire, you had better find a real imam.

Radi looks from Modi to Mani and back. He does not know what to think.

Modi: What is on your mind?

Radi: I don't know how to ask...

Mani: We are all friends here. Go ahead and ask.

Radi: I need to know. May I do my ablutions here and go over the Qur'an with you? If you two are right, then I need to know quickly. Modi, I could have killed you a few minutes ago.

Modi: I know, Radi. But you are my friend. I should never have to watch my words when I speak with you. I speak from my heart. I can see that you trust the wrong people and it looks to me as if you are bound for the fire yourself. Neither Mani nor I want that to happen.

(Modi and Mani join Radi in doing their ablutions. Modi looked at his watch and noted the time. They have about an hour and a half before

Harry J. Sweeney

the Adhan call, which Modi refers to as "Bilal calling" after the first Muezzin, Bilal ibn Ribah.)

Radi: I am a little dizzy after all of that reading and analysis.

Mani: We cannot blame you. It takes quite a lot of effort to read the Holy Book even when you know exactly what verses to read.

Modi: Just imagine some poor people who try to read the Qur'an, manage to stumble their way through it, and think they know it.

Mani: I suggest we throw some water on our faces and try to recover before Mosque.

Modi: Did you ever tell Radi that joke about the red-headed imam?

Mani: I would not tell that one now; no! It is almost time for Mosque and Radi has finished his ablutions. He needed a full body wash because of breaking wind like that.

Modi: Yes. That's the best time.

Mani: OK. Hey Radi, did you hear the one about the red-headed imam?

(Minutes later, Radi was laughing so hard, again the expected happened. He stopped laughing with his eyes wide open and again let out a loud noise. His face contorted up in anger.)

Mani: You know that every time he laughs that hard he can't hold it in. Now he has to do his full body wash all over again. He is livid!

Modi: Come on, hurry before he finishes. He still has his knife.

Mani: It is a good thing we are all friends here.

The Restless Wind and Shifting Sands

<u>Conversation 85: "It is every Muslim's duty to root out sinners and punish them."</u>

Radi is visiting his fiancée, Zaina. Modi and Mani are out of town.

Zaina: I thought you were coming to take us to dinner last night.

Radi: I thought it was tonight.

Zaina: You dufus! When are you going to get things right.

Radi: I managed to go over much of the Qur'an with Modi and Mani this week.

Zaina: Oh, Radi, I am so glad to hear that. Those other pals you have are no good for your blood pressure. By the way, I saw Mani yesterday, probably on the way to Modi's place.

Radi: Did he say anything about me?

Zaina: Radi! You know he cannot say anything to a woman on the street; one of your pals would set up an alarm and beat hell out of both of us.

Radi: I don't understand. I see all kinds of women in foreign dress on the street. They stop and pass the time of day with a man they know.

Zaina: Right. The ones in the foreign dress have families or husbands that are well known and powerful. The looney-tunes know better than to yell at them and beat them. They and their whole families may disappear.

Radi: How can the rich people justify that? On the Last Day, Allah will have them dragged into the fire.

Zaina: And what will you be doing on the Last Day? You will be hiding in a corner somewhere, hoping Allah doesn't spot you.

405

Harry J. Sweeney

Radi: (Puffs out his chest) I will have you know that I am in good standing with Allah. I have gone after many sinners in His name.

Zaina: Radi, how many times have I told you it is not your place to do that? You are not an appointed authority.

Radi: It is every Muslim's duty to root out sinners and punish them.

Zaina: Whoever told you that is way off base. Radi, we have the police force now to go after people who violate the law. They are not really that good yet and many still do not understand that greed and graft are not virtues. Nonetheless, it is better than each person taking it upon himself to punish sinners.

Radi: But Zaina, my love, my flower, our State is not punishing the crimes right. One man last week admitted to being an atheist and he was not even arrested.

Zaina: So? His religion or lack of it is his business. It is certainly none of yours.

Radi: But Zaina, it is against the sharia; he left his religion. He should be killed.

Zaina: Not any more, Radi. If you kill him, you will be in trouble.

Radi: The law says anyone who can gain access to an apostate must kill him.

Zaina: Not any more. We have a Declaration of Human Rights. If you take a look at article XIII, you will see there is no more apostasy.

Radi: What? That cannot be. Nobody can leave this religion.

Zaina: It is the law, Radi. I believe only the Saudis are still holding out about apostasy. I would bet that they have not let their people know about the Universal Islamic Declaration of Human Rights.

The Restless Wind and Shifting Sands

Radi: They cannot abandon the law of apostasy! They just cannot!

Zaina: Are you saying that Islam will not be the same unless we killed someone for leaving it?

Radi: Of course. Nothing will be the same. People can sin and get away with it.

Zaina: I wish Modi were here. I would invite him over so we could talk it out. Meanwhile, Radi, don't you dare go out with those pals of yours again. They are nothing but trouble. One of these days they–and you–will go on the retaliation list for killing the wrong person.

Radi: There is no retaliation for killing sinners.

Zaina: There are no sinners anymore, Radi. There are crimes and criminals. Two or three people in a Salafist group cannot declare anyone a sinner and go after him anymore. If they do, they are responsible for their actions. If they do not accept retaliation, they can go to prison for a long time. I don't think blood-money applies any more.

Radi: If all of these changes were already made, why couldn't you speak to Mani yesterday on the street?

Zaina: Are you kidding? The word has not come down yet to the Neanderthals. They are always the last to learn. I am not going to chance losing an eye or my life because those jerks are still in century seven. I like the new laws, but I will not stand in front of a moving bus to assert my rights not to be run over by the bus.

Radi: You know, now that you mention it, what is wrong with a man and a woman saying hello if they know each other. In fact, look at all the Western films in which unmarried people take each other to dinner without a chaperone.

Zaina: And what is wrong with a man of one religion marrying a

Harry J. Sweeney

woman of another religion and each accompanying his or her spouse to their respective houses of worship every other week.

Radi: Whoa! That is unthinkable! No!

Zaina: Why not? Are you afraid it might lead to someone leaving the religion?

Radi: Yes! That is a terrible sin.

Zaina: No, Radi, please get it through your head that we now have the freedom to believe what we like. There is no more apostasy! Say it!

Radi: There is...no...more...apos... NO! I can't say it.

Zaina: You can say it; it just takes practice. There is no more apostasy! Say it, Radi!

Radi: I can't.

Zaina: I won't dress up in your favorite miniskirt until you learn how to say it.

Radi: Sweetheart! That is cruel. I can't get enough of seeing you in it. Can't I say "there is no more heresy," instead?

Zaina: I am not going to answer that! I told you the way it is. Unless you can say it, Radi, you are no good to any wife. I am not going to let you marry me knowing that before long, you will have a long list of people wanting retaliation for a brother or sister, or even a parent.

Radi: But Zaina...

Zaina: No! When you marry me, Radi, it will be a marriage of peace and of respect for one another. I am drawing the line now. I am not going to have a husband who is an extremist moron.

The Restless Wind and Shifting Sands

Radi: Now what would Modi do?

Zaina: He'd kick your rear and tell you to be thankful that someone like me loves you. Hah! And then he would tell you to grab my hand and quickly say "I marry you," before I got away. Modi's wife was right about that.

Radi: Right about what?

Zaina: Love is not only blind, it's stupid!

Harry J. Sweeney

Conversation 86: Discussing Sura 10.

Modi and Mani have agreed to review the Qur'an with Radi to give him a better understanding of Islam's supreme document. They have been trying to pull him away from his radical friends as a favor to his fiancée, Zaina. They are at Modi's house. Since Radi knew he would be touching and reading the Qur'an, he did his required ablutions before he left his house. Mani and Modi are in the midst of theirs when Radi enters.

Radi: Good morning, you two rascals.

Mani: Look who is talking about rascals. Hand me that towel, Radi.

Modi: I am glad you were able to come over. If you are finished your ablutions, why not take out al-Kitab and get it ready for us. You know where I keep it. We will be finished shortly.

Radi: OK, Modi. Good idea. Yes, I know where it is.

Modi: We were looking at Sura 10, if I am not mistaken.

Radi: Yes. I could not understand ayat 10:15.

"AND [thus it is:] whenever our messages are conveyed unto them in all their clarity, those who do not believe that they are destined to meet us, [are wont to] say, 'Bring us a discourse other than this, or alter this one'."

"SAY, [O Prophet]: It is not conceivable that I alter it of my own volition; I only follow what is revealed to me. Behold, I would dread, were I [thus] to rebel against my Sustainer, the suffering [which would befall me] on that awesome Day of Judgment."

Modi: Allah is saying that people who do not believe in life after death have their own views of right and wrong and want Muhammad to alter the ayats to conform to their view, believing that Muhammad himself was the author.

The Restless Wind and Shifting Sands

Radi: Those fools did not believe that each ayat was a revelation from Allah?

Mani: Truly, Radi. You must remember that most of these people were still one step away from Bedouin nomads, who sometimes carried their gods with them to protect them from others.

Radi: The polytheists had to protect the gods?

Mani: Oh, yes. It is not unknown for another family or tribe to kidnap a "god" if some lucky family ran into some really good fortune after sacrificing something to that god.

Modi: It is also not unknown for a disgruntled believer, disappointed by not receiving a requested favor, to field-kick his "god" right out of the Kaaba. (Mani and Modi laugh. Radi is confused)

Mani: Lighten up, Radi. They were only wooden idols. Today they would be plastic, made in China.

Modi: They would probably be recalled for lead in the paint. (Mani and Modi again laugh)

Radi: Getting back to Sura Ten, ayat 15 is another that I fail to understand.

"Say: 'Had God willed it [otherwise] I would not have conveyed this [divine writ] unto you, nor would He have brought it to your knowledge. Indeed, a whole lifetime have I dwelt among you ere this [revelation came unto me]: will you not, then use your reason?'"

Modi: What Allah said to Muhammad is to tell the cynics that they know that he is not known for telling lies, so why should he attribute a great, inimitable piece of writing like the Qur'an to Allah, when he could take the credit himself, had he written it. In addition, Allah reminded Muhammad that the people knew that he had never authored

Harry J. Sweeney

a single poem or other philosophical work, and indeed was illiterate. How could he possibly have written such a magnificent work?[85]

Radi: Oh, I get it. Some people thought that Muhammad wrote the Qur'an himself, so wanted him to go back and make some changes in it in order to make their lives more comfortable by having the Qur'an agree with their way of thinking.

Mani: Yes, that is a big part of it.

Radi: Right. So, Allah lets Muhammad know that he could always remind those people that a) he does not lie, so why should he give all the credit to another if the credit belongs to him. It made no sense. And b) everyone knows anyway that he never wrote anything because he can't read or write. How can an illiterate person ever have completed something perfect, such as the Qur'an? That is preposterous!

Modi: Now you have it.

Radi: What did I not have before?

Modi: You must know the language of the Qur'an. By knowing the language, I am not just referring to classical Arabic or the number of Aramaic words in the Qur'an, but you must understand the way the Qur'an expresses itself, as if it were made for older people to understand and for us to recognize the words but be unable to decipher the meaning because we are too young or something.

Radi: And how am I supposed to learn the language of the Qur'an?

Mani: There is the hard way or the easy way. The hard way is to keep reading until things start making sense. The easy way is to enroll in a Qur'anic school.

Modi: Of course, that has its problems also, Radi. The Qur'anic school

---

85   note 24, ibid. page 329.

The Restless Wind and Shifting Sands

costs too much and normally requires that you be a *hafiz*, a reciter. You must recite the entire Qur'an from memory without error.

Radi: I can recite most of the Qur'an--I just don't understand all of it. I don't know about the money. But I have one more ayat that mystifies me. I do not understand "sustenance" in ayat 10:59:

"Say: 'Have you ever considered all the means of sustenance which God has bestowed on you from on high--and which you thereby divide into things forbidden and things lawful?'"

Modi: I can understand the confusion here. Allah is talking about the Qur'an and its complete guidance toward the good life and spiritual fulfillment here, and happiness hereafter. But He is a little disconcerted that man has made some of God's blessings forbidden when they should not be.[86] Man should be free to enjoy God's gifts and accept His guidance toward a better life here as well as for the life to come. In other words, Radi, look at this life as well as the next and do not reject God's blessing just because they appear only to help in this life.

Radi: I will have to go over that a few more times. That rejects much of what my friends and their imams have said.

Modi: No doubt, Radi. You cannot dismiss this life as unimportant simply because there will be the next. Allah did not make us to sit in gloom and not appreciate His great works.

Mani: That was a nice touch, Modi.

Modi: Thank you, Mani. We have only a few more ayats to go. Radi, are there any others that give you problems in this sura?

Radi: No, Modi. Thank you. I will close everything up for you. I hope I can spend some uninterrupted time at home with mine. Thank you for what you are doing for me.

---

86   80,81, ibid., pages 338,339

Harry J. Sweeney

Modi: We are doing it for ourselves as well, Radi. We desperately need you to understand reality. Even this sura should tell you that you must really know the Qur'an; you cannot depend on the conjecture of others. Even to hear *"Allahu Akbar"* from every corner of the world is in reality "a consummation devoutly to be wished," and not a goal of a Crusade in reverse. Before that, men must reach perfection. To achieve those goals, we must first aspire to perfection individually.

Mani: I agree. Let's work on that first. Time for lunch and I am buying.

Radi: Perfect. (Laughter)

The Restless Wind and Shifting Sands

<u>Conversation 87: Some thoughts on Sura 11.</u>

Mani and Modi are in Modi's house chatting when Radi arrives. His face is a mess, showing several cuts and bruises, and his clothes are torn. Nonetheless, he is cheerful.

Mani: Radi, you look beat-up; what happened to you.

Radi: I am very dry, Mani, may I trouble you for some water?

Modi: I will get the gourd. Meanwhile, sit down and rest.

Radi: The cool water tastes great. I feel a little better. I managed to have a bit of a scrap with some of my buddies.

Modi: It was about the Qur'an, wasn't it? I suspected that you would have problems with those morons whenever you started disagreeing with their versions.

Radi: Oh, Yes. One of them got on the subject of Allah wanting us to attack Europe and America and making them all believers.

Modi: Let me see, you brought up Sura 11. Let me look it up.

Radi: If you are going to touch your Qur'an, are you purified?

Mani: Radi! That is rude. You know Modi would not touch the Holy Book in a state of impurity. We both are still OK since morning prayers. We will not need ablutions again until later.

Modi: That is OK, Radi. You did not know. I am glad that you asked, though.

Radi: I did not mean anything.

Modi: You are killing me with your new politeness, Radi. You have me disconcerted. Ah, I have it here. You quoted them verse 117:

415

Harry J. Sweeney

"For, never would thy Sustainer destroy a community for wrong [beliefs alone] so long as its people behave righteously [toward one another]."

Mani: Oh, Radi. You really took that verse on? There are lots of arguments about that. Many imams would prefer forgetting that one.

Radi: I have found that out. The imam that was with my so-called friends said that Allah would smile upon friends that would smite people like me, who lie about and obstruct what He has commanded. Even after the dumbbells did their worst, he was still shouting and poking holes in the sky.

Modi: And then you hit him with Muhammad Asad's note about that.

Radi: Well, I had to think about it a little, but yes. And the imam stared at me with his mouth open. I added Razi's two cents' worth:

"God's chastisement does not afflict any people merely on account of their holding beliefs amounting to shirk and kufr, but afflicts them only if they persistently commit evil in their mutual dealings, and deliberately hurt [other human beings] and act tyrannically [towards them]. Hence, those who are learned in Islamic Law hold that men's obligations toward God rest on the principle of [His] forgiveness and liberality, whereas the rights of man are of a stringent nature and must always be strictly observed."[87]

Mani: Dare I ask what happened?

Radi: (Laughs) The imam screamed I was a blasphemer and must be killed outright. He was about to burst a blood vessel, I think. I would have been a goner, but the restaurant owner looked up in his own Qur'an what I had said and showed it to a couple of the knuckleheads. It was too bad that Razi's remarks were not in his Book, but verse 117

---

87   Note 149, Message of the Qur'an, Muhammad Asad, Sura 11, page 374

The Restless Wind and Shifting Sands

was enough to shut the imam up. His face must be really hurting by now.

Mani: Oh, because of the humiliation?

Radi: No, I punched him in the mouth–twice. (Modi and Mani laugh) And then I asked the restaurant owner to back up one sura and read aloud ayat 10:59:

"Verily they who attribute their own lying inventions to God will never attain to a happy state."

Modi: Radi is beginning to scare me, Mani. What have we unleashed on the world?

Mani: You must admit, he is a different kind of monster. I think I liked him better when he was on their side, though.

Modi: That was probably because he was so easy to rile and he just kept saying the same things all the time. It seems the less he knows, the more forcefully and stridently he knows it.

Mani: You know, Modi, I was never sure about Radi's being right until I went through sura 11 with you so long ago. I tried to convince my family, but they are convinced that their own imam is infallible. They equate intelligence and politeness with infallibility.

Modi: I see. Such a gentle person would never hurt anyone. I heard that before. The Banu Quraiza thought that their Arab tribal leader friend would be happy to intercede for them. He did not and they were subsequently murdered.

Radi: Verse 117 is telling everyone that what you said the other day is correct, Modi. Dreaming of the day when *"Allahu Akbar"* is heard from every corner of the world does not mean that we have to run amok through every country, killing everyone in the name of Allah. Remember, *jihad* means to strive to be a better Muslim.

Harry J. Sweeney

Mani: Modi, is Radi really saying that? Am I dreaming?

Radi: Of course, you are dreaming, you dumb cluck. If you think I am falling for this sickly saccharin nonsense, you are as bad as the stupid imam who could not find an answer for a simple verse.

Modi: Well, Radi, you certainly had us fooled. But now if you are so smart, you answer the verse.

Radi: I am not an imam. I have not been taught all the answers. But I know how I feel and when every fiber in my body tells me something is not right, I know it is not right.

Mani: You rely on your bowel and not on your brain?

Radi: See! I turn the tables on you and you insult me already.

Mani: But you opened the door for it. Radi, if you went one step farther in the 11th Sura, in fact to just the next ayat 11:118, you would have read:

"And had the Sustainer so willed, He surely could have made mankind one single community: but He [willed it otherwise, and so] they continue to hold divergent views–[all of them,] save those upon whom thy Sustainer has bestowed His grace."

Modi: And Muhammad Asad noted that God willed it this way, that it represents a God-willed, basic factor of human existence.[88] Since indeed it is God's plan that people differ in various ways, the mass killing and subjugation of humankind would tend to upset His plan and bring upon the heads of those hypocrites charges of hypocrisy and mass murder.

Mani: That should be worth a lifetime in the everlasting fires of hell.

---

88   Note 150, ibid., page 374

The Restless Wind and Shifting Sands

Modi: I do not envy anyone who considers seriously subjugating the world "for Allah."

Mani: Allah knows the world is His already and He can will anything He wants. Only one who has the hubris to think he is better than God would try to outthink Him and kill His people before they have an opportunity to get to know Him.

Modi: Well, we have managed to work longer than we wanted. Bilal is about to call and we should do minimal ablutions before prayer. Radi will not have to wash his feet; he keeps them clean by putting them in his mouth so often.

Radi: You stupid comedian! (Again they run out of the house with Radi close on their heels)

Harry J. Sweeney

Conversation 88: Violent Verses

Mani: I received another letter from my cousin. He has questions about six verses that his friends in America gave to him for clarification.

Modi: [Looks at Mani's list.] Ah, I see what is going on. These all sound pretty nasty when you read them in context as well as out of context. But you really have to know what is going on in order to completely understand them.

Mani: Well, what about this first one, verse 4:56? It sounds awful.

"Those who are bent on denying the truth of Our messages We shall, in time, cause to endure fire: [and] every time their skins are burnt off, We shall replace them with new skins, so that they may taste suffering [in full]. Verily, God is almighty, wise."

Modi: Remember I told you that Muhammad paid a visit to the Jewish scholars in Yathrib, to announce himself as the new Hebrew prophet and that he would be their guide as to the Torah? Well, as you know, it led to a very heated argument that had to have angered Muhammad greatly.

Mani: Yes, I remember how the Jews were excoriated in Sura 2.. They were taken to task again in Sura 4?

Modi: Just listen to the entire message. It is almost as if Muhammad himself wrote the verses–which some people believe, but they are ill-informed. They will discover their error on Judgment Day and be the poorer for it. In 4:46, the people talked about are identified,

"Among those of the Jewish faith, there are some who distort the meaning of the [revealed] words, taking them out of their context and saying, [as it were] 'We have heard, but we disobey,' and, 'Hear without hearkening,' and, 'Hearken thou unto us, [O Muhammad]', thus making a play with their tongues, and implying that the [true] faith is false."

The Restless Wind and Shifting Sands

Again the Jews are excoriated because what Muhammad had told them of his understanding of the Hebrew scriptures differed somewhat from what the scholars' understood of them.

Mani: How could that not be Allah's revelation?   Does that not rise well beyond the level of a mortal? We know Muhammad's anger was enough to send Muslims scurrying away until it was over. So, all of that was directed at the Jewish scholars who humiliated Muhammad. I do not understand why Allah did not just strike them dead right there!

Modi: Yes. Judging from the anger Allah showed, one would think it was enough to mete out terrible punishment right then and there. But then, we are only people and cannot begin to know what Allah had in mind.

Radi: Allah be praised, Modi, are you becoming religious?

Modi: I will ignore that. But let me get back to your second question, 4:89:

"Do not, therefore, take them for your allies until they forsake the domain of evil for the sake of God, and if they revert to [open] enmity, seize them and slay them wherever you may find them."

If any of our people today are using this as an excuse to start trouble, they are way off base. Again, it is only part of the message. Some of the messages, remember, are more than a few verses long. In verse 4:79, Allah talks about what Muhammad had termed the Hypocrites, people who had turned against Muhammad and reminded one of a certain red-faced senator who continually badgered the American President, the younger Bush. Allah reminded Muhammad he wasn't their keeper, and in 4:80, Allah explains how they plot against His Messenger. He continues to talk about them through verse 4:91, apparently trying to tell Muhammad to forget about them and stop trying to convince them or get them on his side. Their cause, it seemed, was hopeless.

"How, then could you be of two minds about the Hypocrites, seeing that God [Himself] has disowned them because of their guilt? Do

Harry J. Sweeney

you, perchance, seek to guide those whom God has let go astray—when for him whom God lets go astray thou canst never find any way? They would love to see you deny the truth, even as they have denied it, so that you should be like them. Do not then take them for your allies until they forsake the domain of evil for the sake of God."

Radi: What was this domain of evil you keep talking about? Europe, America?

Modi: Hello, Radi. We are glad your brain finally showed up. According to Muhammad, in the hijira, he left the "domain of evil" to migrate to Yathrib, a place of goodness. It is a spiritual connection only, as Muhammad Asad notes[89] and is used by the Prophet to indicate leaving a sinful state into something better.

Radi: Darn! For the moment, I thought we had something.

Mani: What about verse 8:39?

"And fight against them until there is no more oppression and all worship is devoted to God alone. And if they desist—behold, God sees all that they do."

Radi: Allah must be talking about the coalition here.

Modi: How could He, Radi? The Qur'an was completed in the seventh century.

Radi: What?

Modi: Yes. In fact, some of the Arabs were rejecting Muhammad's preaching, saying they had heard it all at one time or another. They also wanted some kind of a small sign.

Mani: Why did Allah not give them their sign, or even a miracle? It

---

89   Message of the Qur'an, Muhammad Asad, page 138, note 203.

The Restless Wind and Shifting Sands

would have ended all that consternation from the people and they would all believe.

Modi: I have never understood that, because I am not Allah, but I think it has something to do with taking that first leap of faith. My kids see me every day, know who I am and how I react to different stimuli, so whenever I say something, they know how to take it. There is no great leap on their part to know I mean business sometimes and am very generous at other times.

Radi: So, you are saying that the people do not know Allah, only what Muhammad tells them Allah is revealing to him. How do they know that Muhammad is telling them the truth? How do they know Muhammad is not just fulfilling his own agenda? Oh, I know, it is a leap of faith. That is what separates the believers from the non-believers.

Mani: You have it nailed, Radi. Good work.

Modi: That is right. So Allah continues on until verse 8:36, when He promises to gather all the people who cannot make that leap of faith during their lifetime, into hell for a reunion with others who cannot believe. They are the lost! In 8:38, Allah promises that the rest of the unbelievers still have a chance to come into the fold–and then all will be forgiven.

"But if they revert to their wrongdoing, then let them know what happened to the like of them in times gone by. And fight against them until there is no more oppression and all worship is devoted to God alone."

Radi: That does not sound fair, Modi. Are you sure Allah said that?

Modi: It is written so in the Qur'an, Radi. And you are right; it does not sound fair to ask Arabs to make such a leap of faith when it is contrary to everything they have ever been taught and then condemn them to hell for all eternity because they are unable to leap that far. However, if you read the verse again, the unbelievers are only condemned if they

Harry J. Sweeney

revert to their wrongdoing, not if they simply cannot find belief. By that time, Radi, they will have definitely found their belief.

Mani: What about verse 8:60? Is that about the same?

"Hence, make ready against them whatever force and war mounts you are able to muster, so you might deter thereby the enemies of God, who are your enemies as well, and others beside them of whom you may be unaware [but] of whom God is aware; and whatever you may expend in God's cause shall be repaid to you in full, and you shall not be wronged."

Modi: No, not at all, Mani. Allah is talking about the non-Muslims making agreements between them and the Muslims, and then breaking those agreements by hostile acts. Allah starts with verse 8:56, discussing covenants and agreements with non-Muslims, and then proceeds to talk about possible treachery on their part in Q 8:57 through 8:59. As I said, in context, those verses may never mean what they appear to say alone.

Mani: A friend insisted that verse 24:19 outlawed general immorality.

Modi: Your friend is right.

"Indeed, those who like that immortality should be spread [or publicized] among those who have believed will have a painful punishment in this world and the Hereafter. And Allah knows and you do not."

However, let me quickly add that another translation, this one by Muhammad Asad, differs quite a bit:

"Verily, as for those who like [to hear] foul slander against [any of] those who have attained to faith—grievous suffering awaits them in this world and in the life to come: for God knows [the full truth], whereas you know [it] not."

Mani: Where does the last one, verse 47:4 fit in?

The Restless Wind and Shifting Sands

Modi: Look at the entire message:

"Now when you meet [in war] those who are bent on denying the truth, smite their necks until you overcome them fully, and tighten their bonds; but thereafter [set them free], either by an act of grace or against ransom, so that the burden of war may be lifted: this [shall it be]. And know that had God so willed, He could indeed punish them [Himself]; but [He wills you to struggle] so as to test you [all] by means of one another. And as for those who are slain in God's cause, never will He let their deeds go to waste; <u>He will guide them in the hereafter as well and set their hearts at rest, and will admit them to the paradise which he has promised them</u>. (Underlined is 47:5 and 47:6.)

Allah is simply saying that whenever you have won the battle and taken prisoners, you need not massacre the prisoners. You can ransom some and let the others go if you have the heart to do so. If He wanted them all dead, He could have done it Himself, but it is better all around that you work together for victory. Those who died have not died in vain, something good will come of it on earth, and they will see paradise.

Mani: You were right, Modi. When you look at the complete message, everything is different.

Radi: Speaking of different, I am buying today…hey! Where did everyone go?

Harry J. Sweeney

Conversation 89: Euro – Arab Dialogues, violent verses.

Mani, Modi, and Radi are still interested in Qur'an verses that appear to be warlike or violent and are again discussing them at Modi's house. Hayat has just served coffee.

Radi: The first one, 2:191-193 seems fine to me. I see no problems with it, but Mani does.

> *"And slay them wherever ye find them, and drive them out of the places whence they drove you out, for persecution [of Muslims] is worse than slaughter [of non-believers]...and fight them until persecution is no more, and religion is for Allah."*

Modi: Well, Radi, at the time, Muhammad was reciting for the new Muslims the revelation he received that, like the Ten Commandments, were actions that were expected of Muslims and actions which they should avoid. It started with excoriating the Jews for several verses for not living up to their scriptures, and then turned to ensuring that the new Muslims understand the oneness of Allah and the importance of Judgment Day. And with 2:181, Allah lets the Muslims know that they must prepare for death by ensuring that their parents and other relatives are cared for in their wills. He reminds them of the importance of fasting in verse 2:183, and discourages them from taking advantage of their neighbor's largess during Ramadan, and explains the meaning of true piety in verse 2:189.

Mani: All of this is leading up to verse 2:191?

Modi: Actually, it starts with verse 2:190,

> *"And fight in God's cause against those who wage war against you, but do not commit aggression–for, verily, God does not love aggressors."*

The Restless Wind and Shifting Sands

So, what Allah is really saying is that the Muslims should not start any wars, unless aggression has begun against them, for which there is no alternative but to fight. According to Muhammad Asad (who quotes Razi)[90], "slay them wherever you may come upon them" applies only in the context of hostilities already in progress and the non-Muslims started it. Generally, Muslims agree that the verses that begin with 2:190 are valid beyond the period of the revelation. [91]

Radi: Does that not mean that we could attack an American garrison for attacks their navy made on us during the Barbary Wars?

Modi: Long memories do not count any more, Radi. You cannot decide to attack Americans and then in order to justify it, look for something that happened in the past. That does not work for Allah; He knows what is in your heart. This is a new world and we follow new rules whether we want to or not. The United Nations Charter, Chapter 1, Article 2, paragraphs 3 and 4 prohibits the use or threat of force to resolve disputes.

Radi: But fighters from Saudi Arabia, Yemen, and other Muslim countries have attacked American targets overseas without United Nations sanctions against them.

Mani: You are right, Radi. But you must remember that Europe is bound not to assist the USA in any disputes involving Arab states. Of course, the Arab states in the General Assembly are never going to vote with the Americans—nor is China or Russia.

Radi: What prevents Europe from assisting the USA in Arab disputes?

Mani: The Euro - Arab Dialogues. They are not treaties, but they are treated as such. Modi, what about verse 2:216?

"Fighting is prescribed for you, and ye dislike it. But it is possible

---

90   Note 168, Message of the Qur'an, Muhammad Asad, page 51

91   Note 169, Ibid

Harry J. Sweeney

that ye dislike a thing which is good for you, and that ye love a thing which is bad for you. But Allah knoweth, and ye know not."

Modi: This verse really follows on what was begun with verse 2:190. Allah was referring to the fight with the Meccans. They disallowed Muslims from worshiping in Mecca, which caused followers to flee toYathrib. Allah said in the next verse following, 2:191,

"They will ask thee about fighting on the sacred month. Say: 'Fighting in it is an awesome thing; but turning men away from the path of God and denying Him, and [turning them away from] the inviolable House of Worship and expelling its people therefrom–[all this] is yet more awesome in the sight of God, since oppression is more awesome than killing.'"

Radi: So, what you are saying is that since the Meccans oppressed the Muslims by cutting off their access to their house of worship, the Muslims may have to fight the Meccans to restore their rights. Allah is saying that if someone oppresses you, you can fight.

Modi: It depends just how someone oppresses you. If you are told by the United Nations that you must destroy your nuclear and biological weapons and you do not, it is not oppression if another nation warns you that they will come in and take them if you continue to disobey the world body.

Radi: But Europe and Muslim nations all said that it was against the law for the USA to attack Iraq, especially when they found no such weapons.

Modi: Saddam purposely made everyone think he had them. It was a good defense against a few other nations. He also thought that at the last second, before the Americans attacked, France, Germany, Russia, and China would rush in and stop the Americans. Isn't that what he was paying them for?

The Restless Wind and Shifting Sands

Radi: Nonetheless, Modi, Allah says that if someone oppresses us, we can attack.

Modi: Not really. We must be very cautious about attacking other nations, especially the USA.

Radi: Ha! The US can't even stop the Mexicans from pouring into their borders—and more and more Muslims are settling there and the Americans can't stop them.

Mani: The Americans are a divided country, Radi. There are many people there who do not seem to like their country and their votes often appear less than propitious, as if they prefer to see their country defeated instead of victorious. Their tirades against their country and her policies would probably earn them severe punishment in other countries, but the Americans appear to accept it. And some of the worst offenders are actually part of the government.

Radi: Why does the government put up with it?

Modi: I don't really know. Either one political party is too stupid to know what the other party is doing, or is just too timid to lay it out for the people to understand. The people themselves could use a little backbone to learn what is going on without the newspapers and some dopey commentators telling them what they *want* them to think. Hell, if one of the parties ran Louis Farrakhan, and the newspapers endorsed him, he would get millions of votes.

Mani: We are going a little astray here. What about verse 3:56?

"As to those who reject faith, I will punish them with terrible agony in this world and in the Hereafter, nor will they have anyone to help."

Modi: You know who Allah was talking about. The Meccans were bent

Harry J. Sweeney

on denying the truth. What was addressed here was that if the Meccans kept Allah's message from the people, stifling Muhammad's message, they will "get theirs" and not only in the afterlife. He continued in the next verse, 3:57, which completed the sentence:

"...whereas unto those who attain to faith and do good works, He will grant their reward in full: for God does not love evildoers."

Radi: I have one, Modi, verse 3:151,

"Soon shall We cast terror into the hearts of the Unbelievers, for that they joined companions with Allah, for which He had sent no authority".

Modi: Oh, I forgot about that one. That is a little troublesome. Muhammad Asad translates it a little differently. Now you must remember that Muhammad kept hammering on the idea of the "Trinity" which meant that in God there are three divine persons, Father, Son, and Holy Spirit. The only Christians around were the heretical Christians, who had a different view than mainstreamers. Khadija, Muhammad's beloved wife had been a Christian, but we do not know the extent of her knowledge in that regard. Muhammad did not understand what was meant by the "Trinity" and apparently no one else helped. What Allah seems to be saying is that the "Trinity" is adding two other gods to our one God.

Mani: Here is Asad's translation:

"Into the hearts of those who are bent on denying the truth We shall cast dread in return for their ascribing divinity, side by side with God, to other beings - [something] for which He has never bestowed any warrant from on high; and their goal is the fire - and how evil that abode of evildoers."

Modi: Muhammad always had a thing about the "Trinity," but Allah, as understanding and as merciful as He is, I would think would not

The Restless Wind and Shifting Sands

be as concerned about it. Remember, the idea of the Trinity does not violate the one-God concept, according to the Christians. God just has three natures to Him. If Muslims cannot understand the concept of the Trinity, why should they expect Christians to understand that Allah himself was the author of the Qur'an?

Radi: Why didn't Allah explain His position to Muhammad, so that Muhammad could in turn explain it to the Christians? If I were a Christian and had made a mistake like that, I would not consider roasting in hell a fitting punishment for such a petty error in identity. I might have taken a different course.

Mani: Did you hear what I just heard? Radi disapproved of a punishment?

Modi: Well, look at the situation. The Christians said there are three divine persons in one God. They do not understand it themselves, so they call it a "divine mystery." Well, there are things I do not understand about Islam and I know better than to ask. The Christians can ask questions and get answers. We ask questions and someone becomes very upset. It does not make us evildoers or bad Muslims. It only means we have questions. I believe that our Allah knows what is in our hearts. I am not sure what is in the hearts of our imams.

Radi: But you believe we should have a cleric system, like the Shiites?

Modi: Don't you dare say that! I would never say such a thing.

Mani: Be more careful, Radi. If someone heard you say that, we would be in trouble.

Radi: Now you have me all nervous.

Modi: I will have Hayat bring you some Saudi coffee.

Mani: Me too?

Harry J. Sweeney

Modi: Saudi coffee; the only good thing that ever came out of the Najd[92]

---

92   Region in Saudi Arabia where the al Saud clan originated. An old Arab saying is, "Nothing good ever came out of the Najd." "Saudi coffee" is coffee "spiked" with something stronger. Muslims are not allowed to drink alcohol, but if nobody identifies the ingredients besides coffee, then some Arabs "assume" it is not alcohol. It is another version of "don't ask-don't tell".

The Restless Wind and Shifting Sands

<u>Conversation 90: Violent Verses in Suras 4 and 5.</u>

Modi, Mani, and Radi are continuing to look at the violent verses, this time in Mani's house, where Barma, Mani's wife, has just served tea and refreshments. She is careful not to accidentally touch any of the men; whoever was touched would be required to perform *wudu*[93] *again before touching the Qur'an.*

Mani: I think that verse 4:74 is next on the list, unless you have a more important one.

"Let those fight in the way of Allah who sell the life of this world for the other. Whoso fighteth in the way of Allah, be he slain or be he victorious, on him We shall bestow a vast reward."

Modi: That verse is OK to use as a starting point. In fact, it is a very good starting point. If you back up a little to the same sura, verse 59 (4:59), Allah reminds the Muslims that all moral and political power rests with officials who are appointed over them. Their power is God's, held in trust for Him. In verse 4:71, He reminds them that as Muslims, part of a Muslim community, they always must be on guard against attacks against their state because of its ideological base, a base that other communities consider hostile.[94] Two verses following 4:74 (4:75, 76) in effect say,

"What is wrong with you that you will not fight for so important and so just a cause? Don't you realize that Satan's power materializes only whenever you decide in his favor? There is no excuse for succumbing to his evil suggestions when so many guides are there to help you. Allah provides great rewards for those who fight in His cause, whether they win or are slain."[95]

---

93   *Wudu* means formal ablutions, e.g., before prayers or before touching the Qur'an.
94   Note 87, Message of the Qur'an, Muhammad Asad, Page 135

Harry J. Sweeney

Mani: I see. It is more like "What have you got to lose?"

Radi: Yes, Mani. They are really fighting to defend themselves and their way of life. But, don't forget for a second that the followers were told in no uncertain terms that if something should happen to them on the battlefield or even on the way, the families of the fighters will be secure with part of the booty and the fighters themselves will immediately find themselves, without pain of any kind, in paradise with houris to wait on them and take care of their every need.

Mani: That indeed is a powerful stimulus to fight, Modi. Can we now talk about Verse 4:89? It seems to be fairly close to the first one.

"They but wish that ye should reject Faith, as they do, and thus be on the same footing (as they): But take not friends from their ranks until they flee in the way of Allah (from what is forbidden). But if they turn renegades, seize them and slay them wherever ye find them; and (in any case) take no friends or helpers from their ranks."

Modi: We just spoke of this the other day. Allah was speaking to his Prophet about the Hypocrites who were causing him so much trouble while he had all these other matters to resolve. Allah simply told him he is not their keeper and to stop trying to change them. If they get any worse, then he must do what he must to let others know that there are great punishments for obstructing Allah's messages—even death here and the fires after death. Allah was very keen on His messages being heard and understood by the followers of Muhammad and others. In the Qur'an, Allah spoke out in great anger about those who interfered.

Mani: This one, 4:95, seems to be particularly violent.

"Not equal are those believers who sit (at home) and receive no hurt, and those who strive and fight in the cause of Allah with their goods and their persons. Allah hath granted a grade higher to those who strive and fight with their goods and persons than to those who sit (at home). Unto all (in Faith) hath Allah promised good: But those

---

95   Ibid, Notes 89, 90, page 136

who strive and fight hath He distinguished above those who sit (at home) by a special reward."

Modi: This and associated verses worry people whom the West calls "moderate Muslims." Radi's buddies use it as a sword over everyone's neck to show that Allah does not think much of those who do not join the fighting, If God makes a big thing out of being merciful to the people who fight in His way and forgiving them their sins, the people who do not agree with the issues may eventually learn they will have a hard time reaching paradise. After suffering the indignities of God again in verse 96 and of the angels in verse 97, Allah finally says at the end of verse 97,

"For such then, the goal is hell—and how evil a journey's end."

Radi: Allah is telling me, Modi, if I don't attack US troops I am going to hell. To heck with that, I am getting an AK-47!

Mani: I would not be too sure about that, Radi. I can think of enemies of Iraq and Islam that do not include Americans or Europeans.

Radi: What? How can you say that?

Modi: The American troops could have come through Iraq like a huge, bloody scythe, slaughtering Iraqis wholesale. They did not. They stayed mainly on the high roads and just went after Saddam's armies. Only when they were attacked by irregulars and insurgents did they find themselves forced to take defensive action against irregulars.

Mani: Yes, Radi. Because of the Americans, we now have our own government—an independent government. And if you think they are having a hard time functioning, just ask yourself who is fighting it. It is not the Americans, that's for sure.

Modi: So, we could make a good case for saying that Iraqis and others should be aiming their fighting toward al-Qaida groups and insurgents—oh yes, this is already happening.

Harry J. Sweeney

Mani: And moving right along, we have another warlike verse, same sura, 4:104.

"And be not weak hearted in pursuit of the enemy; if you suffer pain, then surely they (too) suffer pain as you suffer pain...."

Modi: For some reason, God seemed to be more than a little worried that stopping for prayer was going to be a problem for Muslims. In 4:101, He allows Muslims to shorten their prayers if they fear a sneak attack. Following that closely, in 4:102, he suggests allowing half to pray while the other half watch—but nobody should stray too far from their weapons, even if it is raining or they are ill. In 4:103, He insists that once the fear of attack is over, they must go back to praying normally. The full text of verse 4:104 is as follows:

"And do not be faint of heart when you seek out the [enemy] host. If you happen to suffer pain, behold, they suffer pain even as you suffer it; but you are hoping [to receive] from God what they cannot hope for. And God is indeed all-knowing, wise."

Radi: That verse was about war but not particularly warlike. If my imam were to tell me something like the half-verse and not the rest and I was wounded in the fighting and then read the entire text later, I would go after him for retaliation.

Mani: Radi is right. Under the sharia, if someone lies to you and, by so doing, causes you an injury or loss of an eye or limb, you can claim retaliation or indemnity.[96]

Radi: I wonder just how many coalition troops had been killed wrongfully because of these stupid imams calling for attacks, slayings, and massacres because of ayats (verses) that do not even exist.

Modi: Perhaps it is time we had a reckoning, Radi.

---

96   (Sharia) Reliance of the Traveller, A Classic Manual of Islamic Sacred Law, page 585

The Restless Wind and Shifting Sands

Mani: What about verse 5:33?

"The punishment of those who wage war against Allah and His messenger and strive to make mischief in the land is only this, that they should be murdered or crucified or their hands and their feet should be cut off on opposite sides or they should be imprisoned; this shall be as a disgrace for them in this world, and in the hereafter they shall have a grievous chastisement."

Modi: What Allah meant here, using the metaphors of the seventh century, would change the verse somewhat:

"There are many contrary people arrayed against Muslims, in hostile opposition to the teachings of My messenger, and undermining My messages. But they have been found out and punished severely here and We have much more awaiting them in the next life."

Radi: Nobody cut off hands and feet?

Modi: Not really. Reference to amputations is often allegorical, although it was done often enough in earlier centuries. When I was younger, I thought amputations were carried out to force the unfortunate ones to eventually commit suicide because of the hard life they now experienced. Now, I do not really know. When someone says that the American president is going to be crucified by the press, you do not really expect the journalists to be nailing some planks together, do you?

Mani: Hey, some of those bozos might try.

Modi: You may want to read Muhammad Asad's notes 44 and 45 to Sura 5, Message of the Qur'an, page 172. My copy is over on the table there.

Mani: We covered quite a lot today. I am sick at the difference between what evil people today are saying are Muhammad's words. As Radi said, people are being killed because of these words.

437

Harry J. Sweeney

Radi: Look, I have no qualms about bloodying my knife with the likes of a polytheist who is trying to insult Muhammad!

Modi: Radi, the word polytheist is another invective that should bite the dust. Many imams use the term to identify Christians who say Christ is the Son of God. Remember, yesterday we talked about God not authorizing anyone to say that.

Mani: Yes, I remember that the "Trinity" had been an annoying thorn to our prophet.

Modi: And about insulting Muhammad, Radi—anyone who insults our Most Beloved and Allah by ascribing the most vicious lies to them should not only apologize to us, but also be forced to listen to one of our imams some Friday afternoon.

Radi: Oh. I did not expect you to say that. That is punishment!

Barma: I will serve lunch in 15 minutes if you are ready.

Mani: One look at Radi's face tells me he is ready.

Modi: I thought perhaps luncheon before the noon prayer would be OK. Noon prayer will be at 12:06 today.

Radi: That is Friday's time, I think, Modi. I know it is 12:04 today.

Modi: I guess I checked the wrong chart.

CHAPTER 10

Conversation 91: The Truce of Hudaibiyya

Mani: Good morning, Modi. I received a note from another cousin last night. We are invited to spend some time with his family and friends.

Modi: I expected as much, listening to would-be cleric Sadr. I guess they are going to set up some defenses to protect themselves from his militia.

Mani: Actually not. As I understand it, our people want to go after his armory as quickly as possible, especially the one in Sadr City. I will know more about it later on. Don't say any more; here comes Radi.

Radi: Good morning. I have a verse I would like to discuss right off the bat, Modi, Sura 8:57.

"If thou comest on them in the war, deal with them so as to strike fear in those who are behind them, that haply they may remember."

Modi: I remember that one right away. In the Qur'an, Sura 8, Allah appears to be addressing his remarks to His prophet; however, it also seems to be general advice to us all. Again, it is about non-Muslim states or communities who sign treaties with the Muslims. Allah wants the Muslims to know that they must make examples of those who break their treaties, especially if they find them as part of the enemies arrayed against them in war. Others need to know we are not taking it lightly.

Mani: I suspect that it is okay when we do it—the Treaty of Hudaibiyya, for example—but not okay if someone does it to us.

Modi: Good point, Mani. Yes, many Muslims throughout history, including Yassir Arafat, signed treaties they knew they had no intention

Harry J. Sweeney

of keeping. Arafat held up a Camp David document, laughed, and shouted "Hudaibiyya"! All Muslims and Jews instantly knew it was a treaty to be broken. The West had no clue. (Radi laughs at that)

Radi: I have a couple from Sura 9, verses 9:5 and 9:14. The Qur'an seems to be talking about the same situation.

"So when the sacred months have passed away, then slay the idolaters wherever you find them, and take them captives and besiege them and lie in wait for them in every ambush, then if they repent and keep up prayer and pay the poor-rate, leave their way free to them."

"Fight them, Allah will punish them by your hands and bring them to disgrace..."

Modi: Suras 8 and 9 are regarded by some as a single sura; indeed, you will not find *Bismillah* beginning the text, as there is in every other sura. But in any case, Allah begins this sura or part sura declaring that He disavows anyone who ascribes divinity to anyone but Him. In Muhammad's eyes, this would include Christians who believe that Jesus Christ is the Son of God. Some Christian heretics do not believe in the divinity of Christ, and Muhammad could not possibly agree with such a divinity himself because 1) he could not understand the concept of the Trinity, 2) people he knew did not agree with it, 3) as God's messenger/prophet, he would have to explain the concept, and 4) having "The Son of God" in the equation between Allah and him would be rather awkward. It would appear that Allah sympathized with his predicament, so He declared that He alone was God, and there were no sons or daughters, or anyone else to share His divinity. The revelation indeed was a relief for Muhammad.

Mani: I can see that. I read here in verses 1 through 3 that Allah would be very angry with those who still insist on making arguments for Christ's divinity.

Modi: Most assuredly. However, in verse 4, He excludes from His chastisement anyone who makes a treaty with the Muslims, but only if the treaty is kept and the party neither assists nor allies with anyone

The Restless Wind and Shifting Sands

else bent on attacking the Muslims. It seems that it only sets up verse 5. Another way of putting verse 5 could be this way:

"When our yearly traditional four months of cease-fire is up, do everything allowed in warfare to gain victory over these stubborn people. However, if they repent and convert to Islam, or at least pay their jizya tax, then let them go on their way."

Mani: Muslims found that the exorbitant jizya tax paid by dhimmis turned out to be a great idea. By allowing non-believers to live in Muslim lands as third-class citizens, the idea brought in another form of income that became important to them. Because of this, they were not always keen on allowing non-believers to convert; they would lose too much money.

Radi: Are you sure about that, Mani?

Mani: It is part of our history. Modi, I see here that Allah continues to discuss the divinity problem; allowing non-believers to either convert or pay the jizya up through verse 11. In verse 12, He brings up the idea that some of the people with the perverse divinity concept may break their pledges and again attack the Muslims, thus the reason behind verse 9:14:

"Fight against them. God will chastise them by your hands, and will bring disgrace upon them, and will succor you against them; and He will soothe the bosoms of those who believe, and will remove the wrath that is in their hearts."

Radi: So all forms of polytheism, even technicalities such as the Trinity, should be stamped out, unless those unbelievers are friendly with you and have covenants or treaties with you. Eventually, though, you will have to fight them. However, it would be much better to convince them to convert to Islam or to enter dhimmitude with its taxes and humiliations. In either eventuality, you can forget about them. Later on, if they betray us, just step on them again.

Modi: Seems as if you understand it now.

441

Harry J. Sweeney

Mani: I found two that sound particularly eerie, but I think I understand them. They are 9:38 and 39.

"O ye who believe! What is the matter with you, that, when ye are asked to go forth in the cause of Allah, ye cling heavily to the earth? Do ye prefer the life of this world to the Hereafter? But little is the comfort of this life, as compared with the Hereafter. Unless ye go forth, He will punish you with a grievous penalty, and put others in your place."

In this case, Muhammad was not just trying to get up an army to go after some Meccans or Jewish silversmiths. He was intent on attacking a Roman Legion at Tabuk. The people knew the difference and told him so. Abu Bakr and Uthman both gave everything they had to the campaign and spread the word to convince others it was the right thing to do. The people were not stupid; they knew the Muslim army was no match for the Romans. But the verse after verse of revelations descended upon the believers, urging people to enlist and give money, and threatening them if they did not. That is what the verse is all about, along with a companion verse, 9:41, that said,

"Go forth, light-armed and heavy-armed, and strive with your wealth and your lives in the way of Allah! That is best for you if ye but knew."

Modi: You are right. Good job.

Radi: You talked about that several weeks ago, Modi. Considering all of the consternation in the Qur'an about the "coming war" with verses flying hither and thither and Allah demanding more and more money for arms, equipment, and horses, what went on in the minds of the faithful when Muhammad reached Tabuk and there was no one there? Did anyone not ask, if Allah knew the Romans would not be there, why did He create the ruckus?

Mani: He has a good point, Modi.

Modi: As it turned out, my good friends, the Romans knew about the

The Restless Wind and Shifting Sands

Muslims, but to them the Muslim "army" was more like a local band of raiders and was not worth detaching a unit to drive them off or demolish them. They had other things to do. Of course, Muhammad saw it differently and said so. And, since apparently no one else was interested in that area, Muhammad claimed it. The Romans did not know about seizure of the lands; and nearby nations, not privy to the truth, got in line to sign treaties and pledges with the Muslims. They mistakenly thought the Muslims were a new power in the region.

Mani: So, just going there to meet the non-existent Roman Legion, then coming back intact, made everyone believe we were invincible. So, as it turned out, it was good that we outfitted ourselves and went.

Radi: I would like to jump forward a little and look at Sura 48:29. It seems to me, though while others think it rather harsh, I consider it reasonable.

"Muhammad is the messenger of Allah. And those with him are hard (ruthless) against the disbelievers and merciful among themselves"

Modi: I tend to agree with you. You must know that the sura itself was "revealed" to Muhammad during his return to Medina from Hudaibiyya. He would have been very high on what he considered a great victory. And so, from verse one in this sura through verse 28...

Mani: Oh, I know that part of it. Allah spoke of the trials and hardships that led to this "manifest victory." He spoke gently of the believers who volunteered to accompany His prophet on this journey, and chastised those Bedouins who were given the opportunity, but declined.

Radi: Forgive me if I look over your shoulder. I can see that the Meccans were continually described as "those who are bent on denying the truth" or other expressions akin to that, and the Muslims, of course, are the believers.

Modi: I am pleased to have so much help today. Finally, Allah said, as another translation has it,

Harry J. Sweeney

"Muhammad is God's Apostle; and those who are [truly] with him are firm and unyielding towards all deniers of the truth, [yet] full of mercy towards one another. Thou canst see them bowing down, prostrating themselves [in prayer], seeking favor with God and [His] goodly acceptance: their marks are on their faces, traced by prostration."

Allah finishes up by saying,

"[they are] like a seed that brings forth its shoot, and then He strengthens it, so that it grows stout, and [in the end] stands firm upon its stem, delighting the sowers...[Thus will God cause the believers to grow in strength,] so that through them He might confound the deniers of the truth."

Mani: I would not have said it that way, Modi.

Radi: But you are not God, Mani.

Modi: Did you understand that Allah pushed the idea that Muhammad was firm with the Meccans during the treaty negotiations, and that was what the Qur'an meant about being "unyielding to the deniers of the truth."

Radi: Now that you mention it, yes. But why bring that up?

Mani: We just discussed a few verses, Radi, that were printed on posters, and appeared to be very nasty and belligerent, downright warlike. How are we going to make these people stop doing that? They are lying about what the Qur'an is saying and exploiting the lies to further immoral and illegal causes.

Modi: They will never stop no matter what. People who are too stupid to know any better, will stay that way because they are too lazy to learn. That American comedian, Ron White, who we watch a lot on American TV, said it all when he said "You can't fix stupid!"

Radi: What actually does that mean? I don't get it.

The Restless Wind and Shifting Sands

Mani: Case in point.

Modi: Let's saunter down to the restaurant before Radi figures it out.

Mani: Oh, we have time.

Harry J. Sweeney

Conversation 92: Sadr City

Modi: Before Radi arrives, Mani, let me tell you that meeting last night was startling. I think your cousins are taking on quite an assignment.

Mani: Remember, Modi, we are at a crossroads here; either we do something about Muqtada al-Sadr, or we accept a new civil war. I am for taking action against his militia as soon as we have evidence that would be acceptable to a prudent person that it is moving against us. We must destroy his arsenals first, mosque or no mosque.

Modi: You can count me in with you in this endeavor, Mani. How much does the coalition know?

Mani: After the meeting, my cousin assured me that the coalition has not been advised at any step. Less than an hour before the action, we will advise them to look in a different direction and take no action until afterwards. If we achieve success, they can claim a military intelligence coup. If we fail, they knew nothing about it.

Modi: I do believe that if we can destroy his arsenals the government could reinstate that indictment for murder. Here comes Radi.

Radi: Good morning, my good friends. I see Hayat has made coffee. That is great, Modi. Allah's blessings on you.

Modi: I will pass along your blessing to Hayat, Radi. Did you bring the verse you were anxious about?

Radi: Oh, yes. It is Sura 66, ayat 9:

"O Prophet! Strive against the disbelievers and the hypocrites, and be stern with them. Hell will be their home, a hapless journey's end."

Mani: Isn't that "The Sura of the Prophet"? That one is short.

The Restless Wind and Shifting Sands

Modi: That is right. Look at it here, it has only twelve ayats (verses). More importantly, it is almost identical with 9:73. To be *stern* with them (Muhammad Asad translates it as 'adamant') means, do not compromise on matters of principle. If you read the following verse, 66:10, Allah reminds everyone of the parables of Lot's wife and Noah's wife. His point is that being a relative or friend of His Messenger will not save anyone from the fire if he or she is not a believer.

Radi: What about the Bukhari hadith 52:177? I bet the Jews cringe about that one.

Allah's Apostle said,

"The Hour will not be established until you fight with the Jews, and the stone behind which a Jew will be hiding will say, 'O Muslim! There is a Jew hiding behind me, so kill him.'"

Modi: What you are quoting, Radi, is from Bukhari' s Book 4, 52-177, which is for the most part identical with 52-177 that I quote:

Allah's Apostle said, "You (i.e. Muslims) will fight with the Jews till some of them will hide behind stones. The stones will (betray them) saying, 'O 'Abdullah (i.e. slave of Allah)! There is a Jew hiding behind me; so kill him."

It was narrated by Abdullah bin Umar. The words in the *hadith* are not Allah's words but those attributed to Muhammad himself, according to the "narrator" who hears him utter those words.

Mani: Listening to those words, Mani, leads me to believe that Muhammad really hated the Jews.

Modi: I see your profound grasp of the obvious is working, Mani. Yes, Muhammad had a hatred of the Jews. It did not start out that way, but his visit to the Jewish scholars in Yathrib led to an unfortunate schism between the two factions that just could not be repaired. Their denial of him as a Jewish prophet and their rejection of his message and his revelations led to more than just angry words.

Harry J. Sweeney

Mani: I should think so. After that confrontation, Modi, the Qur'an added dozens more verses excoriating the Jews vehemently. This was followed by Muhammad's launching military attacks against the Jews that generally resulted in robbing them of their land and assets, driving them out of the region, and, in one case, mass murder. I would call that hatred.

Radi: And he led a perfect life, which I am enjoined to emulate. See, I am perfectly legal by punishing these sinners by myself. I am only emulating the prophet. And I am watching you two.

Mani: He reminds me of another of Bukhari's hadiths, 52-256. *"The Prophet ... was asked whether it was permissible to attack the pagan warriors at night with the probability of exposing their women and children to danger. The Prophet replied, 'They (i.e. women and children) are from them (i.e. pagans)'"*

Modi: It is like asking, "Can they fly airplanes into the World Trade Center buildings since there certainly will be a plethora of women and children killed?" Muhammad's answer would be simply that the women and children were the wives and offspring of [the men whom we are attacking] and as such are legitimate targets.

Mani: Who was the narrator for the hadith?

Modi: As-Sab bin Jaththama, a creditable witness.

Radi: (Looks at his watch) I need to get along, guys. I told Zaina that I will do the noon prayer at her father's house today. He wanted to have a talk with me after the prayer.

Mani: Uh, oh. That sounds serious. Better pick a day, Radi.

Modi: How many people can your cousin really count on to raid Sadr's mosque?

Mani: It may not exactly be a raid in the mosque. Apparently there are a few of Muqtada's people that are not enamored with the idea

448

The Restless Wind and Shifting Sands

of partisan hostilities. What I hear most is that because of the type of warfare there is no martyrdom involved with it. And if you kill someone else, who is to say that the killing is moral?

Modi: So Muqtada's people are not confident that their leader is the Mahdi or anyone with authority.

Mani: Well look, he is not even a certified cleric. He is the son of a grand ayatollah and the grandson of a prime minister. But aside from family, he has no real credibility, except as prayer leader. Working for him and even doing some incidental thuggery may be acceptable to them to please Sadr or out of respect for his father; however, when it comes to the possibility of spending eternity in the fires of hell, many of them draw the line.

Modi: So that is why the threatened martyr bombing never materialized?

Mani: Yes. He is not Muhammad, and he is not the Mahdi, and he is not even Ayatollah Sistani! It is just not worth risking eternity on whether killing for him is moral. If it is not a moral duty to kill or die for him, a follower could very well spend all eternity writhing and screaming in the fires of hell. It is just not worth it to many followers.

Modi: So some of them just want to prevent a war by allowing the arsenal to disappear. Wow! But it does make a lot of sense. It also shows a little maturity on the part of someone. I bet that person will be doubly blessed by Allah, and considering the lives that will be saved, I bet he almost would be guaranteed martyrdom and paradise.

Mani: The family of course will not reveal who the hero is; however, there are more than just one or two.

Modi: If the situation grows, Mani, it could very well become a movement. Even though it may start as an anti-Sadr movement, it could grow well beyond that and change the face of Iraqi politics.

Harry J. Sweeney

We will need to study this situation and see what we can do to help intensify and spread it.

Mani: How about visiting my family again and talking to them about what you think. I bet my family could help things along by spreading the word on the street.

Modi: Good idea. Some people get their information only that way anyway. They know so little about their own religion, and what they do know is from people on the street.

Mani: Should we go after prayers? Or, wait. Why don't we pray with my family?

Modi: Wonderful. Get them on the phone.

After a phone call, Mani simply smiled and pointed toward the door.

Modi: Well, Mani, something tells me this could be the beginning of a beautiful friendship.

Mani: You said that one time last year.

Modi: Yeah, I know; I just like saying it.

The Restless Wind and Shifting Sands

<u>Conversation 93: "Would you kill him if you knew he would kill children at play?"</u>

Modi: The last two nights have been a little exciting, Mani. We both managed to do some shooting. I am amazed at the number of fighters in that Mahdi Army. I was exhausted last night.

Mani: I really feel bad about shooting at fellow Muslims. I do not think it is right, even if they are Shiites.

Modi: For one thing, Mani, they were shooting at you. Besides that, you cannot consider them Iraqi because they are fighting against our government. They are part of the problem that keeps us from uniting under one banner. If the Americans had not intervened, our government would soon collapse and Iran would send more fighters in to take over. They have already bought up most of the available residential homes here.

Mani: You mean if it comes to another vote, our own Iraqis here may be outvoted by those newcomers?

Modi: You guessed it. But even if the Iranians salted the field, they did it with common people like you and me. If we keep winning against whoever tries to divide us, they will eventually side with the winner, no matter how they got here.

Mani: I am sure we did not win this battle. Whenever I looked around, the government people were either dead or retreating. I don't think we took the arsenal.

Modi: I guessed that we did not. But Maliki's people did not run. Those Sadr people had too much of everything. If we were not in such a good position, we would have moved or retreated; it was too hot. Now that your cousins know better, they will plan better next time.

Harry J. Sweeney

Mani: I hope you are right. Meanwhile, shooting at countrymen is making me ill. What would our most beloved Prophet say about it?

Modi: He would say, "Kill them wherever you find them." Remember, he killed Meccans because they refused to listen to him. His followers raided commercial caravans and killed innocent drivers—fellow Arabs who were not part of the fighting. He killed other people for being Jewish.

Mani: I know that, but it still does not seem right for me to do it.

Modi: You are enjoined to do anything the Prophet did. He was the perfect man who led a perfect life. You know all of this.

Mani: I guess so, but I just do not like it.

Modi: You remember that monster from Zarqaw, right? He was killing Muslims wholesale in the name of Allah. The people were sick of him and finally gave him up to the Americans, who ambushed him and killed him. It is the same thing.

Mani: But they did not pull the trigger.

Modi: Yes, they did. As soon as they gave up his schedule to strangers, he was as good as dead. The Americans were their weapons. Look, how many Iraqis—Shiites and Sunnis alike—Zarqawi would have killed had he lived? It would have been a very high number. How many Sunnis were killed by Sadr's people? That too is a high number. By fighting here, Mani, you are saving the lives of other Muslims, and by helping our government you are helping to further the cause of Islam. You are a hero.

Mani: (Looks directly into Modi's eyes) You are serious about this!

Modi: Quite so. When I squeeze a 7.62 millimeter round off from my Kalashnikov, with one of the insurgent fighters in my sights, I know

The Restless Wind and Shifting Sands

that the person wilting under my fire is a source of trouble for my tribe and my family and is holding back our unity. My wife and kid may live another day, another month, maybe a full lifetime because of what I did last night.

Mani: If we died there, Modi, would we be martyrs?

Modi: Forget all the rumors about that, Mani. We are all human. When good men do good things and it costs them their lives, they will see paradise. Many others who have ulterior motives for putting on a vest and walking onto a bus filled with Jewish children may be unpleasantly surprised after they pass beyond.

Mani: Are they told where to go and when to detonate?

Modi: Of course, some of them think that they control when to detonate, but in reality they do not have total control. For example, if the handler sees the boy developing cold feet and retracing his steps, the handler will probably detonate it quickly. The "bomber" personally might want to pass up a group of kids his age playing nicely together, but the handler might be of a different mind. Such a handler to me is a murderer as bad as Zarqawi.

Mani: I would not do that, Modi.

Modi: But would you kill the handler if you knew he would kill children at play, even if they were Jewish children?

Mani: I don't know. I don't think so. It is none of my business. I might hate the idea that someone is doing it, but I cannot interfere with that brigade. I can say truthfully that I wish they would stop it.

Modi: Had I the opportunity to keep the handler from doing it and have some reasonable chance of escaping notice, I would certainly try to stop him.

Harry J. Sweeney

Mani: What if the handler turned out to be Radi?

Modi: That is an unfair question, Mani, but I will answer it. Since Radi knows me, I would call for him to stop first. If he detonated the bomb anyway without turning around, it would be too late. I could not shoot him even if he lived after he did it; that would be illegal retaliation and his family could file for retaliation against me.

Mani: Would you advocate stopping the homicide bombing?

Modi: Yes, but not by going after the handlers, that would be too dangerous. And if we had protesters outside their headquarters, they would have to send out only one or two bombers, and no one would ever protest there again.

Mani: Then how could you stop it?

Modi: Disband them if possible. If not, blow them up without warning. Have the government notify the brigades that they are now an outlaw organization. Have a fatwa issued that without a government warrant no one may command or support such a brigade. Once the people have been given the word that homicide bombing is a ticket on Hell's express, they will not be so quick to volunteer. If the people in charge would only tell the truth, we would not have this problem.

Mani: The government will have to maintain its own vigilance and find as many imams as possible to sign off on a law prohibiting such slaughter.

Modi: When we are unified and not threatened by imbeciles here and in the American congress, we will be able to do much more than we are doing. I just wish that before an American official speaks to the public he is required to take a polygraph first. We all need the truth.

Mani: Unfortunately, some of them do not know the truth. To them it is only what you can make the people believe.

The Restless Wind and Shifting Sands

Modi: Then it is going to be a long, long war. Here comes Radi.

Radi: Good morning. Are we ready for some breakfast?

Mani: Good idea. I am really starved.

Radi: I have not seen you for a couple of days. Off visiting another cousin?

Modi: We needed to get away from Baghdad for a while.

Radi: I don't blame you. But if you stay around for a while, you may have a chance to get in on the new war.

Mani: New war?

Radi: I think that Iran is going to pull Sadr's strings again. If he is able to back up Maliki's troops and make them look bad, al-Sadr will ask for Iran's help to keep order. Iran, in turn, conceivably could request United Nations' approval to restore or maintain order here. That will put a different face on the war, and the Americans may have to leave. No American president now or later will want to tackle Iran. The Iranians have them confused and scared.

Mani: Iran had better think twice about that one. I think General Petraeus is ready for anything coming out of Iran.

Modi: We know he is tough and unafraid, and so are the US armed forces. But is the American congress ready? Do they know what Iran is?

Radi: Good point, Modi. Perhaps I will have their heads after all.

Mani: It would not be worth the trouble, Radi. They are not warriors by any stretch of the imagination. They are only playing a game of politics and do not seem to realize yet that they do not pick up their

Harry J. Sweeney

marbles and go home when they lose. When they lose this time, they will not have homes. If they are lucky, they will have graves.

Radi: On that note, I say let's go to breakfast. Thinking about beheadings always gives me an appetite.

Modi: Oops. I think I just lost mine.

Mani: Me too!

The Restless Wind and Shifting Sands

Conversation 94: Muqtada Al Sadr

Mani: I did not like losing to Sadr.

Modi: I don't blame you. I feel the same way. It is disgusting that we could not rely on those people to empty that armory.

Mani: It is not their fault. Allah wills what He wants. I will say, however, I just do not understand His purpose in letting Sadr win.

Modi: Why would you think Allah willed it for Sadr to avoid this?

Mani: If it happened, Allah willed it. You know as well as I that everything is already in place and He knows who wins, who loses, and who goes to heaven and who burns in hell.

Modi: Now wait a minute! I though you already rejected predestination when we talked about it months ago.

Mani: I have a new imam and we have gone over this problem again. He calls it *qismah*, the will of Allah. He said that everyone has a life-cycle about which we can do nothing. No matter what befalls us, good or bad, it has already been set—even who goes to heaven and who goes to hell. Allah knows all these things well in advance.

Modi: Are you then telling me that he creates people and puts them on the path to hell? I just cannot accept such a notion.

Mani: The world is his to do with as He pleases.

Modi: It does not sound like the Allah I worship.

Mani: I guess that is one way of putting it. Perhaps He did not plan who goes where, but created a system in which everyone falls in little blocks in the middle of a maze. Perhaps more than one path leads to the fire, but only one leads to paradise. Perhaps He allows newborn

Harry J. Sweeney

souls to fall where they will randomly and they must find their own way out to the fire or to paradise.

Modi: That is a little bleak also, Mani. Is that from your new imam?

Mani: Not exactly, but pretty close. I asked him if we love and worship Allah, keep His laws, and are a benefit to our community, wouldn't Allah go so far as to will us on the right path to avoid a hell we did not deserve? He said that nothing anywhere even hints that He would do that.

Radi: See. You must wade into the unbelievers, your sword flashing in the sunlight or the moonlight. You must kill for Allah and be killed for Allah in order to guarantee paradise.

Modi: Well, that's not encouraging. There must be some way of breaking that life cycle and taking some control without killing people no matter who they are. Why should I care that there are Jews, Christians, and even polytheists and animists in the world? What harm have they done us?

Radi: They have tried to subjugate us and take our lands and our oil. They deserve to die for what they did and are doing.

Mani: I will defend Islam with my life, martyrdom or no martyrdom. But I will not point my AK in the wrong direction. As much as I love my countrymen and hate aggressors, I will pour lead into the chap who straps explosive belts on little kids before I harm a single coalition soldier. Radi, you hated Saddam Hussein and cursed more than a dozen times that someone had not rid us of him.

Modi: Yes, I remember that, Radi. You were miserable under Saddam. He killed at least two of your relatives that I know of. Saddam is dead now because of the Americans. How much oil have they taken? I saw on Fox News that the Americans are paying out billions to stay here

The Restless Wind and Shifting Sands

and fight for us. Mani is right. Some of us Sunnis are hateful beasts that give our people the wrong guidance and ensure they are on the path to hell.

Radi: How can they help being misguided?

Mani: Misguided is no excuse for being stupid. It is written that everyone must know his religion, his community, and the world around him. If one does not learn what he needs to learn, he shares the responsibility for any harm to his community or to Islam.

Modi: Bravo, Mani. You could be an imam.

Mani: But I could also be a radical, Modi. It takes a great deal of effort, too much sometimes, to stay focused. There are too many other imams with agendas that will give us no peace and point to us as if we are the pariahs. You know, it would be so much easier to just throw my hands up, rely on the imams telling me the truth, and just run around blowing up schools and killing people indiscriminately.

Modi: Yes, sometimes it takes every ounce of strength to be a good person. And everyone tries to tell you it is not worth it. And yes, it is much easier to be a Neanderthal.

Radi: You both are confusing me. If I don't die before too long, I must seek to be a martyr. I do not want to take any chances on the fire. I am taking the shortcut!

Modi: I keep hearing that, but I do not believe it. Martyrdom is not zipping on a vest, and then going over to the Israeli side and climbing into a crowded bus. Martyrdom is when you are fighting for Allah with no intention of getting killed, but you catch a bullet or a grenade fragment and die. Once you decide to get yourself killed for one reason or another, that is suicide and you will not see paradise. To the real

Harry J. Sweeney

martyr, life is still dear to him, but he takes the chance because he loves Allah that much.

Mani: Then why would the imam disagree?

Modi: I would guess that his agenda includes recruiting people to use for homicide bombing and the only way he can do that is to lie to his candidates about what constitutes martyrdom.

Mani: It never occurred to me he could be a recruiter.

Modi: There is a lot of money floating around for fighters and for martyr-candidates, Mani. I am certain that some of that wealth can fall into the hands of recruiters.

Mani: That makes me sick, Modi.

Radi: That would not be my way at all. I can see myself wading into a crowd of Jews or Christians, waving my sword and slicing this way and that until I cannot lift my arms to strike again. The Jews will kill me in anger, but I will die smiling.

Mani: Have you ever met a Jew or a Christian, Radi. (Radi frowns)

Mani: I thought so. Radi. Go dress the part and head for Israel. Knock on any door and you will find one of us. They will be Jewish, of course, but nonetheless you will recognize another Modi, yourself, or me.

Modi: Our religion does not make us what we are. There are hundreds of millions of Muslims in this world who would never hurt another person, no matter what religion he is. You will hear "Live and let live," more than you hear "Kill them wherever you find them."

Radi: I have never heard that type of talk before. Just today I sharpened my knife. I may have to use it this day.

The Restless Wind and Shifting Sands

Mani: The world is changing, Radi, and we have already been left behind too long.

Mani: Yes, here we are looking for more 21st century weapons and munitions, but we are led by imams who are still thinking as if we were still in the 7th century. We cannot catch up here.

Modi: You know, Mani, you are right. We cannot catch up here. We are trying to walk upright and live in peace, but we cannot because we are constantly being stirred up by the beasts among us. We must leave.

Mani: Where could we go and live in peace? Egypt? Jordan? Europe? What about our families and our friends? How would we all survive?

Modi: We both have cousins in America. That one cousin in Florida who sent you the photographs of his home and swimming pool, write him and ask for his advice. He brought up his kids in America and has a fine job. He should know.

Mani: I also have a cousin who teaches at the University…

Modi: No, by no means, not him. He probably is giving us a bad name in America already. How can he teach in a university? He is stupid! And he has the attitude of a little Zarqawi.

Radi: Sounds like my kind of guy. (Modi and Mani laugh)

Mani: I have that aunt in Arizona who married the Christian.

Modi: You would have to convince her we are not coming to murder her.

Mani: I will let Radi talk to her. (Modi laughs so hard he falls)

Radi: I will miss you guys if you leave Iraq.

Harry J. Sweeney

Mani: I will talk to Zaina. You two can get married and come with us.

Radi: They might have a price on my head--I am notorious!

Modi: Not to worry; the price on you will be so low, no one will notice.

Radi: Always the comedian, Modi. Ah, Bilal calls.

The Restless Wind and Shifting Sands

Conversation 95: The Hijira

Radi: (At Modi' house, Modi's wife Hayat has just served coffee) Modi, your wife is a jewel and she makes great coffee.

Modi: Thank you, Radi, but you should tell her that. You have my permission.

Radi: I came a little earlier because I am bothered about Muhammad's (peace be upon him) reasons for leaving Mecca for Yathrib. Why were the Meccans so set against his message?

Modi: When he began preaching, Radi, he claimed he was a prophet. Well, the merchants and the families in Mecca were not ready for something like that, not in Mecca. And one of their own, being a prophet, that was too much to expect.

Mani: Wouldn't anyone believe him, besides his family and small circle of friends?

Modi: No. And the Meccan merchants boycotted his entire clan. The clan was not too pleased about that. They warned him continually about the dangers involved in preaching the messages he said was given him. In one place, people actually threw stones at him.

Radi: What? Why did they do that?

Modi: He preached reform, Radi. Mecca was like a wide-open town we see in those wild west films. And along came Muhammad to spoil their fun. With one powerful, angry God they could not see, they could not punch Him or kick Him as they did the little icons that they came to know as gods, when they did not provide the expected favors or relief. In other words, Muhammad wanted them to trade their people-friendly gods for one angry, unseen God who would sweep everyone into hell for disobeying Him.

Harry J. Sweeney

Mani: And with a single God, the merchants stood to lose a great deal of revenue from the pilgrim trade.

Radi: I know all about that, what part of the message affected everyone so badly?

Modi: It was a cultural and social message, building a new civilization based on justice and eliminating the disputes and retaliations of a society almost out of control. But the old, solid tribal and clan lines were also endangered. The rules laid out by God would be the law of the land and not the rules of the family or the tribe. In short, the change was to be dramatic and entirely too much for the Meccans. The allegiance would now be to God and not to the tribe or the family. Dodge City was now to be ruled by the preachers and the temperance ladies.

Mani: We know about the plot to assassinate the prophet and we know about his escaping to Yathrib to become a dispute mediator for the tribes there. But what about Yathrib itself? What sort of place was it before Muhammad got there and changed its name?

Modi: Well, it was close enough to the trade routes to enjoy light trade, but Yathrib relied mostly on agriculture for its survival. Now, as far as the disputes were concerned, that was no small issue. There had been no one in charge for a long period of time and some of the disputes resulted in much violence. Generally, the Jewish tribes had been evicted from their homeland, Canaan, now called Palestina, by the Romans. They settled in Yathrib along with Bedouins, who were just trying out a new life, away from the hazards of nomadic life.

Radi: So between the Jews, the Bedouins, and the settled farmers, it was a very mixed community.

Mani: And so every little problem metastasized into an unacceptable crisis.

Modi: True. But Muhammad found his niche as mediator and found

The Restless Wind and Shifting Sands

himself growing in stature and spreading out into other areas, wherever his management skills were needed.

Radi: What do you mean by his management skills?

Modi: As I mentioned, Yathrib, or now Medina, was now a thriving community of Jewish merchants, Bedouins, and Arab farmers. Before long, added to that were incoming Muslims making their way there from Mecca. Before Muhammad reached Medina, many of this helpers went there first to begin preaching and introducing the new religion. The local Arabs, having heard the talk about the coming of a new prophet, hurried to become a part of this new religion, looking for the salvation that so far was just a rumor. After Muhammad took up residence there, the trickle of people to Yathrib increased little by little.

Mani: That must have been a madhouse.

Modi: You have that right! A madhouse it was. There were more new people coming into Yathrib all the time and it now included the wives and families of Muslims who preceded Muhammad. Food was becoming scarce and so was housing. The old residents were becoming incensed at the new boom-town and they and the Muslims complained about each other.

Radi: I think I know what is coming. Is that when he began raiding caravans?

Modi: Yes, it was. He had to provide for his own people and at the same time ensure that the original residents had customers for their goods and services. The only income available to him there was raiding caravans. With the booty that the robberies provided, each Muslim taking part was able to use his share to provide for his family and at the same time provide profits for the merchants and the farmers.

Mani: That would lead to the Meccans becoming more than just miffed at their losses from the caravans and perhaps fewer people from Syria and other places becoming more reluctant to trade with Mecca.

Harry J. Sweeney

Modi: Mecca had good reason to be angry. Muhammad, an upstart, was giving them fits and they could not get to him to crush him. So they waited patiently for a Muhammad mistake. You and I know that there are no secrets in the Middle East—except to westerners. Muhammad heard about a fat caravan about to leave Syria for Mecca, and they knew the route the caravan was taking. So Muhammad prepared not only to take the caravan, but also to protect the robbers.

Mani: I don't think I heard about that.

Modi: Well if you heard about Badr, you heard the story in a certain way—it was a miracle battle because even though greatly outnumbered, the Muslims won the day. Well, it seems that the leader of the caravan discovered that Muhammad knew his route and had planned to ambush the caravan at a certain place.

Radi: So, did he take a different route?

Modi: Oh yes. However, he also sent a rider ahead to advise the Meccans his caravan was in danger from the Muslims.

Radi: So they assembled their army and rode off to protect the caravan?

Modi: In a manner of speaking, they did. But the army they assembled was only partially Meccan. There were other tribes in the area that had covenants with the Meccans to join them when going into battle. So, the Meccans were not all that many in number starting out, but their numbers grew considerably by the time they reached the caravan rendezvous area. Now here is where things became iffy and why the Meccans needed better management.

Mani: The caravan wasn't there?

Modi: Worse. The caravan was already safe in Mecca and the caravan leader sent word to Badr, where the makeshift army was waiting. When the tribes found out there was no caravan to protect, they took the

The Restless Wind and Shifting Sands

opportunity to leave the scene as fast as their horses would go. They balked at the thought of attacking the Muslim army—whose size and toughness they did not know—without a good reason. Some Meccan units departed as well, leaving the Meccan leader with a force much smaller than he needed.

Radi: So he departed the scene as well?

Modi: He should have, but he stayed around too long and the Muslims attacked him. He had never seen the ferocity that the Muslims brought to the battle. He did not know that his adversary had told his fighters that if they were killed in battle, their families would receive their share of the booty, and they themselves would be in paradise in the blink of an eye with luscious gardens and women ready to wait on them. One fighter, resting from the tough battle is said to have seen the prophet nearby and asked him if it was really true, that he could see those luscious gardens and be waited on hand and foot if he were killed in the battle. When Muhammad replied in the affirmative, the man grabbed his sword and shield, said "Out of my way," and without armor, laid into a group of Meccans. Others followed the man back into the battle and before long, the Meccans were not sure the battle was worth it—the Muslim ferocity was simply too much for them. So they all departed, leaving the field to Muhammad.

Radi: (Laughing) The Muslims were too much for them, I see.

Mani: They were all Arabs and many of them were really neighbors. But look at the situation. The Meccans actually had nothing to fight for. The caravan was safe in Mecca, their allies had disappeared, and there they were trying to keep these mad Muslims from overrunning them.

Modi: Thus passed the opening battle of the Muslims. Even today, as Muslims fight, you can hear them refer to Badr in their shouting and their boasts.

Radi: So that was the beginning of the Muslim battles?

Harry J. Sweeney

Modi: That was it, the Battle of Badr. After Badr, the Meccan leadership knew what they were facing and tried to put together an army they could trust. Unfortunately, neighboring allies had to join each fray, and they were just not as committed as the Meccans. And no one had the incentive that the Muslims showed, to risk their lives as if they were better off if they were killed.

Mani: How can you fight people like that?

Modi: That is the type of fighter the anti-government insurgents use against the Americans. But the Americans can beat those fighters, no matter what they do. The only people that Americans fear are their own leadership. If the "gloom-and-dooms" have their way, the American troops know that Iraq will be gone, along with the rest of the Middle East. Before long, the congressional dummies will become dhimmis, second or third class citizens of the radicals.

Radi: Are we ready for tea and biscuits?

Mani: I need something stronger. (Modi calls for Hayat to bring the Saudi coffee)

(This conversation was adapted from *Legacy of the Prophet*, by Anthony Shadid, Westview Press, 2001, pages 22-25.)

The Restless Wind and Shifting Sands

<u>Conversation 96: Divine mystery, Sunni-Shiite schism, Battle of New Orleans.</u>

Radi: Modi, yesterday we discussed Muhammad's problems and his ability to surmount those problems with just his oratory.

Modi: See, Radi, you misunderstood already. It was not oratory; it was making use of the followers' belief system. Once he established in their minds that indeed he was the messenger of Allah and that he was receiving revelations from Allah they were ready to make leaps of faith.

Mani: Are you saying he exploited their naïveté?

Radi: What? Do I need my dagger?

Modi: Down, boy. I say what I mean, Mani. Please, don't get ahead of me and don't look for hidden meanings.

Mani: Well, please clarify the "leap of faith business."

Modi: Do you understand the "Trinity" of Catholicism—Father, Son , and Holy Spirit in one God?

Mani: Not really. I never have.

Modi: Neither do I, nor do the Catholics. That is why it is called a divine mystery. But understand it or not, Catholics believe it, with a few dissenters. They have taken a *leap of faith* and accepted it. Now, do we accept that the Qur'an was more than just inspired by God, that it was absolutely created by God?

Radi: Of course we do. Everyone accepts that fact.

Modi: No, Radi. We accept it, but we cannot prove it. We have taken a leap of faith that the West cannot take with us. They believe in their respective religions—and we have believers among them—and their

Harry J. Sweeney

religions are fine and wholesome. There is no reason why they should come over to our side when there is nothing wrong with theirs. They must take some faith leaps themselves, but the authorship of the Qur'an is much too difficult a leap for them. If they did believe that God actually created the Qur'an, they would all be Muslims.

Radi: Of course there are many things wrong with their religions that make them our enemies and require that we attack them wherever we find them and kill them. We must lop off their heads!

Modi: We now have a case in point, Radi. Are the Christians constantly on radio and TV shaking their fists and their swords in red-faced rage, shouting that they are going to kill Muslims? I will tell you the correct answer. No, they are not. Do you know what they are doing? They are asking why we are so down on them, and they do not even know us! And what is it that makes us so enraged? Many of them are trying to learn more about us.

Mani: I guess that is the truth, Modi; they don't even know us. And when you look around at the radicals, Radi's buddies, you see outrageous indignation and horrible threats of dismemberment of all those people. It is a wonder they do not all die of fright.

Modi: Funny thing, Radi, the media in America generally try to keep everything from the people, so that very few things get through to alarm them. Look, our beloved Hussein was killed by agents of the same caliph, Mu'awiya, who had Hussein's father killed. Hussein's father was the Caliph Ali, cousin to the prophet and husband of the prophet's daughter.

Mani: Yes, Mu'awiya was the usurper to the throne of the caliph, an illegitimate and secular ruler in defiance of the prophet's wishes.

Modi: That is right, but my point is that it was not over when it was over. They beheaded the holy man, Hussein, the son of the prophet's cousin and daughter, in the year 680, and Ali's faction, the Shiites, have not forgotten. It has been 13 centuries, and one might think it

The Restless Wind and Shifting Sands

happened last week. We remember every crime, every slight; we never forget. I guess the Americans are just too busy.

Radi: You are right about that. They seem to have forgotten the 9/11 attack already.

Modi: I do not think you are right, Radi. Half the Americans do, and the other half seem to have a love affair going with someone who apparently does not think it is important. At any rate, the half in love with the stranger in their midst have forgotten about 9/11 because their political party has buried it deep! They feel that any reminders to the public of what happened on 9/11 would make people realize some of their priorities are askew.

Mani: Yeah! Now that is a leap of faith! They are trading off national defense for the vague promise of some unspecified change that probably is nothing more than a will-o'-the-wisp. He has not said.

Radi: How can the Americans be so damned strong and true in battle, yet be as naïve as Bugs Bunny's *maroons* about politics.

Mani: I think they were born that way; some of them anyway. Remember last year? We did that survey in Europe and found it worse over there.

Modi: Our agents in Europe, radicals all, tried to sell the idea there that the Islam whose representatives were blowing up building, train stations, and people everywhere was the "religion of peace." Well, the Europeans almost laughed us out of the country.

Radi: I noticed that the Americans bought into it though. Don't they ever see what is going on in Europe? I swear, Modi, we are looking at the Banu Quraiza—professional victims—all over again.

Mani: Don't you believe it, Radi. Those radicals may have to fight only half the country, but the half that fights are tough!

Modi: Oh, yes, and there is a precedent for that, Mani. Before the Battle of New Orleans, many people of some northeastern states, with a bit of pressure, would have folded up and surrendered. It was left to the Southwest to put a few people together with their own rifles to represent the entire country against thousands of troops in the most powerful army in Europe, the army that just defeated Napoleon.

Radi: You talked about that issue once before. Did those people really want to surrender—the ones on the East Coast?

Modi: Yep. They had no stomach for a real fight. They looked down their noses at the rest of their country, like some arrogant congressmen are doing now, but when the British lost, so did the American Northeast. They showed their colors, just as they are showing them now.

Mani: But after the Battle of New Orleans, they were all Americans again.

Modi: No, they were all Americans for the first time. They were only liberated colonists before. But many of them soon forgot where their freedom to complain came from. Fortunately for them, they were soon beset with the influx of immigrants from all over the world, enough to drown out the sissies and the cowards. But there they are again. As much as some of us really like those Americans, we just cannot stand those porn-purveyors.

Radi: What if the porn-purveyors were over here in Iraq instead of those magnificent troops?

Mani: Offhand, Radi, I think you would grow tired of cutting off heads.

Modi: Would you really cut off the heads of those who surrender?

Radi: Those are the best kind. I like to hear them begging, bawling, and other things. It is only the smell coming from the seats of their pants that gets to me.

The Restless Wind and Shifting Sands

Mani: Well, thankfully, Radi, only the best are here with us—and I certainly hope they stay. Any group that now goes after those troops will have to face us also.

Modi: With what we have said yesterday and today, can you see the quandary that we are in?

Mani: You mean about our ideology really getting in the way of friendship with the West?

Modi: It is certainly not the religion. It is using some elements of the religion as a sword to threaten the West and to keep it from getting close to us.

Radi: I know some Westerners who have converted.

Modi: It is not that, Radi. Certainly, if you read a few people like Maududi and practice the same religion as many millions of people outside of the Middle East practice it. However, when the radicals visit your mosque and introduce you to a few of their rules, you want out, quickly!

Mani: Yes, and then you discover too late that there is no way "out." And if you just walk away, you know you are under a threat forever.

Modi: Yes, it is the potential for unnecessary violence that turns the West off completely.

Mani: And the women who sometimes just become shadows on the wall to their husbands and their families.

Mani: So, it is not the religion; it is the warlike imams who are also male chauvinists.

Modi: Don't forget the liars, cheaters, thieves, kidnappers, and murderers. We have even had our fill of those people. I imagine the

473

Harry J. Sweeney

West is nonplussed and obsessed with our preference for death over life.

Radi: Don't get Mani talking about that again.

Mani: You are the only one who chooses death over life as a practical matter. I am trying to understand the philosophy.

Radi: Yes. I believe the Prophet. I will be cruel to the unbelievers and kind to the believers.

Mani: Do you really want to be kind to us believers?

Radi: I certainly do.

Mani and Modi: Well then, drop dead!

(The chase is on with Modi and Mani again narrowly avoiding Radi's blade.)

The Restless Wind and Shifting Sands

Conversation 97: The Sharia

Modi: Good morning, Mani, Radi. Peace be unto you.

Radi, Mani: And unto you peace, Modi.

Radi: I would like to know the actual basis for the sharia. I am told that it is only from the Qur'an, which I am inclined to believe. Is that right? The sharia is actually from the Qur'an reworded?

Modi: First you must accept that Islam is a complete life, not a religious component of a life. Where the precepts of Christianity end, the secular law begins.

Radi: I do not understand. What are you saying?

Mani: I can answer that one, Radi. Modi is saying that in the Christian world, there are many nations and cultures. The leaders of Christianity find ways to adjust or tweak their precepts so that the nations and cultures within Christianity can work cooperatively with each other.

Radi: But what about a Christian going from one culture to another? Will he not find differences that may trouble him seriously?

Modi: Good question, Radi, and you are right. I remember reading of a Scotsman, whose traditions included the bearing of a knife[97] worn in their stockings, finding himself in England where the bearing of any arms is illegal. He soon found himself a guest in a British jail, despite the best defense in court about the power of some traditions.

Mani: And closer to home, some of our people continue to emigrate to the United Kingdom and Europe with two or more wives, despite the laws against polygamy in those countries.

---

97   "Sgian dubh" (/skin doo/ 'dagger black') Once worn near the armpit, now worn by Highlanders in the stocking ('stocking dirk')

Harry J. Sweeney

Radi: I have not heard of any deportations for that reason.

Mani: Of course not. Europeans and the British are a little weak when it comes to immigrants breaking their laws. British lawyers for the immigrants have only to state that the polygamists would face prosecution in their own country if they were deported. Some European judges go wacko over that concept and seldom ask for proof.

Modi: Be that as it may, Islam is unlike Christianity in that its precepts go further into each person's life. Islam takes the entire *ummah*, the entire Muslim world, and provides its teachings of the principles of life so that it applies to every aspect of humanity in every nation and culture on the globe. Indeed, Islam is a culture-producing force that also welcomes entire nations to its bosom.[98]

Radi: But what about the Qur'an? Where does that come in?

Modi: According to Muhammad Asad, "From the very outset, Muslim civilization was built on foundations supplied by ideology alone." If you remember, Radi, Prophet Muhammad was building this civilization in Medina while fighting to convert his old hometown, Mecca.

Mani: So it was never a nation by itself, nor was there ever a racial element, so it did not have the "national or racial homogeneity" that organized it into a nation or race.[99]

Modi: And since the Qur'an was the basis of our "ideological civilization", it stands to reason that the Qur'an would also be the basis for all of our laws. The total source of course would be the Qur'an and the Sunnah (words and deeds of Muhammad).

Mani: The other source, Radi, is not really an independent source, but

---

98   *This Law of Ours: And Other Essays*, Muhammad Asad, Islamic Book Trust, Kuala Lumpur, 2001, pp 16, 26.

99   Ibid., page 29.

The Restless Wind and Shifting Sands

a source that must analyze various parts of the Sunnah as they arise in the law.

Radi: That makes as much sense as telling me about aerodynamics.

Modi: Mani means that in some cases pertinent verses or hadiths may not be clear enough to serve as resources. We can then turn to our scholars to study and discuss the situation in order to render a fair decision.

Radi: Oh. Well, that seems clear enough.

Modi: Radi, there is still one more element that is not discussed in the Islamic law books. In cases in which there are relatively new national laws in play, the national governments may determine that in those cases, especially capital cases, prosecution and resulting penalties must be in accordance with the national laws and not the sharia. Even if the nation's constitution states that laws must not conflict with the sharia, in some nations it does not include capital cases.

Radi: What?

Mani: If you take your favorite pastime, killing apostates, you may never do that again in Iraq. Although the sharia not only endorses such killing, but urges it, Iraq and many other Muslim nations do not. Apostasy is not a capital offense in some Muslim countries.

Radi: (Storm clouds appear in his eyes) If the Qur'an and the sharia both call for the killing of apostates, on what authority does any nation prevent it?

Modi: For one thing, Radi, if the nation has signed the International Declaration of Human Rights it may eventually be subject to the ICC on that issue. Second, there is no legal basis for a country, any country, to declare leaving a religion a crime.

Harry J. Sweeney

Mani: In some backwater countries authorities turn a blind eye to the national law and lightly prosecute only if it becomes an international issue.

Radi: I still do not understand the nations' positions in removing apostasy as a capital crime.

Modi: After the Prophet died, many tribes left the religion partially because they considered their covenants a personal bond between themselves and the Prophet, and his death ended the covenants.[100] Caliph Abu Bakr pursued these people vigorously and slew many of them; but he did not refer to them as apostates. He was after their share of the *zakat*, the poor tax.

Mani: Modi, I think Radi is stunned. He is standing there with his mouth open.

Modi: You had better sit down now. I tried to explain this to you once before, but my words did not seem to penetrate. Apostasy by itself is not really a crime; it must be accompanied by something else that makes it one. In the seventh century, an apostate left the religion and either spied for the Meccans or left Medina for Mecca, where he fought the believers. That sort of apostasy was actually treachery, or treason.

Mani: Aha! So you are saying that if you just stop going to mosque on Fridays and eliminate your prayers and the fasting, your neighbors might ostracize you if they found out, but they couldn't remove your head, as Radi wants to do.

Modi: That is about it. However, I would not advise anyone to be open about leaving.

---

100 *Islamic imperialism*, Efraim Karsh, 2007, Yale University Press, p. 30.

The Restless Wind and Shifting Sands

Mani: What about the *zakat*? But, I think that is also considered a state tax also.

Modi: As of today, only the Saudis do that, but soon probably all of the Muslims states will include the *zakat* as an income tax. Well, Yemen maybe, but not Morocco. In Morocco, you must only provide the money to whomever you choose, even if it is your less fortunate relatives.

Mani: I heard that the shops there have coins that will be enough to buy a meal and that a homeless person or one down on his luck need only show up and take one from the shop counter.[101]

Modi: Oh, that is wonderful. Why cannot we all do something like that?

Radi: If it were one of my relatives, he'd be the first one there and take all of the coins.

Mani: See how one person can spoil things for everyone else?

Modi: I am sure that even Radi's relative can be brought into the spirit of things, Mani.

Mani: I suppose so. I will have to forget what he said; he spoiled a beautiful, true story.

Modi: Radicals are known to do just that. I hear Bilal calling. You know what, I will say a special prayer today just for those shopkeepers in Morocco. They deserve a special prayer to Allah.

Radi: I will say a special prayer, too.

Mani: To have Allah bless those Moroccan merchants?

---

101   http://ramadankareem.blogspot.com/2007/09/zAkat-in-morocco.html

Harry J. Sweeney

Radi: No, just to hope any family of mine there finds out about them.

They chase Radi out of the house by bombarding him with cushions.

The Restless Wind and Shifting Sands

Conversation 98: The Crusades

Modi: You fixed up your house, Mani.

Mani: Barma did most of it. Here's Radi now.

Radi: Modi, that new imam I was telling you about; he gave the sermon today and was ranting about how horrible the crusades were.

Modi: The crusades? What do some of these new imams know about crusades?

Mani: But are they not a very somber part of our history?

Modi: A part of our history, yes. But the crusades were hardly a somber part. Very few of our people knew about the crusades, even when they were in progress. For example, in Iraq here, some people may have heard something about the Franks raiding around Palestine or part of Syria, but everywhere else was quiet.

Radi: I don't understand. I thought the crusader wars were terrible catastrophes and many people were slaughtered.

Modi: Hardly, Radi. They actually helped more than they caused harm. Just as soon as they entered the Middle East, the first leaders they came across wanted an alliance of some kind. Our people were still fighting among themselves and calling upon the Franks to help defend against one tribe or another.

Mani: I remember one imam telling us that there was much more trade than fighting going on. In fact the only reason that Saladin attacked the Franks—and it was not much of a battle—is it because they sacked a trade caravan and would not return the goods.

Modi: You are right, Mani, and afterwards, they were all friends again. The Franks did nothing to upset the national, cultural, or political situation throughout the Middle East. If anything, they allowed for opening up markets with other European countries. Don't ever let anyone tell you that the crusades were a catastrophe.

Radi: But one after another imam was ranting about wars and how Saladin saved Islam by defeating the huge Western armies.

Modi: Well, I hate to cut the string on someone's kite, but at no time did any of the crusaders seriously threaten the region or Islam. Islam was never affected at all. As I said, people that came across the crusaders were more interested in trade. Radi, the Shiites and the Sunnis hated each other more than they disliked the Franks.

Mani: Maybe that other imam last year was right. He said that in some cases, because of the Muslim predilection for alliances, it was not unusual for one tribal chief to align himself with the Franks, while another with the British, and still others with whoever else was around.

Modi: You bet. Look, the Fatimids exploited the situation to win back Palestine and Lebanon, which they lost to the Seljuks.

Mani: But what about our great Arab hero, Saladin?

Modi: I have no complaints about Saladin, Mani, but I hate to tell you that he was a Kurd. Not only that, but while his mentor was fighting it out with a Western army, Saladin was consolidating his position with other tribes and cities in the area, sometimes with the compliance or the actual help of the Franks.

Radi: That does not sound like the Saladin that I know.

Mani: Isn't truth the first casualty of war?

Radi: No, the first casualty always winds up being Jewish.

Modi: Look, you guys, Mani is right. Look at the way the imams and leaders from other Muslim countries were characterizing the Iraq War. I remember one peaceful day when Hayat and I were shopping

The Restless Wind and Shifting Sands

downtown Baghdad. We went home and turned on the BBC and were absolutely shocked at the videos and the frantic reporting of what was supposed to be going on in downtown Baghdad—right where we were.

Mani: (laughs) I remember some of that. We used to call it the "BBC Daily War Cinema."

Radi: I am shocked at what you say about Saladin.

Modi: To make you feel better, When the Franks took another trade caravan and again refused to make restitution, Saladin decided the time had come to declare war.

Mani: The whole attack of crusaders wasn't a holy war?

Modi: Certainly not. It was not considered an attack and neither the politics of the Middle East, nor Islam was ever in jeopardy, as I said. Saladin called on his brother's army and a few other alliances and together they won a great battle. Afterwards, however, the alliances fell apart and Saladin turned his attention to Muslim tribes that were giving him trouble.

Radi: I can't believe these imams are such dolts.

Modi: Not all of them, Modi. There are some with agendas that create spin, cover-ups, and downright lies.

Mani: Like that imam in London that time?

Modi: Oh, I forgot about him. He was speaking to some young liberals who were seriously considering converting. Yes, a cousin told me about him.

Mani: I remember that. And he was narrating a hadith of two camel drivers who committed a few crimes and Muhammad tortured them by putting their eyes out, cutting off a hand and foot from alternate

Harry J. Sweeney

sides, and then, because they left the religion, he ordered that they be left in the open to bleed to death. In effect, he ordered the death penalty for apostasy.

Radi: Whoa! That is even a little much for me.

Modi: Well, the imam changed the ending so the young people would not know the penalty for leaving the religion.

Mani: I cannot understand why the scholars do not find a way to undo the penalty for apostasy. I think it is long past time. In addition, who in his right mind would join our religion if they knew they could not leave under penalty of death.

Modi: There are a few changes that should be made, no matter what the imams say. The scholars know that there are some little problems with the basic documents as they have been taught to us. They still discuss them among themselves without resolving anything. Every so often they hint at a conference for wider discussion, but after a few disappear, the others are discouraged… I believe they think we are too stupid to understand anything controversial.

Radi: You mean people really think we need ref…

Mani: Don't you dare say it, Radi. It is not worth it.

Modi: The scholars are not stupid, Mani, and the non-Muslims scholars actually say what our scholars won't. We have a lot to discuss.

Radi: I still do not understand why people get so scared of us.

Mani, **Modi**: It's the violence, stupid!

The Restless Wind and Shifting Sands

Conversation 99: Female Circumcision is Mutilation.

Radi remains unmarried, so Zaina, his fiancée, agreed to host Modi, Mani, and him for coffee, cakes, and conversation, supervised by her father, Mahmoud bin Samir. Zaina has just poured the coffee.

Modi: Radi, this young vision's coffee is so good you need to marry her before others find out. Remember, all it takes is one sentence from you—three little words.

Radi: Don't say things like that in front of her. She will be after me now for days.

Mani: And well she should. We thought you two would be married last year.

Modi: It is not good for men to remain unmarried.

Radi: I have heard all of that. Why can't you guys let me alone about that?

Mani: Just think of all of the young men who would like to be in your place. You have a woman whom you love and who obviously loves you. And you just sit there. Zaina is a great catch. Why Zaina would waste her time with you, I just do not know. Radi, you two right now should be bouncing babies on your knees.

Modi: Yes. I have heard that Zaina had dozens of suitors and could have been happily married with nice kids by now. And there you are.

Mani: One of my cousins was head over heals with a young girl who helped her father with his shop, but he does not have a job and no income, so he could not talk to her family about marriage and could not even talk to her (*haram*). Her father married her to that old fart that has the fish cart. He must be 60 if he is a day.

Harry J. Sweeney

Modi: Oh, yes, I know who you mean. She does not look like a young girl any more. Sad.

Zaina: It is our tradition unfortunately. But what kind of life would a young bride have if she married for love but her husband could not find work and could not house her or feed her?

Modi: Radi has a job and can afford a wife and kids. He drives me crazy. I too had a cousin who was heart broken. He had a little sister whom he loved more than life itself. His father was from the old school and thought that a marriage contract for her when she was only eleven was great, something worthy of bragging.

Mani: Don't tell me. . . .

Modi: Yes, before my cousin could do anything, his father fulfilled the contract, and his little sister was taken away, kicking and screaming. Her husband was in his fifties.

Mani: That poor little girl. She should be playing with dolls.

Radi: You two people are nuts. There was nothing wrong with marrying a girl of eleven. Aisha was younger than that when she married the Prophet (peace be upon him), and she was betrothed to someone else before that. Our Shiite brethren have established nine years as the marriageable age for girls.

Zaina: I always wondered how some people can do their ablutions five times per day, spend all that time praying to Allah, and still remain dirty old men.

Mani: To tell the truth, although I love my little nieces and nephews, I really can't stand being around them for more than a few minutes at a time. How can an older man look at some tyke playing in a sandbox as a wife? What in hell is the matter with our people?

Modi: It is an old tradition. Arabs have always wanted younger girls

The Restless Wind and Shifting Sands

for their wives, even after our Prophet chose, as his first wife, someone fifteen years his senior.

Zaina: Ah, but she was rich. There is something about gold that makes some folks look a lot younger. But I must say that in the case of Khadija, she was an exceptional person. He was lucky.

Mani: Yep. He never looked at another woman during his marriage to her. You know, I was drinking some of Modi's Saudi coffee and happened to mention to Barma that the more I drink of that good stuff, the younger she looked. Then she ran out of the house. When I caught up with her and asked where she was going, she said to get some more Saudi coffee. (Zaina had to laugh at that; Modi smiled)

Modi: I would like to ask Zaina a question, Radi. (Radi nodded).

Zaina, what about your cousin down the street? She was supposed to be married, but something went wrong. What happened?

Zaina: Mutilation, Modi, mutilation. You wonderful guys have been talking about going to the USA and taking us with you. I would like to stay here and try to teach our young girls. I cannot do anything with the older ones. There has to be some role I can play here.

Mani: That is a nice thing to do. But what about the young bride-to-be here?

Zaina: It was butchered so bad it just could not be undone. Any attempt at repairing it led to excruciating pain and screaming.

Modi: What about hospitals here?

Zaina: European medical teams have found that in some areas, 60 to 70 percent of women have been "circumcised." It is a huge problem all over Iraq.[102] The teams have accomplished great things while here, but they cannot cure everyone.

---

102   http://albionmonitor.com/0502a/femalegenitalmutilation3/html

Harry J. Sweeney

Modi: I assume that not only has too much been cut away, but the unsanitary conditions in the procedures and the unprofessional and sometimes bizarre stitching have led to scar tissue that results in impossible odds of repairing.

Zaina: That is what happened here. All of this has been outlawed, and even many imams have declared it is illegal within the religion, but the old know-nothing hags know nothing else but how to cook, sew, and circumcise their granddaughters. Sometimes I think that is their main purpose in life. No wonder some of the Bedouins toss them out to starve.

Mani: Perhaps the Americans will take an interest in what they call FGM (Female Genital Mutilation) and do some studies on how best to repair it.

Zaina: Look how quiet Radi is. I have told him that removing Saddam has been good fortune for Iraqi women. He does not want to hear the Americans are good for us. Yet he wants to go there to live.

Mani: Logic-tight compartments.

Zaina: The Americans and the Europeans and even the Asians have been very good about coming here and helping us, even to the point of repairing it for as many patients as they could see. (Modi and Mani noted tears starting in her eyes.) Little girls dying of blood poisoning, just barely getting to a hospital in time. (She holds her head in her hands, weeping).

Mani: My wife Barma had said a few times that it would be wonderful if our little girls could grow up away from these disgusting old men who keep the rules from changing because of a belief many others do not have. In our Prophet's time, city people sent their boys to Bedouin camps for years to be brought up by the brave, cruel, and unyielding nomads.

The Restless Wind and Shifting Sands

Modi: So you are now advocating sending our little girls to America or somewhere to learn how to be sweet, pretty, little girls.

Zaina: And then you would bring them back here to Iraq, unprepared for the cruelty and savagery of some of our institutionalized slavery factories. What about a family calling their 12-year-old daughter back after four wonder-years in the USA and then telling her they have a contract of marriage with someone over fifty? You teach her how beautiful the world can be and then show her she is nothing but meat.

Modi: We must redo the country, Zaina. But we cannot do it all at once. There are too many people against any type of change or reform. Then we have some ugly Americans who want to abandon us and see all this work stopped and the remarkable people who made so much progress murdered for their efforts.

Zaina: And if both you and your wives leave, that means four people are lost to us; four people who understand the problem and could do something, anything, to help.

Mani: Radi's friends are bad enough, Zaina, but when you add the officials, the radical imams, and the people who will do nothing to help themselves or anyone else, it is not just swimming upstream. It is swimming upstream with hungry bears in the water waiting for us.

Zaina: I guess you guys will have to become imams. You must do something special to help. You do not have a choice. You love your country and your people—and your little nieces to come. We cannot sacrifice any more to those bearded bullies.

(Modi and Mani look at each other. Radi just shrugged his shoulders.)

Modi: Well, Mani, this looks like the beginning of a beautiful . . .

Mani: Oh, shut up!

Harry J. Sweeney

Conversation 100: The Ottoman Empire

Radi: I accuse the West of engineering the demise of the Ottoman Empire.

Mani: And why, pray tell, would the Europeans want to do that, Radi?

Radi: Because they wanted to destroy our religion. We were too powerful for them.

Modi: The reality of the situation, Radi, might shock you. During the extended period of Ottoman decline, the European powers were not slowly picking the Ottoman Empire to pieces, they were trying to shore up our Muslim empire.[103]

Radi: What? That is a terrible lie. Why should the Europeans want to do that?

Modi: Imperialism was important to the imperialists and they did not want a fellow imperialist power to disintegrate before the world. Such a decline would be bad news for other imperialist powers, seeing that such a power could deteriorate without a major war or a terrible catastrophe.

Mani: I can understand that. If you are an imperialist power, you want everyone to know that you are bigger and more powerful than any one or two countries.

Modi: Right. If the Ottomans sank into oblivion, the world would recognize that such a thing is quite possible and that an empire was only as strong as the sum of its parts. You know, the Ottoman Empire

---

103   Islamic Imperialism, Efraim Karsh, Yale University Press, 2007, page 99.

The Restless Wind and Shifting Sands

was threatened by Napoleon III and then by Egypt, and both times the infidels in Europe saved her.

Radi: That is hard to believe. Every imam I know has come down hard on Europe for killing our wonderful Ottoman Empire. They say that anything we do to any European is payback and they deserve it.

Modi: I keep telling you, Radi, that those know-it-alls will drive you crazy if you listen to them. They hate everybody except other Muslims—and they are not too fond of Muslims who are not Salafists, the ones with the seventh century mindset.

Radi: I had seen in writing, Modi, the Ottomans were picked apart. You cannot say they were not. It is a fact.

Modi: Facts are very stubborn things, Radi, but you must get to know them before you introduce them to others. In World War I, the Central Powers of Germany, Austria-Hungary, and Bulgaria were lined up against the Allied Powers of Russia, France, Great Britain, and other smaller nations with the United States coming into the fray later.

Radi: What has that got to do with anything?

Mani: Don't you remember your Muslim history, Radi? The Ottoman Empire at first was neutral.

Modi: Exactly. Virtually all of the most powerful nations had emissaries talking to the Ottomans, assuring them that if they maintained their neutrality, the nations would guarantee her safety during the fighting and would ensure her territorial integrity at the conclusion of hostilities.[104]

Mani: The European powers did not want the Ottoman Empire in the war and just about everyone not associated with Germany told her to stay out for her own interest.

---

104   Ibid., page 107

Harry J. Sweeney

Modi: But somehow she had the idea that Germany would win and after the war she would be in for some great gains in prestige and resources. She did not take into consideration that if she lost, she would lose everything.

Mani: I remember reading that Europeans kept pouring everything they could into the Ottomans to keep them neutral, but to no avail. She came in anyway, on the side of Germany. The Central Powers lost the war and both empires, the Ottomans and Austria-Hungary disappeared.

Radi: And you say that the Europeans tried like crazy to keep her out?

Modi: Right, Radi. And the Ottomans did not have to do anything at all for Europe to give her all those guarantees. She could have just sat out the war and stayed neutral. She might be there still and more powerful than before the war. The Ottomans blew it, Radi.

Mani: So you see, Radi, Europe did not even contribute to the death of the Ottoman Empire. If anything, she committed suicide despite the help and counseling that she received from Europe.

Radi: What about the Armenians. Didn't the Armenians sell them out?

Modi: Absolutely not! Every Armenian church, the masses of Armenians, even the school kids prayed for an Ottoman victory. Even the school kids, Radi. There were only a handful of Armenians that were against an Ottoman victory, and they were not enough to worry about.

Mani: Aha! It was the perception that made the difference!

Modi: Yes, just like now. To the Muslims it was the perception that was the reality. Because of a few disloyal Armenians, millions of faithful Armenians died. Didn't the Americans lock up many Germans and

The Restless Wind and Shifting Sands

Japanese in World War II because the perception was that they would probably be disloyal to the war effort?

Radi: Of course.

Modi: Well, the Ottomans did not lock up their perceived enemies; they slaughtered them by entire villages and towns. Men, women, and children were cut to pieces, burned alive, tortured to death, or otherwise left to the mercy of whoever was in charge of each area. And remember, most of the Armenians were loyal to the Ottomans and prayed for their success in the war.

Radi: But they were not Muslims, so who cares. At the very least, we will not have to deal with them later.

Modi: Let me tell you something, Radi. Islam will never rule the entire world because not all Europeans are incompetent enough not to reverse their dumb programs that let us get this far. Even Europeans learn.

Radi: We should be consolidating our gains now and taking control of the smaller countries. Many European leaders kept pushing for having smaller families while we forever want larger families. We are producing more and more babies while the Europeans are opting to not have children and aborting the ones that manage to get by the firewall.

Mani: But Radi is right about taking the planet for Allah, Modi. He always says that.

Modi: If you go back to the very beginning of our religion and you read the words of our Prophet, he will tell you in his own words that the documents of Judaism and Christianity are the basis for the start and the development of our own religion.

Radi: But he said that the Jewish scholars changed their own scriptures and as a result, Allah had to send another prophet—a final prophet—to straighten them out.

Harry J. Sweeney

Modi: When the prophet visited the Jewish scholars, Radi, he announced to them that he was the new Jewish prophet and he knew the Jewish scriptures. Why did he not establish some rapport with them first? Muhammad was the new force in town and wanted to build a large base of loyal Arabs and Jews. I do not understand what happened to pit both sides against each other.

Mani: What are you trying to say, Modi? Are you arguing with the Qur'an?

Radi: I will have your head if you argue with God's word.

Modi: Not arguing with God's word, Radi, I am just trying to understand it. Usually, I find enough in the verses to make my case.

Mani: What case are you trying to make?

Modi: That the Jews may have been misinterpreting their original scripture over the years, not purposefully changing the scriptures. I am not ready to believe that scholars are easily corrupted. I doubt very seriously that Jewish scholars "mangled" their scripture.[105]

Radi: I am glad I brought my knife.

Modi: Well, I pointed out a few weeks ago when we were discussing each of the suras that quite a lot of anger was displayed in the Qur'an concerning the Jews after our Most Beloved visited them in Yathrib. What happened to the Jews next? One tribe after another was either exiled without their assets, and their land was confiscated; or their land was confiscated and the Jewish "owners" were required to continue working the land for Muslim profit; or in the case of the Banu Quraiza: about 800 were murdered by beheading.

Mani: We know what happened to those Jews, Modi. So what? They deserved it.

---

105   Alan Jones, *The Qur'an*, E. J. W. Gibb Memorial Trust, London, 2007, page 19.

The Restless Wind and Shifting Sands

Modi: Mani, there was no evidence they ever did anything—they were silversmiths, not warriors!

Mani: They were probably spying on Muhammad for the Meccans. Remember, some truths only Allah knows. If it was revealed in the Qur'an, just believe it.

Modi: Is that what you would tell the Jews at Babi Yar, Mani? You and I have agreed that the Holocaust existed, no matter what some of our co-religionists have said. And every time I bring up the Banu Quraiza, I cannot help but see the similarities with Babi Yar.

Radi: I am going to kill him.

Modi: Right, Radi, think like a Neanderthal again.

Radi: Psst, Mani, what is a neon-something—whatever he said?

Modi: Mani and Radi, if you have serious questions about the Torah or either of the Christian Testaments, can you ask the rabbis or priests and get answers?

Mani: Of course.

Modi: If you have serious questions about the Qur'an, Radi, can you ask your friendly imam here why something does not make sense to you?

Radi: No. There are some things you had better not bring up or you would lose your head. Look! It is the word of Allah! Just believe it! Take that leap of faith!

Modi: Can you become a Catholic, leave after a while. Then become a Methodist, or a Baptist, or even just decide to become an atheist without consequences? Can you become a Muslim, decide it is not for you, and then go be something else?

Harry J. Sweeney

Mani: What is your point?

Modi: I guess I am just tired. I love this world and humanity. I also love my religion. I am just tired of being pushed into hating people I don't even know!

The Restless Wind and Shifting Sands

Conversation 101: "Where do we go from here?"

Modi: While we were chatting the other day, Radi, you asked a question that I have been turning over and over in my mind. Where do we go from here?

Radi: Yes, I remember. Suppose the war were to end tomorrow. Where are we? Are we still at war with the West? Do we still have a chance of winning the entire planet for Allah?

Mani: Now that you mention it, I would like to get in on that answer also.

Modi: Mani, you guys have been half-right all along. The Chinese once said, "Do nothing, and all things will be done." Indeed, Mani, that is what your friends were doing—nothing. We could have used your help against Radi's friends, not kicking and screaming and whirling knives around as radicals were doing, but just standing up once in a while and saying that those people do not speak for you.

Mani: Well, they did speak for us, *but not all the time.*

Modi: You had a right, and I would add that you had a duty, to stand up and say that you disagree with what the radicals were saying and doing.

Mani: We did not always disagree with what they were saying and doing. *We would not do it or say it,* but we felt that they had every right to say *what was in the Qur'an and the hadiths,* no matter how terrible it sounded and no matter how many people had to die because of it.

Modi: Because of the hatred shown by Radi's friends and the absolute intolerance they showed to other people of the other great religions, we have turned the clock back again and are not getting the converts we want.

Radi: We are getting plenty of converts. You must be lying.

497

Harry J. Sweeney

Modi: Our religion should be drawing even more, but we are losing more than we are gaining because Radi's friends keep trying to radicalize the new ones who want to be left in peace. If we did not threaten to kill people who want to leave the religion, we might spring a leak because of the present attitudes. Our religion started with Judaism and Christianity and did not do very much that was different, except that we taught that the Qur'an was authored by Allah, while the Christians and Jews go only so far as saying their scriptures were inspired.

Mani: But Modi, the Qur'an was given by Allah by verses to our beloved Prophet over the course of 23 years.

Modi: That is what we have been told; and I have no evidence to the contrary. I guess that too is my leap of faith. But I look around and see many so-called leaders who inspire nothing but fear. Some of those leaders seem to believe that almost any thought, word, and action is a violation of something—a sin against God. How do they know what is a sin against God? They have an agenda; they want to keep us here in the ideology, and they are able to do that because even leaving the religion itself calls for a death penalty. And the pettiness of some of the so-called crimes are hard to believe. For example, Mani, an elderly man was killed because while he was sweeping debris from his yard, someone reported he accidentally touched the mosque wall with the dust. That is not religion! That is just crass homicide!

Radi: That is not homicide; he was rightfully killed for a sin against Allah, blasphemy.

Modi: The man probably loved Allah with all his might but was elderly and probably had bad eyes and shaky hands. But besides that, sweeping dust on a wall? How about if you look at the mosque with dirty glasses? Would that be a sin?

Radi: Hey, it might be. Mani. What do you think?

Mani: I will wait for the film.

The Restless Wind and Shifting Sands

Modi: A friend of mine told me that there are many beautiful things that we should be sharing in our religion; some wonderful thoughts and ideals. But along with the beauty, you must take the ugly: women and non-Muslims as second-class citizens, a death sentence for leaving the religion, death sentences for saying the wrong thing, terrible-looking clothing, death sentences for young girls not marrying whomever their fathers choose, death sentences for being raped, female circumcisions that maim and kill young girls, pre-teen forced marriages, and I can go on and on. But besides all of those, you can also be killed just for saying it is time to reform the ideology and the law.

Mani: We had tried to reform the religion earlier, but it did not work.

Modi: The religion, like Judaism and Christianity, was well on its way to developing into a much more beautiful and tolerant religion when another ill wind blew out of the Najaf and gave us Wahhabism. Mani, we are strong in the Middle East, we are the number 2 religion in Europe, we have many adherents in America—what more do we need? We do not have to take over the world—besides we tried that and bungled the whole thing.

Radi: How do you figure that?

Modi: Read our history, Radi. I just showed you how Europe was trying to prop us up before World War I, stepping in and saving us from our own incompetence more than once. Europe wanted like crazy to keep the Ottomans as a powerful Eastern empire. When we rule, we go crazy and lose everyone's respect because we betray ourselves. We should never rule.

Radi: Are you saying we should be slaves?

Modi: No, Radi. Does the Catholic Church rule? Is there a rabbi pope? No. The religions are just that, religions. They do not rule lands or countries; they do not maintain standing armies and threaten the world. They try to convince everyone that threats and violence, killings and massacres have no place in the world and must stop. The great

Harry J. Sweeney

religions are there not just as guides but as information centers to show how things can be done, and why certain things shouldn't be done.

Radi: You don't mean like the United Nations?

Modi: Don't talk to me about those clowns. We should keep some of the organizations but shut down their administration! If we cannot build a better organization than that, we are a disgrace to our second-grade curriculum.

Mani: So what should we do?

Modi: I do not know for sure, but we must change. First, change the rules on apostasy and blasphemy. As Mao said when he came to power, "Let a thousand flowers bloom, and let a thousand schools of thought contend."

Mani: But won't that lead to chaos?

Modi: Let our people give their opinions and ask their questions without killing them for it! What on earth is wrong with letting go and letting the people live, thrive, and ask lots of questions? It could be lots of fun. If we stop trying to conquer and rule the world, the world might even be given to us. Why not discuss merging with the other monotheistic religions on a trial basis to allow for Islam to flourish and to develop with more people and more ideas? Of course, this is just brainstorming ideas on my part, Mani. Some of it may not work, but some may. We have everything anyone wants in a religion, but we also have too much they don't want.

Radi: Mani, I think Modi is nuts. Should we call the wagon?

Modi: Look, you guys, my Christian friend said that we have the same God, so how come we say ours is always angry and threatening and whipping and cutting off heads? His God is awesome but very tolerant and merciful.

The Restless Wind and Shifting Sands

Radi: God is what He is. We have no choice in the matter. And what are you doing with a Christian friend?

Modi: You still do not get it, Radi. We are not made in God's image. Some nations believe our entire idea of God is created in our image. Religion does not make us. It gives us ideas, but it is the person who makes his religion beautiful. And you must allow for change; if you don't, what would a pond look like after 1300 years of no rain or other fresh water or anyone looking after it? We have wonderful, modern houses now, with showers that indeed make a *ghusl* out of every *wudu*, yet some try to tell me that we cannot use the modern convenience; we must continue with the early way of Muhammad, when our beloved Prophet would be the first to use a convenience that makes the religion easier for everyone. Remember, in hadith 1:38 Muhammad wanted religion to be easy and not burdensome. Sometimes we have to think ahead, not look back. The future is ahead of us wanting us to join it. We can't fix yesterday.

Mani: I must say, Modi, you are all over the planet, but it is beginning to make sense.

Radi: Oh, yeah? Explain it to me.

Modi: Perhaps it is a way of saying, Mani, that we should find a way to love the entire world and everyone in it. And perhaps give them a reason to love us as well.

Radi: Oh, yeah? Who died and left you boss?

Modi: Well, there are exceptions to every rule.

Mani: Yes, I see.

Radi: Why are you both looking at me?

Harry J. Sweeney

Modi: I guess it is time to open the mosques, the churches, and the synagogues and let people look in and take away with them whatever ideas and prayers they like from each religion. And let them all love God and each other the best way they can.

BIBLIOGRAPHY

Qur'an Translations

Ali, Maulana Muhammad. *Introduction to the Study of The Holy Qur'an*, Ahmadiyya Anjuman Ishaat Islam, Dublin, Ohio, 1992

Arberry, A. J. *The Koran*, Touchstone Books, New York, NY, 1969

Asad, Muhammad. *Message of the Qur'an*, The Book Foundation, Bristol, England, 2005

Khan, Dr. Muhammad Muhsin and Al-Hilal, Dr. Muhammad Taqi-ud-Din. *The Noble Qur'an,* Darussalem Publishers and Distributors, Riyadh, Saudi Arabia, 2001

Khan, Muhammad Zafrullah. *The Qur'an,* Olive Branch Press, Brooklyn, NY, 1997

Pickthall, Muhammad M. *The Glorious Qur'an,* Amana Publications, Beltsville, MD, 2006

Rodwell, J. M. *The Koran,* Phoenix, New Clarendon, VT, 2003

About the Qur'an

Kazi, Dr. Mazhar U. *Towards Understanding the Qur'an,* Al-Huda Publications, Richardson, TX, 2004

Maududi, Sayyid Abul A'la. *Towards Understanding the Qur'an,* The Islamic Foundation, Delhi, India, 1997

Harry J. Sweeney

Omar, Abdul Mannan. *Dictionary of the Holy Qur'an*, NOOR Foundation, International, Inc., Hockessin, DE, 2006

Warraq, Ibn. *What the Koran Rally Says*, Prometheus Books, Amherst, NY, 2002

Warraq, Ibn. *Why I Am Not a Muslim*, Prometheus Books, Amherst, NY, 1995

About Muhammad

Center for the Study of Political Islam. *Muhammad and the Unbelievers*, CSPI Publishing, (www) cspipublishing.com, 2006.

Emerick, Yahiya. *Muhammad*, ALPHA (Penguin Books), Indianapolis, IN, 2002

Ernst, Carl W. *Following Muhammad*, University of North Carolina Press, Chapel Hill, NC, 2003

Menezes, Reverend J. L. *The Life and Religion of Muhammad*, Roman Catholic Books, Harrison, NY, 1912

Shadid, Anthony. *Legacy of the Prophet*, West View Press, Boulder, CO, 2001

Spencer, Robert. *The Truth About Muhammad*, Regnery Publishing, Inc., Washington, DC, 2006

Islamic Law

Asad, Muhammad. *This Law of Ours*, Islamic Book Trust, Malaysia, (www) ibtbooks.com, 2001.

The Restless Wind and Shifting Sands

Al-Misro, Ahmad ibn Naqib. *Reliance of the Traveller*: A Classic Manual of Islamic Sacred Law (Sharia), Amana Publications, Beltsville. MD, 1994

Darwish, Nonie. *Cruel and Usual Punishment*: *The Terrifying Global Implications of Islamic Law*, Thomas Nelson, Inc., Nashville, TN, 2008

Psychology of Islam

Abu Sulayman, Abdul Hamid A. *Crisis in the Muslim Mind,* The International Institute of Islamic Thought, Herndon, VA, 1993

Pryce-Jones, David. *The Closed Circle*: *An Interpretation of the Arabs*, Harper Collins Publisher, Chicago, Il, 2002

Mahmud, Dr. Muhammad Abdul Halim. *The Muslim Mind,* New Amsterdam Books, NY, NY, 1990

Nydell, Margaret K. *Understanding Arabs,* Intercultural Press, Yarmouth, ME, 2006

Patai, Raphael. *The Arab Mind,* Harleigh Press, Long Island City, NY, 2002

Islam and Europe

Bawer, Bruce. *While Europe Slept,* Doubleday, New York, NY, 2006

Berlinski, Claire. *Menace in Europe,* Crown Forum, New York, NY, 2006

Blankley, Tony. *The West's Last Chance,* Regnery Publishing, Inc., Washington, DC, 2005

Buruma, Ian. *Murder in Amsterdam: The Death of Theo van Gogh and the Limits of Tolerance,* Penguin Press, New York, NY, 2006

Fetzer, Joel S. and Soper, J. Christopher. *Muslims and the State in Britain, France, and Germany,* Cambridge University Press, New York, NY, 2006

Cesari, Jocelyne. *When Islam and Democracy Meet,* Palgrave MacMillan, New York, NY, 2006

Glenny, Misha. *The Balkans,* Penguin Books, New York, NY, 1999

Laqueur, Walter. *The Last Days of Europe: Epitaph for an Old Continent,* Thomas Dunne Books, New York, NY, 2007

Nielsen, Jørgen. *Muslims in Western Europe,* Edinburgh University Press, Edinburgh, Scotland, 1992

Pargeter, Alison. The *New Frontiers of Jihad: Radical Islam in Europe,* University of Pennsylvania Press, Philadelphia, PA, 2008

Peters, Joan. *From Time Immemorial: The Origins of the Arab-Jewish Conflict over Palestine,* JKAP Publications, Chicago, IL, 2002

Phillips, Melanie. *Londonistan,* Encounter Books, New York, NY, 2006

Scruton, Roger. *The West and the Rest: Globalization and the Terrorist Threat,* ISI Books, Wilmington, DE, 2002

Schweitzer, Yoram and Shay, Shaul. *The Globalization of Terror,* The Interdisciplinary Center for Herzliya Projects, Piscataway, NJ, 2003

The Restless Wind and Shifting Sands

Thornton, Bruce. *Decline and Fall: Europe's Slow-Motion Suicide*, Encounter Books, New York, NY, 2007

Vidino, Lorenzo. *Al Qaeda in Europe. The New Battleground of International Jihad*, Prometheus Books, Amherst, NY, 2006

Ye'or, Bat. *Eurabia: The Euro – Arab Axis*, Associated University Press, Cranbury, NJ, 2005

Terrorism: Iran, Iraq, and Afghanistan

9/11 Commission. *The 9/11 Commission Report*, W. W. Norton & Company, Inc., New York, NY

Arjomand, Said Amir. *The Turban and the Crown: The Islamic Revolution in Iran*, Oxford University Press, New York, NY, 1988

Barnett, Thomas P. M. *The Pentagon's New Map: War and Peace In The Twenty-First Century*, G. P. Putnam's Sons, New York, NY, 2004

Benard, Cheryl. *Veiled Courage: Inside the Afghan Women's Resistance*, Broadway Books, New York, NY 2002

Benjamin, Daniel and Simon, Steven. *The Age of Sacred Terror*, Random House, New York, NY 2002

Berman, Paul. *Terror and Liberalism.* W. W. Norton, New York, NY, 2003

Carafano, James Jay and Rosenzweig, Paul. *Winning the Long War*, Heritage Books, Washington, DC, 2005

Cragin, Kim and Daly, Sara A. *The Dynamic Terrorist Threat: An Assessment of Group Motivations Capabilities in a Changing World*,

Harry J. Sweeney

RAND Corporation, Arlington, VA, 2004 (Prepared for the U.S. Air Force)

Cockburn, Patrick. *Muqtada*: *Muqtada Al-Sadr, The Shia Revival, and the Struggle for Iraq,* Scribner, New York, NY, 2008

Dershowitz, Alan M. *Why Terrorism Works,* Yale University Press, New Haven, CT, 2002

D'Souza, Dinesh. *The Enemy at Home: The Cultural Left and its Responsibility for 9/11*, Doubleday, New York, NY, 2007

Emerson, Steven. *American Jihad*: *The Terrorists Living Among Us*, Free Press (Simon & Schuster), New York, NY, 2003

Feldman, Noah. *After Jihad*: *America and The Struggle for Islamic Democracy,* Farrar, Straus, and Giroux, New York, NY, 2003

Flynn, Stephen. *America the Vulnerable*: *How Our Government Is Failing to Protect Us From Terrorism*, Harper Collins, New York, NY 2004

Gabriel, Mark. *Islam and Terrorism*: *What the Qur'an really teaches About Christianity*, violence and the goals of the Islamic Jihad, Front Line, Lake Mary, FL, 2002

Gertz, Bill. *Breakdown*: *The Failure of American Intelligence to Defeat Global Terror,* Penguin Group (PLUME), New York, NY, 2003

Gabriel, Brigitte. *Because They Hate: A Survivor of Islamic Terror Warns America,* St. Martin's Press, New York, NY, 2006

Gabriel, Brigitte. *They Must be Stopped*: *Why We Must Defeat Radical Islam and How We Can Do it*, St. Martin's Press, New York, NY, 2008

Gold, Dore. *Hatred's Kingdom*: *How Saudi Arabia Supports the New Global Terrorism,* Regnery Publishing, Inc., Washington, DC, 2003

The Restless Wind and Shifting Sands

Hanna, John U. *Cancer in America: The Enemy Within*, Trafford Publishing, Victoria, B.C. Canada, 2004

Horowitz, David. *Left Illusions*, Spence Publishing Company, Dallas, TX, 2003

Horowitz, David. *Unholy Alliance: Radical Islam and the American Left*. Regnery Publishing Company, Washington, DC, 2004

Lewis, Bernard. *The Crisis of Islam: Holy War and Unholy Terror*. Modern Library, Random House, New York, NY, 2003

Lewis, Bernard. *What Went Wrong: The Clash Between Islam and Modernity in the Middle East*, Harper-Collins Press, New York, NY, 2002

Lewis, Bernard. *From Babel to Dragomans: Interpreting the Middle East*, Oxford University Press, New York, NY, 2004

McInerney, Lt. General Thomas and Vallely, Maj. General Paul. *Endgame: The Blueprint for Victory In The War On Terror*, Regnery Publishing, Inc., Washington, DC, 2004

Patterson, Lt. Col. Robert "Buzz". *Reckless Disregard*, Regnery Publishing, Inc. Washington, DC, 2004

Pollack, Kenneth M. *The Threatening Storm: The Case for Invading Iraq*, Council On Foreign Relations, Random House, New York, NY, 2002

Rosen, Nir. *In the Belly of the Green Bird*: The *Triumph of the Martyrs in Iraq*, Free Press (Simon & Schuster), New York, NY, 2006

Stern, Jessica. *Terror in the Name of God: Why Religious Militants Kill*, Harper Collins, New York, NY, 2003

Verstappen, Stefan H. *The Thirty-Six Strategies of Ancient China*, China

Harry J. Sweeney

Books & Periodicals, Inc., South San Francisco, CA, 2004 (Note: Deception strategies in warfare)

Wright, Robin. *Sacred Rage: The Wrath of Militant Islam*, Touchstone Books, New York, NY, 1985 (Updated)

General Books on Islam: History and Culture

Ahmed, Akbar S. *Islam Today: A Short Introduction to the Muslim World*, I. B. Tauris & Co, Ltd., New York, NY, 2001

Algar, Hamad. *Wahhabism: A Critical Essay*, Islamic Publications International, Oneonta, NY, 2002

Ali, Maulana Muhammad. *The Muslim Prayer Book,* Ahmadiyya Anjuman Ishaat Islam (Lahore) USA, Dublin, OH, 1998

Ali, Ayaan Hirsi. *Infidel*, Free Press, New York, NY 2007

Ashraf, SH. Muhammad. *Salat: Islamic Prayer Book*, SH. Muhammad Ashraf Publishers, Lahore, Pakistan, 1997

Baker, Raymond William. *Islam Without Fear: Egypt and the New Islamists*, Harvard University Press, Cambridge, MA, 2003

Belloc, Hilaire and Oussani, Gabriel: *Moslems: Their Beliefs, Practices, and Politics,*
Roger A. McCaffrey Publishing, Ridgefield, CT, 2002 (original Imprimatur 1907)

Bostom Andrew G. *The Legacy of Islamic Antisemitism: From Sacred Texts to Solemn History*, Prometheus Books, Amherst, NY, 2008

Carol, Dr. Steven. *Middle East Rules of Thumb: Understanding the complexities of the Middle East*, iUniverse, Inc., New York, NY, 2008

Cramer, Richard Ben. *How Israel Lost: The Four Questions*, Simon & Schuster, New York, NY, 2004

Fallaci, Oriana. *The Rage and the Pride*, Rizzoli International Publications, Inc., New York, NY 2003

Fallaci, Oriana. The Force of Reason, Rizzoli International Publications, Inc., New York, NY, 2007

Gibb, H. A. R. *Mohammedanism: A Historical Survey*, Oxford University Press, New York, NY, 1970

Glubb, John Bagot. The Story of the Arab Legion, Hodder and Stoughton, London, 1948

Gold, Dore. *The Fight for Jerusalem: Radical Islam, the West, and the Future of the Holy City*, Regnery Books, Inc., Washington, DC, 2007

Haneef, Suzanne. *What Everyone Should Know About Islam and Muslims*, KAZI Publications, Inc., Chicago, IL, 1996

Hasan, Asma Gull. *American Muslims: The New Generation*, The Continuum International Publishing, New York, NY, 2001

Housani, Albert. *A History of the Arab Peoples*, The Belknap Press, Harvard University Press, Cambridge, MA, 1991

Kaplan, Robert D. *The Arabists: The Romance Of American Elite*, The Free Press, New York, NY, 1995

Kimball, Charles. *When Religion Becomes Evil,* Harper San Francisco, New York, NY, 2003

Harry J. Sweeney

Lammens, H., S.J. *Islam Beliefs and Institutions,* Oriental Books, New Delhi, India, 1979

Lamp, Walter. *Koranic Verses,* Running Light Publishing Company, Reno, NV, 2009

Karsh, Efraim. *Islamic Imperialism: A History,* Yale University Press, New Haven, CT, 2007

Kepel, Gilles. *Jihad: The Trail Of Political Islam,* The Belknap Press, Harvard University Press, Cambridge, MA, 2002

Maududi, Sayyid Abu'l A'La. *Towards Understanding Islam,* The Islamic Foundation, Leicester, UK, 2004   (KAZI Publications, Chicago, IL)

Murk, Jim. *Islam Rising, Book One. The Never-Ending Jihad Against Christianity,* 21st Century Press, Springfield, MO, 2006

Murk, Jim. *Islam Rising, Book Two. The Never-Ending Jihad Against The Jews and Israel,* 21st Century Press, Springfield, MO, 2007

Newby, Gordon D. *A Concise Encyclopedia of Islam,* OneWorld Publications, Oxford, England 2002

Oren, Michael B. *Power, Faith, and Fantasy: American in the Middle East 1776 to the Present,* W.W. Norton & Company, New York, NY, 2007

Peres, Shimon. *The New Middle East,* Henry Holt & Company, New York, NY, 1993

Qutb, Sayyid. *Milestones,* The Mother Mosque Foundation, Cedar Rapids, IA, 2006

Qutb, Sayyid. *Social Justice in Islam,* Islamic Publications International, Oneonta, NY, 2000

Rabbani, Faraz Fareed. *The Absolute Essentials of Islam: Faith, Prayer & The Path of Salvation According to the Hanafi School*, White Thread Press, Santa Barbara, CA, 2005

Gartenstein-Ross, Daveed. *My Year Inside Radical Islam: A Memoir*, Tarcher/Penguin, New York, NY, 2007

Sadat, Anwar. *In Search of Identity: An Autobiography*, Harper & Row, New York, NY, 1979

Schindler, Colin. A *History of Modern Israel*, Cambridge University Press, New York, NY, 2008

Shipler, David K. *Arab and Jew: Wounded Spirits in a Promised Land*, Times Books, 1986

Trifkovic, Serge. *The Sword of Islam: Islam History, Theology, Impact on the World*, Regina Orthodox Press, Inc., Boston, MA, 2002

Internet Resources

About Islam. http://islam.about.com/

Ali, Yusuf (et al): *The Qur'an,* Internet Edition: http://www.oneummah. net/quran and www. quranexplorer.net/quran/

Daily Iraq News. http://www.iraqinews.com and www.mnf-iraq.com.

Guide to Understanding Islam: http://www.thereligionofpeace.com/ Quran/015-slavery.htm

Islam 101: http://islam101.net/

Jihad Watch: http://www.jihadwatch.org

Harry J. Sweeney

Middle East Radio Forum: http://www.middleeastradioforum.org.

The Noble Qur'an, Saheeh International English Translation: http://www.imaanstar.com.

Portal to Islam: http://www.islam.com/

Servier, André. *Islam and the Mind of the Musulman:* http://musulmanbook/blogspot.com/ 2005/read-this-first-about-book-islam-and.html, 1923.

About Ablutions: http://strangerinthisdunya.wordpress.com/2008/08/29/wiping-over-the-socks-in-wudu/

ABOUT THE AUTHOR

Harry Sweeney attended Yale University, studying at the Yale Institute of Far Eastern Languages. Following those studies, he found himself a member of the translator/analyst community in Japan, Okinawa, the Philippines, Taiwan, and Berlin during the next 18 years. The foreign assignments were occasionally relieved by a return to Yale and Defense Language Institute for additional studies, an assignment as instructor at the Intelligence School, and a special assignment as Advisor, Strategic Air Command.

Following his intelligence career, Harry was recruited by the Department of HEW (now U.S. Department of Education) to find and resolve severe problems plaguing the department. He succeeded in fulfilling this first task, and then continued on to another successful career, retiring as chief of a very important region.

The 9/11 tragedy was the trigger that brought him back into the field of scholars and writers, resolved to learn not only the reasons for the terrible tragedy, but to learn about the religion and the culture behind the actors in that tragedy, and the reasons why an attack on this country was so critical to them. He again showed success in this new endeavor and has been productive in essays, speeches, and radio, always providing easy to understand insights into the world of the Middle East. *The Restless Wind and Shifting Sands* is his first major published work and will quickly find its place among the other outstanding works on Islamic culture

LaVergne, TN USA
26 January 2010
171124LV00006B/2/P